ANNUAL EDITIONS

Dying, Death, and Bereavement 13/14
Fourteenth Edition

EDITORS

George E. Dickinson, PhD
College of Charleston

George E. Dickinson, Professor of Sociology at the College of Charleston, received his Ph.D. in sociology from LSU in Baton Rouge (LA) and his M.A. in sociology and B.A. in biology from Baylor University (TX). He came to the College of Charleston in 1985, having previously taught in Minnesota and Kentucky. Dickinson has presented more than 70 papers at professional meetings and has been the author/co-author of over 80 articles in professional journals, primarily on end-of-life issues. In addition, he has co-authored/co-edited 22 books/anthologies (with Michael R. Leming), including *Understanding Dying, Death and Bereavement* (7th ed., Wadsworth/Cengage, 2011). His research and teaching interest in end-of-life issues goes back to 1974 when he taught a course on death and dying and in 1975 when he began research on medical schools and physicians. He is on the editorial boards of *Mortality* (U.K.) and the *American Journal of Hospice & Palliative Medicine* (U.S.). He was the 2002 recipient of the Distinguished Teacher/Scholar Award and the 2008 Distinguished Research Award at the College of Charleston, a South Carolina Governor's Distinguished Professor Award in 2003 and 2008, and the Death Educator Award from the Association for Death Education and Counseling in 2009. In 1999 he was a Visiting Research Fellow in palliative medicine at the University of Sheffield's School of Medicine (UK), in 2006 at Lancaster University's Institute for Health Research (UK), and in 2013 at the University of Bristol's Veterinary School (UK). Earlier, Dickinson did postdoctoral studies at Pennsylvania State University (gerontology), at the University of Connecticut (medical sociology), and at the University of Kentucky's School of Medicine (thanatology).

Michael R. Leming, PhD
St. Olaf College

Michael R. Leming is Professor of Sociology and Anthropology at St. Olaf College. He holds degrees from Westmont College (B.A.), Marquette University (M. A.), and the University of Utah (Ph.D.) and has done additional graduate study at the University of California in Santa Barbara. Leming's research has primarily focused on the sociology of religion, the sociology of the family, and social thanatology. He has written or edited 27 books and numerous articles about cross-cultural and comparative studies of kinship, religion, death rituals, and bereavement behavior. The books he has worked on include *Understanding Families: Diversity, Continuity, and Change; Understanding Dying, Death, and Bereavement; The Sociological Perspective: A Value-Committed Introduction; Handbook of Death and Dying;* and the *Encyclopedia of Death and the Human Experience.* Most of his published work has been co-authored with George E. Dickinson.

Dr. Leming was the founder and former director of the St. Olaf College Social Research Center, former member of the board of directors of the Minnesota Coalition on Terminal Care and the Northfield AIDS Response, and has served as a hospice educator, volunteer, and grief counselor. Leming was promoted the rank of Professor Emeritus in 2012 and after his retirement will continue to devote the rest of his career to studying and teaching about the people of Asia, most notably Thailand. He produced a documentary film titled *The Karen of Musikhee: Rabbits in the Mouth of the Crocodile.* For the past twelve years Dr. Leming has directed the Spring Semester in Thailand (*SpringSemesterInThailand.com*) program that is affiliated with Chiang Mai University and lives in Thailand during Minnesota's coldest months.

While teaching and research has been his vocation, community development and service to others has been Leming's passion and primary calling. He (and his Santa Claus persona) led efforts to raise money to create sustainable development and reforestation programs, and build water supplies, churches, and three schools in Karen, Lahu, and Akha villages in Thailand. The success of these projects inspired him to work on bringing a performing and visual arts center for the disabled to Thailand. His tenacity was rewarded with a $6.9 million grant for the project from the Thai government.

D1472827

ANNUAL EDITIONS: DYING, DEATH, AND BEREAVEMENT, FOURTEENTH EDITION

Published by McGraw-Hill, a business unit of The McGraw-Hill Companies, Inc., 1221 Avenue of the Americas, New York, NY 10020. Copyright © 2014 by The McGraw-Hill Companies, Inc. All rights reserved. Previous edition(s) © 2012, 2011, and 2010. Printed in the United States of America. No part of this publication may be reproduced or distributed in any form or by any means, or stored in a database or retrieval system, without the prior written consent of The McGraw-Hill Companies, Inc., including, but not limited to, in any network or other electronic storage or transmission, or broadcast for distance learning.

Some ancillaries, including electronic and print components, may not be available to customers outside the United States.

This book is printed on acid-free paper.

Annual Editions® is a registered trademark of The McGraw-Hill Companies, Inc.
Annual Editions is published by the **Contemporary Learning Series** group within the McGraw-Hill Higher Education division.

1 2 3 4 5 6 7 8 9 0 QDB/QDB 1 0 9 8 7 6 5 4 3

ISBN: 978–0–07–805130-2
MHID: 0–07–805130-4
ISSN: 1096–4223 (print)
ISSN: 2162–1829 (online)

Acquisitions Editor: *Joan L. McNamara*
Marketing Director: *Adam Kloza*
Marketing Manager: *Nathan Edwards*
Developmental Editor: *Dave Welsh*
Senior Project Manager: *Joyce Watters*
Buyer: *Nichole Birkenholz*
Cover Designer: *Studio Montage, St. Louis, MO*
Content Licensing Specialist: *DeAnna Dausener*
Media Project Manager: *Sridevi Palani*

Compositor: Laserwords Private Limited
Cover Image Ingram Publishing (inset), Ingram Publishing (background)

Editors/Academic Advisory Board

Members of the Academic Advisory Board are instrumental in the final selection of articles for each edition of ANNUAL EDITIONS. Their review of articles for content, level, and appropriateness provides critical direction to the editors and staff. We think that you will find their careful consideration well reflected in this volume.

ANNUAL EDITIONS: Dying, Death, and Bereavement 13/14
14th Edition

EDITORS

George E. Dickinson
College of Charleston

Michael R. Leming
St. Olaf College

ACADEMIC ADVISORY BOARD MEMBERS

Editors/Academic Advisory Board continued

Preface

In publishing ANNUAL EDITIONS we recognize the enormous role played by the magazines, newspapers, and journals of the public press in providing current, first-rate educational information in a broad spectrum of interest areas. Many of these articles are appropriate for students, researchers, and professionals seeking accurate, current material to help bridge the gap between principles and theories and the real world. These articles, however, become more useful for study when those of lasting value are carefully collected, organized, indexed, and reproduced in a low-cost format, which provides easy and permanent access when the material is needed. That is the role played by ANNUAL EDITIONS.

Dying, death, and bereavement have been around for as long as humankind, yet as topics of discussion they have been "offstage" for decades in contemporary American public discourse. In the United States, dying currently takes place away from the arena of familiar surroundings of kin and friends, with approximately 80 percent of deaths occurring in institutional settings such as hospitals and nursing homes. Americans have developed a paradoxical relationship with death: We know more about the causes and conditions surrounding death but have not equipped ourselves emotionally to cope with dying, death, and bereavement. The purpose of this anthology is to provide an understanding of dying, death, and bereavement that will assist in better coping with and understanding our own deaths and the deaths of others.

Articles in this volume are taken from professional/ semiprofessional journals and from popular publications written for both special populations and a general readership. The selections are carefully reviewed for their currency and accuracy. Many of the articles have been changed from the previous edition through updating and responding to comments of reviewers. Most of the articles refer to situations in the United States, yet other cultures are represented. We strive to have current articles, though a few may be earlier, due to readers' requests to maintain them in this updated issue.

The reader will note the tremendous range of approaches and styles of the writers, from personal, firsthand accounts to more scientific and philosophical writings. Some articles are more practical and applied, whereas others are more technical and research-oriented. If "variety is the very spice of life," this volume should be a spicy venture for the reader. Methodologies used in the more research-oriented articles range from quantitative (e.g., surveys/questionnaires) to qualitative (e.g., interviews/observation). Such a mix should especially be of interest to the student majoring or minoring in the social sciences. If a particular article seems too technical for your background, do not bog yourself down with the statistical analysis; rather, look ahead to the discussion and conclusions.

These articles are drawn from many different periodicals, thus exposing the reader to a variety of publications in the library. With interest stimulated by a particular article, the student is encouraged to pursue other related articles in that particular journal.

This anthology is organized into six units to cover many of the important aspects of dying, death, and bereavement. Though the units are arranged in a way that has some logical order, one can determine from the brief summaries in the table of contents and the cross-references in the topic guide whether another arrangement would best fit a particular teaching situation. The first unit is on issues in dying and death. Unit 2 takes a life-cycle approach and looks at the developmental aspects of dying and death at different age levels. The third unit concerns the process of dying. Unit 4 covers selected ethical issues, while Units 5 and 6 discuss funerals and bereavement, respectively.

Annual Editions: Dying, Death, and Bereavement, Fourteenth Edition is intended for use as a supplement to augment selected areas or chapters of textbooks on dying and death. The articles in this volume can also serve as a basis for class discussion about various issues in dying, death, and bereavement.

Annual Editions: Dying, Death, and Bereavement is revised periodically to keep the materials timely as new social concerns about end-of-life issues develop. Your assistance in the revision effort is always welcome. Please complete and return the postage-paid article rating form at the back of the book. We look forward to your input.

George E. Dickinson
Editor

Michael R. Leming
Editor

The Annual Editions Series

VOLUMES AVAILABLE

Adolescent Psychology

Aging

American Foreign Policy

American Government

Anthropology

Archaeology

Assessment and Evaluation

Business Ethics

Child Growth and Development

Comparative Politics

Criminal Justice

Developing World

Drugs, Society, and Behavior

Dying, Death, and Bereavement

Early Childhood Education

Economics

Educating Children with Exceptionalities

Education

Educational Psychology

Entrepreneurship

Environment

The Family

Gender

Geography

Global Issues

Health

Homeland Security

Human Development

Human Resources

Human Sexualities

International Business

Management

Marketing

Mass Media

Microbiology

Multicultural Education

Nursing

Nutrition

Physical Anthropology

Psychology

Race and Ethnic Relations

Social Problems

Sociology

State and Local Government

Sustainability

Technologies, Social Media, and Society

United States History, Volume 1

United States History, Volume 2

Urban Society

Violence and Terrorism

Western Civilization, Volume 1

Western Civilization, Volume 2

World History, Volume 1

World History, Volume 2

World Politics

Contents

Preface   *v*

Series   *vi*

Correlation Guide   *xii*

Topic Guide   *xiii*

Internet References   *xvii*

UNIT 1
Issues in Dying and Death

Unit Overview   **xxii**

1. **The Dead, the Living, and Those Yet to Come,** Charles Lemert, *Contexts, 10*(4), Fall 2011
   A prominent social theorist draws on classic sociological texts to explore what he calls the **Society of the Dead**—the one group we must all inevitably join.   **2**

2. **The Cycle of Death,** Vince Beiser, *Pacific Standard,* May/June, 2012
   Some 40 years ago, Americans' moral qualms almost ended the **death penalty.** Now we are abandoning **capital punishment** again, but not because we object to executions, according to Beiser.   **6**

3. **How We Bury the War Dead,** Yochi J. Dreazen and Gary Fields, *The Wall Street Journal,* May 29, 2010
   To bring home the **war dead** for burial has not always been the case for the U.S. military. This article traces the **history** of war dead body disposition and gives the current situation.   **8**

4. **Grief in the Age of Facebook,** Elizabeth Stone, *The Chronicle Review,* March 5, 2010
   Technology gives us a new way to express **grief** following a death: Facebook.   **11**

5. **Brain Death Guidelines Vary at Top US Neurological Hospitals,** Susan Jeffrey, *Medscape Medical News,* 2008
   A recent survey reveals widespread **brain death** guidelines in U.S. hospitals.   **13**

6. **Criteria for a Good Death,** Edwin Shneidman, *Suicide and Life-Threatening Behavior, 37*(3), 2007
   The late Edwin Shneidman outlines ten criteria for a **good death.**   **15**

7. **The Emergence of Thanatology and Current Practice in Death Education,** Luciana M. Fonseca and Ines Testoni, *Omega, 64*(2), 2011–2012
   A **history** and evolution of **thanatology** in Western society is outlined.   **17**

UNIT 2
Dying and Death Across the Life Cycle

Unit Overview   **24**

8. **Teaching Children about Death and Grief: Children Can Learn about Grief and Dying from Teachable Moments,** Kirsti A. Dyer, Help a Child Cope with Loss or Death, Suite101.com
   Presents **teachable** moments regarding **children** and death.   **26**

The concepts in bold italics are developed in the article. For further expansion, please refer to the Topic Guide.

9. **Death in Disney Films: Implications for Children's Understanding of Death,** Meredith Cox, Erin Garrett, and James A. Graham, *Omega, 50*(4), 2004–2005

   Examines the potential influence of Disney films on **children's concepts of death,** using **a content analysis** of Disney animated films.   28

10. **Death and Dying in the Curriculum of Public Schools: Is there a place?,** Ethel L. King-McKenzie, Journal of Emerging Knowledge on Emerging Markets, 3, 2011

    Dying and death have traditionally been somewhat **taboo topics** in American culture. Should such a topic be addressed with **children** in **pubic schools?**   35

11. **Needs of Elderly Patients in Palliative Care,** Helle Wijk and Agneta Grimby, American *Journal of Hospice and Palliative Medicine, 29*(2), April/May 2008

    A **pilot study** of **elderly patients'** end-of-life needs in a **Swedish geriatric palliative care** unit concluded that elimination of **physical pain** was a primary need of the patients.   40

12. **Good Mourning,** George Dickinson, *College of Charleston Magazine, 15*(2), Spring 2011

    The article discusses the role of a **veterinarian** in the **death of a pet** and also the seriousness that should be given by everyone to the death of a **child's companion animal.**   45

13. **Through the Touch of God: Child Death and Spiritual Sustenance in a Hutterian Colony,** Joanne Cacciatore and Rebecca Ong, *Omega, 64*(3), 2011–2012

    This **ethnographic study** of Hutterites in South Dakota uses **participant observation** and **interviews** in focusing on the **death of children.**   47

14. **End-of-Life Concerns and Care Preferences: Congruence Among Terminally Ill Elders and their Family Caregivers,** Daniel S. Gardner and Betty J. Kramer, *Omega, 60*(3), 2009–2010

    An examination of **end-of-life** issues and care preferences of **terminally ill older persons** and their **caregivers.**   56

UNIT 3
The Dying Process

Unit Overview   68

15. **Dying on the Streets: Homeless Persons' Concerns and Desires about End-of-Life Care,** John Song et al., *Journal of General Internal Medicine,* 22(4), April 2007

    In-depth interviews with 53 **homeless** individuals in Minnesota regarding end-of-life care concluded that they worry about dying and **end-of-life care.**   70

16. **Death and Dying across Cultures,** Gihan ElGindy, MinorityNurse.com. http://www.minoritynurse.com, 2010

    Discusses the importance of **nurses'** being sensitive to unique **religious** and **cultural** needs of patients with **terminal illnesses.**   79

17. **The Promise of Presence,** Paul Rousseau, *American Journal of Hospice and Palliative Care,* 28(6), 2011

    A **physician** laments his promising to return to check on a **terminally ill patient,** yet realizes later on that he did not return, only to then find out it was too late. This caring individual warns that if medical doctors **promise presence,** then they must be present.   82

The concepts in bold italics are developed in the article. For further expansion, please refer to the Topic Guide.

18. **When Death Strikes without Warning,** Jennifer Couzin, *Science, 321,*
    July 4, 2008
    Presents information about the devastating effect of **epilepsy** and **sudden death.**   84

19. **Are They Hallucinations or Are They Real? The Spirituality of Deathbed
    and Near-Death Visions,** L. Stafford Betty, *Omega, 53*(1–2), 2006
    Do the living really **see the dead?** The author looks into this "twilight zone" to determine
    if this is real or a mere **hallucination.**   87

20. **Beyond Terror and Denial: The Positive Psychology of Death
    Acceptance,** Paul T.P. Wong and Adrian Tomer, *Death Studies, 35,* 2011.
    Death is ubiquitous, yet whether the American society **accepts or denies death** is
    the question. The authors argue that **psychologists** need to focus more on death
    acceptance. They discuss **terror management theory** and **meaning management
    theory.**   94

UNIT 4
Ethical Issues of Dying and Death

Unit Overview   98

21. **Ethics and Life's Ending: An Exchange,** Robert D. Orr and Gilbert
    Meilaender, *First Things,* August/September 2004
    This article provides a point–counterpoint discussion of the quality-of-life arguments for
    passive euthanasia and the right to die. Knowledge from both points of view challenge
    the student who is attempting to formulate an understanding of the complex issues sur-
    rounding this controversy.   100

22. **Obituary for Jack Kevorkian,** Associated Press. *Minneapolis Star
    and Tribune,* June 4, 2011
    This is the obituary for the famous and controversial Jack Kevorkian, "Dr. Death," who
    caused the American public to deal with legal issues related to physician-assisted sui-
    cide. The article discusses Kevorkian's philosophy and social activism to do something
    about human suffering for terminal patients.   107

23. **At the Bottom of the Slippery Slope,** Wesley J. Smith, *The Weekly
    Standard,* July 4/July 11, 2011 (in CLS Digital Library held by McGraw-Hill)
    Smith argues that once society accepts euthanasia/organ harvesting, we will soon
    see agitation to pay seriously disabled or dying people for their organs, a policy that
    Kevorkian advocated.   109

24. **Hospitals Embrace Palliative Care,** Bridget M. Kuehn, *Journal of the
    American Medical Association, 298*(11), 1263–1265, September 19, 2007
    This article presents the argument that palliative care is the best form of competent care
    for patients living with a terminal illness. Providing a new model for palliative care, the
    article gives special attention to meeting psychological and physical needs of the dying
    patient.   111

25. **Cannabis Use in Long-Term Care: An Emerging Issue for Nurses,**
    Roxanne Nelson, *American Journal of Nursing, 111*(4), 19–20, April 2011.
    When dealing with patients in end-of-life care and marijuana, many nurses' protocol is
    "don't ask, don't tell."   114

26. **I Was a Doctor Accustomed to Death, But Not His,** Marc Agronin, *Salon,*
    February 5, 2011.
    Son tells his story of dealing with his own father as patient. It was a real lesson in caring
    for the dying.   116

The concepts in bold italics are developed in the article. For further expansion, please refer to the Topic Guide.

UNIT 5
Funerals

Unit Overview   **118**

27. **The Contemporary American Funeral,** Michael R. Leming and George
E. Dickinson, *Understanding Dying, Death, and Bereavement,* Wadsworth-
Cengage, 2010
This article provides an overview of the present practice of funeralization in American
society, including the traditional and alternative funeral arrangements. The functions of
funerals relative to the sociological, psychological, and theological needs of adults and
children are also discussed.   **120**

28. **Building My Father's Coffin,** John Manchester. *Salon,* June 4, 2010
"My body is to be placed in a plain pine box. I would like my children to make the box."
William Manchester knows that grief work is best when done as a family.   **123**

29. **Dealing with the Dead,** Jennifer Egan, *The New Yorker,* October 11, 2010
It is possible to facilitate our grieving by remembering dead relatives by wearing clothes
and jewelry that once belonged to them to their funerals.   **125**

30. **Mourning in a Digital Age,** Bruce Feiler, *The New York Times,*
January 12, 2012
This article discusses the way in which families can communicate with their potential
supporters in the event of a death within their families, and how their friends can use the
Internet to provide social support.   **126**

31. **10 Burdens Funeral Directors Carry,** Caleb Wilde,
http://connectingdirectors.com/articles/35386-10-burdens-funeral-
directors-carry and http://connectingdirectors.com/articles/35479-10-ways-funeral-
directors-cope-caleb-wilde   **128**

32. **Memorial Videos Give Lasting Farewell,** Jeff Strickler, *Minneapolis Star
and Tribune,* June 6, 2011,
http://www.startribune.com/lifestyle/relationship/123142533.html?page=all&prepage=
1&c=y#continue
Now you can speak at your own funeral and tell your mourners how your really feel.   **130**

33. **Speaking from Beyond the Grave; High-tech Headstones Use QR Codes
to Link to Photos and Videos of the Dearly Departed,** Jeff Strickler,
Minneapolis Star and Tribune, July 15, 2012, http://www.startribune.com/
lifestyle/162485776.html
With high-tech tombstones and QR codes, the deceased can talk back to those who
visit their graves.   **132**

UNIT 6
Bereavement

Unit Overview   **134**

34. **The Grieving Process,** Michael R. Leming and George E. Dickinson,
Understanding Dying, Death, and Bereavement, Wadsworth-Cengage, 2010
This article discusses the seven basic coping strategies related to the bereavement
process (shock and denial, disorganization, volatile emotions, guilt, loss and loneliness,
relief, and reestablishment) and the four tasks of bereavement (accepting the reality
of the loss, experiencing the pain of grief, adjusting to an environment in which the
deceased is missing, and the withdrawing of emotional energy and reinvesting it in other
relationships).   **136**

The concepts in bold italics are developed in the article. For further expansion, please refer to the Topic Guide.

35. **The Normal Process of Grieving,** Harvard Medical School, *Harvard Mental Health Letter,* December 2011.
This article discusses experiences that are part of the normal spectrum of grieving, lasting from six to twelve months.　　140

36. **A Guide to Getting Through Grief,** Harvard Medical School, *Harvard Mental Health Letter,* December 2011.
Dr. Michael Hirsh, a psychiatrist at Massachusetts General Hospital, offers advice for enabling people who are grieving to work through the bereavement process.　　142

37. **Disenfranchised Grief,** Kenneth J. Doka, *Disenfranchised Grief: Recognizing Hidden Sorrow,* Lexington Books, 1989
Kenneth Doka discusses the unique situation of bereaved survivors whose loss is not, or cannot be, openly acknowledged, publicly mourned, or socially supported.　　144

38. **Challenging the Paradigm: New Understandings of Grief,** Kenneth J. Doka, 2007
Kenneth Doka discusses five significant ways in which earlier understandings of or paradigms of grief have been challenged. He also discusses three current challenges to the field of thanatology and two others that are likely to occur in the not-too-distant future.　　148

39. **We've Been Misled about How to Grieve,** Nicholas Köhler, *Maclean's Magazine,* February 21, 2011
This article discusses much of the misinformation most people assume about grieving.　　155

40. **Shades of Grief: When Does Mourning Become a Mental Illness?,** Virginia Hughes, *Scientific American,* June 7, 2011, http://www.scientificamerican.com/article.cfm?id=shades-of-grief
This article discusses the *Diagnostic and Statistical Manual of Mental Disorders* (DSM) and how it addresses "Complicated Grief Disorder," also known as traumatic or prolonged grief. The important question addressed is, When does normal grieving become pathological?　　158

41. **11 Ways to Comfort Someone Who's Grieving,** Harvard Medical School, *Health Beat,* August 24, 2010
If you find yourself tongue-tied or uncertain of what to do in the face of someone's loss, here are some steps to try.　　160

Test-Your-Knowledge Form　　162

The concepts in bold italics are developed in the article. For further expansion, please refer to the Topic Guide.

Correlation Guide

The *Annual Editions* series provides students with convenient, inexpensive access to current, carefully selected articles from the public press. **Annual Editions: Dying, Death, and Bereavement 13/14** is an easy-to-use reader that presents articles on important topics such as *the dying process, funerals, bereavement,* and many more. For more information on *Annual Editions* and other *McGraw-Hill Contemporary Learning Series* titles, visit www.mhhe.com/cls.

This convenient guide matches the units in **Annual Editions: Dying, Death, and Bereavement 13/14** with the corresponding chapters in our best-selling McGraw-Hill Political textbooks by DeSpelder/Strickland.

Annual Editions: Dying, Death, and Bereavement 13/14	The Last Dance: Encountering Death and Dying, 9/e by DeSpelder/Strickland
Unit 1: Issues in Dying and Death	**Chapter 1:** Attitudes toward Death: A Climate of Change **Chapter 4:** Death Systems: Mortality and Society **Chapter 15:** The Path Ahead: Personal and Social Choices
Unit 2: Dying and Death Across the Life Cycle	**Chapter 2:** Learning about Death: The Influence of Sociocultural Forces **Chapter 10:** Death in the Lives of Children and Adolescents **Chapter 11:** Death in the Lives of Adults **Chapter 13:** Risks, Perils, and Traumatic Death
Unit 3: The Dying Process	**Chapter 4:** Death Systems: Mortality and Society **Chapter 5:** Health Care Systems: Patients, Staff, and Institutions **Chapter 7:** Facing Death: Living with Life-Threatening Illness **Chapter 14:** Beyond Death/After Life
Unit 4: Ethical Issues of Dying and Death	**Chapter 5:** Health Care Systems: Patients, Staff, and Institutions **Chapter 6:** End-of-Life Issues and Decisions
Unit 5: Funerals	**Chapter 3:** Perspectives on Death: Cultural and Historical **Chapter 8:** Last Rites: Funerals and Body Disposition
Unit 6: Bereavement	**Chapter 9:** Survivors: Understanding the Experience of Loss

Topic Guide

This topic guide suggests how the selections in this book relate to the subjects covered in your course. You may want to use the topics listed on these pages to search the Web more easily.

On the following pages a number of websites have been gathered specifically for this book. They are arranged to reflect the units of this Annual Editions reader. You can link to these sites by going to www.mhhe.com/cls.

All the articles that relate to each topic are listed below the bold-faced term.

Advance directives
21. Ethics anFd Life's Ending
22. Obituary for Jack Kevorkian
23. At the Bottom of the Slippery Slope
26. I Was a Doctor Accustomed to Death, But Not His

Animals and death
9. Death in Disney Films: Implications for Children's Understanding of Death
12. Good Mourning

Assisting grievers
14. End-of-Life Concerns and Care Preferences: Congruence Among Terminally Ill Elders and their Family Caregivers
18. When Death Strikes Without Warning
28. Building my father's coffin
29. Dealing with the Dead
30. Mourning in a Digital Age
34. The Grieving Process
35. The Normal Process of Grieving
36. A guide to getting through grief
37. Disenfranchised Grief
38. Challenging the Paradigm: New Understandings of Grief
39. We've Been Mislead about How to Grieve
40. Shades of Grief: When Does Mourning Become a Mental Illness?
41. 11 Ways to Comfort Someone Who's Grieving

Attitudes toward death
9. Death in Disney Films: Implications for Children's Understanding of Death
19. Are They Hallucinations or Are They Real? The Spirituality of Deathbed and Near-Death Visions
21. Ethics and Life's Ending
22. Obituary for Jack Kevorkian
23. At the Bottom of the Slippery Slope

Bereavement and grief
4. Grief in the Age of Facebook
9. Death in Disney Films: Implications for Children's Understanding of Death
18. When Death Strikes Without Warning
28. Building my father's coffin
29. Dealing with the Dead
30. Mourning in a Digital Age
34. The Grieving Process
35. The Normal Process of Grieving
36. A guide to getting through grief
37. Disenfranchised Grief
38. Challenging the Paradigm: New Understandings of Grief
39. We've Been Mislead about How to Grieve
40. Shades of Grief: When Does Mourning Become a Mental Illness?
41. 11 Ways to Comfort Someone Who's Grieving

Brain death
5. Brain Death Guidelines Vary at Top US Neurological Hospitals

Capital punishment
2. The Cycle of Death

Caregivers
11. Needs of Elderly Patients in Palliative Care
14. End-of-Life Concerns and Care Preferences: Congruence Among Terminally Ill Elders and their Family Caregivers
18. When Death Strikes Without Warning
22. Obituary for Jack Kevorkian
23. At the Bottom of the Slippery Slope
25. Cannabis Use in Long-Term Care: An Emerging Issue for Nurses
26. I Was a Doctor Accustomed to Death, But Not His.
30. Mourning in a Digital Age
34. The Grieving Process
35. The Normal Process of Grieving
36. A guide to getting through grief
37. Disenfranchised Grief
38. Challenging the Paradigm: New Understandings of Grief
40. Shades of Grief: When Does Mourning Become a Mental Illness?

Cemeteries
1. The Dead, the Living, and Those Yet to Come
3. How We Bury the War Dead
33. Speaking from beyond the grave

Children
8. Teaching Children about Death and Grief
9. Death in Disney Films: Implications for Children's Understanding of Death
10. Death and Dying in the Curriculum of Public Schools: Is there a place?
12. Good Mourning
13. Through the Touch of God: Child Death and Spiritual Sustenance in a Hutterian Colony
18. When Death Strikes Without Warning
28. Building my father's coffin
29. Dealing with the Dead

Communication
8. Teaching about Death and Grief
9. Death in Disney Films: Implications for Children's Understanding of Death
12. Good Mourning
14. End-of-Life Concerns and Care Preferences: Congruence Among Terminally Ill Elders and their Family Caregivers
21. Ethics and Life's Ending
26. I Was a doctor accustomed to death, but not his.
30. Mourning in a Digital Age
32. Memorial videos give lasting farewell
33. Speaking from beyond the grave

Coping
12. Good Mourning
13. Through the Touch of God: Child Death and Spiritual Sustenance in a Hutterian Colony
18. When Death Strikes Without Warning
20. Beyond Terror and Denial: The Positive Psychology of Death Acceptance
26. I Was a doctor accustomed to death, but not his.
28. Building my father's Coffin
29. Dealing with the Dead
30. Mourning in a Digital Age
32. Memorial videos give lasting farewell

33. Speaking from beyond the grave
34. The Grieving Process
35. The Normal Process of Grieving
36. A guide to getting through grief
37. Disenfranchised Grief
38. Challenging the Paradigm: New Understandings of Grief
39. We've Been Mislead about How to Grieve
40. Shades of Grief: When Does Mourning Become a Mental Illness?
41. 11 Ways to Comfort Someone Who's Grieving

Counseling

22. Obituary for Jack Kevorkian
23. At the Bottom of the Slippery Slope
34. The Grieving Process
35. The Normal Process of Grieving
36. A guide to getting through grief
37. Disenfranchised Grief
38. Challenging the Paradigm: New Understandings of Grief
39. We've Been Mislead about How to Grieve
40. Shades of Grief: When Does Mourning Become a Mental Illness?
41. 11 Ways to Comfort Someone Who's Grieving

Cultural situations

11. Needs of Elderly Patients in Palliative Care
16. Death and Dying Across Cultures
18. When Death Strikes Without Warning
19. Are They Hallucinations or Are They Real? The Spirituality of Deathbed and Near-Death Visions

Dead human remains

23. At the Bottom of the Slippery Slope
28. Building my father's coffin

Death Attitudes

2. The Cycle of Death

Death defined

19. Are They Hallucinations or Are They Real? The Spirituality of Deathbed and Near-Death Visions

Death denial

7. The Emergence of Thanatology and Current Practice in Death Education
20. Beyond Terror and Denial: The Positive Psychology of Death Acceptance

Death education

7. The Emergence of Thanatology and Current Practice in Death Education
8. Teaching about Death and Grief: Implications for Children's Understanding of Death
10. Death and Dying in the Curriculum of Public Schools: Is there a place?

Death fear/anxiety

9. Death in Disney Films: Implications for Children's Understanding of Death
14. End-of-Life Concerns and Care Preferences: Congruence Among Terminally Ill Elders and their Family Caregivers
15. Dying on the Streets: Homeless Persons' Concerns and Desires about End-of-Life Care

Disadvantaged dying

15. Dying on the Streets: Homeless Persons' Concerns and Desires about End-of-Life Care

Dying individuals

11. Needs of Elderly Patients in Palliative Care
18. When Death Strikes Without Warning

21. Ethics and Life's Ending
22. Obituary for Jack Kevorkian
23. At the Bottom of the Slippery Slope,
26. I Was a doctor accustomed to death, but not his.

Economic Issues

Elderly persons

11. Needs of Elderly Patients in Palliative Care
14. End-of-Life Concerns and Care Preferences: Congruence Among Terminally Ill Elders and their Family Caregivers
25. Cannabis Use in Long-Term Care: An Emerging Issue for Nurses

End-of-life care

11. Needs of Elderly Patients in Palliative Care
14. End-of-Life Concerns and Care Preferences: Congruence Among Terminally Ill Elders and their Family Caregivers
15. Dying on the Streets: Homeless Persons' Concerns and Desires about End-of-Life Care
21. Ethics and Life's Ending
22. Obituary for Jack Kevorkian
23. At the Bottom of the Slippery Slope,
25. Cannabis Use in Long-Term Care: An Emerging Issue for Nurses
26. I Was a doctor accustomed to death, but not his.

Ethical issues

21. Ethics and Life's Ending
22. Obituary for Jack Kevorkian
23. At the Bottom of the Slippery Slope,
25. Cannabis Use in Long-Term Care: An Emerging Issue for Nurses

Ethnography

13. Through the Touch of God: Child Death and Spiritual Sustenance in a Hutterian Colony

Etiology (Causation)

9. Death in Disney Films: Implications for Children's Understanding of Death

Euthanasia

12. Good Mourning
21. Ethics and Life's Ending
22. Obituary for Jack Kevorkian
23. At the Bottom of the Slippery Slope,

Funerals

1. The Dead, the Living, and Those Yet to Come
27. The Contemporary American Funeral
28. Building my father's coffin
29. Dealing with the Dead
30. Mourning in a Digital Age
31. 10 Burdens Funeral Directors Carry
32. Memorial videos give lasting farewell
33. Speaking from beyond the grave
34. The Grieving Process
35. The Normal Process of Grieving
36. A guide to getting through grief
37. Disenfranchised Grief
38. Challenging the Paradigm: New Understandings of Grief

Funeral Directors

31. 10 Burdens Funeral Directors Carry
32. Memorial videos give lasting farewell
33. Speaking from beyond the grave
34. The Grieving Process
37. Disenfranchised Grief
38. Challenging the Paradigm: New Understandings of Grief

Good death

6. Criteria for a Good Death
14. End-of-Life Concerns and Care Preferences: Congruence Among Terminally Ill Elders and their Family Caregivers
22. Obituary for Jack Kevorkian
23. At the Bottom of the Slippery Slope
25. Cannabis Use in Long-Term Care: An Emerging Issue for Nurses
26. I Was a doctor accustomed to death, but not his.

Healthcare

11. Needs of Elderly Patients in Palliative Care
22. Obituary for Jack Kevorkian
23. At the Bottom of the Slippery Slope
25. Cannabis Use in Long-Term Care: An Emerging Issue for Nurses
26. I Was a doctor accustomed to death, but not his.

History

3. How We Bury the War Dead
7. The Emergence of Thanatology and Current Practice in Death Education
18. When Death Strikes Without Warning

Humor and death

9. Death in Disney Films: Implications for Children's Understanding of Death

Intervention

5. Brain Death Guidelines Vary at Top US Neurological Hospitals
11. Needs of Elderly Patients in Palliative Care
22. Obituary for Jack Kevorkian
23. At the Bottom of the Slippery Slope
25. Cannabis Use in Long-Term Care: An Emerging Issue for Nurses
30. Mourning in a Digital Age
31. 10 Burdens Funeral Directors Carry
35. The Normal Process of Grieving
36. A guide to getting through grief
37. Disenfranchised Grief
38. Challenging the Paradigm: New Understandings of Grief
40. Shades of Grief: When Does Mourning Become a Mental Illness?
41. 11 Ways to Comfort Someone Who's Grieving

Legal issues

21. Ethics and Life's Ending
22. Obituary for Jack Kevorkian
23. At the Bottom of the Slippery Slope
25. Cannabis Use in Long-Term Care: An Emerging Issue for Nurses

Life after death

19. Are They Hallucinations or Are They Real? The Spirituality of Deathbed and Near-Death Visions

Meaning of life-death

9. Death in Disney Films: Implications for Children's Understanding of Death
22. Obituary for Jack Kevorkian
23. At the Bottom of the Slippery Slope
26. I Was a doctor accustomed to death, but not his.
34. The Grieving Process

Media and death

9. Death in Disney Films: Implications for Children's Understanding of Death
21. Ethics and Life's Ending

22. Obituary for Jack Kevorkian
30. Mourning in a Digital Age
32. Memorial videos give lasting farewell
33. Speaking from beyond the grave

Medical ethics

22. Obituary for Jack Kevorkian
23. At the Bottom of the Slippery Slope
25. Cannabis Use in Term Care: An Emerging Issue for Nurses

Memorials

32. Memorial videos give lasting farewell
33. Speaking from beyond the grave

Memorial service

32. Memorial videos give lasting farewell

Mourning

12. Good Mourning
28. Building my father's coffin
29. Dealing with the Dead
30. Mourning in a Digital Age
32. Memorial videos give lasting farewell
33. Speaking from beyond the grave
34. The Grieving Process
35. The Normal Process of Grieving
36. A guide to getting through grief
37. Disenfranchised Grief
38. Challenging the Paradigm: New Understandings of Grief
39. We've Been Mislead about How to Grieve
40. Shades of Grief: When Does Mourning Become a Mental Illness?
41. 11 Ways to Comfort Someone Who's Grieving

Multicultural

16. Death and Dying Across Cultures
18. When Death Strikes Without Warning

Near-Death Experiences

19. Are They Hallucinations or Are They Real? The Spirituality of Deathbed and Near-Death Visions

Nurses

16. Death and Dying Across Cultures
25. Cannabis Use in Long-Term Care: An Emerging Issue for Nurses

Organ transplants

22. Obituary for Jack Kevorkian
23. At the Bottom of the Slippery Slope

Palliative care

11. Needs of Elderly Patients in Palliative Care
26. I Was a doctor accustomed to death, but not his.

Pain Control

11. Needs of Elderly Patients in Palliative Care
14. End-of-Life Concerns and Care Preferences: Congruence Among Terminally Ill Elders and their Family Caregivers

Pets

12. Good Mourning

Physicians

5. Brain Death Guidelines Vary at Top US Neurological Hospitals
17. The Promise of Presence
21. Ethics and Life's Ending

22. Obituary for Jack Kevorkian
23. At the Bottom of the Slippery Slope

Physician-assisted suicide

21. Ethics and Life's Ending
22. Obituary for Jack Kevorkian
23. At the Bottom of the Slippery Slope

Policies

22. Obituary for Jack Kevorkian
23. At the Bottom of the Slippery Slope
25. Cannabis Use in Long-Term Care: An Emerging Issue for Nurses

Preplanning funerals

28. Building my father's coffin
32. Memorial videos give lasting farewell
33. Speaking from beyond the grave
34. The Grieving Process

Religion and spirituality

16. Death and Dying Across Cultures
19. Are They Hallucinations or Are They Real? The Spirituality of Deathbed and Near-Death Visions

Research methods

9. Death in Disney Films: Implications for Children's Understanding of Death
11. Needs of Elderly Patients in Palliative Care
13. Through the Touch of God: Child Death and Spiritual Sustenance in a Hutterian Colony
14. End-of-Life Concerns and Care Preferences: Congruence Among Terminally Ill Elders and their Family Caregivers
15. Dying on the Streets: Homeless Persons' Concerns and Desires about End-of-Life Care

Rituals

9. Death in Disney Films: Implications for Children's Understanding of Death
28. Building my father's coffin
30. Mourning in a Digital Age
32. Memorial videos give lasting farewell
34. The Grieving Process
35. The Normal Process of Grieving
36. A guide to getting through grief
37. Disenfranchised Grief
38. Challenging the Paradigm: New Understandings of Grief

Spiritual/Religious

11. Needs of Elderly Patients in Palliative Care
13. Through the Touch of God: Child Death and Spiritual Sustenance in a Hutterian Colony
15. Dying on the Streets: Homeless Persons' Concerns and Desires about End-of-Life Care
16. Death and Dying Across Cultures
19. Are They Hallucinations or Are They Real? The Spirituality of Deathbed and Near-Death Visions

Sudden, unexpected death

18. When Death Strikes Without Warning

Support groups

14. End-of-Life Concerns and Care Preferences: Congruence Among Terminally Ill Elders and their Family Caregivers
28. Building my father's coffin
30. Mourning in a Digital Age
31. 10 Burdens Funeral Directors Carry
34. The Grieving Process
35. The Normal Process of Grieving
36. A guide to getting through grief
37. Disenfranchised Grief
38. Challenging the Paradigm: New Understandings of Grief
40. Shades of Grief: When Does Mourning Become a Mental Illness?
41. 11 Ways to Comfort Someone Who's Grieving

Teaching about dying and death

8. Teaching Children about Death and Grief
9. Death in Disney Films: Implications for Children's Understanding of Death

Technology and death

4. Grief in the Age of Facebook
30. Mourning in a Digital Age
32. Memorial videos give lasting farewell
33. Speaking from beyond the grave

Terminally-ill Patients

11. Needs of Elderly Patients in Palliative Care
14. End-of-Life Concerns and Care Preferences: Congruence Among Terminally Ill Elders and their Family Caregivers
17. The Promise of Presence

Theories on dying and death

1. The Dead, the Living, and Those Yet to Come
7. The Emergence of Thanatology and Current Practice in Death Education
10. Death and Dying in the Curriculum of Public Schools: Is there a place?
19. Are They Hallucinations or Are They Real? The Spirituality of Deathbed and Near-Death Visions

Timing of death

18. When Death Strikes Without Warning

Veterinarians

12. Good Mourning

War

3. How We Bury the War Dead

Internet References

The following Internet sites have been selected to support the articles found in this reader. These sites were available at the time of publication. However, because websites often change their structure and content, the information listed may no longer be available. We invite you to visit www.mhhe.com/cls for easy access to these sites.

Annual Editions: Dying, Death, and Bereavement 13/14

General Sources

An Introduction to Death and Dying
www.bereavement.org

This electronic book was created to help those who grieve and those who provide support for the bereaved. Sections include Grief Theories, Death Systems, Ritual, and Disenfranchised Grief.

Yahoo: Society and Culture: Death
http://dir.yahoo.com/Society_and_Culture/Death_and_Dying

This Yahoo site has a very complete index to issues of dying and a search option.

Unit 1: Issues in Dying and Death

Association for Death Education and Counseling, The Thanatology Association
www.adec.org

The Association for Death Education and Counseling, The Thanatology Association, is one of the oldest interdisciplinary organizations in the field of dying, death, and bereavement. Its nearly 2,000 members include a wide array of mental and medical health personnel, educators, clergy, funeral directors, and volunteers.

Bardo of Death Studies
www.bardo.org

Bardo of Death Studies assists in the development of discourse, discussion, and archival materials related to personal experiences in death and dying. We serve as a friendly net repository for these personal reflections (both from the professional and the lay public) and a crossroads resource for others who happen by in search for personal reflection in their own time of need.

Death and Culture
http://en.wikipedia.org/wiki/Death_and_culture

This article is about death in the different cultures around the world as well as ethical issues relating to death, such as martydom, suicide, and euthanasia. Death and its spiritual ramifications are debated in every manner all over the world. Most civilizations dispose of their dead with rituals developed through spiritual traditions.

Kearl's Guide to Sociology of Death and Dying
www.trinity.edu/~mkearl/death.html

An internet resource on the Sociology of Death and Dying that includes issues of dying and death, such as death in the natural order, is found here.

Yahoo: Society and Culture: Death and Dying
http://dir.yahoo.com/Society_and_Culture/Death_and_Dying

This Yahoo site has a very complete index to issues of death and dying and a search option.

Unit 2: Dying and Death across the Life Cycle

American Academy of Child & Adolescent Psychiatry
http://aacap.org/page.ww?name=Children+and+Grief&section=Facts+for+Families

The American Academy of Child & Adolescent Psychiatry provides important information as a public service to assist parents and families in their most important roles. This article "Children and Grief" is one such resource, written in English, Spanish, and French.

Child Bereavement Charity
www.childbereavement.org.uk/home_page

The Child Bereavement Charity site provides support for families and educates professionals for bereaved families, including miscarriage, stillbirth, neonatal death, and termination for abnormality.

Children with AIDS Project
www.aidskids.org

The Children with AIDS Project offers a deeper understanding of children with, and at risk of, AIDS, including the medical, psychosocial, legal, and financial issues. The mission of the organization is to develop local and national adoptive, foster- and family-centered care programs that are both effective and compassionate.

The Compassionate Friends
www.compassionatefriends.org/resources/links.aspx

The Compassionate Friends site is a self-help organization for bereaved parents and siblings. There are presently hundreds of chapters worldwide.

Grief Net
http://rivendell.org

This website provides many links on the bereavement process, resources for grievers, and information concerning grief support groups.

Motherloss
www.freewebs.com/motherloss/front.htm

This site is a support group started to help with the grieving issues for women whose mothers have died.

Raindrop: Death Education for Children of All Ages
http://iul.com/raindrop

This site presents an explanation of "What happens when we die?" a question by children of all ages for the unexplainable phenomenon of life and death.

Yahoo: Society and Culture: Death and Dying
http://dir.yahoo.com/Society_and_Culture/Death_and_Dying

This Yahoo site has a very complete index to issues of death and dying and a search option.

Internet References

Unit 3: The Dying Process

Thanatolinks
http://netsociology.tripod.com/thanalinks.htm

This site contains links to some of the best sites related to death and dying on the internet.

Yahoo: Society and Culture: Death and Dying
http://dir.yahoo.com/Society_and_Culture/Death_and_Dying

This Yahoo site has a very complete index to issues of death and dying and a search option.

Centers for Disease Control and Prevention
www.cdc.gov

Centers for Disease Control and Prevention (CDC) provide informational material to protect people and communities health, through health promotion, prevention, and preparedness.

Agency for Healthcare Research and Quality
www.ahrq.gov

Agency for Healthcare Research and Quality provides information on the dying process in the context of U.S. health policy.

The Natural Death Centre
www.naturaldeath.org.uk

This is a nonprofit charitable project launched in Britain in 1991, with three psychotherapists as directors. It aims to support those dying at home and their caregivers and to help them arrange funerals. It also has a more general aim of helping improve "the quality of dying."

Project on Death in America
www.soros.org/resources/articles_publications/publications/pdia_20040101

Project on Death in America (PDIA) has the goal to help people understand and transform the dying experience in America.

Kearl's PARADIGM: Enhancing Life near Death
www.trinity.edu/~mkearl/paradigm.html

This internet resource does not suggest that there is one particular way of dying well. However, it is possible to identify some general developmental tasks that the dying person can accomplish if dying well is the goal.

The Living Will and Values History Project
www.euthanasia.cc/lwvh.html

The Living Will and Values History Project was set up in response to an alarming growth and proliferation of living will documents that bore little correlation to academic and empirical data on their usefulness or effectiveness. It attempts to collate, analyze and apply research in this area, acting as an adviser and resource base, as well as publishing its own document.

Hospice Foundation of America
www.hospicefoundation.org

Hospice Foundation of America provides general information about hospice and specific information on the Foundation.

Hospice and Palliative Nurses Association
www.hpna.org

Hospice and Palliative Nurses Association (HPNA) is an international professional association with the mission of promoting excellence in hospice nursing.

National Prison Hospice Association
www.npha.org

National Prison Hospice Association promotes hospice care for terminally ill inmates and those facing the prospect of dying in prison. The goal of the association is to support and assist corrections professionals in their continuing efforts to develop high-quality patient care procedures and management programs.

Larson's Compilation of Great Ideas
www.scu.edu/Hospice/greatideas.html

Dale Larson's compilation of Great Ideas submitted from a wide variety of sources.

Hospice-Care
www.hospice-cares.com

The Hospice-Care website includes an extensive collection of links to hospice resources.

American Academy of Hospice & Palliative Medicine
www.aahpm.org

American Academy of Hospice and Palliative Medicine (AAHPM) is the only organization in the United States for physicians dedicated to the advancement of hospice/palliative medicine, its practice, research, and education.

The Zen Hospice Project
www.zenhospice.org

This site organizes programs dedicated to the care of people approaching death and to increasing the understanding of impermanence. The Zen Hospice Project also runs a small hospice in a restored Victorian house near the San Francisco Zen Center.

VNA of Hudson Valley, NY
www.vnahv.org

Visiting Nurse Association of Hudson Valley website provides quality healthcare to all people in their communities regardless of ability to pay, in a manner that recognizes the whole person and their environment. A primary focus is to maximize resources for the organization for the benefit of the patient. The VNAHV strives to foster independence and choice for all individuals with the overall goal of improving the quality of life by assuming a proactive advocate role.

The Connecticut Hospice
www.hospice.com

Founded in 1974 as the nation's first Hospice, today The Connecticut Hospice, Inc., offers a state-wide hospice home care program and the state's only 52-bed inpatient hospice care center that accepts referrals from throughout the United States and the world. Being a leader in palliative medicine, The Connecticut Hospice became the first and only accredited teaching hospice offering training and consultation to professionals from around the world through its teaching arm, the John D. Thompson Hospice Institute for Education, Training, and Research, Inc.

Houston Hospice
www.houstonhospice.org

The Houston Hospice website offers and provides, regardless of ability to pay, the highest quality of care for patients with life-threatening illnesses and their families through a well-qualified interdisciplinary team of professionals and volunteers.

Internet References

Hospice Service of Santa Barbara
www.hospiceofsantabarbara.org

The Hospice Service of Santa Barbara, Inc. is a program of the Santa Barbara Visiting Nurse Association.

Unit 4: Ethical Issues of Dying and Death

Moral Debates of Our Times
www.trinity.edu/~mkearl/death-5.html#eu

Moral Debates of our Times is an internet resource on biomedical issues.

Biomedical Ethics and Issues of Euthanasia
http://pwa.acusd.edu/~hinman/euthanasia.html

A website dedicated to biomedical ethics and issues of euthanasia.

Yahoo: Society and Culture: Death and Dying Euthanasia
http://dir.yahoo.com/Society_and_Culture/Death_and_Dying/Euthanasia

This Yahoo site has a very complete index to issues of euthanasia related to death and dying and a search option.

Deathnet
www.deathnet.com

Deathnet is an internet searchable website containing many links to many biomedical topics including living wills, "how to" suicide, euthanasia, mercy killing, and legislation regulating the care for the terminally ill.

Thanatolinks
http://netsociology.tripod.com/thanalinks.htm

This site contains links to some of the best sites on the internet related to death and dying.

Living Will (Advance Directive)
www.mindspring.com/~scottr/will.html

Living Will contains the largest collection of links to living wills and other advance directive and living will information. Living wills (advance directives) and values histories help medical staff and others to make decisions about care and treatment of the seriously ill who are unable to speak for themselves. In some circumstances, living wills may become legally binding on healthcare staff. The Living Will and Values History Project was set up in response to an alarming growth and proliferation of living will documents that bore little correlation to academic and empirical data on their usefulness or effectiveness. It works on a nonprofit basis and attempts to collate, analyze, and apply research in this area, acting as an adviser and resource base, as well as publishing its own document.

Euthanasia Research & Guidance Organization
www.finalexit.org/index.html

Euthanasia Research & Guidance Organization (ERGO) provides links to right to die organizations worldwide.

Euthanasia in the Netherlands
www.euthanasia.com/netherlands.html

Website dedicated to the issues of euthanasia as practiced in the Netherlands.

The Choice in Dying
www.choices.org

The Choice in Dying is an organization that provides information to patients interested in active and passive euthanasia.

Last Rights Organization
http://lastrights.info

Last Rights Organization publishes electronically the complete texts of many of the key legal documents concerning the dying patient's right to die.

Euthanasia and Christianity: Christian Views of Euthanasia and Suicide
www.religionfacts.com/euthanasia/christianity.htm

Roman Catholic perspective and view about euthanasia and suicide.

Not Dead Yet!
www.notdeadyet.org/pressrel.html

Americans with Disabilities have a website to mobilize American's against euthanasia and mercy killing. They say, "We don't want your pity or your lethal mercy."

Patients Rights Council
www.patientsrightscouncil.org

International Anti-Euthanasia Task Force that provides more links to internet resources which oppose euthanasia.

United Network for Organ Sharing
www.unos.org

The website of the United Network for Organ Sharing Transplantation Information Site.

TransWeb
www.transweb.org

TransWeb is a website all about transplantation and organ donation.

Unit 5: Funerals

Personal Impacts of Death
http://www.trinity.edu/~mkearl/death-6.html#funerals

Personal Impacts of Death is an internet resource regarding funeral guides and planning.

Willed Body Program
www.utsouthwestern.edu/utsw/home/pcpp/willedbody

The Willed Body Program is a universal program in which people can donate their body for medical science, after death. The program is a division of the Department of Anatomy and Neurobiology at the University of California, Irvine's College of Medicine.

Mortuary Science
www.alamo.edu/sac/mortuary/mortuarylinks.htm

A list of some internet links.

Funerals: A Consumer Guide
www.ftc.gov/bcp/edu/pubs/consumer/products/pro19.shtm

Funerals: A Consumer Guide presents facts for consumers produced by the Federal Trade Commission.

Internet References

Funeral Net
www.funeral.net/info/notices.html

Funeral Net's intention is to provide an avenue to the general public to gain a basic understanding of the funeral and grief process so that they may be better equipped, emotionally, psychologically, and mentally to deal with the closure of significant relationships in their lives.

The Internet Cremation Society
www.cremation.org

The Internet Cremation Society contains statistics on cremations and links to funeral industry resources.

Cremation Consultant Guidebook
www.funeralplan.com/funeralplan/cremation/options.html

The Cremation Consultant Guidebook provides information to families who are interesting in cremation and memorial services.

National Academy of Mortuary Science
www.drkloss.com

The National Academy of Mortuary Science informs how you can enroll in funeral school to gain mortuary service employment.

Alcor
www.alcor.org

Alcor is the world's largest cryonics organization.

CyroCare
www.cyrocare.org

CyroCare is a website dealing with cryonics.

Funerals and Ripoffs
www.funerals-ripoffs.org

Funerals and Ripoffs is a website that is very critical of the funeral industry and specializes in exposing funeral home financial fraud.

The Making of a Classic
www.monitor.net/monitor/decca/death.html

The Making of a Classic is an internet resource that provides a critical perspective on the funeral industry in America.

The End of Life: Exploring Death in America
http://www.npr.org/programs/death/index.html

The End of Life: Exploring Death in America provides assistance for families who want a "do-it-yourself" funeral. They assist families in providing in conducting their own legal, uncomplicated, dignified, and inexpensive funeral without advanced planning or professional help.

Forensic Entomology
www.forensic-entomology.com

Forensic Entomology provides information concerning what happens to the human body after death and the process of body decomposition.

Hospice: A Guide to Grief Bereavement, Mourning, and Grief
www.hospicenet.org/html/grief_guide.html

Hospice: A Guide to Grief Bereavement, Mourning, and Grief is an informational resource to learn about the different ways people cope with the loss of a loved one.

Growth House
www.growthhouse.org

Growth House is a nonprofit organization working with grief, bereavement, hospice, and end-of-life issues.

Directory of Grief, Loss and Bereavement: Support Groups
www.dmoz.org/Health/Mental_Health/Grief,_Loss_and_Bereavement/Support_Groups

The death of a loved one is an emotionally devastating time for survivors. But not knowing what to expect can often lead to unnecessary additional pain. To alleviate some of the confusion, to begin to examine the many issues that are often hard to discuss and to find all the help bereaved individuals need as they begin this journey, we created the most comprehensive book, the first of its kind, to assist them with resources and answers—all in one place.

Bereaved Families of Ontario
www.bereavedfamilies.net

Bereavement self-help resources guide indexes resources of the center along with over 300 listings to other resources and information.

Death Notices
www.legacy.com/NS

Death Notices is a placement of death notices for information purposes.

Burial Insurance
www.burialinsurance.org

Burial Insurance is a website that informs about final expense insurance standard policy that many use to cover the cost of a funeral.

Unit 6: Bereavement

After Death Communication Research Foundation
www.adcrf.org

This website includes information and resources regarding after death communication, bereavement, grief, life after death.

Thanatolinks
http://netsociology.tripod.com/thanalinks.htm

This site contains links to some of the best sites on the internet related to death and dying.

Hospice: A Guide to Grief Bereavement, Mourning, and Grief
www.hospicenet.org/html/grief_guide.html

Hospice: A Guide to Grief Bereavement, Mourning, and Grief is an informational resource to learn about the different ways people cope with the loss of a loved one.

Growth House
www.growthhouse.org

Growth House is a nonprofit organization working with grief, bereavement, hospice, and end-of-life issues.

Grief in a Family Context
www.indiana.edu/~famlygrf/sitemap.html

Grief in a Family Context is an internet resource provided with links to various grief issues.

Directory of Grief, Loss and Bereavement: Support Groups
www.dmoz.org/Health/Mental_Health/Grief,_Loss_and_Bereavement/Support_Groups

The death of a loved one is an emotionally devastating time for survivors. But not knowing what to expect can often lead to unnecessary additional pain. To alleviate some of the confusion, to begin to examine the many issues that are often hard to

Internet References

discuss and to find all the help a bereaved individuals need as they begin this journey, we created the most comprehensive book, the first of its kind, to assist them with resources and answers—all in one place.

Bereaved Families of Ontario
www.bereavedfamilies.net

Bereavement self-help resources guide indexes resources of the center along with over 300 listings to other resources and information.

Grief Net
http://rivendell.org

This website provides many links on the bereavement process, resources for grievers, and information concerning grief support groups.

Child Bereavement Charity
www.childbereavement.org.uk/home_page

The Child Bereavement Charity site provides support for families and educates professionals for bereaved families, including miscarriage, stillbirth, neonatal death, and termination for abnormality.

Core Principles for Helping Grieving Children
www2.cfalls.org/hs_pdf/core_principles_for_helping_grieving_children.pdf

Core Principles for Helping Grieving Children provides core principles for helping grieving children.

The Compassionate Friends
www.compassionatefriends.org/resources/links.aspx

The Compassionate Friends site is a self-help organization for bereaved parents and siblings. There are presently hundreds of chapters worldwide.

American Academy of Child & Adolescent Psychiatry
http://aacap.org/page.ww?name=Children+and+Grief&section=Facts+for+Families

The American Academy of Child & Adolescent Psychiatry provides important information as a public service to assist parents and families in their most important roles. This article "Children and Grief" is one such resource; written in English, Spanish, and French.

Children with AIDS Project
www.aidskids.org

The Children with AIDS Project offers a deeper understanding of children with, and at risk of, AIDS, including the medical,

psychosocial, legal, and financial issues. The mission of the organization is to develop local and national adoptive, foster- and family-centered care programs that are both effective and compassionate.

Rites of Passage: Our Fathers Die
www.menweb.org/daddie.htm

The Men Web-M.E.N. Magazine posts an article "Rites of Passage: Our Fathers Die" written by Bert H. Hoff

Motherloss
www.freewebs.com/motherloss/front.htm

This site is a support group started to help with the grieving issues for women whose mothers have died.

Widow Net
www.widownet.org

Widow Net is an information and self-help resource for, and by, widows and widowers. Topics covered include grief, bereavement, recovery, and other information helpful to people of all ages, religious backgrounds and sexual orientations who have suffered the death of a spouse or life partner.

Web Healing
www.webhealing.com

Tom Golden of the Crisis, Grief, and Healing Page brings you A Place to Honor Grief. This is a website where people write concerning the grief they are experiencing at the death of a loved-one.

Dearly Departed
http://dearlydprtd.com

Dearly Departed is a free service, dedicated to the memory of those loved ones who passed away from this life, but not from our hearts—a virtual internet mausoleum.

In Memory of Pets
www.In-Memory-Of-Pets.Com

In Memory of Pets website includes poems, tributes, and resources.

Burial Insurance
www.burialinsurance.org

Burial Insurance is a website that informs about final expense insurance standard policy that many use to cover the cost of a funeral.

UNIT 1

Issues in Dying and Death

Unit Selections

1. **The Dead, the Living, and Those Yet to Come,** Charles Lemert
2. **The Cycle of Death,** Vince Beiser
3. **How We Bury the War Dead,** Yochi J. Dreazen and Gary Fields
4. **Grief in the Age of Facebook,** Elizabeth Stone
5. **Brain Death Guidelines Vary at Top US Neurological Hospitals,** Susan Jeffrey
6. **Criteria for a Good Death,** Edwin Shneidman, PhD
7. **The Emergence of Thanatology and Current Practice in Death Education,** Luciana M. Fonseca and Ines Testoni

Learning Outcomes

After reading this unit you should be able to:

- Better explain how Facebook has contributed to grief in today's world.

- Discuss how brain death guidelines vary in hospitals.

- Wrestle with the issue of a good death.

- Identify how the different veterinary schools in the United States prepare future veterinarians to deal with end-of-life issues.

- Present something of the history of thanatology and the current status of death education.

- Talk about why the United States is seemingly abandoning the death penalty.

- Share knowledge of the role of the dead in the world of the living.

- Trace the history of the final disposition of the bodies of the war dead.

Student Website

www.mhhe.com/cls

Internet References

Association for Death Education and Counseling, The Thanatology Association
www.adec.org
Bardo of Death Studies
www.bardo.org
Death and Culture
http://en.wikipedia.org/wiki/Death_and_culture
Sociology of Death and Dying
www.trinity.edu/~mkearl/death.html
Yahoo: Society and Culture: Death and Dying
http://dir.yahoo.com/Society_and_Culture/Death_and_Dying

Death, like sex, is a rather taboo topic. British anthropologist Geoffrey Gorer's writing about the pornography of death in the mid-20th century seemed to open the door for publications on the subject of death. Gorer argued that death had replaced sex as contemporary society's major taboo topic. Because death was less common in the community, with individuals actually seeing fewer corpses and being with individuals less at the time of death, a relatively realistic view of death had been replaced by a voyeuristic, adolescent preoccupation with it. Our modern way of life has not prepared us to cope any better with dying and death. Sex and death have "come out of the closet" in recent decades, however, and now issues are discussed and presented in formal educational settings. Baby Boomers are aging and changing the ways we handle death. In fact, end-of-life issues are frequently discussed in the popular media, as evidenced by the numerous documentaries and other drama series about hospitals and emergency rooms as well as series about crime scenes. Yet, we have a long way to go in educating the public about these historically taboo subjects.

We are beginning to recognize the importance of educating youth on the subject of dying and death. Like sex education, death education (thanatology, literally "the study of death") is an approved topic for presentation in elementary and secondary school curricula in many states, but the topics (especially death and dying) are optional and therefore rarely receive high priorities in the classroom or in educational funding. With terrorist attacks around the world, the war in Afghanistan, and various natural disasters, an increased interest in death and dying in the curricula could have a positive impact on helping to cope with these various megadeath-related situations.

Just what is a "good death?" Edwin Shneidman in "Criteria for a Good Death," addresses this topic, although it will vary significantly between cultures and individuals within cultures.

When is a person dead? The "brain death" definition of death is one of the more definitive definitions of death, yet brain death guidelines vary in U.S. hospitals, as noted in "Brain Death Guidelines Vary at Top US Neurological Hospitals" by Susan Jeffrey.

Other issues discussed in this section include the impact of technology, particularly the Internet and Facebook, on how death and grief are handled, the role of the dead in the world of the living, capital punishment, burying the war dead, and the emergence of thanatology.

© Ingram Publishing/SuperStock

The Dead, the Living, and Those Yet to Come

CHARLES LEMERT

One late summer afternoon some years ago, I visited the graves of those who had brought me up. The last of them died in 1995, and I had not been to my hometown since. Cincinnati, Ohio, like many hasn't changed much over 20 years, especially within the confines of Spring Grove Cemetery. Cemeteries fill up, but otherwise, they remain much as they were when the Dead came for their rest.

That summer, I was of an age when one pauses before the surprising idea that he too will return to the ground of all beings. Those I visited had been thus grounded a good while. It was Florence who died most recently, about twenty years after Helen went Home (as Florence would have put it, with a capital H). That was 1975; just months after Gertrude had passed (as she would have put it, in a discreet lower case). And Grandmother Gertrude lay next to Blaine. He was grandpa; she was grandmother. I never knew why (nor thought much about it). Grandpa had purchased this family plot when World War II made burial ground a particular concern, and he bought places for four—no more. This he did in the assurance that the intended would not refuse to join him. He died in 1948. Blaine and Gertrude, parents to Charles, lay side-by-side alongside their son and Helen, his wife. Florence and Adele were elsewhere in the yard. No place had been made for them in the tight circle of family respectability. Neither had their second son, Edwin, nor my brother and I (much less our wives and children) been invited. This place wasn't for just anyone.

The family burial place was a choice address in one of the nation's most lovely cemeteries. When they were among the Living, these four had made a judicious show of their slight progress beyond the American postwar normal. Gertrude, whom I had never known to read a book, kept a subscription to *The New Yorker* until the day she died. Blaine, from small-town Ohio, wanted an address in Cincinnati's best neighborhood. He got it, but his was the smallest house on the avenue. Charles, who bought a new car every year, once bought a Jaguar. In those days, such a prize meant an hour's drive each way for maintenance at a dealership closer to the city's truly wealthy. The year after the Jaguar, he went back to Oldsmobiles. His wife Helen decorated our homes in expensive reproduction furniture and art, using an interior decorator, even when the interiors decorated were no more than a living room and a dining alcove. Each of these four had their way of hinting at the good luck of their inconsiderable fortunes, and they chose their final resting-place so as to perpetuate a status that outran their means. In this, they were like thousands of men and women of their times: good (or at least well-intended) people who wanted more than their circumstances would permit. In life, they had had a lot, but less than they thought they deserved. In death, their family plot was meant to close the gap.

Spring Grove Cemetery was designed in the mid-nineteenth century when landscape architecture was a new art. Its architect was the man who finished second to Fredrick Law Olmstead for the prize of landscaping New York's Central Park—an emblematic outcome for a city like Cincinnati, so accustomed to coming second. Today, Spring Grove is as it was when Charles bought the biggest house in a declassed neighborhood. It made us all miserable. Today, that house is in shambles. He, like his father Blaine, may well have applied the rule to the place of their deaths as if proximity to the better-off Dead promises a perpetual gain in long-term status. But who exactly did they suppose would notice or otherwise pay the dividend? Might they have hoped that their plot, so near the road but overlooking a lovely pond amid splendid plantings, would cause strangers to tip their hats? What were they thinking, if they thought at all, about the place they would inhabit forever?

The Dead are not exactly absent from the communities of the living. Many of them lie or are scattered in special places around town. People will swear on their dead. We visit them. Huge sums are paid to manage their remains. While they remain above ground, the Living meant to be: an arboretum of 700 acres for about 200,000 interments since 1845. That's about 1,200 bodies a year, 250 an acre. Like the neighborhoods in which most of the Dead here gathered had lived, Spring Grove is an exclusive address in a suburban sort of way—hard to get into, and a bit crowded, though tastefully so. No plastic flowers.

At my family's perpetual address, their graveyard neighbors generally have the bigger monuments. The first rule among nouveau house hunters is that long-term profits accrue to the smallest house on a block of bigger homes.

Down through the ages, since at least Homer had Ulysses visit the underworld, the world of the Dead has preoccupied the Living. To write or speak of the underworld is, as novelist Margaret Atwood puts it in *Negotiating with the Dead,* grave digging. "Everyone can dig a hole in a cemetery, but not everyone is a grave-digger. The latter takes a good deal more stamina and persistence. It is also, because of the nature of the activity, a deeply symbolic role. As a grave-digger, you are not just a person who excavates. You carry upon your shoulders the weight of other people's projections, of their fears and fantasies and anxieties and superstitions." While Atwood is referring to her work as a writer, the wisdom applies just as well to the murkiness of living in the shadow of a nether world that can be explored only in the faint light of signs and symbols.

In *The Living and the Dead,* W. Lloyd Warner, one the most thoughtful of modern writers on the society of the Dead, said: "In the context of the sacred ceremonial, the funeral, and the consecrated ground of the cemetery, the name of the departed becomes the sacred symbol which helps unite the secular living with the sacred dead." Warner went on to explain how the burial grounds of the Dead were deeply embedded in the social order of Yankee City, his pseudonym for the New England town he studied as carefully as any town has been studied.

Questions of the social worlds of the Dead may seem to entail some sort of religious sentiment. Yet, Lloyd Warner, who took religion very seriously, was quite clear that the graveyard united the secular living with the sacred dead. The society of the Dead, whatever may be its status in the order of enduring things, is not reserved either for the righteous or the religious. All die. All join the company of the Dead. Whatever may be believed about the state of their souls, the Dead are not, in themselves, religious beings (if they are beings at all). Whatever may be sacred about them is a given of their condition. They have done nothing to earn the status. The indefinite location of the Dead in but not of the worlds of the Living may explain why they disturb the sober space between faith and doubt.

Though polling evidence can be fickle, well into the twenty-first century one Harris poll reported a majority of Americans believed in ghosts (a 2009 Pew poll found that fewer did but, inexplicably, the number of those who believed had more than doubled in the first decade of the century). Even the notoriously irreligious believe in ghosts.

As long ago as 1852, in *The Eighteenth Brumaire,* Marx wrote of the force of ghosts in human society assigns fungible value to any given commodity, least of all to the treasure of life itself? The source of value dies before our eyes at the very moment we catch a glimpse of it, then lingers as structures that haunt. What then are these ghosts, and what is their relation to the society of the Living? Simply put, they are the ghouls of the one social fact that we the Living cannot think—that we will die, all and without exception. Yet, as Marx put it, the Dead (our dead) press on us as we try to live in history.

The Dead comprise that one society all the Living must join and to which, whilst living, we are bound by the irony of the breach on both sides of the imperceptible line between. They are lost to us; we to them. The very necessity of it is the most fundamental of hauntings. We know that the Dead are waiting for us, but we know it only in that instant when we allow (or cause) that insight to disappear.

In *Ghostly Matters,* a modern classic in the study of ghosts, Avery Gordon sharpens the point well: "The ghost is not simply a dead or missing person, but a social figure, and investigating it can lead to that dense site where history and subjectivity make social life. The ghost or the apparition is one form by which something is lost, or barely visible, or seemingly not there to our supposedly well-trained eyes, makes itself known or apparent to us, in its own way, of course. The way of the ghost is haunting, and haunting is a very particular way of knowing what has happened or is happening." Could there be a better adumbration of what C. Wright Mills called the "sociological imagination"?

Whether in practical or professional work we must live in the between of our subjective or personal troubles and the reality of historical structures we can only imagine (if we will). The fact of all social matters is that we know something is happening before (and if) we come to know what it is. This is the truth of structural effects. Whatever they may be when we experience them, the deep structures of the worlds about are long dead by history: "The tradition of all dead generations weighs like a nightmare on the brains of the living." Thereafter ghosts have lurked here and there in the shadows of social theory. More recently, in *Spectres of Marx,* Jacques Derrida wrote an invitation: "Let us situate ourselves for a moment in that place where the values of value (between use-value and exchange-value), secret mystique, enigma, fetish, and the ideological form a chain in Marx's text, singularly in Capital, and let us try at least to indicate (it will be only an indicator) the spectral movement of this chain. The movement is staged there where it is a question, precisely, of forming the concept of what the stage, any stage, withdraws from our blind eyes at the moment we open them." Why is it that the mystery of social life rests on the unfathomable fact that we cannot ever know directly the exact structural forms by which the time they get under our skin. Like all ghosts, they haunt the guts well before some word of them forms in mind or mouth.

To say that the Dead haunt all that we know is not the undomesticated idea it might at first appear to be. We cannot ponder the long, tragic history of race in America without a thought of the dead slaves of long before. We cannot study the modern world-system or globalization without consideration of its deep past in the ghosts of the colonial system. We cannot look into the face of inequalities without casting an eye on the flawed dream of modern equalities. Some might want to call these hauntings the necessity of history. •

To live wittingly in the days we may have is hard skating on the thin evidence we garner from hints and clues found in the attics and stacks wherein history's dusty archives languish. The first among equals of social historians was Max Weber who, in 1917 in "Science as a Vocation," remarked that the scientist must be willing to make countless calculations for months on end before, in its own good time, an idea dawns. So it is for all. Social facts are truths buried in a past perfect. They work their way toward us and our destinies only through the hauntings of dead social structures. Some think they have earned the goods they have. Others believe that they need what they need because they did something wrong or bad. The curve that falls from the presumption of merit to the shame of poverty measures the truth of social inequalities. It counts the arrogant in and the shamed out with no sense of irony that all social measures are ghosts of the past. We belong to the Dead. This is what an apparition is— the appearance as if it were a reality that is always somewhere in the offing. Elvis, like JFK, like all who die before their time, is out there somewhere, beckoning. These totemic figures may be perfectly content. It is we who cannot let them grow old.

In what may be the best recent essay by a sociologist on the subject, Zygmunt Bauman in *Mortality, Immortality and Other Life Strategies,* joins a long lineage of thinkers going back at least to Augustine of Hippo. The single most distinctive quality of human consciousness, says Bauman, is that "we not only know but we know that we know" and this, he continues, is why death is so terrifying. Death, insofar as the living can know it, obliterates precisely this knowledge of ourselves as beings who know that they know (the very quality that makes us rational). If death is so fearsome as to be the object of a culturally induced denial and, as Bauman adds, the inspiration to creative thinking and living, then why shouldn't the Dead be treated for what they are—as at once the symbolic shifters that return us to life and the phantoms of that life lived with others? An honest living accrues only to those who calculate their worth against the collective Dead who, in turn, are the only ones able to supply the facts of the structural past to an illusory social present. Could there be any subject, however slippery, more fundamental to the social study of these worlds than the hold the world of the Dead has upon our living? To be sure, that hold is the suffocating grip of denial, as the cultural anthropologist Ernest Becker put it in *Denial of Death.* Cultures that deny the welcoming embrace of their dead are themselves morbid—a morbidity that works its nasty charms by sneaking up in those flickering moments of awareness. In the end (so to speak), to try to think of the society of the Dead is to demand a certain rigor of, if not definition, hypothesis as to what such a society might be. Ironically put, that hypothesis would be that ultimately everything social is hypothetical. It is not sheer cleverness that leads to this conclusion, but the reality of our work as we do it, or as we ought to be doing it. Everything we touch—every fact mined, every passing thought, every test of our significance, every calculus of net worth, everything—ought to be kept in the realm of the hypothetical. Yet, in the course of our practical lives, it seldom works this way. Perhaps it's not because we long so for certainties that will resurrect us from the land of the anonymous Dead. We want to be known, remembered. The ordinary living might not stare straight on into the land of the Dead, but, whatever they think they are doing, they take Abrahamic leaps of faith in the risks of bearing children, making love, looking for work, daring to beg. To give birth, to undress, to work, to try is to live facing if not the society of the Dead, the uncertainty that our efforts will somehow endure— and they do not, at least not to a degree that warrants cutting off the land of the Dead as if it were unreal.

Still, it is a challenge to think about this society we cannot know but without which we cannot be. It may be that we must think of the Dead as they appear to us as hauntings from a nether world. In *The Dominion of the Dead,* Robert Pogue Harrison, the brilliant Stanford professor of Italian Literatures, ties the knot that Lloyd Warner put in place but could not bind. If there is a symbolic bond between the Living and the Dead, then how does that symbolic reality affect the work of Living itself? Harrison's answer: "In the human realm the dead and the unborn are native allies, so much so that from their posthumous abode—wherever it be—the former hound the living with guilt, dread, and a sense of responsibility, obliging us, by whatever means necessary, to take the unborn into our care and to keep the story going, even if we never quite figure out what the story is about, what our part in it is, the end toward which it is progressing, or the moral it contains." This contains everything necessary, if not sufficient, unto one of the social mysteries of the communion we share with the Dead. Why we, in our collective human nature, care about and for the unborn cannot be so simple as the reason the salmon swim hard against the current to reproduce their kind. Instinct may be part of it, but caring for the unborn is far more social, in the human sense, than mere species reproduction. To be sure, some among us don't give a damn. But the human Living and our Dead are a community that cannot rely on outliers for either survival or meaning.

Societies rely on their norms, as Emile Durkheim said early in the twentieth century, even when, as Erving Goffman said much later, they do not require all members to be normal. The normal is a crypto-statistical condition. Norms are the substance of the social contract—that vast, impossible unborn ideal that is beyond historical evidence yet without which societies cannot think themselves. Collective self-knowledge is, as again Durkheim discovered, a very different thing from the psychology of self-consciousness. We may, as individuals, know that we know, but in the long run of life what matters is that those with whom we constitute a society know that together we do not know everything, least of all the truth of our relations with the Dead. Herein is where and how the Dead join us to the unborn. It's not a formal rule, so much as an essential, affective experience that societies care for those yet to come. We cannot say exactly what the Dead feel, but we can suppose that, wherever they are, they await those as yet unborn to their realm as we await those yet to come to the land of our Living.

The norm of a social contract is, thus, tested most severely by a society's willingness to care for its unborn. They may not come from the body of our personal relations, but they do come and they must be cared for. Hence, the society of the Dead is the social fact that in caring for what happens to our Dead, we engage them and their society in their responsibility to care for us. Otherwise, we will not keep the story going. We may not understand what it all means, but we know that we are haunted by this story that continues for however long until whatever comes next. Where we came from and where we are going aren't challenges to our minds but to the primordial, even pre- (or post-) verbal states of our being. Marx had it backwards. The dead weigh upon us not as nightmares but as life itself. Warner got it right. We live among the Dead, and they live among us.

Recommended Readings

Bauman, Zygmunt. *Mortality, Immortality, and Other Life Strategies* (Stanford University Press, 1992). The great Polish-English social theorist's gripping meditations on death and society—and their moral implications.

Bell, Michael Mayerfeld. "The Ghosts of Place," *Theory and Society* (1997) 26: 813–836. A neglected but important article on ghosts and social space, published in the same year as *Ghostly Matters*.

Gordon, Avery. *Ghostly Matters: Haunting and the Sociological Imagination* (University of Minnesota Press, 1997). Easily the modern classic on ghosts, this book is notable in its range, insight, and literary grace.

Harrison, Robert Pogue. *The Dominion of the Dead* (University of Chicago Press, 2005). Drawn from classical and modern literatures, Harrison's book is a stunningly original exposition of the social place of the dead among the living.

Warner, W. Lloyd. *The Living and the Dead: A Study of the Symbolic Life of Americans* (Yale University Press, 1959). Part of Warner's classic multivolume community study of Yankee City, this is perhaps the single most important empirical study of the social order of the dead among the living.

Charles Lemert is an emeritus professor at Wesleyan University and a senior fellow at Yale University's Center for Comparative Research. He is the author, most recently, of *Why Niebuhr Matters*.

Critical Thinking

1. How is socioeconomic status displayed in cemeteries—in death as in life?

2. What is the role of the dead within the community of the living?

3. How does a cemetery help to make the name of the dead a sacred symbol that helps unite the secular living with the sacred dead?

From *Contexts*, vol. 10, no. 4, 2011, pp. 16–21. Copyright © 2011 by the American Sociological Association. Reprinted by permission of Sage Publications via Rightslink.

The Cycle of Death

Forty years ago, Americans' moral qualms almost ended the death penalty. Now we're abandoning it again— but not because we object to executions.

VINCE BEISER

You may have noticed something about the debate over the death penalty in the presidential race: there's hardly been one. That speaks volumes about how this persistent institution is quietly fading away in the U.S.—for the second time in history.

Most Americans support capital punishment, in principle. That majority, however, has shrunk from 80 percent in 1994 to 61 percent today. And when faced with actually using the ultimate sanction, the country is increasingly squeamish.

The number of death sentences imposed by judges and juries has plummeted to record lows. Last year's total was 78, according to the Washington, D.C.-based Death Penalty Information Center—down from a high of 315 in 1996, and the smallest annual total in decades. Only 43 inmates were executed last year, half the number of a decade ago. Meanwhile, Illinois became the fourth state in as many years to abolish executions, joining New Mexico, New Jersey, and New York.

But Americans aren't abandoning the death penalty because of an upsurge in concern over taking killers' lives. Thanks largely to DNA testing and other technological advances, an estimated 140 condemned men and women have been exonerated in recent years. Proof that the system can fail so badly has made juries, judges, prosecutors, and the public wary of exacting the ultimate punishment.

Forty years ago, when the U.S. briefly abolished capital punishment, it was for very different reasons. Consider Robert Page Anderson. A small-time lowlife with a lengthy rap sheet, Anderson walked into a San Diego pawnshop one morning in 1965, picked out a rifle from the gun display, loaded it, and shot the store's two clerks. One died instantly. When police cars pulled up in front of the store, Anderson grabbed a few more guns, barricaded the doors, and started blasting. What ensued was the biggest firefight ever on the streets of San Diego. In its course, a journalist dropped dead of a heart attack, Anderson wounded a cop, and then was shot by another.

A black man who shot a white cop and killed a storekeeper would, at most times in American history, have found himself on a fast trip to death row. But Anderson had the good fortune to have committed his crime when Americans were turning against the death penalty to an unprecedented extent.

In the late 1960s, with the injustices highlighted by the civil rights movement prominent in the public consciousness, polls found that more Americans opposed capital punishment than supported it. The NAACP and other groups were challenging the constitutionality of executions. Several states had banned the practice, and prominent politicians denounced it. Even the U.S. Attorney General called for its abolition. In a 1968 ruling, a Supreme Court justice dismissed death penalty advocates as a "dwindling minority." That year, for the first time in the nation's history, not a single prisoner was executed.

In 1972, Anderson's case came before the California Supreme Court. There was no question about his guilt; what was in question was the morality of capital punishment itself. The court declared that, loathsome as his crime was, Anderson would not be executed, because execution was a "cruel and unusual" punishment that "degrades and dehumanizes all who participate in its processes." By then almost every industrialized nation had scrapped the death penalty. "It is now, literally, an unusual punishment among civilized nations," noted the state's justices. More than 100 California inmates had their death sentences commuted to prison terms, including Anderson—who was subsequently paroled in 1976 after 11 years behind bars.

A few months later the U.S. Supreme Court struck down capital punishment. As part of that ruling, Justice Thurgood Marshall declared that if they were properly informed, "the great mass of citizens would conclude . . . that the death penalty is immoral and therefore unconstitutional."

Only a few years later, however, the nation began an about face. The U.S. didn't just bring back the death penalty—it embraced it. In 1976, the Supreme Court declared that states could reinstitute capital punishment, as long as they updated their laws to eliminate the more egregious injustices. Dozens of states did just that.

Why the reversal? By the mid-1970s, much of middle America had grown deeply anxious about how society seemed to be unraveling. Drug use and crime were rising. Minorities women, and homosexuals were demanding power and respect. In this milieu, politicians increasingly learned that crime could pay—for them. From federal candidates to county sheriffs, would-be officeholders began vying to out-tough each other on law-and-order issues.

Capital punishment became a litmus test of a candidate's law-and-order bona fides. Michael Dukakis was slammed for opposing it in the 1988 presidential elections, and was trounced by George H.W. Bush, who advocated executing drug dealers. Then-Governor Bill Clinton took notice; in 1992, he made a point of leaving the campaign trail to return to Arkansas to personally sign an inmate's death warrant. Shortly afterward, Newt Gingrich declared that the keys to building a conservative majority in the U.S. were "low taxes and the death penalty."

By the 1990s, a record majority of Americans favored capital punishment. Courts were handing down hundreds of death sentences every year, and dozens of new crimes were being made capital offenses. By the start of the new millennium, the number of annual executions shot up to nearly 100.

Those years turned out to be the high-water mark of the resurgence. One exoneration after another began exposing how fallible the system is. "Although the dissatisfaction with capital punishment has many roots, the common and principal concern heard throughout the country is the risk that innocent people may be caught up with the guilty," declared a 2007 Death Penalty Information Center study based on a poll of 1,000 adults. Even among death penalty supporters, nearly two-thirds are worried about that risk, a 2011 Rasmussen Reports poll found.

For capital punishment abolitionists, this is grounds for optimism. They hope the public's growing concerns will lead to a complete ban, something 16 states have already enacted.

But the pendulum could just as easily swing the other way again. As DNA testing becomes more widespread, the number of wrongful convictions is likely to drop. That might bolster capital punishment's advocates, who could claim the process has been perfected.

Unlike 40 years ago, Americans don't object to executing criminals; they object to executing innocent people. Unless that changes, the death penalty seems certain to remain on the books—even if it is an increasing rarity in courtrooms.

Critical Thinking

1. The number of deaths through capital punishment has decreased significantly in recent years. If not a change in attitudes toward capital punishment, what scientific breakthrough has contributed to this?

2. Who are we as human beings to practice capital punishment and terminate intentionally the lives of someone else? What is your opinion of the death penalty?

How We Bury the War Dead

Bringing fallen troops home is a fairly modern idea. Today, the military sees it as a sacred duty

YOCHI J. DREAZEN AND GARY FIELDS

The U.S. military didn't always bring home its dead. In the Seminole Indian Wars in the early 1800s, most of the troops were buried near where they fell. The remains of some dead officers were collected and sent back to their families, but only if the men's relatives paid all of the costs. Families had to buy and ship a leaded coffin to a designated military quartermaster, and after the body had been disinterred, they had to cover the costs of bringing the coffin home.

Today, air crews have flown the remains of more than 5,000 dead troops back to the U.S. since the conflicts in Iraq and Afghanistan began.

For those charged with bringing out the dead, it is one of the military's most emotionally taxing missions. The men and women of the Air Force's Air Mobility Command function as the nation's pallbearers, ferrying flag-draped remains to Dover Air Force Base in Delaware from battlefields half a world away.

The missions take a heavy toll on the air crews, but many of the pilots and loadmasters say their work is part of a sacred military obligation to fallen troops and their families. Air Force Capt. Tenaya Humphrey was a young girl when her father, Maj. Zenon Goc, died in a military plane crash in Texas in 1992. She remembers his body being flown to Dover before his burial in Colorado.

Capt. Humphrey and her husband, Matthew, are now C-17 pilots who regularly fly dead troops back to the U.S. and then on to their home states for final burial. "It's emotional for everyone who's involved," she says. "But it's important for the family to know that at every step along the way their loved one is watched over and cared for."

Bringing fallen troops home is a relatively modern idea. Until the late 19th century, military authorities did little to differentiate and identify dead troops. Roughly 14,000 soldiers died from combat and disease during the Mexican-American War of 1846, but only 750 sets of remains were recovered and brought back, by covered wagon, to the U.S. for burial. None of the fallen soldiers were ever personally identified.

The modern system for cataloguing and burying military dead effectively began during the Civil War, when the enormity of the carnage triggered a wholesale revolution in how the U.S. treated fallen troops. Congress decided that the defenders of the Union were worthy of special burial sites for their sacrifices, and set up a program of national cemeteries.

During the war, more than 300,000 dead Union soldiers were buried in small cemeteries scattered across broad swaths of the U.S. When the fighting stopped, military authorities launched an ambitious effort to collect the remains and rebury them in the handful of national cemeteries.

The move "established the precedent that would be followed in future wars, even when American casualties lay in foreign soil," Michael Sledge writes in "Soldier Dead," a history of how the U.S. has handled its battlefield fatalities.

The first time the U.S. made a serious effort to repatriate the remains of soldiers killed overseas came during the Spanish American War of 1898, when the military brought back the remains of thousands of troops who were killed in places like the Philippines and Cuba.

The relatives of fallen troops in both world wars were given the choice of having their loved ones permanently interred in large overseas cemeteries or brought back to the U.S. for reburial.

Those who wanted their sons or husbands returned to them were in for a long wait. Fallen troops had been buried in hundreds of temporary cemeteries near the sites of major battles throughout Europe. When World War I ended, the families of 43,909 dead troops asked for their remains to be brought back to the U.S. by boat, while roughly 20,000 chose to have the bodies remain in Europe. The war ended in 1918, but the first bodies of troops killed in the conflict weren't sent back to the U.S. until 1921.

World War II posed a bigger logistical challenge, since American war dead were scattered around the globe. Nearly 80,000 U.S. troops died in the Pacific, for example, and 65,000 of their bodies were first buried in almost 200 battlefield cemeteries there.

Once the fighting ended, the bodies were dug up and consolidated into larger regional graveyards. The first returns of World War II dead took place in the fall of 1947, six years after the attack at Pearl Harbor. Eventually, 171,000 of the roughly 280,000 identified remains were brought back to the U.S.

Today, the remains of 124,909 fallen American troops from conflicts dating back to the Mexican-American war are buried at a network of 24 permanent cemeteries in Europe, Panama, Tunisia, the Philippines and Mexico.

The military reshaped its procedures for handling war dead during the Korean War, when territory changed hands so many times that temporary U.S. battlefield cemeteries were at constant risk of falling into enemy hands. In the winter of 1950, the U.S. launched a policy of "concurrent return," which called for flying the bodies of fallen troops back to the U.S. as quickly as possible.

The military now goes to tremendous lengths to recover the remains of fallen troops. In March 2002, a Navy Seal named Neil Roberts fell out of the back of a Chinook helicopter in Afghanistan and was cornered and killed by militants on the ground. The U.S. sent in a second helicopter to attempt a rescue, but six members of its crew were killed in the ensuing firefight.

Then-Brig. Gen. John Rosa, the deputy director of operations for the Joint Staff, told reporters that U.S. commanders ordered the high-risk recovery mission to ensure that Petty Officer Roberts' body didn't fall into enemy hands.

"There was an American, for whatever reason, [who] was left behind," Gen. Rosa said at the time. "And we don't leave Americans behind."

The military's system of concurrent return is basically still in use today, with modern technology cutting the lag time between when troops die in the field and when they are returned to their families down to as little as one day.

On May 16, Navy Petty Officer Zarian Wood, a 29-year-old medic who had deployed overseas less than a month earlier, died from wounds suffered in a bomb blast in southern Afghanistan's Helmand Province. Marine Cpl. Nicolas Parada-Rodriguez, the son of immigrants who moved to the U.S. two decades ago, was killed in Helmand that same day.

The following evening, the remains of both men were slowly lowered from the cargo deck of a civilian 747 that the military had chartered to fly their bodies back to Dover. Cpl. Parada-Rodriguez's relatives could be heard weeping as the transfer case carrying his body was taken off the plane.

The plane that brought the two men back to their families was operated by Evergreen International Airlines Inc., a military contractor. The Pentagon employs four other companies, including UPS and Federal Express, to help bring bodies back to Dover. Officials at the base say that 70% of the dead are flown back on the civilian planes, with the remainder coming home aboard military aircraft.

The military doesn't have air crews who are assigned specifically to the mission of bringing out the nation's war dead. Instead, the work is assigned to crews depending on their locations and the speed with which they can stop at bases in Afghanistan and Iraq to pick up fallen troops and their military escorts.

Air crews are tight-knit groups of men and women who typically pass the long hours in the air and on the ground telling jokes and needling each other. But veterans of the repatriation missions say the mood among the flight crew changes immediately after they get orders to pick up fallen troops.

"You can sense it in the crew," says Maj. Brian O'Connell, a C-17 pilot who has flown the remains of a half-dozen soldiers and Marines. "As soon as everybody knows about it, the attitude changes, a lot."

The long flights from the war zones mean that the air crews spend hours with the flag-covered remains. Air Force Tech Sgt. Donny Maheux, a C-17 loadmaster, says he often finds himself staring at the metallic transfer cases holding the bodies of the dead soldiers and wondering what kind of people they were. "I'm looking at [the remains] the whole flight," he says. "Sometimes I wonder, 'What if it was my family on the receiving end?'"

When they land at Dover, the crews often choose to remain with their plane until the families of the dead troops arrive to see the bodies of their loved ones taken off of the plane. Since the planes land late at night and early in the morning, it can sometimes be hours before the families arrive for the transfer ceremonies.

Carrying and preparing the dead exacts a toll on the Dover personnel, according to Col. Robert Edmondson, who commands the Air Force's Mortuary Affairs Operations Center at the base. "It's a chronic stress and it never goes away," he says.

The base launched a new "resiliency" program a year ago after two of the Air Force personnel assigned to Dover "broke" from the strain of dealing with so much death, Col. Edmondson says, and had to go through intensive counseling. Now there are five chaplains and three mental health technicians available at all times for the mortuary affairs personnel.

For the Shea family of Frederick, Md., the repatriation of their only son Kurt's body to Dover capped a wrenching 2½ days that began when two Marines, accompanied by an Army chaplain, knocked on their front door the night of May 9th.

Cpl. Kurt Shea's mother, Linda, had volunteered in a Marine Corps support group for the mothers of fallen troops, so she immediately knew why the officers were there. "They don't come to your door if they're injured," she said.

Cpl. Shea, who was deployed to the Helmand Province, had sent her a Mother's Day message through Facebook around noon that same day.

"Hey mom, Happy Mother's Day. Hope everything is going well," he wrote.

He was shot dead less than five hours later.

On Tuesday, May 11, Mrs. Shea, along with her husband and daughter, drove to the base with a pair of military escorts. Last year, the military began paying the travel costs of bereaved families and dispatching troops to accompany them from the moment they leave to their home until they arrive at Dover.

"That had to be the longest drive in my life," Mrs. Shea says. "What do you say? What do you talk about? It was three hours of silence."

The family and the military escorts spent the night in a hotel and arrived at Dover early the following morning. The rear ramp of a gray C-17 Globemaster cargo plane stood open as Mrs. Shea and her husband and daughter were driven onto the runway. Marines wearing white gloves carried the flag-draped transfer case holding her son's body off the plane. Inside the C-17, the air crew that had flown Cpl. Shea back to the U.S. saluted as his remains were placed into a waiting military van.

"Nothing prepared us for the reality of it," Mrs. Shea says. "Nothing prepares you to see your child in a silver box with a flag over it."

The family returned home after the transfer but was asked several days later if they wanted to return to Dover to accompany their son's body on the three-hour trip home. They declined.

Linda Shea and her husband saw their son's body for the first time shortly before a memorial service near their home.

"When I peeked in the room where Kurt was laying I know I cried out, 'Baby boy, what happened? What happened to you?' He looked like he was sleeping," she recalls. "Whoever prepared him, he was at peace. He looked like Kurt, just not moving, just laying there."

Cpl. Shea was buried May 19 in the Resthaven Memorial Gardens with full military honors. He was 21 years old.

Critical Thinking

1. Should we bring home the war dead for burial or would not it be more practical to simply bury them near where they died, as was one time the case?

2. Should we segregate the war dead in cemeteries such as Arlington Cemetery or integrate them into cemeteries with others?

3. Do you believe that families of the war dead should be allowed to meet the plane bringing the caskets into Dover Air Base?

Grief in the Age of Facebook

ELIZABETH STONE

On July 17 last year, one of my most promising students died. Her name was Casey Feldman, and she was crossing a street in a New Jersey resort town on her way to work when a van went barreling through a stop sign. Her death was a terrible loss for everyone who knew her. Smart and dogged, whimsical and kind, Casey was the news editor of the *The Observer,* the campus paper I advise, and she was going places. She was a finalist for a national college reporting award and had just been chosen for a prestigious television internship for the fall, a fact she conveyed to me in a midnight text message, entirely consistent with her all-news-all-the-time mind-set. Two days later her life ended.

I found out about Casey's death the old-fashioned way: in a phone conversation with Kelsey, the layout editor and Casey's roommate. She'd left a neutral-sounding voice mail the night before, asking me to call when I got her message, adding, "It's OK if it's late." I didn't retrieve the message till midnight, so I called the next morning, realizing only later what an extraordinary effort she had made to keep her voice calm. But my students almost never make phone calls if they can help it, so Kelsey's message alone should have raised my antenna. She blogs, she tweets, she texts, and she pings. But voice mail? No.

Paradoxically it was Kelsey's understanding of the viral nature of her generation's communication preferences that sent her rushing to the phone, and not just to call boomers like me. She didn't want anyone to learn of Casey's death through Facebook. It was summer, and their friends were scattered, but Kelsey knew that if even one of Casey's 801 Facebook friends posted the news, it would immediately spread.

So as Kelsey and her roommates made calls through the night, they monitored Facebook. Within an hour of Casey's death, the first mourner posted her respects on Casey's Facebook wall, a post that any of Casey's friends could have seen. By the next morning, Kelsey, in New Jersey, had reached *The Observer*'s editor in chief in Virginia, and by that evening, the two had reached fellow editors in California, Missouri, Massachusetts, Texas, and elsewhere—and somehow none of them already knew.

In the months that followed, I've seen how markedly technology has influenced the conventions of grieving among my students, offering them solace but also uncertainty. The day after Casey's death, several editorial-board members changed their individual Facebook profile pictures. Where there had been photos of Brent, of Kelsey, of Kate, now there were photos of Casey and Brent, Casey and Kelsey, Casey and Kate.

Now that Casey was gone, she was virtually everywhere. I asked one of my students why she'd changed her profile photo. "It was spontaneous," she said. "Once one person did it, we all joined in." Another student, who had friends at Virginia Tech when, in 2007, a gunman killed 32 people, said that's when she first saw the practice of posting Facebook profile photos of oneself with the person being mourned.

Within several days of Casey's death, a Facebook group was created called "In Loving Memory of Casey Feldman," which ran parallel to the wake and funeral planned by Casey's family. Dozens wrote on that group's wall, but Casey's own wall was the more natural gathering place, where the comments were more colloquial and addressed to her: "casey im speechless for words right now," wrote one friend. "i cant believe that just yest i txted you and now your gone . . . i miss you soo much. rest in peace."

Though we all live atomized lives, memorial services let us know the dead with more dimension than we may have known them during their lifetimes. In the responses of her friends, I was struck by how much I hadn't known about Casey—her equestrian skill, her love of animals, her interest in photography, her acting talent, her penchant for creating her own slang ("Don't be a cow"), and her curiosity—so intense that her friends affectionately called her a "stalker."

This new, uncharted form of grieving raises new questions. Traditional mourning is governed by conventions. But in the age of Facebook, with selfhood publicly represented via comments and uploaded photos, was it OK for her friends to display joy or exuberance online? Some weren't sure. Six weeks after Casey's death, one student who had posted a shot of herself with Casey wondered aloud when it was all right to post a different photo. Was there a right time? There were no conventions to help her. And would she be judged if she removed her mourning photo before most others did?

As it turns out, Facebook has a "memorializing" policy in regard to the pages of those who have died. That policy came into being in 2005, when a good friend and co-worker of Max Kelly, a Facebook employee, was killed in a bicycle accident. As Kelly wrote in a Facebook blog post last October, "The question soon came up: What do we do about his Facebook profile? We had never really thought about this before in such a personal way. How do you deal with an interaction with someone who is no longer able to log on? When someone leaves us, they don't leave our memories or our social network. To reflect that reality, we created the idea of 'memorialized' profiles as a place where people can save and share their memories of those who've passed."

Casey's Facebook page is now memorialized. Her own postings and lists of interests have been removed, and the page is visible only to her Facebook friends. (I thank Kelsey Butler for making it possible for me to gain access to it.) Eight months after her death, her friends are still posting on her wall, not to "share their memories" but to write to her, acknowledging her absence but maintaining their ties to her—exactly the stance that contemporary grief theorists recommend. To me, that seems preferable to Freud's prescription, in "Mourning and Melancholia," that we should detach from the dead. Quite a few of Casey's friends wished her a Merry Christmas, and on the 17th of every month so far, the postings spike. Some share dreams they've had about her, or post a detail of interest. "I had juice box wine recently," wrote one. "I thought of you the whole time: (Miss you girl!" From another: "i miss you. the new lady gaga cd came out, and if i had one wish in the world it would be that you could be singing (more like screaming) along with me in my passenger seat like old times."

It was against the natural order for Casey to die at 21, and her death still reverberates among her roommates and fellow editors. I was privileged to know Casey, and though I knew her deeply in certain ways, I wonder—I'm not sure, but I wonder—if I should have known her better. I do know, however, that she would have done a terrific trend piece on "Grief in the Age of Facebook."

Critical Thinking

1. How can Facebook serve as a therapeutic device for grieving individuals?
2. Facebook makes the grief process more public. How is this helpful and how might it not be therapeutic?
3. How does grief via Facebook differ from traditional ways of grieving?

ELIZABETH STONE is a professor of English, communication, and media studies at Fordham University. She is the author of the memoir *A Boy I Once Knew: What a Teacher Learned From Her Student* (Algonquin, 2002).

Brain Death Guidelines Vary at Top US Neurological Hospitals

SUSAN JEFFREY

A new survey shows wide variation in brain death guidelines among leading neurological institutions in the United States, differences that may have implications for the determination of death and initiation of transplant procedures, the researchers say.

Under the Uniform Determination of Death Act, guidelines for brain death determination can be developed at the institutional level, leading to potential variability in practice, David M. Greer, MD, from Massachusetts General Hospital, in Boston, and colleagues report. Although there are guidelines on brain death determination from the American Academy of Neurology (AAN), they are not binding at the local level.

Results of this survey, published in the January 22 issue of *Neurology,* now suggest that substantial variation is in fact present even among top US hospitals.

"It was very concerning that there was a huge mismatch between what is set forth in the practice parameters from the AAN and what is actually being stipulated at local hospitals," Dr. Greer told *Medscape Neurology & Neurosurgery* when their findings were first presented in October 2007 at the 132nd Annual Meeting of the American Neurological Association.

Although it is possible that actual performance at these hospitals is better than what is suggested by the protocols, he noted, "We have no evidence of that."

Top 50 Hospitals

For the study, the authors requested the guidelines for determination of death by brain criteria from the *US News and World Report* top 50 neurology/neurosurgery institutions in 2006. There was an 82% response rate to their request, from 41 institutions, but 3 did not have official guidelines, leaving protocols from 38 hospitals for evaluation.

The guidelines were evaluated for 5 categories of data: guideline performance, preclinical testing, clinical examination, apnea testing, and ancillary tests. They compared the guidelines directly with the AAN guidelines for consistencies and differences.

"Major differences were present among institutions for all 5 categories," the authors write. "Variability existed in the guidelines' requirements for performance of the evaluation, prerequisites before testing, specifics of the brain-stem examination and apnea testing, and what types of ancillary tests could be performed, including what pitfalls and limitations might exist."

For example, with regard to preclinical testing, it was surprising to find that the cause of brain death was not stipulated in a large number of guidelines, they note. "Of concern was the variability in the apnea testing, an area with the greatest possibility for inaccuracies, indeterminate testing, and potentially even danger to the patient," they note. "This included variability of temperature, drawing of an [arterial blood gas sample] ABG prior to testing, the proper baseline [partial pressure carbon dioxide] pCO_2, and technique for performing the test. Although a final pCO_2 level was commonly stated (most often 60 mm Hg), specific guidelines in a situation of chronic CO_2 retention, clinical instability, or inconclusive testing were commonly lacking. A surprising number (13%) of guidelines did not specify that spontaneous respirations be absent during the apnea test."

In the category of guideline performance, there was a "surprisingly low rate of involvement of neurologists or neurosurgeons in the determination." Further, the requirement that an attending physician be involved was "conspicuously uncommon."

"Given a technique with some complexity as well as potential medical-legal implications, we find it surprising that more institutions did not require a higher level or more specific area of expertise," they write.

Their findings suggest that stricter AAN guidelines may be in order, they conclude. "Given the fact that the guidelines put forth by the AAN are now 13 years old, perhaps now is the time that they be rewritten, with an emphasis on a higher degree of specific detail in areas where there is greater variability of practice. Furthermore, perhaps now there should be standards by which individual institutions are held more accountable for their closeness to, or variability from, national guidelines."

Coauthors on the study were Panayoitis Varelas, MD, PhD, and Shamael Haque, DO, from Henry Ford Hospital, in Detroit, Michigan, and Eelco Wijdicks, MD, PhD, from the Mayo Clinic, in Rochester, Minnesota.

A "Disturbing Pattern of Nonuniformity"

In an editorial accompanying the paper, James L. Bernat, MD, from Dartmouth-Hitchcock Medical Center, in Lebanon, New Hampshire, points out that Greer and colleagues have shown that "physicians declaring brain death in leading neurology departments in the United States practice with a disturbing pattern of nonuniformity."

Some of these variations are inconsequential, he notes, but some could make a serious difference in outcomes. "Practices that do not require demonstrating an anatomic lesion sufficient to explain the clinical findings, do not rigorously exclude potentially reversible metabolic and toxic factors, do not properly test brain-stem function, or do not require proper apnea testing are consequential because they could yield an incorrect determination of death," he writes.

Although brain death has to be determined correctly to maintain confidence in high-quality medical care and the organ-procurement enterprise, he writes, in addition to accuracy, "it is desirable to achieve a uniformity of practice using the optimal guidelines."

"I suggest that the AAN, the American Neurological Association, and Child Neurology Society jointly empanel a task force to draft evidence-based guidelines, including specific recommendations for conducting the clinical and confirmatory tests for brain death," Dr. Bernat continues. "Once these guidelines have been accepted and published, neurologists should act as envoys to ensure that they become incorporated into hospital policies throughout the country and help implement them locally."

This task force could also update the guidelines at intervals to accommodate emerging technologies as they are validated, such as noninvasive neuroimaging tests measuring the absence of intracranial blood flow, he writes. "The most daunting global problem of establishing worldwide uniformity of brain death guidelines is a task for the World Federation of Neurology."

Critical Thinking

1. How do the guidelines for brain death vary in U.S. hospitals?

2. Why would a uniformity of hospital practice in brain death guidelines be useful?

3. What is the Uniform Determination of Death Act? Was this a wise act to pass?

Dr. Greer reports receiving speaker honoraria from Boehringer-Ingelheim Pharmaceuticals Inc. Disclosures for coauthors appear in the paper.

Criteria for a Good Death

This brief paper advances the concept of a "good death," outlines ten specific criteria for a good death, and proposes a simple golden rule for optimal dying.

EDWIN SHNEIDMAN, PHD

By almost universal common consent, death has a bad reputation. Words like awful and catastrophic are practically synonymous with death. Good and death seem oxymoronic, incompatible, mutually exclusive. Given all this, what then can it mean to speak of a good death? Are some deaths better than others? Can one plan to improve on one's death? My answer to these questions is yes, and that is what this brief paper is about.

In a previous article about a related topic (Shneidman, 1998), I discussed how *suicide*—the meaning and connotations of the A good death is one word—had palpably changed over the last 230 years. The entries on suicide traced in fifteen different editions of the *Encyclopedia Britannica* indicate that suicide has mutated from being a sin and a crime (involving the punishment of the corpse and the survivors) to being a mental health issue meriting the therapeutic and sympathetic response of others. Death is the over-arching topic of suicide and is more culturally gyroscopic, slower to change, yet subject to shifts in the cultural zeitgeist. If one begins, somewhat arbitrarily, in the Middle Ages with another related topic—courtly love, specifically courtship (DeRougemont, 1940)—one sees that there were elaborate rules for courtly love and for courtly deportment in general. The goal was to be able to do admittedly difficult tasks with seeming effortlessness and without complaint (Castiglione, 1528/1959); in other words, with grace.

The challenge for this paper is to propose some criteria for a good death—a sort of report card of death, a fantasied optimal dying scenario—and to provide a chance to debate what a good death ought to be.

There is no single best kind of death. A good death is one that is appropriate for that person. It is a death in which the hand of the way of dying slips easily into the glove of the act itself. It is in character, on camera, ego-syntonic. It, the death, fits the person. It is a death that one might choose if it were realistically possible for one to choose one's own death. Weisman (1972) has called this an appropriate death.

A decimal of criteria of a good death can be listed. The ten items include (see also Table 1):

1. *Natural.* There are four modes of death—natural, accident, suicide, and homicide (NASH). Any survivor would prefer a loved one's death to be natural. No suicide is a good death.

2. *Mature.* After age 70. Near the pinnacle of mental functioning but old enough to have experienced and savored life.

3. *Expected.* Neither sudden nor unexpected. Survivors-to-be do not like to be surprised. A good death should have about a week's lead time.

4. *Honorable.* Filled with honorifics but not dwelling on past failures. Death begins an ongoing obituary, a memory in the minds of the survivors. The Latin phrase is: *De mortuis nil nisi bonum* (Of the dead [speak] nothing but good).

5. *Prepared.* A living trust, prepaid funeral arrangements. That the decedent had given thought and made arrangements for the necessary legalities surrounding death.

6. *Accepted.* "Willing the obligatory," that is, accepting the immutables of chance and nature and fate; not raging into the night; acceding to nature's unnegotiable demands.

7. *Civilized.* To have some of your loved ones physically present. That the dying scene be enlivened by fresh flowers, beautiful pictures, and cherished music.

8. *Generative.* To pass down the wisdom of the tribe to younger generations; to write; to have shared memories and histories; to act like a beneficent sage.

9. *Rueful.* To cherish the emotional state which is a bittersweet admixture of sadness, yearning, nostalgia, regret, appreciation, and thoughtfulness. To avoid depression, surrender, or collapse; to die with some

Table 1 Ten Criteria for a Good Death

Natural	**Accepted**
A natural death, rather than accident, suicide, or homicide	Willing the obligator; gracefully accepting the inevitable
Mature	**Civilized**
After age 70; elderly yet lucid and experienced	Attended by loved ones; with flowers, pictures, and music for the dying scene
Expected	**Generative**
Neither sudden nor unexpected; some decent warning	To have passed the wisdom of the tribe to younger generations
Honorable	**Rueful**
Emphasis on the honorifics; a positive obituary	To experience the contemplative emotions of sadness and regret without collapse
Prepared	**Peaceable**
A living trust; prearranged funeral; some unfinished tasks to be done	With amicability and love; freedom from physical pain

projects left to be done; by example, to teach the paradigm that no life is completely complete.

10. *Peaceable.* That the dying scene be filled with amicability and love, that physical pain be controlled as much as competent medical care can provide. Each death an ennobling icon of the human race.

I end with a sweeping question: Is it possible to formulate a Golden Rule for a good death, a maxim that has the survivors in mind? I would offer, as a beginning, the following Golden Rule for the dying scene: Do unto others *as little as possible.* By which I mean that the dying person consciously try to arrange that his or her death—given the inescapable sadness of the loss-to-be—be as little pain as humanly possible to the survivors. Along with this Golden Rule for dying there is the copperplated injunction: Die in a manner so that the reviews of your death speak to your better self (as a courtier distinguished by grace) rather than as a plebian marked by coarseness and complaint. Have your dying be a courtly death, among the best things that you ever did. It is your last chance to get your neuroses under partial control.

References

Castiglione, B. (1959). *The book of the courtier.,* trans. Charles S. Singleton. Garden City, NY: Anchor Books. Originally published in 1528.

DeRougemont, D. (1940). *Love in the western world.* Princeton, NJ: Princeton University Press.

Shneidman, E. S. (1980). *Voices of death.* New York: Harper & Row.

Shneidman, E. S. (1998). Suicide on my mind; Britannica on my table. *American Scholar,* 67(3), 93–104.

Weisman, A. (1972). *On dying and denying.* New York: Behavioral Publications.

Critical Thinking

1. How is a "good death" defined? What is your own definition of a "good death?"

2. Present an argument, both for and against, of suicide being a "good death."

3. Discuss the pros and cons of this statement: "The all-American way to die is very unexpectedly while sleeping in one's bed at night, having had a normal, healthy day prior to going to bed."

EDWIN S. SHNEIDMAN is professor of Thanatology Emeritus, UCLA and founder of the American Association of Suicidology.

Address correspondence to Edwin S. Shneidman, 11431 Kingsland St., Los Angeles, CA 90066.

The Emergence of Thanatology and Current Practice in Death Education

Known as the study of death, thanatology is an interdisciplinary approach that encompasses various areas of study. The aim of thanatology is to construct a scientific comprehension of death, its rites, and its meanings. An alternative definition of thanatology, "the study of life with death left in," was proposed by Kastenbaum (1993, p. 76).

LUCIANA M. FONSECA AND INES TESTONI

The word thanatology is of Greek origin. In mythology, Thanatos (death) was the son of Nyx (night) and Chronos (time) and was the twin brother of Hypnos (sleep). Ancient Greeks began to use thanatos as a generic word for death (DeSpelder & Strickland, 2007). In 1903, Metchnikoff proposed two new areas of investigation, borrowing from the Greek gerontos and thanatos to coin the names gerontology and thanatology (Golden, 1998; Kastenbaum, 1988, 1993; Kastenbaum & Costa, 1977). However, unlike gerontology, thanatology did not gain broad acceptance as a science until the 1950s. An analysis of thanatology's journey from its inception to its current status as an interdisciplinary science must include an evaluation of our relationship with death and how that relationship has changed over time. Although the science of thanatology is relatively new, death has always been a subject of interest to humans. The early philosophers and poets were perplexed by the very idea of death, as evidenced by Socrates' discussions on the soul's immortality and by the omnipresence of the theme of death in Seneca's letters (Postiglione, 2008). However, the drastic transformations that modern society underwent in the last century have contributed to a social construct in which death has become a theme that is considered off-limits (Gorer, 1955; Sozzi, 2009). The changes in how people think of and deal with death constituted one of the factors that triggered the thanatology movement. Morin (1951/2002) emphasized the relationship between the denial of death and the focus on individuality, which occurred simultaneously in the second half of the 19th century, a period marked by the transition from a theocentric to an anthropocentric understanding of reality and life; it became evident that human beings considered themselves to be at the center of the universe and therefore could not conceive of their own finitude (Testoni, 2007).

Throughout history, death on a grand scale has always compelled us to reflect on our own mortality, as illustrated by important works on death published during or after historical events involving wholesale death, such as Freud's *Thoughts for the Times on War and Death* (1915/1957), written and published during the First World War; Gorer's *The Pornography of Death* (1955), written a few years after the Second World War; and the many books and articles on the theme written immediately after the World Trade Center attacks, such as *Precarious Life: The Powers of Mourning and Violence* (Butler, 2004) and the new chapter added to *Death, Society, and Human Experience* (Kastenbaum, 2004).

In recent decades, there has been a notable increase in the preoccupation with physical perfection and in the scientific impulse to explain and measure everything, as well as a considerable increase in life expectancy. However, our inability to cope with death grew in direct proportion to our capacity to postpone it. People want to live longer but want to remain youthful. Death began to be considered a failure, and the weakening of the body, a natural consequence of aging, has been interpreted as imperfection (Elias, 1982/2001; Feifel, 1959; Kastenbaum, 2000; Morin, 1951/2002). In this cultural atmosphere, the debates surrounding death have taken on greater importance. In this era of technological control over nature and human life, there is, more than ever, a need for the science of thanatology, a completely new area of study, the scope of which encompasses all of the encounters between life and death. Beginning at the end of the 20th century, thanatology turned the philosophical, poetic, and secular debate on death into a scientific field of study that touches on other realms of interest, such as philosophy, psychology, medicine, sociology, anthropology, nursing, bioethics, history, architecture, education, archeology, and law.

The objective of the present review was to describe the history of thanatology from its inception, as well as to evaluate the theories and practices in the related field of death education. To that end, we analyzed the literature on these topics.

Thanatology and the Contemporary Denial of Death

Although death has always puzzled humankind, the practice of thanatology, as an interdisciplinary science, gained acceptance only after the Second World War (Kastenbaum, 1993), in the historical context of the 20th century denial of death (Aries, 1974). The emergence of this science was closely linked to the moment in history and the human relationship with death at that time.

Over the course of history, the way in which we deal with death has changed significantly (Aries, 1974; Elias, 1982/2001; Gorer, 1955; Kastenbaum, 1995; Kovács, 2003a; Lifton, 1975; Morin, 1951/2002; Parkes, Laungani, & Young, 1997; Pine, 1986). Aries (1974) maintained that throughout human history, even if changes were subtle during certain periods of time, our attitude toward death has changed substantially from the Middle Ages to the present: the customs of the former evoked greater familiarity with death, whereas death is currently considered a frightening concept.

In earlier times, death was in evidence, underscored by routine: death was an event that occurred at home, shared by the family and the community as a whole (Fulton & Owen, 1988). According to Elias (1982/2001), what comforted the dying and their relatives was being able to share the experience with others. Therefore, in those times, death was not a lonely experience.

Religion plays a major role in the way in which we deal with death, by creating various death rituals and providing explanations that give believers the sense that they understand the meaning of death (Parkes et al., 1997). In each religion, these rituals and teachings have undergone many changes over the years (Aries, 1974). In general, cultural frameworks guide individual attitudes and behaviors: different religions construct different representations of death, leading to different patterns of social interaction (Greenberg, Koole, & Pyszczynski, 2004). Darwin's work in the 19th century marked a shift from a theological to a natural and biological approach (Lifton, 1975). In the contemporary age, all religions are suffering, because scientific and technological advances have demonstrated that the world can be explained without reference to a god or gods and can be controlled without divine intervention ("God is dead"—Nietzsche, 1896). One of the greatest changes was the transition between death being dealt with as a familial matter and the care of the dying being carried out by professionals (Aries, 1974; Morin, 1951/2002; Sozzi, 2009). Near the end of the 19th century, death began to be displaced from the home to the hospital (Aries, 1974). Previously functioning as places of healing, hospitals began to have the secondary function of receiving the dying. In the hospitals, death lost much of its ritual and ceremony (Aries, 1974). Together with the changes in mentality and efforts to set the death event itself apart from social life, one of the causes of death becoming distanced from society was the displacement of cemeteries from inter-urban areas to areas on the outskirts of cities (Sozzi, 2009). Motivated by the hygienist ideas of the period, authorities decreed that cemeteries should be located far from populated areas, thereby imposing the need for hearses in order to transport the bodies of the deceased (Sozzi, 2009). In Western society, the structure of cemeteries is no longer influenced by religion, as it was in medieval Europe and in pre-modern Islamic societies, but is determined by public health concerns (Walter, 1997). Advances in science, technology, and medicine have extended life spans by many years, not only postponing the event of death but also allowing individuals to ignore the very idea of it (Kovács, 2003a). The spread of the paradoxical "religious secularization" also changed our relationship with death (Walter, 1997). After the Industrial Revolution, death began to be viewed as the failure of the body machine (Kastenbaum, 1995).

According to Gorer (1955), by the middle of the 20th century, death was being ignored and the concept itself was therefore in danger of becoming obsolete. As it became acceptable to discuss sexuality, death took its place as the forbidden subject (Gorer, 1955; Lifton, 1975). Prior to that time, all of the sciences, with the exception of anthropology, had overlooked the concept of death (Kastenbaum & Costa, 1977). When it became clear that there was a crisis involving our relationship with death and that all aspects of death were being neglected, researchers and educators were inspired to stimulate discussions on the topic and to promote death education (Noppe, 2007a).

At the apex of the crisis in our relationship with death, science began to be employed as a weapon in the battle against death. The concepts of health and death became dichotomous concepts, death being considered a sickness, as pathos. Within this context, growing old was correlated with physical malfunction and was equated with death (Elias, 1982/2001; Kastenbaum, 2000; Morin, 1951/2002). In recent times, this mentality has made it common to "treat" old age, for either health or esthetic reasons, as if abolishing old age would allow us to live forever, or at least to live within that illusion. Many authors have stated that, in addition to the biological process, the psychosocial and cultural aspects of death should be taken into consideration (Kellehear, 2008). In many societies, social death follows the physical event, whereas, in Western society, this chronology is increasingly being inverted, social death often preceding the biological fact (Sweeting & Gilhooly, 1992).

Throughout the scientific literature, the theme of death is being discussed, and the scientific community is making an effort to reintroduce the concept of death as a social reality. However, thanatology has often been practiced in a manner that depicts death as being disconnected from life (Kastenbaum, 1993). The Japanese word for thanatology is shiseigaku, which means the study of death and life (DeSpelder & Strickland, 2007). Death studies and reflections on death must integrate the concepts of life and death in order to reintegrate death into the social context, effectively redefining death and altering its symbolic significance in our complex Western society (Elias, 1982/2001; Sozzi, 2009).

Theory and Practice in Death Education, History, and Evolution

In a sense, death education has been practiced informally throughout the history of humanity. Prior to being connected with religious representation or formal teaching, the concepts inherent to the relationship between life and death were transmitted to the individual by the group through family values and rites of passage. Each individual was thus initiated into the symbolic apparatus shared by the community. Since law became a science, religion has been relieved of the responsibility of initiating individuals into their social roles, which has been entrusted to the school system. In recent years, that same system has progressively taken over the responsibility for educating individuals on the concepts of death and dying.

Regarding formal death education, Herman Feifel (1959), Elisabeth Kübler-Ross (1969/1993), and Cicely Saunders (2000) played important historic roles. First published in 1959, the book *The Meaning of Death,* edited by Feifel, was what many authors consider the first work of the death awareness movement (Kastenbaum, 1995; Pine, 1986; Wass, 2004), which envisions multidisciplinary study in the area. The death awareness movement was seen as a synonym for death education (Wass, 2004). In 1967, Saunders founded what came to be known as the first modern hospice, the St. Christopher Hospice in London. Hospice is a philosophy of care that aims to introduce quality of care into the dying process, bringing together scientific data, palliative care, and humanity at the end of life (Doka, 2007; Parkes, 1997). The philosophy of hospice includes the entire family and can be applied in the home or in a facility that also allows personal care (Kastenbaum, 1995). The hospice movement and the death education movement have had a parallel history in society (Pine, 1986). The hospice movement was clearly initiated as a response to the impersonal and high-tech way of dealing with death in Western society (Kastenbaum, 1995). Two years after the foundation of the first modern hospice, Kübler-Ross published her book *On Death and Dying* (1969/1993), in which she interviewed 200 dying patients to learn what they knew of the experience of being near death. She emphasized the fact that the fear of death is universal and that humans have always lived in the shadow of death but went on to state that the more we have denied death and have tried to distance ourselves from it—institutionalizing and thus depersonalizing it—the more we have suffered emotionally and the more death has become a subject that is suppressed in our society. Kübler-Ross' now famous theory of the five stages of death (Denial, Anger, Bargaining, Depression, and Acceptance) was widely criticized because of its lack of methodological rigor (Corr, 1993; Doka, 2007; Kastenbaum, 1995; Thorson, 1996). Kübler-Ross herself underscored the didactic objective of the stages theory and of the stage dynamics, stating that, in many cases, not all of the stages occur or the stages occur in a different order. Nevertheless, many people have applied her theory in a rigid way. Caregivers and families tend to qualify the dying process on the basis of the stages, which puts unnecessary pressure on the dying individual to complete the five phases in an "appropriate" manner (Kastenbaum, 1995). However, the greatest value of Kübler-Ross' work was not in categorizing the stages of dying but in creating space for a humanistic approach to death and end-of-life care (Corr, 1993; Doka, 2007; Kastenbaum, 1995; Thorson, 1996).

The first few college courses on death education appeared in the United States in the 1960s (Kastenbaum, 1995; Noppe,

2007a; Pine, 1986). Dickinson (2007) showed that, despite the fact that medical and nursing schools in the United States have traditionally had a limited emphasis on the theme, the number of death education courses has recently increased at such institutions, over 90% of their students now taking some courses related to end-of-life care.

Beyond formal instruction, death education encompasses everything people learn about death during their lifetime (Wass, n.d.). It is part of everyday life and culture, through which individuals begin to realize that their lifespan is limited (Noppe, 2007b). The first source of death education is the family, which exerts its influence throughout the life of the individual (Gilbert & Murray, 2007).

Various scientific journals have been established in the interest of disseminating knowledge related to thanatology. Examples include *Omega: Journal of Death and Dying and Death Studies* (originally named Death Education), which were the pioneers in the area, first published in 1970 and 1977, respectively (Wass, n.d.). A more recent example is the *European Journal of Mortality,* which was first published in 1996.

Theory and Practice

In recent years, there have been major contributions to the theoretical foundations of thanatology. The advances in thanatology include a wide range of aspects, from the increase in death education at the university and professional training levels to the use of hospice programs as an alternative means of caring for dying patients (Saunders, 2000). Although it is clear that thanatology know-how has improved, the accumulated knowledge on death, dying, and grief has yet to be fully applied to the education of neglected groups, such as school-age children and older adults (Wass, 2004).

In death education, there is a gap—a lack of "crosstalk"—between practice and research. Thanatology deals with a very personal subject, the fact that everyone will die and that everyone needs to deal with bereavement. Therefore, it is of great importance that practitioners integrate their own experiences into the death dialogue, being able to address the question from the standpoint of humanity (Jordan, 2000; Schim, Briller, Thurston, & Meert, 2006; Silverman, 2000; Wolfe & Jordan, 2000). Currier, Holland, and Neimeyer (2008) evaluated 119 end-of-life practitioners and found that, although many acknowledged the importance of empirical findings, they often expressed concern that the theory is not always consistent with the practice. Integrating the contributions of researchers with those of practitioners could be mutually advantageous. Researchers, being removed from practice, might have a more objective point of view of clinical practice (Kastenbaum, 1995). Likewise, practitioners who remain abreast of the latest developments in research, could suggest new lines of research based on their practical experience (Kastenbaum, 1988). A mix of quantitative and qualitative studies would best represent theories and practices: evidence-based practices should be applied and demonstrated, whereas the qualitative investigations should be complemented by quantitative studies (Thorson, 1996).

Hospices have played an important role in death education (Noppe, 2007a; Wass, n.d.). However, in many countries, public health authorities have not established end-of-life policies, whereas those in other countries have attempted to incorporate the hospice philosophy, but, without proper adaptation, the process failed to achieve many of its objectives and death is rarely discussed in palliative care facilities (Campione, 2003, 2004). Therefore, reflecting upon thanatology and discussing the application of death studies in various environments is fundamental to adapting practice to different realities. Thanatology theory took shape as death studies and research, whereas thanatology practice manifests primarily as formal death education, end-of-life care, and bereavement counseling.

In poor countries, there is also a great demand for palliative end-of-life care, which still competes for resources with other basic necessities. In countries with greater social and health problems, this inequality is also visible in research and practices in death education. The development of new public policies that include death education in many different settings will also require a change in the current mentality of certain practitioners. Hospice and palliative care, for example, require interdisciplinary efforts involving equal contributions from various fields and the sharing of knowledge. In some countries, in addition to the precarious social conditions that complicate the use of palliative care, as well as that of other types of treatment and equipment, there is resistance from many physicians who have difficulty in accepting this horizontal model of interdisciplinary collaboration (Kovács, 2003a).

Areas of Difficulty and Neglected Groups

Death education is spreading to many areas, such as school classrooms, college courses, and education for health professionals, as well as training of grief counselors and public educators (Wass, n.d.). However, there is still a vast amount of work to be done in the field. For school-age children in some countries, there are still many barriers such as reluctance on the part of teachers or parents and the lack of adequate training (Noppe, 2007b). Many people still think that death education for young children would be better taught at home, despite the fact that the most common way to deal with the subject of death in the modern home is through silence (Noppe, 2007b). Researchers believe that, in some countries and cultures, death is not contemplated or talked about in elementary schools because it is related to non-traditional teaching and is considered to be within the purview of the family (Testoni, Tranquilli, Salghetti, Marini, & Legrenzi, 2005). In professional health education, the situation has improved but has yet to meet expectations. Death education should be considered for individuals of all ages. However, in the area of gerontology, there have been even fewer studies of death education, because there are fewer death education programs targeting the elderly (Noppe, 2007b, Wass, 2004).

Death Education, Media, and Politics

The media currently has a fundamental influence on death education. As the need for death education came to be recognized, it became an informal theme for a sensationalist media (Noppe, 2007b). The most common venues for discussions on death are currently television, advertisements, games, and print (Sofka, 2007). Television and violent video games marketed to children present death as something cruel and aggressive (Fulton & Owen, 1988; Testoni et al., 2005; Young & Papadatou, 1997). Gilbert and Murray (2007) showed that the informal death education presented by the media is unrealistic and should be carefully evaluated in formal settings and by families. On television, images of death appear back-to-back with margarine advertisements and are described as "illusively fantastical and frightening real" (Fulton & Owen, 1988, p. 383).

At present, the media and government play a major role in the sphere of information and education. The public sector can determine whose death is worth counting—or recounting (Butler, 2004). During the Vietnam War, for example, deaths were reported by the American media as if they occurred in a mythical place, almost as a fiction (Fulton & Owen, 1988). During the Gulf War, the public was almost completely shielded from the reality of war deaths because the American government wanted to maintain public support for the war. Consequently, the distinction between human beings and objects was blurred, and the idea of death was minimized through the use of euphemisms and ambiguity, as well as through strict control of media news, the dehumanization of people, and the personification of equipment (Umberson & Henderson, 1992).

Noppe, Noppe, and Bartell (2006) studied adolescents' responses to terrorism and underscored the need for community support and educational windows of opportunity to discuss the theme with teenagers, as they pass into maturity and form the bases of the concepts they will carry with them in adulthood. In cases of great tragedies and everyday violence, activating community support is crucial to collective life and should be a primary focus of death education programs.

Because of the mystery of death and the human fear of annihilation, the concept of death has great influence on our social system. In the hands of politicians or members of the clergy, it is a powerful tool that can be used as a control mechanism. That is why there is a need for death awareness programs. Death education can be used to open the debate and illuminate various images of death, leading to personal reflection. However, when misused, it can also serve to distort reality, obscuring the theme for political purposes, as it was by the Nazis during the Second World War and by others during other wars, in the name of racial cleansing, for stereotyping, and in the interest of mass destruction (Becker, 1973; Parkes et al., 1997). Therefore, promoting discussion and raising consciousness of death is a basic goal of thanatology practice.

Discussion

Since its emergence, the science of thanatology has been entwined with the way in which we dealt with death and inextricably linked to the history of that relationship. Economics, politics, theology, social concerns, and cultural factors have influenced the way in which we live and the way in which we die. The gradual changes throughout human history and the rapid transformations in recent decades have made it necessary to formally consider the concept of death and to embrace the interdisciplinary nature of the field of thanatology. During the development of this study, it became clear that there is a strict correlation between the declining involvement in structured religions and the emergence of thanatology as a science. In our complex society, the current death rites are ineffective in meeting our need to mourn and to express our feelings of grief. Religion is not as influential as it was in earlier times (Sozzi, 2009). New death rituals that take contemporary feelings and behaviors into consideration are not yet available (Elias, 1982/2001). The death system is going through a phase of hesitation and adjustment (Kastenbaum, 1995). We must therefore consider new customs that can replace the previous ones (Sozzi, 2009). The current lack of religious faith can be also thought of as a daring shift toward a more realistic view of death. Modern culture and the current technology, which often allows people to live longer, also support the decline of religious defenses against the reality of death, encourage formal death education, and promote the thanatology movement.

The way in which human beings deal with death is deeply rooted in individual cultural contexts (Irish, Lundquist, & Nelsen, 1993). Therefore, when working in death education and providing end-of-life care, it is important to recognize these differences in background (Rosenblatt, 1993, 1997). When working in big cities, it is hard to define a local population, because migration tends to create multi-cultural societies. This has led to a broad demand for cultural awareness on the part of professionals, as well as for opportunities to share experiences and knowledge (Irish et al., 1993). There is great need to extend the scope of research to include different ethnic communities (Kastenbaum, 2000).

More and more people are living longer and longer, and their quality of life is not always satisfactory. The consequent rising costs of end-of-life care have captured the attention of policy makers around the world (Kastenbaum, 1996). Palliative care services are not necessarily more expensive than the hospital-based services they replace. Public policies related to end-of-life care and death education should be broader in order to encompass presumed realities. Expanding death education in countries that still suffer from more basic problems of health care and general education is a great challenge (Bromberg, 2001; Kovács, 2003b). Death education must be broadened in order to address the concept of death in other specific contexts and settings, such as urban violence, poverty, and slums, all of which have a greater impact in such countries than in developed countries.

If we use Feifel's landmark book (1959) as the benchmark, the formal interdisciplinary study of dying, death, and loss is now entering its 5th decade. Therefore, it is certainly appropriate and timely to review the present status of the field. Here, we have provided the general framework of thanatology and death education from a historical perspective. The need for thanatology was found to be implicit in the way in which society deals with death (Aries, 1974; Gorer, 1955; Kastenbaum, 1993). The desire to ponder the concept of death and to alleviate the suffering caused by death anxiety, together with the growing scientific impulse to quantify and qualify our world, contributed to the emergence of thanatology. We have shown that death studies and practices are important instruments to promote death awareness and life reflection. Nevertheless, there is a need for deeper and more meaningful analyses in this field (Wogrin, 2007). Although we found an extensive number of remarkable works on death education in general, there have been few studies giving attention to current death customs or focusing on the historical aspects of society's response to large-scale death. There is a need for further studies that would promote a dialogue on updating the fundamental concepts of thanatology. In a science that is growing so rapidly, theoretical reviews that consolidate its accumulated findings are of extreme importance.

References

Aries, P. (1974). The Western attitudes toward death: From the Middle Ages to the present (P. M. Ranum, Trans.). Baltimore, MD: The Johns Hopkins University Press.

Becker, E. (1973). The denial of death. New York: Free Press Paperback.

Bromberg, M. H. P. F. (2001). Guest editorial: Death studies in Brazil. Mortality, 6(1), 5–6.

Butler, J. (2004). Precarious life: The powers of mourning and violence. London: Verso. Campione, F. (2003). Contro la morte [Against death]. Bologna: CLUEB.

Campione, F. (2004). Research note: To die without speaking of death. Mortality, 9(4), 345–349.

Corr, C. A. (1993). Coping with dying: Lessons that we should and should not learn from the work of Elisabeth Kübler-Ross. Death Studies, 17, 69–83.

Currier, J. M, Holland, J. M., & Neimeyer, R. A. (2008). Making sense of loss: A content analysis of end-of-life practitioners' therapeutic approaches. Omega, 57(2), 121–141.

DeSpelder, L. A., & Strickland, A. L. (2007). Culture, socialization and death education. In D. Balk (Ed.), Handbook of thanatology (pp. 303–314). London: Routledge.

Dickinson, G. E. (2007). End-of-life and palliative care issues in medical and nursing schools in the United States. Death Studies, 31, 713–726.

Doka, K. J. (2007). Historical and contemporary perspectives on dying. In D. Balk (Ed.), Handbook of thanatology (pp. 19–25). London: Routledge.

Elias, N. (2001). The loneliness of the dying (E. Jephcott, Trans.). New York: Continuum. (Original work published 1982)

Feifel, H. (1959). The meaning of death. New York: McGraw-Hill.

Freud, S. (1957). Thoughts for the times on war and death. In J. Strachey (Ed. & Trans.), The standard edition of the complete psychological works of Sigmund Freud (Vol. 14, pp. 275–300). London: Hogarth Press. (Original work published 1915)

Fulton, R., & Owen, G. (1988). Death and society in twentieth century America. Omega, 18(4), 379–395.

Gilbert, K. R., & Murray, C. I. (2007). The family, larger systems and death education. In D. Balk (Ed.), Handbook of thanatology (pp. 345–353). London: Routledge.

Golden, R. L. (1998). Sir William Osler: Humanistic thanatologist. Omega, 36(3), 241–258.

Gorer, G. (1955, October). The pornography of death. Encounter, 5(4), 49–52.

Greenberg, J., Koole, S. L., & Pyszczynski, T. (Eds.). (2004). Experimental existential psychology. New York: Guilford Press.

Irish, D. P., Lundquist, K. F., & Nelsen, V. J. (1993). Ethnic variations in dying, death and grief: Diversity in university. Philadelphia: Taylor & Francis.

Jordan, J. R. (2000). Introduction. Research that matters: Bridging the gap between research and practice in thanatology. Death Studies, 24, 457–467.

Kastenbaum, R. (1988). Theory, research and application: Some critical issues for thanatology. Omega, 18(4), 397–410.

Kastenbaum, R. J. (1993). Reconstructing death in postmodern society. Omega, 27, 75–89.

Kastenbaum, R. J. (1995). Death, society, and human experience (5th ed.). Boston: Allyn & Bacon.

Kastenbaum, R. (1996). A world without death? First and second thoughts. Mortality, 1(1), 111–121.

Kastenbaum, R. (2000). The psychology of death (3rd ed.). New York: Springer.

Kastenbaum, R. (2004). Death, society and human experience (8th ed.). Boston: Pearson.

Kastenbaum, R., & Costa, P. T. (1977). Psychological perspectives on death. Annual Reviews, 28, 225–249.

Kellehear, A. (2008). Dying as a social relationship: A sociological review of debates on the determination of death. Social Science & Medicine, 66, 1533–1544.

Kovács, M. J. (2003a). Educação para a morte. Temas e reflexoes [Death education. Themes and reflections]. São Paulo: Casa do Psicologo, Fapesp.

Kovács, M. J. (2003b). Educação para a morte. Desafio na formação de profissionais de saúde e educação [Death education. Challenges in health and educational professional training]. São Paulo: Casa do Psicologo, Fapesp.

Kübler-Ross, E. (1993). On death and dying. New York: Collier Books. (Original work published 1969)

Lifton, R. J. (1975). On death and the continuity of life: A psychohistorical perspective. Omega, 6(2), 143–159.

Morin, E. (2002). L'uomo e la morte (A. Perri, & L. Pacelli, Trans.). Paris: Le Seuil. [Original work published 1951; original title, L'Homme et la Mort (Man and death)]

Nietzsche, F. W. (1896). Thus Spake Zarathustra—A book for all and none. (A. Tille, Trans.). New York: Macmillan.

Noppe, I. C., Noppe, L. D., & Bartell, D. (2006). Terrorism and resilience: Adolescents' and teachers' responses to September, 11, 2001. Death Studies, 30, 41–60.

Noppe, I. C. (2007a). Historical and contemporary perspectives on death education. In D. Balk (Ed.), Handbook of thanatology (pp. 329–335). London: Routledge.

Noppe, I. C. (2007b). Life span issues and death education. In D. Balk (Ed.), Handbook of thanatology (pp. 337–343). London: Routledge.

Parkes, C. M. (1997). Help for the dying and the bereaved. In C. M. Parkes, P. Laungani, & B. Young (Eds.), Death and bereavement across cultures (pp. 206–217). New York: Routledge.

Parkes, C. M., Laungani, P., & Young, B. (1997). Death and bereavement across cultures. New York: Routledge.

Pine, V. R. (1986). The age of maturity for death education: A socio-historical portrait of the era 1976–1985. Death Studies, 10, 209–231.

Postiglione, A. (2008). Della bella morte [The good death]. Milan: Bur.

Rosenblatt, P. C. (1993). Cross-cultural variation in the experience, expression and understanding of grief. In D. P. Irish, K. F. Lundquist, & V. J. Nelsen (Eds.), Ethnic variations in dying, death and grief: Diversity in university (pp. 13–29). Philadelphia: Taylor & Francis.

Rosenblatt, P. C. (1997). Grief in small-scale societies. In C. M. Parkes, P. Laungani, & B. Young (Eds.), Death and bereavement across cultures (pp. 27–51). New York: Routledge.

Saunders, C. (2000). The evolution of palliative care. Patient Education and Counseling, 41, 7–13.

Schim, S. M., Briller, S. H., Thurston, C. S., & Meert, K. L. (2006). Life as death scholars: Passion, personality, and professional perspectives. Death Studies, 31(2), 165–172.

Silverman, P. R. (2000). Research, clinical practice and the human experience: Putting the pieces together. Death Studies, 24, 469–478.

Sofka, C. J. (2007). Death education: Ethical and legal issues. In D. Balk (Ed.), Handbook of thanatology (pp. 355–367). London: Routledge.

Sozzi, M. (2009). Reinventare la morte. Introduzione alla tanatologia [Reinventing death. Thanatology's introduction]. Bari: Laterza.

Sweeting, H. N., & Gilhooly, M. L. M. (1992). Doctor, am I dead? A review of social death in modern societies. Omega, 24(4), 251–269.

Testoni I. (2007). Autopsia filosofica [Philosophical autopsy]. Milan: Apogeo.

Testoni, I., Tranquilli, R., Salghetti, M., Marini, L., & Legrenzi, A. (2005). L'educazione alla morte come momento di incontro psico-socio-culturale tra scuola, famiglia e territorio [Death education as a psycho-socio-cultural encounter among school, family and territory]. Famiglia Interdisciplinarità Ricerca, 10(3), 313–322.

Thorson, J. A. (1996). Qualitative thanatology. Mortality, 1(2), 177–190.

Umberson, D., & Henderson, K. (1992). The social construction of death in the Gulf War. Omega, 25(1), 1–15.

Walter, T. (1997). Secularization. In C. M. Parkes, P. Laungani, & B. Young (Eds.), Death and bereavement across cultures (pp. 166–187). New York: Routledge.

Wass, H. (2004). A perspective on the current state of death education. Death Studies, 28, 289–308.

Wass, H. (n.d.). Death education. Retrieved June 3, 2009, from http://www.deathreference.com/Da-Em/Death-Education.html

Wogrin, C. (2007). Professional issues and thanatology. In D. Balk (Ed.), Handbook of thanatology (pp. 371–386). London: Routledge.

Wolfe, B., & Jordan, J. R. (2000). Ramblings from the trenches: A clinical perspective on thanatological research. Death Studies, 24, 569–584.

Young, B., & Papadatou, D. (1997). Childhood death and bereavement. In C. M. Parkes, P. Laungani, & B. Young (Eds.), Death and bereavement across cultures (pp. 191–205). New York: Routledge.

Critical Thinking

1. Throughout history, death has compelled us to reflect on our own mortality. How is your taking a course in thanatology impacting on your own feelings toward your death?

2. Does the Western world today tend to deny or accept death? Highlight the pros and cons of this argument.

3. What factors have contributed to an increase in death education offerings throughout academe?

Acknowledgements—The authors would like to thank the professors and students of the University.

UNIT 2

Dying and Death Across the Life Cycle

Unit Selections

8. **Teaching Children about Death and Grief,** Kirsti A. Dyer
9. **Death in Disney Films: Implications for Children's Understanding of Death,** Meredith Cox, Erin Garrett, James A. Graham
10. **Death and Dying in the Curriculum of Public Schools: Is there a place?,** Ethel L. King-McKenzie
11. **Needs of Elderly Patients in Palliative Care,** Helle Wijk, RN, PhD and Agneta Grimby, PhD
12. **Good Mourning,** George Dickinson
13. **Through the Touch of God: Child Death and Spiritual Sustenance in a Hutterian Colony,** Joanne Cacciatore and Rebecca Ong
14. **End-of-Life Concerns and Care Preferences: Congruence Among Terminally Ill Elders and their Family Caregivers,** Daniel S. Gardner, PhD and Betty J. Kramer, PhD

Learning Outcomes

After reading this unit you should be able to:

- Discuss teachable moments to teach children about death.

- Explain how animated characters in Disney films can help in a child's understanding of death.

- Describe how death is depicted in Walt Disney films.

- Present a case for offering death and dying in the curriculum of public schools.

- Enumerate how caregivers can be helped to lessen their assignment of dealing with a dying family member and what kinds of support are available for caregivers.

- List particular needs of elderly persons in a palliative care unit.

- Discuss the role of the veterinarian in the death of a pet.

- Understand how a Hutterite colony relates to the death of a child.

Student Website

www.mhhe.com/cls

Internet References

Wonder on the Web
http://wonder.cdc.gov
Children with AIDS Project
www.aidskids.org
Yellow Ribbon Suicide Prevention Program, Light for Life Foundation International
www.yellowribbon.org
National SUID/SIDS Resource Center
www.sidscenter.org
Palliative Care for Children
http://pediatrics.aappublications.org/content/106/2/351.full

Death is something that we must accept, though no one really understands it. We can talk about death, learn from each other, and help each other. By better understanding death conceptualization at various stages and in different relationships within the life cycle, we can help each other. It is not our intent to suggest that age should be viewed as the sole determinant of one's death concept. Many other factors influence this cognitive development such as level of intelligence, physical and mental well-being, previous emotional reactions to various life experiences, religious background, other social and cultural forces, personal identity and self-worth appraisals, and exposure to or threats of death. Indeed, a child in a hospital for seriously ill children is likely to have a more sophisticated understanding regarding death, as she/he may be aware of dying and death, more so than an adult who has not had such experiences. Nonetheless, we discuss dying and death at various stages from the cradle to the grave or, as some say, the womb to the tomb.

The death of a child and the death of a spouse are both toward the top of a list of 100 stresses that an individual has in life. The death of a child is so illogical, as the child has not lived through the life cycle. One can anticipate attending the funeral of a grandparent and then a parent. We do not, however, anticipate attending the funeral of a child, since the adult is expected to die before the child. Such is the rational sequence of the life cycle.

Research on very young children's conceptions of death does not reveal an adequate understanding of their responses, yet young children are often more sophisticated regarding death than we give them credit. Adults, many decades later, recall vivid details about their first death experiences, whether a pet or a person, and for many it was a traumatic event filled with fear, anger, and frustration. How might we help with such situations? "Death in Disney Films" might aid in working with children trying to understand dying and death. Additionally, "Teaching Children about Death and Grief" address these issues. Whether to offer thanatology in the curriculum of public schools to help children better cope with death is addressed in Ethel L. King-McKenzie's article. When a child (or an adult) must go to the veterinarian to terminate the life of a pet, what role does the veterinarian play in the decision making? This topic is addressed in "Good Mourning." How a Hutterite colony in South Dakota addresses the death of a child is presented in Cacciatore and Ong's article.

As individuals move into the "autumn" of their lives and are classified as "elderly," death surrounds them, and they are especially made aware that they are reaching the end of the tunnel. Though old age is often pictured as gloom and doom, it can be viewed as "the best is yet to be," as poet Robert Browning noted.

© Liquidlibrary/Dynamic Graphics/Jupiterimages

The aging professional athlete Satchel Paige observed years ago that aging is really mind over matter—as long as you don't mind, it really doesn't matter. You are as old (or young) as you feel. Research suggests that the elderly are accepting of death, having lived a normal life span, and are grateful for the life they have had. Some of these issues are addressed in "Needs of Elderly Patients in Palliative Care" and in "End-of-Life Concerns and Care Preferences: Congruence Among Terminally Ill Elders and their Family Caregivers."

Teaching Children about Death and Grief

Children Can Learn about Grief and Dying from Teachable Moments

Kirsti A. Dyer

For a child learning how to cope with loss, with death and with grief are some of the most important life lessons that parents, grandparents, teachers can teach them.

For many children, the first loss they may experience is the death of a grandparent or a pet. The death of a treasured pet may be more real for many children than the death of a distant grandparent.

One simple way for children to learn about death before they may be exposed to a death is for parents to take advantage of the teachable moments in life that present themselves, like discovering a dead bird or dying plant.

Using Teachable Moments to Teach Children about Death

A teachable moment is a brief instant when something happens that causes a child to be uniquely and specifically interested in a particular thing or idea and more likely to learn something. A teachable moment is a special educational opportunity.

Teachable moments occur unexpectedly. Children's grief expert Phyllis R. Silverman points out in her 1999 book, *Never Too Young to Know* [Oxford University] "We cannot always choose our moments. Children raise questions as they think of them and when they are ready. They ask questions about things for which we have not answers, such as what is death."

According to Silverman, "If these moments are utilized well, children learn to be respected as mourners and that they have a legitimate role as part of their community."

Examples of Teachable Moments

Opportunities for teaching children about death may arise when parents least expect it. Parents should be ready to use teachable moments that occur in conversations about news, watching television, or reading books to talk to your child about death. Teachable moments can be used to explain the parents' beliefs about death and how they may feel when something or someone dies.

There may be a news story in the newspaper, a dying person on a television program, in a movie or a book. Seeing a dead lizard, butterfly or bird in the yard can be used to explain to children how death comes to all living creatures.

Many children struggled to understand death when the beloved Crocodile Hunter, Steve Irwin died suddenly or when some of the more popular Harry Potter characters were unexpectedly killed. Older parents may remember learning about death by watching *Bambi* or reading *Charlotte's Web*.

The death of a family pet is often very traumatic for a child. Parents can talk about how death has ended the pet's life. Being exposed to a death helps children see that death is final and irreversible and that their pet will not come back to life the way it does on television. Parents can encourage the child, plan and carry out a pet burial to cope with the loss.

Teaching with "The Circle of Life" or Life Cycles

Elton John and Tim Rice helped parents to explain living with loss and death and the circle of life to their children by bringing up the topic in their song, "The Circle of Life" written for the 1994 movie, *The Lion King:*

> *"Some of us fall by the wayside*
> *And some of us soar to the stars*
> *And some of us sail through our troubles*
> *And some have to live with the scars"*

Animals and nature can be one of the best tools for teaching children about the circle of life and death providing a wide variety of teachable moments. When out in nature, one becomes more aware of the life cycle, by seeing decay and death, but also by seeing renewal and rebirth. Birth and death are a part of the life cycle.

The changing seasons can be used as a concept to explain life cycles. Parents can talk about what happens with the changing seasons, how plants grow or animal babies are born in spring.

Leaves wither and fall in the autumn and plants hibernate in the winter. When spring returns again there is evidence of new life growing from the dust and decay of the old plants.

Create a Safe Environment to Teach about Death

Fortunately, most children, even those exposed to loss and death, are quite resilient. Teachable moments that present themselves can be a good way for parents to explain death and their family's death beliefs to children.

By creating a safe, open environment where children feel free to ask questions and talk about feelings, parents can help their children learn about loss, death and grief.

Resource

Dyer KA. Help a Child Cope with Loss or Death: Helping Children Deal with Life's Losses and Tragedies. Suite 101.

Critical Thinking

1. Recall your first childhood death experience. Was it a pet or a person? How old were you? How did you react? How did your parents/guardians relate to this experience?

2. What "teachable moments" regarding death did you have as a child? How well do you recall that your "teacher" (mom/dad/whoever) handled this?

3. How might the death of a pet differ from that of a person (e.g., your grandfather)?

Death in Disney Films: Implications for Children's Understanding of Death

MEREDITH COX, ERIN GARRETT, AND JAMES A. GRAHAM

Introduction

Death is an aspect of life that is not only inevitable but also painful, especially for children. Children do not have the knowledge or experience that adults have; thus, they are often unprepared to deal with the death of a loved one or even of a beloved cartoon character in a movie. Furthermore, it is not until about 10 years of age that healthy children achieve an understanding that death is irreversible, permanent, and inevitable (Brent, Speece, Lin, Dong, & Yang, 1996).

If death is a concept that many young children do not have a working understanding of, then why is it such a prominent theme in children's media, specifically in Disney movies? Do Disney's portrayals influence children's comprehension of death? The current content analysis describes and analyzes the portrayal of death in selected animated Disney films. In order to examine the possible affect that death scenes in Disney films might have for children, it is necessary to understand how children conceive of death.

Children's Understanding of Death

Many of the classic Disney movies target young audiences who do not have very developed or accurate concepts of death. For instance, many children younger than five years old do not understand that death is final, and inevitable (Grollman, 1990; Speece & Brent, 1984). Between the ages of five and nine, children who do acknowledge the permanence and inevitability of death see death as something that only applies to older adults (Grollman, 1990; Speece & Brent, 1984). Some children who do not have a complete understanding of death often will fill in gaps in understanding with fantasy elements (Baker, Sedney, & Gross, 1992), which may be taken from the media that children view, such as Disney movies. If the media, specifically some Disney films, convey unrealistic messages about death, then aspects of those portrayals are likely to be internalized by children. These less than desirable notions about death may have an impact on how children will view later instances of death.

In general, children's comprehension of death depends on two factors: experience and developmental level. First, children's experiences with death (i.e., actual experience and what they have been told about death) are critical to their understanding of death (Speece & Brent, 1984). Second, the developmental level of the child also must be taken into account when examining the comprehension of death (Brent et al., 1996; Willis, 2002). For example, Willis pinpointed four aspects of death that children and adults do not view in the same way: irreversibility, finality, inevitability, and causality. Children may not understand that death is permanent and that it cannot be "fixed" or reversed. They also do not have enough life experience to realize that death is inevitable for all living things. Furthermore, because they do not think abstractly, some young children do not understand the causality of death.

There is much support to the idea that children have a very limited understanding of death (e.g., Baker et al., 1992; Brent et al., 1996; Grollman, 1990; Speece & Brent, 1984; Willis, 2002), and the partial understanding they do have is often based on fuzzy logic (Brent et al., 1996). Brent et al. found that most children do not fully understand that death is a universal, irreversible, and nonfunctional state (meaning that dead beings cannot do the things that the living do) until the age of 10 years. Interestingly, it was also found that even after children reach this level of understanding they might continue to struggle with the idea that death is final, possibly because of certain religious beliefs. However, this may suggest a more mature understanding of death rather than a less mature one (Brent et al., 1996). Children with immature, binary concepts of death see people as either alive or dead, and do not consider the idea that there may be any other options based on religious values and ideas about afterlife.

According to Baker et al. (1992), the process of grieving after a loss and coming to understand death is a process that consists of psychological tasks that children progress through to eventually overcome their grief. The first stage involves *understanding what death is,* knowing its characteristics, and being able to recognize when it has happened. At this stage, it is important for children to feel self-protected, meaning that they need to know that just because someone or something has died does not mean the child or his or her family is in any immediate danger.

The middle phase involves *understanding that death is a reality and accepting the emotions that come along with that realization.* This may include reflecting on times spent with the deceased loved one and coming to terms with the fact that he or she is gone while still maintaining memories and an internal connection to that person. Thus, we should not give children the false hope that a loved one may "come back" after death, and we should not discourage them from remaining emotionally attached to the deceased individual (Baker et al., 1992). This phase shows a marked difference in the way that children and adults grieve. Many adults move through the process more quickly than children do because they may understand and have more actual experience with the concept of death. Thus, many adults do not have to spend as much time figuring out what has happened when a loved one is suddenly gone, as would a child.

The last phase of this process involves a *reorganization of a child's sense of identity and his or her relationships with others and with the environment.* The child will also be able to invest emotionally him- or herself in relationships with others without being overly afraid of losing that person to a death. At this stage, a well-adjusted child still remembers the loved one without fearing excessively that others will die and is able to cope with those memories and any sadness associated with them (Baker et al., 1992).

Parents' Role in Children's Comprehension of Death

There are other reasons why children may misunderstand death beyond the obvious cognitive limitations. Many children tend not to discuss death with their parents or friends because they think the subject is too unpleasant, frightening, or even unnecessary (Wass, Raup, & Sisler, 1989). The manner in which some parents communicate with their children about death may influence the child's comprehension of it. When it comes to talking about death, a lot of parents do so in a way that is very confusing and potentially harmful to children (Ryerson, 1977; Willis, 2002). It seems that some parents' main objective shifts from explaining and teaching to *protecting.* For instance, rather than telling children why and how people die they may focus on downplaying the emotionality, seriousness, and reality of death.

Though their intentions are good, many adults often hinder children's understanding of death by using confusing terms and abstract language to explain the concept to them. They may say that someone has "passed away," which does not convey a realistic portrayal of death to children (Willis, 2002). They may use euphemisms (such as "sleeping for a long time" or "taken a long trip") in an attempt to downplay the impact of death in order to protect children, which only serves to confuse them. These phrases convey to the young child that the loved one who has "passed away" may "wake up" from their long nap or "come home" from their voyage (Willis, 2002). Furthermore, describing death to children as a long "sleep" is not only confusing but may foster a fear of going to sleep among children (Grollman, 1990).

Ryerson (1977) points out that sometimes parents avoid the topic of death altogether and are very awkward about discussing it with children. Many parents' hesitation to talk to children about death in a straightforward way likely stems from their own fears of death, which may have origins in the way that their own parents spoke to them about it. The implication is that this matter-of-fact manner of explaining death is likely to perpetuate a cycle of faulty communication between parents and children. Ryerson describes the mourning process in children as well as ways to help children cope with death. The use of fairy tales may be a source of identification and interest for children, and they can be used to facilitate discussion between children and adults about death and grieving.

The fairy tale has served as the most honest and clear-cut managing of death available to children over the ages (Dobson, 1977). According to Dobson (1977), its main purpose is to stimulate children's intellect and help them tackle their "darkest and scariest thoughts about separation, rejection, abandonment, and death" (p. 175). Fairy tales often contain non-threatening references to death, which makes them appropriate for use with children. Fairy tales, many of which have inspired many Disney films, present interesting and somewhat controversial portrayals of death and grieving.

Popular Children's Films, Children's Grieving Processes, and Death Education

The present study is an exploratory analysis of death from animated Disney movies. In general, there is limited research that examines the relationship between popular children's films and children's comprehension of death. For instance, Sedney (1999) examined the portrayal of grief in young characters in children's films. The films all had hopeful messages showing the possibility for a happy life following the death of a loved one. However, the films showed differing degrees of grieving. Sedney points out that sometimes deaths are unacknowledged completely, which is an aspect that is common to children's films, especially among those with missing parents. In other cases, there is an acknowledgment of death, but it is not grieved, as in *Bambi.* In contrast, in *The Lion King,* death *is* acknowledged and the young character grieves and displays a gamut of typical grieving emotions ranging from self-blame and anger to profound sadness. Sedney describes the merits of *The Lion King's* grief portrayal because it offers a realistic view of grief as well as a resolution to sadness. For this reason, this particular film has the potential to be an effective teaching tool to serve as a basis of discussion on the topic of death with children.

In contrast with Sedney (1999, 2002) who found positive aspects of portrayals of death in children's films, Schultz and Huet (2001) examined the highest grossing American films and Academy Award nominees and concluded that the majority of portrayals of death are unrealistic and sensational, and are rarely accompanied by realistic and normal grief reactions. This was true about some children's films as well. Many of the films did not either acknowledge death or use "death terminology," lending further support to the idea that our culture has taboos about discussing death in a straightforward manner

(Schultz & Huet, 2001). Interestingly, Schultz and Huet point out that the Motion Picture Association of America (MPAA) does not distinguish between types of violence and death when considering ratings, which also affects audiences, and most notably children.

As previously emphasized, the amount of research done on the media's influence on children's understanding of death is very limited. Many death educators propose some form of death education for children (Wass et al., 1989). How is this education to be initiated? We propose that using popular animated Disney films may be one way to intervene and may provide a foundation for discussion between children and adults about death. Specifically, we examined the portrayal of death and grieving in Disney films geared toward children, focusing on five factors: character status, depiction of death, death status, emotional reaction, and causality.

Method
Film Selection
The analyzed content consists of 10 Disney Classic animated full-length feature films. The movies were selected only if a death occurred or was a theme in the plotline. The movies were chosen from various decades in order to sample the portrayal of death across time in Disney films. The first animated Disney full-length feature film was released approximately 60 years ago; thus, films were selected from both the first 30 years of production (pre-1970s) and from the last 30 years (post-1970s). Due to a lack of full-length films with death scenes released before the 1970s, only three movies were selected from that period, whereas seven were selected from more recent decades. This limited selection could also be attributed to the fact that full-length animated Disney movies were released on an average of three per decade in the past, whereas 14 were released in the 1980s and 1990s. The films were not chosen haphazardly; rather, the researchers went through the plot outlines of all animated Disney Classic films and chose from that list, being careful to select both older classics and more modern films that children are familiar with today. The movies examined for this study were: *Snow White and the Seven Dwarfs* (1937), *Bambi* (1942), *Sleeping Beauty,* (1959), *The Little Mermaid* (1989), *Beauty and the Beast* (1991), *The Lion King* (1994), *The Hunchback of Notre Dame* (1996), *Hercules* (1997), *Mulan* (1998), and *Tarzan* (1999).

Coding Categories
Two coders watched the movies together and coded the data individually. Each character's death was analyzed by the following five coding criteria.

Character Status
This category refers to the role the character that died played in the plot. We coded for two different types of characters. First, a *protagonist* is a character that is seen as the "good guy," hero/heroine of the movie, or the main character whom the story revolves around. An *antagonist* is a character who is seen as the "bad guy," villain, nemesis, or enemy of the protagonist.

Depiction of Death
Refers to how the character's death was shown in the film. In an *explicit death* the audience sees that the character is definitely dead because the body is shown being physically damaged/killed and/or the dead, motionless body is shown on screen. An *implicit death* refers to one in which the audience can only assume that the character is dead based on the fact that they do not appear again in the film and/or that they have encountered something that would presumably result in death. Examples include seeing a shadow of a dead body or a character falling off a cliff. *Sleep death* refers to an instance in which a character falls into a state of prolonged sleep. Generally, this is the result of a spell due to an original intent to kill.

Death Status
This category refers to if a death was a true end of life or if it was shown as something negotiable that does not necessarily represent the absolute end of life. A *permanent/final* death is one in which the character does not return in any form. A *reversible* death is one where a character returns in one of two ways. A *reversible-same form* death is one in which the character seemingly comes back from a dead or seemingly dead state in his or her original body. In a *reversible-altered form* death, the character returns either in a physically transformed state or in the form of a spirit.

Emotional Reaction
Refers to how the other characters in the movie responded to or dealt with death. *Positive emotion* refers to a character or characters being visibly happy (e.g., smiling, cheering) or showing signs of relief. *Negative emotion* refers to a character or characters reacting with frustration, remorse, anger, or with general signs of sadness (e.g., crying). *Lacking emotion* refers to characters reacting to death as if it is inconsequential or the death is not dealt with or acknowledged by all characters.

Causality
Causality refers to what led to or caused the death and whether the death was portrayed as being justified or unjustified. In a *purposeful* death, a character dies as the result of another character's intent to harm or kill him or her. An *accidental* death refers to one where the death was unintentional and was the result of an unplanned event. In addition to being either purposeful or accidental, death events were also coded as being either *justified* or *unjustified*. *Justified* deaths were ones in which the character who died had done something that warranted punishment; the general message conveyed was that they "deserved" to die. *Unjustified* deaths were ones in which the character did not do anything wrong; there was a sense that they did not deserve to die.

Intercoder Reliability
Two coders rated the selected films. Intercoder reliability was judged as acceptable if the raters achieved more than 70% agreement on all categories, using Cohen's Kappa. The reliability between coders was tested on a randomly selected subsample of

Table 1 Depiction of Death by Character Type

Depiction of Death	Protagonist	%	Antagonist	%	Total
Explicit death	7	63.64	4	36.36	11
Implicit death	3	30.0	7	70.0	10
Sleep death	2	100.0	0	0	2
Total	12	52.17	11	47.83	23

Note. Percentages are row percentages.

Table 2 Death Status by Character Types

Death Status	Protagonist	%	Antagonist	%	Total
Reversible/Same	4	100	0	0	4
Reversible/Altered	2	100	0	0	2
Permanent/Final	7	41.18	10	58.82	17
Total	13	56.52	10	43.48	23

Note. Percentages are row percentages.

four films (40% of the sample). Intercoder reliability was computed for each of the five categories of interest: character status ($K = 1.00$), depiction of death ($K = 0.92$), death status ($K = 1.00$), emotional reaction ($K = 1.00$), and causality ($K = 0.87$).

Results

Our study examined the portrayal of death and grieving in Disney films geared toward children, and focused on five factors.

Character Status

A total of 23 death scenes occurred in the 10 Disney films analyzed. Protagonists and antagonists were portrayed nearly equally in those scenes. Out of the 23 characters who died, 52% were protagonists ($n = 12$) and 48% ($n = 11$) were antagonists (see Table 1).

Depiction of Death

Implicit death accounted for 43% of total deaths ($n = 10$) and explicit death ($n = 11$) accounted for 48%. We found that 64% of explicit deaths occurred among protagonists ($n = 7$) while only 36% of explicit deaths were the deaths of antagonists ($n = 4$). In contrast, implicit deaths occurred more among antagonists: 70% of antagonists died in implicit death scenes ($n = 7$), whereas only 30% of protagonists did ($n = 3$). Sleep death was not nearly as common as "real" death portrayals, occurring in 9% of death instances ($n = 2$). Both sleep deaths occurred among protagonists (see Table 1).

Death Status

A large majority of deaths (74%) were portrayed as permanent, final, and irreversible ($n = 17$). Out of the permanent deaths, 59% were those of antagonists ($n = 10$) and 41% were

protagonists ($n = 7$). Reversible death occurred in 26% of death scenes ($n = 6$). Of the six reversible deaths, 67% ($n = 4$) of characters returned in their same form and 33% ($n = 2$) reappeared in altered forms. All of the reversible deaths were among protagonists (see Table 2).

Emotional Reaction

In terms of reactions to a character's death, the most prevalent type of emotion displayed by characters was negative emotion, which occurred in 48% of death scenes ($n = 11$). Negative emotions included typical grieving responses such as fear, crying, and expressing anger or frustration over a loss. Out of the negative emotional responses, 91% ($n = 10$) were for the deaths of protagonists, whereas only 9% ($n = 1$) resulted from the death of an antagonist. Positive emotion, indicated by happiness, relief, or celebration of a loss, occurred in only 13% of deaths ($n = 3$). Positive emotion resulted solely from the deaths of antagonists.

Interestingly, neutral or lacking emotion occurred in 39% of death scenes ($n = 9$), which is nearly as frequently as grieving/negative emotion did. The majority of instances of lacking emotion (78%) were associated with the deaths of antagonists ($n = 7$), whereas only 22% of protagonist deaths resulted in neutral or lacking emotion ($n = 2$) (see Table 3).

Causality

Purposeful deaths occurred most frequently, i.e., 70% ($n = 16$) of all deaths. Out of these purposeful deaths, 38% ($n = 6$) were justified and 62% ($n = 10$) were unjustified. Accidental deaths made up 30% of total deaths ($n = 7$). Out of accidental deaths, 71% ($n = 5$) were justified and 29% ($n = 2$) were seen as unjustified. When justification was considered, regardless of motivation or cause of death, it was found that the respective prevalences of justified and unjustified deaths were nearly

Table 3   Emotional Reactions by Character Type

Emotional Reaction	Protagonist	%	Antagonist	%	Total
Positive emotion	0	0	3	100	3
Negative emotion	10	90.9	1	9.1	11
Lacking emotion	2	22.22	7	77.78	9
Total	12	52.17	11	47.83	23

Note. Percentages are row percentages.

Table 4   Cause of Death by Character Type

Cause of Death	Protagoniste	%	Antagonist	%	Total
Accidental–justified	0	0	5	100	5
Accidental–unjustified	2	100	0	0	2
Purposeful–justified	0	0	6	100	6
Purposeful–unjustified	10	100	0	0	10
Total	12	52.17	11	47.83	23

Note. Percentages are row percentages.

equal: justified deaths accounted for 48% of all deaths ($n = 11$) and unjustified deaths accounted for 52% of deaths ($n = 12$).

When both aspects of the causality category were considered together (purposeful/accident and justified/unjustified), the following was found: all purposeful, justified deaths resulted in the death of an antagonist ($n = 6$), and all purposeful, unjustified deaths were those of the protagonists ($n = 10$). All of the accidental, justified deaths were to antagonists ($n = 5$) and the accidental, unjustified deaths were to all protagonists ($n = 2$) (see Table 4).

Discussion

The purpose of our content analysis was to examine the depiction of death in Disney movies. Based on the content analysis of 23 death scenes in 10 Disney films, several trends were observed. Each of the five aspects of death portrayals is discussed separately.

Character Status

The deaths shown in the films were comprised of almost equal numbers of protagonists and of antagonists. This demonstrates a fair distribution of the portrayal of "good" and "bad" characters, showing that both character types are susceptible to death. Many children viewing these scenes receive the message that even good characters that we care about may also die (Brent et al., 1996; Willis, 2002).

Depiction of Death

The depictions of explicit and implicit deaths were fairly equal. Explicit deaths were seen more in scenes where protagonists died. This can be viewed as a positive point because these scenes demonstrate real, explicit deaths of characters to whom the viewer has developed an attachment. However, this can be potentially traumatic for some children because they actually must witness a death. An example is seen in *The Lion King,* where a child must watch as Mufasa is thrown to his death.

The fact that implicit deaths occurred mostly among antagonists may send the message that their deaths are inconsequential in comparison to those of the protagonists. This can perhaps be seen as negative due to the fact that the antagonists' deaths are often merely implied (rather than being explicitly described).

Though sleep deaths only occurred twice out of 23 total deaths, it is important to discuss the implications of this type of portrayal. The sleep deaths occurred in two older films: *Sleeping Beauty* and *Snow White,* which is likely due to the fact that before the 1970s presenting death to audiences in animated films was not considered as big of an issue as it is today. Instead, the issue was dealt with through the use of the sleep deaths, in which spells meant to incur death were magically altered to produce only sleep in characters, rather than death. The fact that sleep deaths did not occur in Disney films released post-1970s may be an indication that children's exposure to death has increased and is now a somewhat less taboo issue in our society.

Death Status

The majority of deaths shown in the selected Disney films were permanent. This is a positive message because it enforces the idea that death is a permanent phenomenon, a concept that many young children do not fully grasp (Baker et al., 1992; Brent et al., 1996; Grollman, 1990; Willis, 2002). Seeing this in Disney films might help some children develop this understanding sooner. However, if they are left unaided in understanding these scenes, they may be upset at the permanence of death. Therefore, because many young children lack the cognitive abilities and experiences required to comprehend the concept of death fully, it is important for parents or teachers to guide them through the processes of learning about death.

Of the deaths that occurred, only six were shown as reversible. All of these reversible deaths occurred among protagonists, showing that antagonists or "bad guys" do not get a second chance at life, at least in some Disney films. Protagonists, on the other hand, fare much better. Half of the protagonists that had died in all 10 films "came back" in some way. An example of a scene that represents this concept is one in which Mufasa returns to communicate with Simba in *The Lion King*. This shows many children that loved ones can always be a part of them, even after death. However, young children may confuse this idea with the notion that the deceased may actually return (Worden & Silverman, 1996).

Emotional Reaction

In terms of emotion shown over death, almost all of the negative emotion was shown as a result of protagonist's deaths. This may provide some children who lack experience with death with a model of grieving (Baker et al., 1992). Presumably, when children see characters grieve and show sadness or frustration over the deaths of loved ones, they may learn that these are acceptable and normal behaviors.

Positive emotional reactions to death occurred solely for antagonists. However, this was not common; the deaths of only three "bad guys" resulted in positive emotion such as visible happiness and relief over their deaths. Most of the deaths that lacked any real emotional reactions were those of antagonists. This shows that the death of a character that is disliked may not warrant clapping and cheering but that it is not worth recognizing it at all. In addition, when one of these deaths *is* acknowledged, it is done in a positive and celebratory manner.

Causality

It was found that all of the justified deaths within the 10 Disney films were those of antagonists. This further demonstrates the trend in Disney films to vilify the antagonists to a point where they are seen as deserving their death. Along the same lines, all unjustified deaths were those of protagonists, showing that good characters never deserve to die.

The deaths of antagonists often result from accidents. However, we are made aware by the films that the antagonists deserve to die because they have done negative things, usually to a protagonist. The fact that they die accidentally allows them to "get what they deserve" while still allowing the protagonists to look good. In other words, protagonists are too good to kill others; thus, the antagonists must die accidentally. For example, in *Beauty and the Beast*, Gaston (the antagonist) stabs the Beast (the protagonist). The Beast, writhing in pain, "accidentally" causes Gaston to lose his balance on the castle tower, which results in Gaston falling to his implied death. When protagonists died, antagonists most often purposely killed them. This further demonstrates the evil of the antagonists.

Conclusions

The purpose of this content analysis was to examine how death is depicted in Disney films. This study is limited in scope, but it serves as a good starting point for the work of others in the area of animated film and children's understanding of death. We are not making conclusive statements about the effects of media on actual children; however, we are suggesting possibilities worth further examination. Our conclusions, based on the content analysis of 10 Disney films containing 23 death scenes, indicate that Disney's portrayal of death may be both good and bad; yet they can serve as effective learning tools for children. Some portrayals of death in Disney films send ambiguous messages about death and may be confusing to many young children. As stated earlier, some young children do not have the cognitive ability or experience to understand death fully (Brent et al., 1996; Speece & Brent, 1984; Willis, 2002). Furthermore, many animated Disney films contain moral implications. The results from this content analysis indicate that the antagonists ("bad guys") deserve to die. These aspects of death in the film may serve as discussion points for parents to talk about their own family's beliefs and morality.

These films may give children something to relate to when they are experiencing a loss. Watching films in which characters die may help children understand real death in a way that is less traumatic and threatening. Based on many of the movie scenes, children may better learn how to deal with death in terms of grieving and understanding what has happened when someone or something dies.

Depictions of death may also serve as springboards for discussion between children and adults about death. As previously mentioned, many parents try to downplay the severity and reality of death when discussing it with children (Grollman, 1990; Ryerson, 1977; Willis, 2002). However, using Disney movies may be a more comfortable way of discussing this difficult topic for both parents and children. Even films with unrealistic messages about death can be used as tools for pursuing discussion about death. Parents can watch Disney films with their children and verbally walk them through a death scene, deconstructing aspects that may be unrealistic and clarifying points that are exaggerated or confusing. This idea of using Disney films to discuss death can be extended to educational and counseling settings as well.

Though our content analysis provides interesting insight into the portrayal of death in Disney films, there are some limitations of this study that should be addressed. First, because the current study focused solely on Disney movies that were known to contain death, our sampling method was one of convenience. Future research may benefit from examining a wider variety of children's media. In addition, due to the small sample of films, the results may not generalize to other animated features. Continuing studies should be done on other types of animated films besides Disney movies.

Further studies may be done utilizing concrete hypotheses based on current findings. The findings from this and future studies can be used to implement new ways of educating children about death, both in home and counseling settings, possibly using Disney films as springboards for discussion. It may also be interesting to examine the next wave of Disney films, as they are released, to determine whether Disney's past and current trends in death portrayals remain the same. Although findings in this area may someday enlighten the creators of Disney movies to their potential to impact children's conceptions of death.

References

Baker, J. E., Sedney, M. A., & Gross, E. (1992). Psychological tasks for bereaved children. *American Journal of Orthopsychiatry, 62,* 105–116.

Brent, S. B., Speece, M. W., Lin, C., Dong, Q., & Yang, C. (1996). The development of the concept of death among Chinese and U.S. children 3–17 years of age: From binary to "fuzzy" concepts? *Omega: The Journal of Death and Dying, 33,* 67–83.

Dobson, J. (1977). Children, death, and the media. *Counseling and Values, 21*(3), 172–179.

Grollman, E. A. (1990). *Talking about death: A dialogue between parent and child* (3rd ed.). Boston: Beacon Press.

Ryerson, M. S. (1977). Death education and counseling for children. *Elementary School Guidance and Counseling, 11,* 165–174.

Schultz, N. W., & Huet, L. M. (2001). Sensational! Violent! Popular! Death in American movies. *Omega: The Journal of Death and Dying, 42,* 137–149.

Sedney, M. A. (1999). Children's grief narratives in popular films. *Omega: The Journal of Death and Dying, 39,* 315–325.

Sedney, M. A. (2002). Maintaining connections in children's grief narratives in popular film. *American Journal of Orthopsychiatry, 72,* 279–288.

Speece, M. W., & Brent, S. B. (1984). Children's understanding of death: A review of three components of a death concept. *Development, 55,* 1671–1686.

Wass, H., Raup, J. L., & Sisler, H. H. (1989). Adolescents and death on television: A follow-up study. *Death Studies, 13,* 161–173.

Willis, C. A. (2002). The grieving process in children: Strategies for understanding, educating, and reconciling children's perceptions of death. *Early Childhood Education Journal, 29,* 221–226.

Worden, J. W., & Silverman, P. R. (1996). Parental death and the adjustment of school-age children. *Omega: The Journal of Death and Dying, 33,* 91–102.

Critical Thinking

1. Think back to Disney films you saw as a child. How do you recall that they impacted on your own thinking about dying, death and grief?

2. How sensitive do you feel that Walt Disney was when producing films on death for children? For example, how did you react to Bambi's mother's death (assuming you saw it as a child)?

3. What is your thinking regarding the importance of an adult always watching films (Disney or otherwise) with a small child, rather than letting the child view them alone?

Death and Dying in the Curriculum of Public Schools: Is there a place?

Ethel L. King-McKenzie

Over the past few decades, death has frequently visited our school campuses and nation in alarming ways. During these times there has always been a sense of despair and uncertainty about how to react to this visitor. Willis (2002) contends that people from the American culture often have a difficult time discussing death and dying and dealing with grief, as it is a somber topic with many different emotions attached to it. Death and dying has become a tabooed subject as people are afraid and cannot comprehend what lies beyond it. People are scared that if they acknowledge death or that merely mentioning the word might bring about their own demise. Death is not a myth but a reality of life and living; something we cannot and will not escape. Clearly, there is no resisting, no fighting against it or hating it that will eliminate it from our lives. Death and dying is a common destiny that at some point all the humankind will experience; and the reality is that everyone eventually dies regardless of their age, gender, race, religion, color, creed, or socio-economic status as death is fate equal to all.

Willis (2002) observes that American children grow up in a culture that tries to avoid grief and denies the inevitability of death. These children are growing up in a world in which death, dying, and violence have become synonymous. Death is hardly ever mentioned or spoken about in schools except when it happens as a national trauma or disaster such as in the killing of children in the schools at Columbine in 1999, Paducah in 1997, the shooting of Amish children in Pennsylvania in 2006, the Virginia Tech shooting (2007) and more recently when children commit suicide because of bullying and name calling, the explosion of Challenger in 1986, the Oklahoma bombing in 1995, and the attacks on the World Trade Center in 2001. When such catastrophes happen teachers and school counselors get into crisis-mode, because they are unprepared to deal with the calamity. Often as humans we tend to be able to visualize other people's death but we are either unwilling or unable to see our own immortality. We are all dying, as death comes to all of us and this life and living is but for a brief moment.

This paper proposes the inclusion of death and dying as a topic to be covered in the curriculum of all public schools. Inclusion in the curriculum will enhance the discourse and conversation about death and dying and thus will hardly be treated with such shock and awe when it appears. This paper will explore two key issues: why death and dying in the curriculum, and how it should be integrated into the public school curriculum. Death education can be offered at various levels of the educational system in elementary, middle and high school levels. It can also be offered at the post-secondary education level where teachers are prepared and as short-term seminars or workshops as part of professional development for in-service teachers. According to the *Encyclopedia of Death and Dying* (2010), death education addresses the life and problems of people of today and help students to learn skills to solve them. Understanding and appreciating oneself, others and life; learning ways to manage anger and frustration; developing attitudes of tolerance, respect and empathy and compassion all contribute to a high quality of life. These may be the basic ingredients of long-term primary prevention of destructive behavior and serve as an antidote to the distorted perception children form from the entertainment media.

The paper is divided into three sections. The first section presents a theoretical framework used as the lense to discuss inclusion of death and dying in the curriculum. The second section discusses the reasons for inclusion of the topic and how it may be integrated into the curriculum of public schools. The third section presents the conclusion.

Theoretical Framework

This article uses Pinar's (1992) theory that the "concept and realities of death need to be integrated in everyday conversation and in everyday curriculum, and not treated as exotic topics of extreme anxiety" (p. 99). Pinar argues that it is when death is treated as distant that it becomes terrible and provokes fear. As life leads to death, he asks us not to tempt death but invites us to perhaps make friends with it.

Kubler-Ross (1997) asserts that every man will attempt in his own way to postpone questions and issues until he is forced to face them and will only be able to change things if he can start to conceive his own death. Today families and school personnel, as Baker, Sedney and Gross (1992) mention, have to help children, even young children, deal with death and grief on a far too regular basis. Gordon and Klass (1979) made a sound argument for teaching the basic facts about death and dying in the school system. However, they caution that schools should not teach about the religious aspect and beliefs of death and dying but allow parents to do so at home.

Why Death and Dying in the Curriculum?

This paper proposes that death and dying should be addressed in the school curriculum the same way we teach about the big bang theory, patriotism, sex, character and moral education. Over the last few decades death has frequently walked the corridors of our schools either through murders, suicide or natural causes as stated above. It has bombarded the nation in ways that were not expected. Though we are never happy when death visits, we cannot deny its imminence and that it is essential to address the topic in schools so that students and teachers may be better able to cope when it comes visiting, especially on our school campuses. Society tends to treat death as a distant cousin, a stepchild, and the proverbial mother-in-law or as even an enemy. For many people death is a difficult topic to discuss. People are scared to talk about death and dying especially with our students as they are afraid of what parents will say since it is not listed as a topic to be taught in the curriculum guidelines. The inclusion of the topic in the curriculum will therefore help teachers and students to address it freely and openly. Crase and Crase (1977) assert that if education contributes to the ultimate goal of human happiness and overall well-being, then death education should be part of the process. Death education is as much a requisite for a complete education as education for human sexuality, nutrition education, environmental education or drug education (Crase & Crase, 1977).

Cox, Garrett and Graham (2005) mention that children may misunderstand death beyond the obvious cognitive limitations because many tend not to discuss death with their parents or friends because they think the subject is too unpleasant, frightening, or even unnecessary. Thus, education about death and dying should begin in school during the early years as many children have certain knowledge and experience about it. Many students have experienced the passing of family members and friends. However, Cox, Garrett and Graham (2005) argue that the manner in which some parents communicate with their children about death may influence the child's comprehension of it as many parents do so in a way that are very confusing and potentially harmful to children. When children ask questions about death it is better to gently tell them the truth than to tell them some make-believe story about grandmother not being here because she is gone to visit 'Uncle Charlie' and will be away for a long time. To tell them someone is gone visiting or gone to sleep confuses them. Eventually, that child is going to realize that we have lied and then learn to distrust the one who lies to them. Cox, Garrett and Graham (2005) assert that adults often hinder children's understanding of death by using confusing terms and abstract language to explain the concept to them. Adults tend to protect children from life's realities but

we must also realize that we cannot shield them from death. Daily they are bombarded with the happenings on television and in the printed media. Take for instance the current wars in Afghanistan and Iraq—Operation Iraqi Freedom. How do we protect or shield our children from what is happening? They view the carnage on television each day. Children need to know that death and dying really happens and it is not some television movie or a game in which the bad guys get killed. Pointing at the parents' common weakness, Cox, Garrett and Graham (2005) argue that rather than telling children why and how people die many parents focus on downplaying the emotionality, seriousness and reality of death.

I recall my friend, the mother of a three-year-old girl, saying she was sitting and watching a children's program with her daughter, Madison, that fateful morning of September 11, 2001. The children's program was interrupted with breaking news and before the mother realized what was happening she was enthralled by the airplanes flying into the towers. Her daughter was sitting on her lap and the mother was so caught up with what was happening that she was brought back to reality only when her little girl said, "Mommy, will anyone die?" She did not know that her daughter even knew the word "die" or if she understood the concept but this was a teachable moment, so rather than trying to protect her daughter by turning off the television, she used the opportunity to tell the child about death as best she thought she would comprehend. The three-year-old was not scared. A few months later, Madison lost her grandmother, who was sick with cancer and she was able to tell me then, "Grandma was sick and she died and is gone to be with the angels". Imagine my shock when she continued, "Everybody dies, you are going to die, and I am going to die. Mommy and Daddy are going to die. We will then see Grandma." Madison has grasped the concept.

Death comes to everybody, so why treat it as a stranger or a disgusted, hated enemy? Teachers and parents need to find ways to expose children to the reality of death, as it will be better for them. I understand that children should not be robbed of their innocence but telling them about death will empower them. A curriculum that fails to address a topic as important as death and dying is in itself dead. Society changes and our schools and curriculum must adapt to these changes. Education should recognize, assume responsibility for, and maximize the consequences of the awareness of man's temporality (Huebner, 1975). The reality is, sooner or later everyone faces death and we cannot hide from it. If we talk about death to our children they will come to know that we are on this terrestrial ball for only a time and no doubt lead better lives. Heidegger (quoted in Pinar, 1992) tells us "meditation on the fact of death brings this life into focus." Pinar (1992) adds, "It makes this moment we share together, precious worthy of caring, worthy of presence" (p. 99).

Many of us live our lives as if we are fixed on this planet and unfortunately our families come to believe the same, so when the "grim reaper" comes to get us there is this total hopelessness. Had we been taught to live our lives and expect death at any time our whole living would be different. We know what is taught should be age appropriate but we should not neglect the teaching. In her Commencement address "Dancing the Circle" at the Cambridge School, Mary Aswell Doll (1991) reminds us that:

> *Death indeed highlights life. Life is not as organized as a set curriculum. . . Nor is death as end-stopped as we fear. We are all on journeys, destinations, unknown. What better opportunity for students to begin to come to terms with life than by writing about the dying they have experienced along the way. We need death in our lives to define our living. (pp. 13–14).*

The 21st century with its societal transformations demands that new topics be added to the curriculum to accommodate these changes. Paradoxically, death has not changed, human life has been devalued and death now walks the halls and grounds of our campuses as man take the lives of their fellow man without thinking twice.

In the fall of 2002, I offered *"Death and Dying"* as an Inquiry Seminar while on the faculty of a university. Although the course was advertised all over two campuses, it was noticed that two weeks before the class should have started only two students had inquired about taking the course. That summer students were told about the seminar with the hope that they would consider taking it. Many of them inquired why anyone would want to teach a seminar with such a title. Some even went as far as to say that they would not take the course as they thought that it was morbid of me for wanting to teach such a seminar. One student retorted, "It is very freaky and spooky. Who would want to talk about death and dying?" Another cynically asked, "Where will you go for fieldtrips. . . the cemetery?" We indeed went on field trips to the cemetery. Field trips were taken from the cradle to the grave. Students visited the pediatric wards, kindergarten classes, elementary, middle and high schools, nursing homes, mortuary and cemeteries.

Finally, two students registered for the course and I had a consultation with them. They asked if I would consider holding the seminar for them, as they were very interested in the topic. They expressed that they were not surprised that more students had not signed up for the seminar, as it is something entrenched in the psyche of people for not wanting to discuss death. "They are scared that if they acknowledge death, or that merely mentioning the word might bring about their own demise," one student remarked. "It is the same thing with cancer," the other student joined in. "No one will come out and say, I have cancer. They are afraid to say it, but will tell you that I have the big "C" and they never use the word cancer." Cancer for them is the onset of death and they are afraid of death and dying. Many people consider cancer a death warrant and so they will not name it, for to do so is to sign that death certificate, they believe. Not mentioning the word "death" will not prolong our lives or let us live forever. In the midst of life and living we are in death and we are all dying and the statistics are there to prove it.

If we learned to make friends with death, perhaps we would not treat the elderly as we do. They will not be sent off to nursing homes, as used commodities that are no longer needed or valued. As I visit these nursing homes I am moved to tears when I see the aged grandmothers, grandfathers, mothers and fathers who are abandoned there. We pay the money for them to be provided for but we do not find time to visit and sit for a while and talk with them. They are lonely souls who have nurtured and cared for their families and now that they need to be cared for with love and patience they are ushered off to spend their final days with strangers. I have spoken with many of these elderly who have not seen the face of a loved one for days, weeks and even months. They feel dejected and exported as rejects. Why do we hide our loved ones in nursing homes? "Just as we evade the fact of our deaths we look the other way at the dying around us. We hide them in nursing homes, hospitals, even on the streets, where we look the other way as outstretched arms and voices beg for life" (Huebner, 1975). Are we afraid to experience the presence of those who are dying? We should not be, as this is an experience of our own dying also.

In Randy Pausch's *Last Lecture* at Carnegie Mellon University in the Fall of 2007, facing pancreatic cancer and the likelihood that he would only live a month or two, Randy summed up his life's wisdom for his kids (then 1, 2, and 5 years of age). In that lecture he said,

> *"We cannot change the cards we are dealt, just how we play the hand. If I don't seem as depressed or morose as I should be, sorry to disappoint you. . . assure you I am not in denial. It's not that I am not aware of what is going on. My family, my three kids, my wife we just decamped. We bought a house in Virginia. . . better place for the family to be, down the road. . . "*

As Pausch continued his lecture he seemed more at peace than his audience. He handled the news of his dying with such grace and poise and seemed to have come to terms with his dying. If more of us come to terms with our death then we would be able to do the things that Pausch did to make sure his family would be comfortable when he was no longer with them. In the book *Tuesdays with Morrie,* Albom (2002) gives an account of visits with Morrie who had asked him to give his eulogy. In their discussion Morrie speaks about his death and dying and that everyone is aware that they will eventually die, though no one actually believes it. Morrie makes a profound statement to Mitch ". . . the truth is. . . if you accept that you can die at any time—then you might not be as ambitious as you are" (p. 83). This kind of acceptance comes only if we are educated about death and dying and realize that we are living in the shadow. People have lived to be seventy, eighty years and older and have children, grandchildren and have departed this life without telling loved ones their wishes. Some are hooked up to technology to prolong their lives. Worst, many have made no plans for death and die leaving relatives behind in debts from which they have a hard time emerging. Our days or lives here will end. We will all experience death, either that of a friend, relative, co-worker and our own dying. Though there are technological advances to prolong life, death is still certain. We have learned to defy gravity, we have traveled to the moon and back, we make trips to outer space, but death is still a reality. Doctors now probe the human body and replace body parts and organs as technicians do in motor vehicles. However, in the long run we will die. Scientists have cloned animals and are thinking about cloning humans. Even if scientists succeed in human cloning, we will still die. *Dolly,* the cloned sheep died. There will be no discovery to let anyone live forever.

How to Integrate Death and Dying in the Curriculum

To integrate death and dying in the school curriculum, death education should be a part of every teacher education preparation program, as teachers have the task of comforting children when they have dead pets, friends or relatives. According to Wolfelt (1996), children at a very young age are not able to understand about death and dying, however, their distress is real when someone they are close to dies. Cox, Garrett and Graham (2005) state that death is an aspect of life that is not only inevitable but also painful, especially for children. Children, as they mention, do not have the knowledge or experience that adults have; consequently they are often unprepared to deal with the death of a loved one or even of a beloved cartoon character in a movie.

Death and dying by its very nature lends itself to a multidisciplinary approach. The topic could be integrated into various learning areas including the Social Studies, Science or English curriculum. The interdisciplinary aspect of such a topic is staggering and warrants a place in the curriculum. Students need to be exposed to the reality of death and the school must play a role through its education process. Willis (2002) states that children can and do learn to talk about their feelings, although they may not use words or phrases as adults do. Furthermore, Willis argues that young children benefit from the freedom of expressing their feelings by being able to draw or color, even if they are scribbling.

Beginning in elementary school very young children, kindergarteners through the fifth grade, can be encouraged to talk about the death of their pets. Whether we flush the goldfish down the toilet or bury other pets in the backyard we can talk to the children about the passing of a friend. In the middle/junior high school classes the topic could be addressed in the Science curriculum as a part of the discussion on suicide. This paper argues that the suicide rate among adolescents is as high as it is because the students have no understanding of the finality of death. Many believe that the very same principle of killing off opponents and enemies in a video game applies to life. At the end of the game they hit the "start over" button and all the characters are alive again and a new game begins. Students think they can kill themselves and their friends and start life over. It is my belief that teaching about death and dying to them would remove this misconception and considerably reduce the suicide rate. Students would learn that life is not a game and we live only once and there are no second chances to life.

High school students could be allowed to pursue the topic from many different angles as they are more mature. Business majors could look at such things as pre-planning services, the cost of hospice, cost of funerals, making living wills and

trusts. Science can look at the biology, chemistry, and ecology/recycling—what happens to dead animals and plants. What of whales in the ocean? What happens to them at the bottom of the ocean floor when they die? In Social Studies it can be examined for the social customs of different cultures/societies and how death influences behavior—from the death of public leaders to death in war as a mobilizing force for a country to fight. Mathematics can look at statistics, figures and trends and graphs, all of which can be on the proficiency test, making the topic relevant to all students and justifiable in the curriculum. The topic should be addressed without emphasis on multi-theological ways, as everyone dies, regardless of one's own spirituality or religious beliefs. The point is to discuss death and dying, not to talk about life after death or anyone's religious understanding or beliefs thereof.

Teachers and students do not have to address the topic in a morbid way. A few years ago I taught English Literature in a high school in Louisiana. One of the books that the students were asked to read was, *Beowulf,* the oldest surviving epic from British Literature. Anyone who has read that book will agree that a teacher has to be creative and innovative to hold the interest of today's student. There were students who complained about the antiquated language of the text. I had to come up with a plan to make the lesson creative, understandable and connected to real life. I had students make connections with their lived experiences, the dailiness of their lives, by reading the obituaries in newspapers, writing letters of sympathy, willing their belongings, making living wills and writing what they would want written as their epitaphs. We even had mock memorial services. All this was done to ensure that the students would be able to grasp an understanding of this rich fabric of fact and fancy. Students who were not interested in the book because of the Old English quickly got a grasp of the story. They were also learning about death, dying and life. It was several weeks after that some students came to me and confessed that the activities we did in that class not only helped them to understand the text but also had helped them in allaying their fears of death. Then I was not teaching to lessen the fear of death or dying but simply trying to find a way to teach the story of the book. It is interesting that the activities we did taught them something about death and dying. Clearly, schools should be proactive in preparing students by giving them information on death and dying before they are in a panic and distress mode from traumas.

Conclusion

Discussing death and dying can provide both students and teachers an outlet for mending the torn fabric for those who grieve and those who comfort them when someone dies. Death is the surest event of our lives from the moment we take our first breaths into this world. When we talk about our lives we use a lot of "maybe," "if" and "perhaps." Maybe we will go to school; maybe we will grow up, go to college and maybe even get married; maybe we will have children. The "maybes" and "perhaps" of life are endless. There is, however, no maybe about our death and dying. We say, "when we die." We should therefore embrace our death and our dying. Death can be a beautiful and a less painful experience if we come to befriend it as we do our living. According to de Hennezel (1997), "death can cause a human to become what he or she was called to become. It can be in the fullest sense of the word, an accomplishment." Death puts life and living into focus. "There is life amid death, life in death, life from death" (Pinar, 1992, p. 94).

Death and dying is a mystery that man will never solve or uncover. Does not nature itself teach this? Animals and plants die and scientists have not been able to bring them back to life. It is inevitable and our students need to be taught and to know about it. Schools should be the place where they learn about death and dying as part of the curriculum. The content of the death and dying education programs can range from discussion of a pet in kindergarten classroom to the study of human death, burial and bereavement as the children get older. The sooner we learn to accept this the better we will live with each other each day as we will acknowledge that we live in the shadow of our dying. We will begin to treat everyone we come in contact with differently. We will live each day as if it is the last day of our lives; not as sad people but with a love, respect and an appreciation for life. The moments we spend on this earth are precious and we "should make the time we share together precious, worthy of caring, worthy of presence" (Pinar, 1992, p. 93).

References

Albom, M. (2002). *Tuesdays with Morrie: An old man, a young man, and life's greatest Lesson*. New York: Doubleday.

Baker, J.E., Sedney, M.A., & Gross, E. (1992). Psychological tasks for bereaved children. *American Journal of Orthopsychiatry, 62,* 105–116.

Bowie, L. (2002). Is there a place for death education in the primary school curriculum? *Pastoral Care in Education, 18*(1) 22–26

Cox, M., Garrett, E., & Graham, J. A. (2005). Death in Disney film. An implication for children's understanding for death. *Omega,* 50(4), 267–280

Crase, D. R., & Crase, D. (1985). Death education in the schools for older children. In H. Wass & C. A. Corr (Eds.), *Childhood and death* (pp. 345–61. New York: Hemisphere.

DeHennezel, M. (1997). *Intimate death: How the dying teach us how to live.* New York: Alfred A. Knopf.

Doll, M.A. (1995). *To the lighthouse and back: Writings of teaching and living.* New York: Peter Lang.

Gordon, A.K., & Klass, D. (1979). *They need to know: How to teach children about death.* Englewood Cliffs, NJ: Prentice-Hall.

Huebner, D. (1975). Curriculum theorizing as a concern for man's temporality. In W.F. Pinar (Ed.), *Curriculum theorizing: The reconceptualists* (pp. 237–250). Berkley: McCutchan.

Kubler-Ross, E. (1997). *On death and dying.* New York: Simon & Schuster Inc.

Pinar, W.F., & Reynolds, W.M. (Eds.). (1992). *Understanding curriculum as a phenomenological and deconstructed text.* New York: Teachers College Press.

Pausch, R., & Zaslow.J. (2008). *The last lecture* New York: Hyperion

The *Encyclopedia* of Death and Dying. (2010). Death education. Retrieved online: http://www.deathreference.com/Da-Em/Death-Education.html

Willis, C.A. (2002). The grieving process in children: Strategies for understanding, educating, and reconciling children's perception of death. *Early Childhood Education Journal, 29*(4), 221–227.

Wolfelt, A. (1996). *Helping children cope with grief.* Bristol, PA: Accelerated Development.

Critical Thinking

1. Sex education is offered in public schools. Why not offer death education? What is your reflection on this issue?

2. Did you have death education in elementary or secondary school? If so, would you then recommend that death education be included throughout public school curricula?

3. If asked to develop an outline for a death education course for fourth graders, what would you include? What would you not include?

From *Journal of Emerging Knowledge on Emerging Markets*, Vol. 3, November, 2011, pp. 511–520. Copyright © 2011 by Ethel King-McKenzie. Reprinted by permission of the author.

Needs of Elderly Patients in Palliative Care

HELLE WIJK, RN, PHD AND AGNETA GRIMBY, PHD

Europe's population is aging and more people are dying from chronic diseases. Still, the range and quality of palliative care services remain rather limited and inadequate. According to the World Health Organization, many Europeans who are terminally ill die in unnecessary pain and discomfort because their health systems lack skilled staff and do not widely offer palliative care services.

Even though evidence may be lacking and the empirical studies characterized by a high degree of heterogeneity, some important areas seem to stand out considering the elderly patient's views and needs in the terminal phase of life.[1] Assessments of quality of life have shown that the lowest scores are related to the physical domain, followed by the existential, supportive, and social domains.[2] A similar trend can be observed among people wishing to hasten death.[3] Actions to avoid nutritional and pain problems are also crucial at the end-of-life stage, as are avoiding inappropriate prolongation of dying and having a sense of control.[4]

To be able to provide high-quality palliative care, it is important for the health care staff to see and understand the special needs and wishes of the patients; however, knowledge, methods, and programs for this are sparse. The patients themselves seem not to be the one to blame.[5] On the contrary, studies have demonstrated that older people are willing to talk about death and dying in a rather spontaneous way.[6]

Existing empirical evidence on elderly patients' thoughts about death and dying has so far mostly been collected after cross-sectional, quantitative, or qualitative designs, mainly using personal interviews. Open conversations are considered the optimal way of learning about needs at the end-of-life stage. The method, however, is time consuming for daily practice, where somewhat more fixed estimates of needs may be preferred.

Identifying desires and needs of the palliative patient may provide increased quality of care. This pilot study about needs at the end of life aims at describing the individual reports from 30 elderly palliative patients on their needs and their ranking of these needs by degree of concern.

Method
Participants

Thirty consecutively chosen patients, admitted for palliative care at the Geriatric Department, Sahlgrenska University Hospital in Gothenburg, Sweden, were willing to join the study. Inclusion criteria were strength enough to perform an interview and Swedish mother tongue. Exclusion criteria were aphasia, dementia, or lack of strength. The respondents (15 men and 15 women) were an average age of 79 years (75 for men, 81 for women) and had a 50:50 background of manual labor and white-collar jobs.

The primary diagnosis was different types of cancer, with a variation of length of illness of 1 month to several years. All but 1 of the patients were admitted to the palliative unit from another health care institution. All patients signed an informed consent before they participated in the study. The study was approved by the Ethics Committee of the Faculty of Medicine, University of Gothenburg, Sweden.

Procedures

The survey included demographic data and information about reason for admittance and state of health at the time of admittance, reactions to the admittance, and awareness of illness. The information was retrieved partly through patients' files and partly through patient interviews.

Individual needs were identified by semistructured interviews by a research nurse (PhD student) at the palliative unit of the Geriatric Department at Sahlgrenska University Hospital. Most of the interviews were conducted, if possible, once a week and at daytime between 9:00 AM and 2 PM. Interview length was 20 to 30 minutes in 50%; 30% lasted 30 to 60 minutes, 2 interviews lasted for more than an hour, and 2 were very short due to the patient's fatigue.

The introductory question was "How do you feel today?" This was followed by questions about (1) the patient's ranking of important needs for the moment, (2) things in particular that the patient wanted help with at the moment, and

(3) things in particular that the patient wanted to speak about at the moment. The patient was asked to try to rank the different needs by the degree of concern. The answers were categorized according to physical, psychologic, social, and spiritual needs.

Statistical Analysis

For statistical trend tests, the Fisher exact test and permutation trend tests were used.[7] All results given refer to $P < .05$ unless otherwise stated.

Results

Most patients (61%) wanted to spend their last days in their own home, whereas the rest preferred to stay at an institution where "one would receive the best help." The most common symptoms before admission were pain, lack of appetite, anxiety, sleeplessness, fatigue, vomiting, cough, and shortness of breath (Table 1). At admission, more than 50% of the patients were not quite sure of their diagnosis; of the transition from curative to palliative care, 30% were completely sure, and 20% were completely unsure. The figures were very similar among the relatives. This was mostly due to incomplete former information, not to language or communication problems.

Before admission, 11% of the patients needed practical help with most daily services, but 20% had not been in need of any help at all. The helpers were next of kin (63%), a close friend (10%), and different people (11%). Most patients considered the help to be pretty good or good, but 5 of the patients were less satisfied. More than 50% of the patients considered it pleasant to receive professional care. A few patients felt it as a relief not being a burden to their family; 4 felt resigned or depressed.

Most interviews were experienced as less strenuous. All of the patients reported some type of need. If only 1 kind of need was reported, this was rated as a primary one. More patients ranked the physical needs as primary compared with the psychologic needs, which in turn were more important than the social needs (Table 2). Spiritual needs were only mentioned by 1 person. In the first interview, 14 patients ranked their physical needs as primary, 6 as secondary, and 2 as tertiary. Ten patients ranked their psychological needs as primary, 8 ranked them as secondary, and 1 as tertiary. Social needs were ranked as primary by 6 patients; just as many patients ranked them as secondary as well as tertiary. The rankings were equal in interviews II and III.

In the continued interviews, which comprised a reduced number of patients, the ranking changed in favor of the nonphysical dimensions of need. There was no significant trend related to the kind of need; they varied extensively from 1 interview to another. Correlation analysis on primary needs and symptoms/troubles resulted in no significant outcomes apart from nausea, which was related to physical need ($P < .025$). No significant correlations were found

Table 1 Reported/Registered Symptoms and Problems at the First Interview with 30 Patients

Symptom	Patients, n	Little	Some	Much	Missing Data
Pain	12	3	7	8	0
Shortness of breath	21	1	3	5	0
Cough	23	2	1	4	0
Vomiting	9	7	4	11	0
Loss of appetite	4	5	12	8	1
Diarrhea	20	4	4	2	0
Obstipation	15	3	7	5	0
Incontinence, fecal	25	2	3	—	0
Incontinence, urinary	21	—	2	4	3
Fever	27	—	2	1	0
Bleeding	28	1	1	—	0
Pressure sores	30	—	—	—	0
Bad smells	29	1	—	—	0
Lack of energy	16	2	4	8	0
Depression	21	6	3	—	0
Nervousness	10	10	8	2	0
Sleeplessness	17	7	3	3	0
Confined to bed	12	9	6	3	0
Caring need	4	15	7	4	0
Comatose	29	1	—	—	0
Other[a]	20	3	2	5	0

[a]unsteadiness, 5 patients; infection, cramps, swollen legs, personality change, 1 patient.

between the remaining primary needs (psychologic, social, and spiritual) and symptoms or troubles.

Physical Needs

Many of the physical needs ranked as primary were related to pain. Quotes from different patients reveal a fear of pain, which for many patients seemed to be equal to the experience of pain itself. Other types of needs of a physical character ranked as primary were often related to severe nausea or feebleness. Shortness of breath and a feeling of choking resulted in agony of death. Cough, phlegm, and oral hygiene problems were a recurrent source of irritation for some patients. The lack of opportunities for taking care of personal hygiene made some of the men and women feel in physical decay. Others complained about being cold, that they didn't get any better, or that they wanted to get well and be discharged. A few of the patients had more unusual requests of a physical character.

Table 2 Reported Primary, Secondary, and Tertiary[a] Needs of Patients at the Geriatric Palliative Ward

Interview	Respondents	Physical Needs	Psychologic Needs	Social Needs	Spiritual Needs
I	30	14-6-2	10-8-1	6-6-6	0-0-0
II	20	10-6-3	6-5-1	4-3-2	0-0-0
III	10	6-0-0	3-2-1	1-2-1	0-0-0
IV	4	2-0-1	1-2-0	1-1-0	0-0-0
V	2	2-0-0	0-1-0	0-0-0	0-0-0
VI	2	1-1-0	0-0-0	0-1-0	1-0-0
VII	1	0-0-0	1-0-0	0-1-0	0-0-0
VIII	1	0-1-0	1-0-0	0-0-1	0-0-0

[a]The combinations of figures refer to the number of patients reporting primary, secondary, and tertiary types of needs, respectively.

The physical needs of a secondary nature (ie., the second most important need) were often similar to the primary ones, which may or may not have been attended to.

Tertiary physical needs mainly concerned the feeling of feebleness. A few patients emphasized the importance of appearance and getting good food.

"I suffer from such perspirations, sometimes I'm soaking wet. To remain without any pain the rest of my days! Shortness of breath and pain make me scared. Spare me this feebleness, feels awful, may as well finish the old man."

"Don't want to be so tired [falls asleep several times during the conversation], that's the only thing!"

"I want to feel cleaner, don't even have the strength to care for my personal hygiene! My only wish is that I get to lie comfortably, but now I have been given a comfortable mattress."

"There is a draft from the fan. I get cold easily, at the same time I perspire a lot. I suffer a lot from it. The nausea is troublesome, but it comes and goes. I want my hair to grow back. The scalp is itchy from the wig and it is so hot. Some people say that the hair may turn blond and curly when it grows out, we'll have to wait and see [laughs]."

Psychologic Needs

Anxiety, uncertainty, and security were explicit and frequent primary psychologic needs among many of the patients. A feeling of longing was often directed towards their home environment, belongings, and "the ordinary" and "freedom." But at the same time, staying at home was associated with anxiety and worry. The wish for taking 1 day at a time and not having to contemplate the future occurred quite frequently.

There was a need for seclusion to get some peace and quiet, maybe to have the opportunity to see relatives, and to be freer to express emotions and reactions to the situation.

A common wish was to think back on their lives, maybe to recapitulate. Some of the patients pointed to psychosocial needs, for example, to restore broken relationships and becoming reconciled before it was too late.

Physical and psychologic fatigue often went hand-in-hand, and they often seemed to have a reciprocal effect. The power of initiative sometimes fell short, but if conquered, there was a feeling of great victory. For example, a patient who had been lying in a draft found the greatest triumph (primary need) when he succeeded at closing the vent. "I knew I could make it. One should never give up!" Worries could also be directed towards variations in psychologic functions such as memory and cognitive functioning.

The psychologic needs to find a meaning in life, feel security, or have opportunities to go out were ranked as second most important (secondary). So were also worries about the future for the spouse and other relatives. Pleasurable needs could include the opportunity to have a good meal. Moreover, there were also expressed needs for contemplating, thinking over their life and to summing up things, and finally, to having their life substantiated by telling others of what their life had been like.

Quite a few psychologic needs were given a tertiary ranking, for example, a mixed anxiety and expectation when awaiting a move to a nursing home or feeling the need to keep their private room.

"What is it going to be like? Where will I end up? What if I didn't have to worry about what the future is going to look like. Want to avoid the anxiety of feeling nauseous and vomiting all the time, don't dare to go anywhere, not even to the hairdresser."

"Want to avoid thinking ahead, just want to relax, take it easy, one day at a time."

"There is no point in wishing to see what the future holds; how my grandchildren will do in life or what is going to happen to the world. No use in worrying; better to live in the present and to take one day at a time."

"I only want to be left in peace."

"I lack the strength to both think and do things now. It's a shame."

"If only I didn't have to wait for answers about everything and being worried about people at home!"

Social Needs

The primary needs of a social nature were often associated with visits from family and close friends, reunions, and practical and economical tasks when moving back home or to a nursing home.

Social needs of a secondary nature often included, as did the primary ones, contact with or care for the family. For a few of the patients, that meant reunion or reconciliation. Practical tasks related to finances or accounting also came up as well as being given some privacy.

Social needs, which had been ranked as tertiary, were also similar to primary and secondary wishes; that is, they comprised troubles about family and finances, the longing for their relatives and privacy, but also retrieving parts of their former way of life.

"Mostly I wish to come home to friends and family. I do have to think about my wife, to help each other and to be together!"

". . . to see my brother, never told you that I have a brother, did I? I regret not staying in contact with him during all these years. But I do hear from my son now. It made me happy and moved me. But is it too late now?"

"I need to have someone to talk to about anything but illness all the time!"

"I want the caravan to be ready, cleaned and connected to the car. I need to sort my finances. I don't have a will, do I?"

"Mostly, I'm worried about the boy; what's going to happen when I'm gone. How will he do in school?"

"Want to be able to handle my bills and finances."

Spirituality

One person had a primary need of a spiritual nature. However, spiritual needs of secondary and tertiary rank did not occur.

"I've started to ponder. Ask myself if I'm religious. I've never thought about those things before, but I do now."

Discussion

During the 4 months of observation, the initial (at admission) general state seemed to be dominated by a rather extensive need for care, bad physical condition with nausea, emaciation, pain, anxiety, and feebleness. The palliative care, however, appeared to have had a rapid and intended effect on the physical troubles. Because the observations were made only at the ward, the state and needs of the patients were recorded most thoroughly during the first period after admission. A small portion of the patients could be interviewed for a longer period, a few of them until their deaths.

To have the opportunity to speak about one's fear of being in pain and to have it confirmed that pain relief could be guaranteed seemed to dominate the physical picture of need and was just as prominent as the need of pain relief itself. These findings may suggest that adequate pain relief was accomplished but that the memory of the pain itself was very dominating and strong. Perhaps it points to a need for assurance of relief of recurrent pain. However, the frequent wishes of reduced nausea and increased energy were more difficult to fulfil because of type and course of illness.

Successful pain relief and other types of palliative care may be behind the fact that a great number of psychologic needs were reported. The relief of physical needs may have facilitated the expression of needs of security when being cared for in the hospital. One patient did even admit of pleasurable aspects of life, for example, to allow oneself to long for something or somebody, or maybe to have that feeling of longing fulfilled. It could mean having satisfied the need to come back home to well-known things or being offered a good meal. Many of those who had been uneasy at the time of admission later seemed to have improved their abilities to better specify needs and wishes of psychologic nature, particularly if symptoms of the disease did not stand in the way.

Social needs bore a clear socioeconomic touch. Many patients wished to be with their life partner or children, as well as to look over and secure their future lives. To make sure there were enough pension benefits and savings for continuous care also seemed be important. Moreover, patients expressed a longing for having things taken care of. Issues that had been ignored for a lifetime were now of highest priority, maybe because the patient suspected that not much time was left.

Very few of the patients were interviewed when they were in the very final stage of their lives. Maybe that was one of the reasons why only 1 patient expressed a wish to talk about existential issues and their relation to divine powers (spiritual-existential needs). Great psychologic torment, remorse over the past, and a wish for forgiveness or understanding from significant individuals was also expressed.

Interpreting and describing a strict mapping or preference of needs in the terminal stage of life is risky, however. Depending on the state of illness, identifying and reporting needs can be difficult. Boundaries between categories of needs can become blurry, and the intensity of wishes can be hard to perceive. There may be rapid and wide variations in needs, and individual and unstable preference on wishes can vary under different circumstances.

Conclusion

Despite the limitations of the study, considering the small number of patients, certain tendencies could be noticed in the outcome. Physical pain overshadows everything, at least in the very last stage of life. Furthermore, pain seems to hinder the recognition of other psychologic, social, and spiritual needs. Merely the fear of physical pain, originating from prior experiences of pain, may be the most common feeling to be relieved from. Other important needs appear when pain and other health problems, for example, vomiting and shortness of breath, no longer generate fear of death. The feeling of security mediated by the presence of loved ones, as well as worries about their future, seems to occupy a severely ill person's mind even during the last days of his or her life.

The study was small, and the results may not be accurate for all types of palliative units; however, it did seem to confirm former, unrecorded observations of the priorities of needs among our patients. We intend to repeat the study including a larger number of patients to further investigate end-of life needs.

Notes

1. Hallberg, RI. Death and dying from old people's point of view. A literature review. *Aging Clin Exp Res.* 2004;16:87–103.
2. Lo RS., Woo J., Zhoc KC., et al. Quality of life of palliative care patients in the last two weeks of life. *J Pain Symp Man.* 2002;24:388–397.
3. Kelly B., Burnett P., Pelusi D., Badger S., Varghese F., Robertson M. Terminally ill patients' wish to hasten death. *Palliat Med.* 2002;16:339–345.
4. Singer PA., Martin DK., Kelner M. Quality end-of-life care: patients' perspectives. *JAMA.* 1999;281:163–168.
5. Ottosson JO. *The Patient-Doctor Relationship* [Swedish]. Stockholm, Sweden: *Natur och Kultur.* 1999:282–308.
6. Thomé B. *Living with Cancer in Old Age: Quality of Life and Meaning.* Thesis. Lund University, Faculty of Medicine; 2003.
7. Cox DR., Hinkley DV. *Theoretical Statistics.* London: Chapman & Hall; 1974.

Critical Thinking

1. Just what is palliative care all about? How might this holistic approach to relating to the elderly (or anyone else) be beneficial to the patient?

2. What are the four needs of geriatric patients as discussed in the article? How does palliative care attempt to satisfy these needs?

3. What are some limitations of this study (how it might have been improved)?

From the Institute of Health and Care Sciences, Sahlgrenska Academy, University of Gothenburg and Sahlgrenska University Hospital (HW) and Department of Geriatric Medicine (AG), Sahlgrenska University Hospital, Gothenburg, Sweden.

Address correspondence to: Helle Wijk, Sahlgrenska University Hospital, Röda stråket 8, 413 45 Göteborg, Sweden; e-mail: helle .wijk@vgregion.se.

Acknowledgments—This study was facilitated by grants from the Coordinating Board of Swedish Research Councils, the Swedish Medical Research Council, Medical and Social Services Administrations, the Helge Axson Johnson Foundation, and the Hjalmar Svensson Foundation. Thanks are due to Valter Sundh, BSc, for statistical discussions and invaluable help with the data processing.

Good Mourning

For more than three decades, George Dickinson has been exploring the ways Americans handle death and end-of-life issues. So, we asked the 2009 Death Education Award recipient and acclaimed scholar to talk about one of his latest research interests—the issues surrounding the passing of a pet.

GEORGE DICKINSON

For many of us, a pet is a significant member of the family. We talk to pets and care for them as if they were our children. We tend to have a very human bond with our companion animals. Pets often live with us as many years as our children live at home before leaving for college or emancipation. Pets can make us feel needed, can relieve loneliness and can serve as friends and companions. Therefore, the death of a pet is a traumatic experience. As occurs with any other member of the family, that death leaves a huge void.

Our first childhood death experience typically is around the age of 8. And that first experience is often a pet. Recollections of this event are among our more vivid childhood memories. The death of a pet presents a good opportunity for a parent to explain death to a small child: The animal is immobile, not breathing, not eating or drinking because it is dead. This situation provides a setting for the parent to be a role model by being open with the child about what happened. If the parent cries, this lets the child know that crying is OK. It's helpful if the parent is involved in a burial, if earth burial is the chosen means of final body disposal.

Our children had guinea pigs. A guinea pig's lifespan is short, thus we had a lot of funerals for guinea pigs at our house. In our routine, I was the official grave digger; the children wrapped the animal in a cloth (shroud), placed it in the hole, covered it with dirt and then put a rock or something else over it to mark the spot in the backyard. As the ceremony progressed and the children related a memory of the pet, each of us felt tears rolling down our cheeks. Such parental participation showed my children that our companion animals had importance.

For adults, and especially the elderly, pets can be excellent companions. A dog, for example, typically wags its tail and genuinely seems happy to see its owner enter the house. The pet can help lessen a feeling of isolation and loneliness for a person living alone. The companion animal does not seem to get out of sorts about the stresses in life. A pet can be most relaxing for an individual stroking it and thus even contribute to better health for the individual. The loss of a beloved pet, therefore, can certainly be traumatic for the owner, who—no longer being needed by the companion animal—may feel a true sense of emptiness.

Unlike the person who loses a friend or relative and receives outpourings of sympathy and support, one who loses a pet is often ridiculed for overreacting or for being foolishly emotional. Such an unsympathetic response is called disenfranchised grief (grief not openly acknowledged, socially sanctioned or publicly shared). Today, however, the death of a pet is being recognized in many circles similarly to that of the death of a human—as evidenced by the recent development of Hallmark sympathy cards for owners of deceased pets. Grieving for a pet and for a human has many similarities: feeling preoccupied, experiencing guilt and mistaking shadows and sounds as being from the dead companion.

The death of a pet is experienced uniquely by veterinarians —especially when they are performing euthanasia, granting "merciful relief" from irreversible pain or an incurable malady. Though the states of Oregon and Washington now allow physician-assisted suicide, medical doctors are not allowed to practice euthanasia; and, for them, their role ends when the patient dies, as the follow-up functions are handled by medical staff, then the mortuary. Veterinarians, however, are often asked to dispose of the animal's body. Additionally, veterinarians have the added pressure of a client asking for advice as to whether or not to "put the pet to sleep" (*sleep,* an interesting euphemism for *death*), and if so, when. The owner of the companion animal does not wish to euthanize too quickly, yet does not want to wait beyond the time when death perhaps should have occurred. Thus, veterinarians give advice, themselves not knowing when is "just right" for the death. Such stress is somewhat limited to the veterinary medicine profession.

From the veterinarian's perspective, the most legitimate reasons for euthanizing a companion animal revolve around the animal's quality of life. The final decision, however, rests with the human guardian. Following a decision to euthanize, the owner often has a feeling of regret for having given permission for euthanasia, no matter the severity of the illness or the animal's incapacity.

Together with Paul and Karin Roof, I recently conducted an end-of-life survey of 463 veterinarians in the Southeast, and found that the average veterinarian practices euthanasia 7.53 times per month. The majority of companion animal owners opt to stay with the animal during the procedure, and two-thirds of owners leave the pet with the veterinary clinic for disposal. Those who leave the animal at the clinic more often choose cremation, while those who take the dead animal away typically bury the animal. It also found that veterinarians feel that more education on end-of-life issues is needed in veterinary school, though the more recent graduates feel more favorable toward their end-of-life education than earlier graduates. Currently, the 28 veterinary medicine schools in the United States average 15 hours on end-of-life issues within their curriculum. This is similar to U.S. baccalaureate nursing schools' 14 hours and U.S. medical schools' 12 hours on end-of-life issues.

Good, open communication by professionals is pivotal in any end-of-life discussion, be it involving a companion animal or a human. Whether the terminally ill family member is a human or a pet, the process of dying and the event of death are among the more stressful experiences humans have. We can be supportive of each other and remember that a death—pet or human—should not be reacted to as disenfranchised grief; rather, it should be socially sanctioned and publicly shared.

Much like those for humans, hospices for pets are evolving in the 21st century. Some of these hospice programs focus on teaching pet owners how to care for their terminally ill pets at home, yet others handle the pet at a free-standing hospice facility. If euthanasia isn't an option (the owner "simply cannot put Fido down"), hospice care might be the solution for a terminally ill companion animal. Palliative care within a hospice setting, where pain control is paramount, presents a peaceful way for an animal to die. And who wants to see anything/anyone die in pain when analgesics are a reasonable option? Is not quality of life better than quantity of life?

Pets—like family members—leave a tremendous void in our lives when they die. Life goes on, however, and we must cope with the loss. We should talk openly about our feelings. Grief shared is grief relieved. We don't "get over" the loss of a family member, pet or human, but we simply learn to live with the fact that that member will no longer be literally present. Through memories, however, the human or companion animal "lives on." Gone but not forgotten.

Critical Thinking

1. How did your family handle the death of your pets when you were a child?

2. What is your experience with veterinarians regarding their role in the death of one of your pets?

3. Should we have hospice facilities for pets, as we now have for humans?

GEORGE DICKINSON is a professor of sociology.

Through the Touch of God: Child Death and Spiritual Sustenance in a Hutterian Colony

JOANNE CACCIATORE AND REBECCA ONG

General Ethnographic Background

History

The Hutterites, like the Mennonites, the Amish, and the Brethren in Christ, had their beginnings during the Reformation in the 16th century as a part of the Anabaptist movement, whose core beliefs include adult baptism and pacifism. In 1528, a group of Anabaptist refugees, fleeing persecution in Austria and led by Jacob Wiedemann and Philip Jager, established an assembly of 200 people under a communal ownership of property, or a "full community of goods," in Moravia in the present-day Czech Republic. In time, members of this Moravian assembly and other Anabaptist refugees organized into a church led by Jacob Hutter, from whom the group took their name.

Following a "Golden Period" of expansion and economic prosperity in the mid-to-late 1500s, a succession of wars and religious persecution caused the Hutterites to abandon communal life on several occasions and move further east to Slovakia, Hungary, and present-day Romania, seeking safety and religious freedom. Bruderhöfe, or colonies, established in Russia in the Ukraine renewed the practice of communal living and community of goods under the leadership of Michael Waldner in 1859. In the 1870s, following the passage of a Russian law making military service compulsory, the Hutterites emigrated to North America, where today there are approximately 45,000 Hutterites living in over 450 colonies (Hofer, 1998; Hutterian Brethren Schmiedeleut Conference, 2006; Janzen 2005; Packull, 1999; Rhodes, 2009).

Social Structure

At first glance, a Hutterian colony appears to be a contradiction. Their faith, values, manner of dress, and language have been maintained for centuries despite persecution and through mass migration. Yet this reverence for history and tradition is juxtaposed with a business acumen equal to that of a modern capitalist business and a willingness to embrace the most modern agricultural technology.

The Hutterites have three distinct subgroups, or "Leut," which were established around the time of emigration from the Ukraine to North America: Schmiedeleut, Dariusleut, and Lehrerleut. These three groups share a common belief system, each is its own denomination with its own unique culture and discipline. The Schmiedeleut are named after their leader Michael Waldner, a blacksmith (schmied) and preacher; the Dariusleut, after minister Darius Walter; and the Lehrerleut, after their leader Jakob Wipf, who was a teacher (Lehrer). The Schmiedeleut live primarily in North and South Dakota, Minnesota, and Manitoba, while the Dariusleut and Lehrerleut colonies are located mainly in Alberta, Saskatchewan, Montana, and the state of Washington (Hofer, 1998). A fourth subgroup, known as the Prairieleut, are the descendants of the Hutterites who emigrated from the Ukraine but established privately-held homesteads and individual Hutterite congregations that were eventually absorbed into Mennonite and other communities. In 1992, the Schmiedeleut were divided into two separate groups, the "progressives," also known as the Hutterian Brethren, led by Jacob Kleinsasser, and the "traditionalists" or "Committee Hutterites," because they function without the leadership of a single elder (Hofer, 1998; Janzen, 2005).

The hierarchy of the Hutterian community is based on a literal interpretation of the Bible, in which the order of relationships places the community authority over the individual, older people over younger people, and men over women (Janzen & Stanton, 2010). Each Hutterian Leut is led by a senior male elder called a vorsteher, or preacher, who is responsible for the spiritual leadership of all the Leut's colonies and its members. At the colony level, authority is based on a male hierarchy of economic and spiritual responsibilities. A preacher and assistant preacher work closely with an elected council of five or six men who hold key administrative positions in the colony, such as financial manager, field manager, and the German schoolteacher. Other elected posts include department manager positions, such as the head mechanic, cattle boss, and lead carpenter. Only the congregation's baptized men, collectively known as the brethren, are able to vote on colony decisions and elect leaders. Unbaptized men, like all the women, have no official authority in the colony, although they may exert informal influence (Hofer, 1998; Janzen & Stanton, 2010; Peter, 1987).

A colony's population can range from 60 to 160 individuals, with the average being about 90 people or 15 families. The labor force of the colony is organized according to gender and age and, in particular, gender roles are clearly proscribed and never challenged. Men are responsible for farm operations, manufacturing, and carpentry, while women perform the domestic work, such as cooking, baking, and sewing. Teenagers and children are assigned chores as appropriate to assist their elders (Hofer, 1998; Janzen & Stanton, 2010). While a colony is not completely self-sufficient, the community is able to supply much of its own food, furniture, repairs, and clothes through the skilled labor of its members.

The physical size of a Hutterian colony depends on its location and the type of crops and industry in which it is engaged, but can range in size from 5,000 to 20,000 acres. The Hutterites are successful farmers who are particularly known for their large-scale poultry and livestock production, where they have adopted the use of the most modern equipment available. Despite their centuries-old traditions, the Hutterites believe that new technologies can be embraced so long as the entire colony benefits and full community of goods is maintained (Hofer, 1998). In general, animal barns, machine shops, grain storage, and other farm buildings are located on the periphery of the colony, offering more privacy to the church building, schoolhouse, dining hall, communal kitchen, and homes located at its heart. Janzen and Stanton (2010) point out that the Hutterian kitchen and dining hall are "the functional center of every colony . . . where important information is exchanged" (p. 202). Meals are prepared by the colony women and eaten communally, with men and women dining separately.

Spirituality

Faith in God is the centerpiece of Hutterian life, and their Christian beliefs are woven into every aspect of their daily lives. The watershed principles of communal living, shared property, and collective ideologies are laid out in the Hutterites' confession of faith, the Ordnungen (church rules), Lehren (sermons), and Lieder (hymns). One Hutterian sermon proclaims, "Just as wine is made of many grapes, pressed, crushed, joined, and merged together in one pure liquid, so also we have been called together from many peoples with many opinions" (Janzen & Stanton, 2010, p. 76). Hutterian spirituality is expressed through their untiring and cooperative work ethic predicated in humility and honesty, as well as formally through daily worship.

Formal Hutterian worship has two formats: the Gebet, a service that takes place daily before the evening meal, and the Lehr, the longer service that occurs on Sunday mornings. Seating is arranged according to gender and age, with men and women separated and children toward the front. All services include devotional singing, hymns, and a sermon delivered in High German. Most sermons were written by their forefathers and date back to the 16th and 17th centuries. These are still in use today (Hofer, 1998; Janzen & Stanton, 2010).

Family Life

The Hutterian definition of family is influenced by their tradition of communal living. In a sense, an entire Hutterite Leut is seen as a large extended family, and this perception is especially true for each specific colony. It is common for a Hutterite man's father, sons, and uncles to live at the same colony for most of their lives, since Hutterite women relocate to their husbands' colonies after marriage (Hofer, 1998; Janzen & Stanton, 2010).

Each nuclear family lives in its own separate home or apartment, furnished by the community. Despite claims from outsiders of the patriarchal nature of Hutterian society, husbands and wives work together as partners in raising children. Although men and women are separated during the most of the work day and at meals, time is set aside in the evenings and on weekends for families to spend time together. The Hutterites cherish both male and female children and tend to have larger families compared to mainstream society (Hofer, 1998; Janzen & Stanton, 2010; Peter, 1987; Stahl, 2003).

In addition to their close relationships with their parents, Hutterite children are also nurtured and disciplined by other adults and older children in the colony. For example, new Hutterite mothers typically take 6-week maternity leaves to bond with their newborns before returning to their regular colony duties. At that time, childcare may be provided by the sorgela (young female childcare providers), who are chosen to serve the colony on the basis of age, character, and trustworthiness. According to Janzen and Stanton (2010), the relationship between the sorgela and child is often remembered for life. Additionally, elder men and women in the colony may assist in childcare and adopt the role of "grandpa" and "grandma," regardless of blood relation. In this way, the Hutterites have a broad interpretation of family that sustains and bolsters their communal ties.

Birth and Death in the Hutterian Colony

According to Larsen and Vaupel (1993), the Hutterian mortality rate is comparable to that of the U.S. average. The Hutterites' fertility rate is noted to be exceptionally high, with families having a median number of 10 children in the 1950s. However, in recent years, young Hutterite men and women are both delaying marriage by 3 to 4 years and having fewer children, usually less than 6 or 7, as compared to 50 years ago (Janzen & Stanton, 2010; Morgan, 1983).

Most Hutterites do not fear death. Rather, physical death is viewed as the beginning of a new existence, and the general perception is that those who have tried to live a principled, virtuous, and spiritual life are reasonably assured a place in heaven (Janzen & Stanton, 2010). The "ideal" death, as summarized by one Hutterite, is a prolonged death, not a sudden death. In his words, "[the Hutterites] want to have plenty of time to consider eternity and to confess and make everything right. We don't like to see a grownup go suddenly" (Hostetler, 1974, p. 248). There is a dearth of literature on Hutterian perceptions of and reactions to infant and child death, and the little that exists merely mentions the topic in passing. For example, in comparison to the death of adults, Stephenson (1983) observed that "Hutterites prize the deaths of children while we [non-Hutterites] abhor them" (p. 129). In sum, based on a thorough review of the literature, no cultural portrait exists on the ways in which this unique culture-sharing group experiences the deaths of children on the colony.

Methodology
Purpose Statement

This is an ethnographic exploration into the experience of infant and child death on a Midwestern Hutterian colony that will describe, analyze, and interpret observations. This study will incorporate both the emic and the etic to provide a holistic cultural portrait.

Access and Rapport

According to Bogdan and Biklen (1992), gatekeepers are the key to access and thus researchers have an obligation to provide the following information: Why was the site chosen? How much time will be needed? Will the researcher be intrusive? Where will the results be reported? And, is there reciprocity?

The principal investigator's access to the colony was granted through the farm manager ("boss"), the gatekeeper for this closed system. Initial contact was made through a letter informing the boss of my area of interest, research, and practice. The boss was very interested and invited a telephone conversation that included an extensive discussion about me as an individual, my research agenda, and service within my community for a nonprofit organization that aids parents whose children died. Then, mindful to address all five of the suggestions posited above, we discussed the absence of research in this area of colony life, and I described how much time I would need in order to effectively collect data. I explained that I would remain a participant observer, and would minimize disruption to their daily lives. I explained the end result would be a publication in a peer-reviewed journal that would illuminate the culture-sharing group's response to child death on the colony. Finally, to attend to reciprocity, I offered to bring bibliotherapeutic materials specific to parental bereavement to the colony for his perusal in order to disseminate to members. I read the consent form over the phone, and subsequently mailed one to arrive a few weeks prior to my stay at the colony. The boss and I had two more phone conversations beginning in the Spring of 2010, prior to the beginning of the study in June of 2010, and after IRB approval.

As an outsider, I was humble, mindful, and reflexive in my approach with members of the colony (Cacciatore, 2010). Namely, I engaged in active and intentional empathy through facial, vocal, and postural mimicry (Hatfield, Rapson, & Le, 2009), and in culturally-aware interaction that adopted participants' primary style of communication (Cacciatore, 2009). In addition, I was intentionally willing to engage in therapeutic personal disclosure to build trusting relationships with colony members.

Data Collection

The holistic perspective is one of circumspect, according to Fetterman (1998), and integrates cultural history, spirituality, politics, economics, and social function. The approach used is realist ethnography, a paradigm often employed by cultural anthropologists, and characterized by Van Maanen (1988) as objective participant observation. Unlike other qualitative methods, the ethnography focuses on hearing the stories of the individual "within the context of their culture and cultural sharing group" (Creswell, 2007, p. 76).

Data collection lasted for 12 days during the summer of 2010. This study utilized five methods of fieldwork to collect data in a systematic order of occurrence:

1. gatekeeper intake;
2. group interviews;
3. individual interviews;
4. key leader interviews; and
5. participant observation.

During the gatekeeper intake, upon arrival at the study site, I met with the boss in his home for several hours talking about our families and building rapport. He provided information specific to this colony and its heritage and culture. Once comfortable with me, he made an announcement about the group interview in the church building over the public announcement system. He spoke in German, so I was unable to understand exactly what he said; however, he said that he had "many families waiting to talk with you."

Fetterman (1998) recommends beginning with the "big net" approach in ethnographic research, accomplished through the second method for data collection, group interviewing. The boss walked me to the church, where I was greeted by several male members of the council in the foyer area. The boss walked me to the front of the church where 36 women and 2 men (out of 115 total colony population) sat in the pews. I first introduced myself to the group and my reason for being on the colony, established rapport, and then invited others to share their stories. The group interview lasted just under 4 hours. All members remained for the entire duration of the group interview except for one bereaved mother who left after 3 hours because she was in charge of meal preparation for the day.

The third mode of data collection included seven, unstructured, open-ended interviews with individuals and families, representing the deaths of ten children, from newborn to 19 years of age. Each interview lasted anywhere from 30 minutes to 6 hours. All of these interviews took place with bereaved mothers. Interview data were noted, recorded, and kept in the form of:

1. field notes;
2. memos;
3. public documents;
4. photographs; and
5. other artifacts, including mementos shared by the family members.

The fourth mode utilized unstructured, open-ended interviewing with three key leaders on the colony who included the colony boss, preacher, and an elder woman in the community. Finally, participant observation data were recorded each day in a journal using headers for essential materials, descriptive notes, and reflective notes that occurred in situ. In addition, data also included subsequent personal letters from participants.

Data Analysis

Data management was the first step toward analysis, and included reading through all the materials—field notes, memos, documents, photographs, and daily journals—before organizing the data based on code segments that best described patterned regularities in the data (Wolcott, 1994). Those segments were placed into a matrix that delineated five thematic categories:

1. details of the actual death experience;
2. emotional and physical reactions to the loss;
3. individual, familial, and communal response;
4. coping and rituals; and
5. spirituality category.

Then came the interpretive processes of the culture-sharing group within their specific cultural context as well as within the larger context of scholarly evidence published on child death. To increase internal validity, I engaged in member checking, or respondent validation, a crucial step in establishing the credibility of the findings (Lincoln & Guba, 1985), with the colony boss and one of the interviewees.

Results
Specific Description of the Culture-Sharing Group

The specific colony studied is nestled in more than 5,000 acres of prairie farmland in South Dakota where each individual is "provided for equally and nothing is kept for personal gain" (farm manager, personal communication, June 27, 2010); this agrarian Hutterian colony flourishes with more than 23 families and a population of 115 people. Run by a church council of six members, this Schmiedeleut colony is one of five local colonies, one of which is the "mother colony," all within a 30-mile range. Statewide, there are 51 colonies in total and expanding. It is a place where both forgiveness and gratitude are constantly sought attributes, and the daily ritual of collective "prayer to keep the law of faith and good works inspired by God" is accomplished with "trembling and humility" (farm manager, personal communication, June 27, 2010).

As "strong advocates of education," there is a main school with a kindergarten located on the colony grounds where 36 children attend beginning at age 2. The concept of prayer, peace, sharing are the "main lessons of school" (farm manager, personal communication, June 27, 2010). Colony members speak High German as their primary language, so English speaking, non-Hutterites from local school districts teach classes in English beginning at age 6. Children on the colony are said to have four mothers: their birth mother and three older women "who look after them and who specialize in prayer, song, and discipline" (farm manager, personal communication, June 27, 2010). These women are viewed as partners in child rearing by colony members, and their focus is to teach children about the "afterlife, forgiveness, and service." The terms "grandpa and grandma" are used often in many non-kin relationships. There is "zero tolerance" on the colony for the use of expletives, and each member is expected to act with integrity and respect for others. Adultery, theft, and petty crimes are virtually non-existent, and no one locks their home (farm manager, personal communication, June 27, 2010).

Beginning at age 15, young men are inducted into a husbandry apprenticeship. At the same age, young women begin to learn practical skills such as knitting, sewing, cooking, and canning, "until every member finds his or her place of most usefulness" (farm manager, personal communication, June 27, 2010). Visits from guests, colony business, and meal times are communicated through a public address system. Meals are eaten together in one room, with men on one side and women on the other. Following lunch, each member returns home for a nap at 2:30 p.m. There is one landline phone that is housed in the home of the farm manager, and each member is allowed up to 10 minutes per day to use the phone. There are no computers, cellular phones, or other forms of social technology. Medical care, however, is sought outside the colony.

This colony has two large wind generators and it shares its electricity with the local rural power company. In addition to the farmland, there are several large gardens yielding produce for the colony's use including potatoes, onions, asparagus, and sweet corn. This colony has an extensive dairy cow farm, and organically raises hogs, turkeys, and chickens for market. Their domestic commodities are prolific, producing, for example, 70,000 turkeys in one year. The farm manager, or the "colony boss," oversees all matters social, economic, and agricultural, and often members seek his guidance, even about issues related to bereavement and loss. The preacher is the second key leader, and he manages all things spiritual.

The Hutterites on this colony attend church every day for 30–45 minutes, and for 1 hour or more on Sunday. There is no music in church; however, there is often accappella singing, praying, and reading of scripture and traditional Hutterite teachings. Children study both German and religion after school hours each day, and most adults are baptized at age 21. They are sociopolitical pacifists who believe that "Christ commanded that we love God above all else and your neighbor as yourself" and "everything belongs to everyone" (farm manager, personal communication, June 30, 2010). These canons also manifest outside the colony. Several such examples of altruistic traditional acts include blood donation every 8 weeks and organ donation of their deceased loved ones in order to save a non-Hutterite life. Autopsies are exceedingly rare on the colony and only occur in "highly suspicious deaths." These decisions are "left to the family."

Five Thematic Categories
Details of the Actual Death Experience

> *I heard someone, a girl outside, scream. It was terrifying. And I felt a strong knowing that it was him, that something happened to him. I ran out of the house praying "dear God please help me" over and over. (Mother of a 10-year-old boy who died in a farm accident)*

Three families experienced the deaths of multiple children. One lost a stillborn baby in 1980 to unknown causes, and subsequently her 5-year-old son died as a result of a neuroblastoma. She described both children's deaths in detail, noting of her 5-year-old's death, though anticipated: "I thought I was prepared but it wasn't as I thought." Another mother experienced the stillbirth of her twin boys just 4 months prior to the study. She described holding and naming the babies, noting that "I couldn't have handled it if I didn't hold them." Another mother lost all four of her children in a fire 20 years earlier in 1990, stating that "I questioned God but I prayed." Her husband, she said, "was completely hysterical." He later died at age 53, an event she described as "even harder" than the deaths of her four children. Four other families lost a single child: one lost her 19-year-old son in a farm accident, noting he was her only boy of five children and that she was "still struggling"; another lost her 10-year-old son in a farm accident; and two others lost their children from terminal illnesses.

This theme was the first to emerge in every narrative, both in the group interview and in the one-on-one interviews. Participants seemed to want to tell their story repeatedly, working through the details and expressing, quite openly, their traumatic experiences.

Emotional and Physical Reactions to the Loss

> *I went through so much pain even though he died peacefully. Even today I cry thinking of it. I felt depressed. I tried Zoloft but it didn't help. There were many, many tears and even my other children suffered. (Mother of a toddler who died of cancer)*

> *I have a lot of bad days. Occasionally, I have good days. But even on the good days I feel so sad underneath the smile and there is so much pain. . . . I think of them every single day. I will never forget them. (Mother of twins who were stillborn at 6 months gestation)*

Each mother described psychological processes congruent with those that emerge in mainstream studies on parental bereavement, identifying specific emotional experiences such as guilt, denial, despair, and sadness (Cacciatore, DeFrain, Jones, & Jones, 2008). They also expressed profound emotional reactions to their losses during both the group and individual interviews. One mother, whose 10-year-old son was "dragged under a tractor," said that she "collapsed" under the weight of the "shock and grief." She described the need to ride in the ambulance with her son, not wanting to leave him alone, noting that, "I had to be near him." Ten years later, she says she continues to "cry and miss him and feel the sadness." A mother who lost twin sons to early stillbirth talked about her pain being exacerbated by the "constant reminder" of her sister's twins, born around the same time her babies were due. At this point, she became very emotional and wept openly during the group interview. Another mother found herself withdrawing after her young child's death, and like many others described physical symptoms such as lethargy, headaches, nausea, and weight gain. Individual interviews affirmed these emotional and physiological symptoms.

Interestingly, during the course of the group interview not a single participant mentioned one salient emotion in current research on parental bereavement: anger. Thus, I inquired specifically about anger; however, the participants appeared nonplussed, many simultaneously declaring they had never experienced anger.

During each subsequent individual interview I intentionally inquired, at the end of the interview, about anger. Each person again explicitly eschewed anger. Three mothers discussed how their surviving children, however, went through periods of "anger and rebellion" following the death of their siblings, and that the process was "hard on them" not only because of their own grief, but also as witnesses to their "mother's grief." Another thing I noted was that participants discussed having "nice dreams," rather than nightmares. Idiosyncratic posttraumatic stress symptoms, specifically avoidance, hypervigilance and startle, and intrusion, did not appear to be part of their current or past symptomatology. Only one mother, who had lost her four children in a house fire, described a brief period of nocturnal hyperarousal that endured for several days.

Familial and Communal Response

> *With the help of my husband and my family and a lot of colony support, I have made it. He was my only son, and it helps that so many people valued his place in the colony. (Mother of 19-year-old who died in a farming accident)*

During the group interview, many colony members attended who did not directly lose a child. However, as mothers discussed their losses, other colony women collectively and openly mourned with them as they told their stories, reaching out to touch them on the back or on the hand. Some of the non-bereaved-parent participants remembered and spoke of details that several mothers had forgotten since the loss. I noted they were expressive, used the dead child's name, and obviously experienced their own grief as extended members of a larger family system. Participants openly discussed the ways that each family member responded differently to the death. Many mothers spoke of gender differences in mourning: "My husband and I grieved so differently." Others spoke of the struggles of surviving and subsequent children: "Our younger daughter always wants to visit him in the cemetery." The four older siblings of the twins who died in utero "took it very hard," and the mother felt as if she "had to comfort them, but I needed comforting." Some siblings did experience what the mothers identified as anger or rebellion, quickly quelled by social proscriptions of colony life. Mothers whose children died years earlier described how important it was to them that their subsequent children knew the story of their sibling who died: "Our children remember him and we keep him alive and part of our family." One mother who lost her four children in a fire noted that her husband "grieved more" than she did and that she "spoiled" her "next child" because of her losses.

Hospital bills and any other final expenses are paid through the common colony fund, and the mother and father of the child who died are "relieved from work duties" for as long as necessary. Most people are "held up" for 2 weeks then gradually resume their responsibilities as able, although "life is never the same." Fellow colony members and relatives appear "overwhelmingly supportive," "sympathetic," and "willing to listen." The bereaved are never alone unless they ask for solitude. Participants described an incontrovertible trust in one another, as they "eat together, laugh together, cry together, and pray together" from birth until death.

No participant mentioned the transgressions of others in their narratives. Nearly every participant, however, expressed gratitude repeatedly for the kindnesses of others, Hutterite and non-Hutterite, in the aftermath of their losses. Their focus often seemed to be on recognizing others' compassion: "At all times, someone was hugging me," "The doctor was so helpful and he knelt down in front of us and told us," "Everyone in our path was so caring," and "He told us with sad, caring eyes our son died."

Coping and Rituals

Everyone from miles and miles around came to his funeral, and my sisters and I talk about him all the time. We look at his photographs and we remember the things he said or did. Sometimes we laugh, sometimes we cry. But we do it together. (Mother of an 8-year-old who died of cancer)

Shared ritualization plays a key role in coping for grieving families on the colony. Funerals as last rites are a very important part of the Hutterite tradition. Caskets are made by the colony woodsmith, and each colony has its own cemetery where family members are often buried near one another. The deceased's body is kept in the family home until the evening wake. From 8:00 until 11:00 p.m., colony members attend a wake in the church. The body is then carried back to the family home, followed the next day by a "mostly open casket" funeral where every person "walks around the family of the dead" as a sign of support. The funerals of the dead are attended by Hutterites from all surrounding areas, usually between 400–600 people, who eat lunch together prior to the funeral. Only the colony minister speaks at the funeral and the eulogy is often brief, focusing on "what we are doing with our lives and ensuring we don't have unfinished business." Prior to burial, the family will have many opportunities to say goodbye: "We are given alone time with our dead ones." The headstones are designed by the family of the

deceased and are often written in German. The funeral services of babies and young children, under age 5, are different from those of older children who die. "Fewer people attend" because "fewer people knew" the child. Every mother described how important it was to say goodbye: "I am so glad that I had that time with the twins. I cannot imagine where I'd be if I hadn't."

Mementos were important to all the families. Both during the individual and group sessions, bereaved mothers shared photo albums, poetry, scrapbooks, and other tangible keepsakes documenting their child's life and death. One mother told the story of how painful it was for her as she watched her son's 8th grade class graduate, and they intentionally kept his photo on the wall with the five other graduating students. Another colony member mentioned it to her, acknowledging his absence, and the mother wept: "It means so much—those little times—when others remember him." The same mother modified their most recent family photograph to include her son's picture because she "couldn't bear the family photo without him." Parents describe such microritualistic mementos as: "memory books, special candles, angel bears, curio cabinet, and special poetry" that serve the purpose of "helping stay connected" to their child who died: "We have a lot of reminders of the twins in our house. It brings me comfort."

There is narrative evidence of posttraumatic growth in the data. The desire to discover meaning through helping others, both inside and outside the colony, was a common aspiration for many bereaved families. One family donated their young son's organs to three donors. She described the emotional process for her and her husband as they approached first the minister, then the doctor, and then the hospital with their decision. The mother currently corresponds with one of the donors who received a liver transplant and says that she lived "because of [him]." This young woman then went on to have a baby who was named after the young boy who died. Another woman donated because it is "what he would have wanted." Mothers described how they "get together and drink tea" and share their mementos with one another. This collective reprocessing appeared to serve as a type of bonding time between colony women where the "older grieving mothers comfort the newer grieving mothers" with song, and food, and prayer.

Spirituality

We put more into our spiritual life and our entire community revolves around our spiritual connection to God. When I drive down the road and see a beautiful crop, I thank God and see His hand in it. We pray morning and night, twice with each meal, and at church. We thank God all the time and we are very grateful for everything we have. We trust God's will because without God we have nothing. (Farm manager)

Spirituality emerged as the most salient variable in the narratives of parentally bereaved Hutterite families, both individually and collectively, noting that "Faith in God is the most important to us" and "We survived because of the touch of God." Bereaved mothers acknowledged "God's goodness" through their struggles, even if "it still hurts." The mothers described having a "little questioning toward God," tempered by "faith that God has a plan for us, even if it's hard." The mothers seem firmly committed to faith in a reunion with their children, comforted that "they went to Heaven without sin." The Hutterites believe that "babies and children go straight to Heaven" because "who could be more innocent," and they "trust God's plan" even when it's "painful."

Forgiveness is a cornerstone principle of their theological culture. One family who lost their son when a fellow colony member inadvertently activated a piece of farm machinery approached the man and offered their forgiveness, assuring him it was not his fault and that "it was [their son's] time to die." While "some on the outside can't understand," the Hutterites collectively "accept and trust in God's will" unconditionally.

Ex Post Facto

As part of reciprocity, I brought about 25 copies of bibliotherapeutic materials specific to parental bereavement to the colony. Those items included psycho-educational brochures, bereaved parent newsletters, and grief specific books. Within minutes of offering them, the materials were taken by individuals who were both directly bereaved and indirectly bereaved. The ones who did not receive copies were palpably disappointed and in my field notes I wrote, "Hungry for information!" They asked me to send more, and I agreed. Several of the bereaved mothers sent thank you cards within the few months following data collection: "How do I begin to say thank you for hearing my story?"; "I hope you'll come again."; and, "The things you sent were so helpful for us, thank you."

In addition, 4 months following the conclusion of data collection, the colony boss contacted me seeking additional bibliotherapy materials for a family whose 8-year-old died in a farm accident in October. As a researcher and practitioner, it was apparent throughout my experience on the colony, and even months later, that leaders of the community recognize the unique pain of a family experiencing infant and child death, and they are willing to seek help from non-Hutterites to find help.

Discussion

Previous literature suggests that "children who die young are envied for having avoided life's temptations and struggles" (Ingoldsby, 1999, p. 388) and that children's deaths are "prized" not "abhorred" in Hutterian society (Stephenson, 1983). Yet, the results of this study depict a more nuanced story. While no bereaved father's voice was recorded as it relates to infant or child death on the colony, the voices of mothers, both individually and collectively, suggest that infant and child death are exceedingly painful experiences for families. Despite their spiritual beliefs that "babies go straight to heaven" and that "most mothers accept that it was meant to be" (key leader, personal communication, July 1, 2010), the effects of child death "never go away." During both group and individual interviews, mothers openly mourned for their dead babies and children, expressing emotional experiences ranging from sadness, guilt, and disbelief to "a little questioning of God" and even social

withdrawal. Though anger was not expressed by participants, it is possible that this emotion may be constrained by sociocultural norms. Thus, its disavowal within the colony may result in sublimation or some other means of psychopathological expression that is, perhaps, not easily recognizable.

It is interesting to note that previous research suggests, however, a very low prevalence of psychopathology, including schizophrenia and anxiety, among the Hutterites when compared to non-Hutterite populations (Eaton & Weil, 1955; Torrey, 1995), and suicide is exceedingly rare for colony members (Stephenson, 1997). Researchers attribute this to high cohesion and low dispersion. Eaton and Weil (1955) estimated that more than 97 percent of Hutterites had never experienced mental illness other than depressive symptoms, a condition they know as anfechtung. Anfechtung symptoms include weeping, difficulty sleeping, loss of appetite, and seeking solitude. And, most importantly, "as soon as the behavior associated with anfechtung begins to be displayed, the [colony] enfolds the suffering individual within a set of support individuals and practices" that help them overcome their angst (Stephenson, 1997, p. 111) through empathy and compassion. Because those with anfechtung are not stigmatized, some assert that the colony qualifies as a therapeutic community which can "ameliorate the serious consequences of mental disorders or disability" (p. 110). Yet, importantly, colony members seem to differentiate anfechtung from bereavement, despite the fact that the losses may have occurred years ago. Mourning is perceived as a justified act of love while anfechtung derives from endogenous, not reactive, sadness (farm manager, personal communication, July 1, 2010). Nevertheless, whether the emotional despair is reactive or endogenous, the community responds mindfully, intentionally, and with compassion.

This shared processing often manifests through rituals. And, these acts have a distinct purpose in social bonding and thus are not "empty performances." Rather, they are imbued with "meaning, symbolism, and moral consequences" and bind members together in a common moral language (Sosis, 2003, p. 98). These shared practices create a very different environment for processing grief in the wake of a child's death, one in which the death is openly acknowledged and felt by the entire community. This may be because on the colony "Hutterites have a specific system for taking care of every member from birth to death" (Freese, 1994, p. 55). The bereaved are never left alone unless they specifically ask for solitude, and there is genuine willingness among colony members to be present and share with another's sorrow. Furthermore, they are given as much time off from their colony responsibilities as needed, in contrast to mainstream culture, which has a socially dictated mourning period and often rigid bereavement leave policies (Pratt, 1981).

While it is one thing for the Hutterites to believe that children are assured a "place in heaven upon death" and to find a measure of consolation in that belief, it is quite another to say that the deaths of children are "prized," which disregards the depth of grief and suffering of the bereaved parents and family. Despite their isolation from mainstream culture, the Hutterian experiences of traumatic infant and child death and their expressions of loss are similar to those of non-Hutterites. The emotional cadence following the death of a child appears to be a universal part of the human experience.

Limitations

This study is cross sectional, and no causal conclusions can be drawn. Additionally, some of the deaths occurred years prior to the study, and thus are subject to memory bias. The study occurred in one Hutterite community and thus may not represent the total population of Hutterite colonies globally. Finally, because of the reluctance of Hutterite males to interact with non-Hutterite females on very personal matters (in this case, the primary investigator), no fathers' voices were recorded in the study; thus, only the mothers' perspectives were actually recorded in first person. Despite the limitations, this study illuminates many important, previously undiscovered data with regards to infant and child death among the Hutterite population, and offers some interesting insights to the larger community about the process of shared mourning, forgiveness, gratitude, and spirituality.

Conclusion

Grief can be expressed differently, individually and collectively, in traditional societies versus modern societies. In traditional societies, usually small villages, there is a greater degree of cohesion and familiarity as everyone knows and relies on everyone else in a "dense human sphere" (Stephenson, 1997, p. 116). Demonstrations of empathic support are expressed and perceived in more tangible ways and daily rituals, such as shared meals, stories, and spiritual worship. A loss within a small community—and the resultant emotional anguish—may be easier to acknowledge openly. By contrast, in contemporary, urban society, intimate social circles are likely to be smaller, more fragmented, spanning several locations. Consequently, loss and mourning can be a more isolating experience for the bereaved. While "private" grief is experienced by only a small circle of individuals directly impacted by the loss, "shared" grief is where the death is recognized and mourned by the entire community (Walter, 2007). There is also narrative evidence that, for the Hutterites, focusing on the numinous aspects of loss seem to foster posttraumatic growth.

In sum, the Hutterites' spiritual beliefs play a significant role in their daily lives, thus they also influence their experiences of grief. Several examples of this may be the seeming and remarkable absence of both anger and PTSD symptomatology. Additionally, their profuse and contemplative expression of gratitude, even for small gestures of kindness, was a salient theme in this study. And the tangible communal trust during periods of mourning is influenced by their unmitigated trust in God over their losses. Hutterian colonies exist in a unique intersection of traditionalism and modernity, an agrarian culture amidst a modern, geographically mobile, and increasingly urbanized society. While this study suggests that parental grief is no less anguishing than in mainstream culture, the Hutterite community's response to child death is markedly open in their support and sharing of the mourning experience.

This cultural portrait of the Hutterites illustrates the ways in which community, social support, and spirituality help the bereaved process their loss. It is imperative for clinicians to be cognizant of the role of spirituality and faith in the course of grief. While the dominant society may be quick to dismiss their way of life as "quaint," the ways in which these bereaved families speak of their deceased children and the comfort and strength they derive from their faith demonstrate the healing power of collective compassion, shared ritualization, and the "touch of God."

References

Bogdan, R., & Biklen, S. (1992). Qualitative research for education: An introduction to theory and methods. Boston, MA: Allyn and Bacon.

Cacciatore, J. (2009). Appropriate bereavement practice after the death of a Native American child. Families in Society, 90(1), 46–50.

Cacciatore, J. (2010). Stillbirth: Clinical recommendations for care in the era of evidence-based medicine. Clinical Obstetrics and Gynecology, 53(3), 691–699.

Cacciatore, J., DeFrain, J., Jones, K., & Jones, H. (2008). The couple and the death of a baby. Journal of Family Social Work, 11(4), 351–370.

Creswell, J. W. (2007). Qualitative inquiry and research design (2nd ed.). Thousand Oaks, CA: Sage.

Eaton, J., & Weil, R. (1955). Culture and mental disorders. Glencoe, IL: Free Press.

Fetterman, D. (1998). Ethnography step-by-step (2nd ed.). Thousand Oaks, CA: Sage.

Freese, B. (1994). All things in common. Successful Farming, 92(10), 54–61.

Hatfield, E., Rapson, R. L., & Le, Y. L. (2009). Primitive emotional contagion: Recent research. In J. Decety & W. Ickes (Eds.), The social neuroscience of empathy. Boston, MA: MIT Press.

Hofer, S. (1998). The Hutterites: Lives and images of a communal people. Saskatoon, Saskatchewan: Hofer Publishers.

Hostetler, J. (1974). Hutterite society. Baltimore, MD: Johns Hopkins University Press.

Hutterian Brethren Schmiedeleut Conference. (2006). Hutterite history. Hutterian Brethren Schmiedeleut Conference: Decker Colony, Shoal Lake, Manitoba. Retrieved 10/24/2010 from www.hutterites.org/HutteriteHistory/index.htm

Ingoldsby, B. (1999). The Hutterite family in transition. Paper presented at the Communal Studies Association annual meeting, St. George, Utah.

Janzen, R. (2005). The Hutterites and the Bruderhof: The relationship between an old order religious society and a twentieth-century communal group. Mennonite Quarterly Review, 4, 506–541.

Janzen, R., & Stanton, M. (2010). The Hutterites in North America. Baltimore, MD: Johns Hopkins University Press.

Larsen, U., & Vaupel, J. W. (1993). Hutterite fecundability by age and parity: Strategies for frailty modeling of event histories. Demography, 30(1), 81–102.

Lincoln, Y. S., & Guba, E. G. (1985) Naturalistic inquiry. Beverly Hills, CA: Sage.

Morgan, K. (1983). Mortality changes in the Hutterite Brethren of Alberta and Saskatchewan, Canada. Human Biology, 55(1), 89–99.

Packull, W. O. (1999). Hutterite beginnings: Communitarian experiments during the Reformation. Baltimore, MD: Johns Hopkins University Press.

Peter, K. A. (1987). The dynamics of Hutterite society. Edmonton, Alberta: University of Alberta Press.

Pratt, L. (1981). Business temporal norms and bereavement behavior. American Sociological Review, 46(3), 317–333.

Rhodes, R. (2009). Nightwatch: An inquiry into solitude. Intercourse, PA: Good Books.

Sosis, R. (2003). Why aren't we all Hutterites? Costly signaling theory and religious behavior. Human Nature, 14(2), 91–127.

Stahl, L. M. (2003). My Hutterite life. Helena, MT: Farcountry Press.

Stephenson, P. H. (1983). "He died too quick!": The process of dying in a Hutterian colony. Omega, 14(2), 127–134.

Stephenson, P. H. (1997). The Hutterites. In I. Al-Issa & M. Tousignant (Eds.), Ethnicity, immigration, and psychopathology. New York: Plenum Press.

Torrey, E. F. (1995). Prevalence of psychosis among the Hutterites. Schizophrenia Research, 16(2), 167–170.

Van Maanen, J. (1988). Tales of the field: On the ethnography. Chicago, IL: University of Chicago Press.

Walter, T. (2007). Modern grief, postmodern grief. International Review of Sociology, 17, 123–134.

Wolcott, H. F. (1994). Transforming qualitative data: Description, analysis, and interpretation. Thousand Oaks, CA: Sage.

Critical Thinking

1. The Hutterites tend to not fear death. Why do you think this is the case?

2. Why do the Hutterites not display anger at the death of a child? What might we learn from this communal, Christian group?

3. Why do Hutterites tend to envy a child who died young? What behavioral expressions do we non-Hutterites typically display upon the death of a child?

End-of-Life Concerns and Care Preferences: Congruence Among Terminally Ill Elders and their Family Caregivers

DANIEL S. GARDNER, PhD AND BETTY J. KRAMER, PhD

Introduction

In the past several decades, it has become clear that there are substantial disparities between the way older Americans wish to die and the way their last days are realized. This discrepancy is due, in part, to well-documented gaps in the quality of care that people receive at the end of life (Field & Cassel, 1997; SUPPORT, 1995). Although most people prefer to die in their own homes (Higginson & Sen-Gupta, 2000; Tang & McCorkle, 2003; Thomas, Morris, & Clark, 2004), a majority of deaths occur in hospitals or nursing homes (Gallo, Baker, & Bradley, 2001; Pritchard, Fisher, Teno, Sharp, Reding, Knaus, et al., 1998). And despite considerable advances in medical and supportive approaches to pain management, a significant number of older adults with advanced and terminal illness experience serious pain and discomfort (SUPPORT, 1995; Teno, Clarridge, Casey, Welch, Wetle, Shield, et al., 2004). In an effort to better understand the needs and enhance the care of dying individuals and their families, end-of-life researchers have explored these and other disparities between end-of-life preferences and outcomes.

Barriers to quality end-of-life care include the unpredictable nature of terminal illness, communication difficulties in familial and social relationships, and the complex care needs of dying patients and their families (Kramer & Auer, 2005). Quality care is also hindered by systemic-level factors, including the emphasis on curative and life-sustaining intervention over quality of life and supportive care, health care financing and service delivery structures that move patients between multiple care settings with minimal coordination and poor continuity of care, a lack of providers trained in the fundamentals of palliative care (e.g., biopsycho-social-spiritual aspects of grief and loss, effective clinical communication, attention to family systems), and the absence of evidence-based practice knowledge in this area (Emanuel, von Gunten, & Ferris, 2000; Field & Cassel, 1997; Morrison, 2005). Further, end-of-life care models that represent the standard of care—hospice and palliative care—are underutilized and often inaccessible to the poor, racial and ethnic minorities, and elders with uncertain disease pathways.

Less is known about the subjective end-of-life experiences, concerns, and preferences of older patients and their family members (Cohen & Leis, 2002; Singer, Martin, & Kellner, 1999; Vig, Davenport, & Pearlman, 2002). Recently there have been calls for research to better understand factors that affect patients' and families' perceptions of quality of life and quality of care at the end of life (Field & Cassel, 1997; Kramer, Christ, Bern-Klug, & Francoeur, 2005; NIH, 2004; SUPPORT, 1995). This study explores the challenges, concerns, and preferences of low-income elders receiving palliative care, and focuses on congruence and incongruence between the elders and their primary family caregivers.

Quality of Life and Care at the End of Life

The Institute of Medicine defined a "good death" as one with minimal suffering, which satisfies the wishes of dying patients and their families, while adhering to current medical, cultural and ethical standards (Field & Cassel, 1997). Researchers often operationalize a good death as the degree to which an individual's dying experiences correspond with their preferences for quality of life and quality of care at the end of life (Engelberg, Patrick, & Curtis, 2005). A growing literature has sought to shed light on the aspects of care that are most important to terminally ill elders and their family members (Heyland, Dodek, Rocker, Groll, Gafhi, Pichora, et al., 2006; Laakkonen, Pitkala, & Strandberg, 2004).

When faced with advanced life-threatening illness, most people wish to be free of pain and symptoms (Heyland et al., 2006; Vig & Pearlman, 2004), to be treated with dignity and respect (Chochinov, Hack, Hassard, Kristjianson, McClement,

& Harlos, 2002; Steinhauser, Christakis, Clipp, McNeilly, McIntyre, & Tulsky, 2000), and to maintain a sense of autonomy and control over their last days (Singer et al., 1999; McSkirmning, Hodges, Super, Driever, Schoessler, Franey, et al., 1999; Vig & Pearlman, 2004). Nearly all prefer to be informed of their prognoses and have time to put their affairs in order (Heyland et al., 2006; McCormick & Conley, 1995; Terry, Olson, Wilss, & Boulton-Lewis, 2006). Dying elders hope to avoid becoming burdens to their families (McPherson, Wilson, & Murray, 2007; Vig & Pearlman, 2004) and typically eschew the use of artificial means to prolong life (Heyland et al., 2006; Singer, et al., 1999; see Steinhauser et al., 2000 for divergent findings). There is, however, a great deal of heterogeneity in what constitutes a "good death." Ultimately, end-of-life preferences are individual, dynamic and multidimensional, and vary across contexts such as age, gender, disease course, care setting, financial resources, and social and familial relationships (Thomas et al., 2004).

Congruence in Patient and Family Perspectives

During the course of advanced and terminal illness, elders increasingly rely on family members to identify and communicate their emotional and physical needs and concerns (McPherson, Wilson, Lobchuk, & Brajtman, 2008; Waldrop, Kramer, Skretny, Milch, & Finn, 2005). Much of the research on patients' end-of-life care preferences is also based on the report of family surrogates or healthcare proxies (Teno et al., 2004). However, the accuracy of family members' assessments of dying patients' concerns and preferences is uncertain. Studies have documented significant incongruence between patients and family members on their evaluations of quality of life (Farber, Egnew, Herman-Bertch, Taylor, & Guldin, 2003; McPherson & Addington-Hall, 2003), frequency and severity of pain and other physical and psychological symptoms (McPherson et al., 2008; Mularski, Curtis, Osborne, Engelberg, & Ganzini, 2004; Sneeuw, Sprangers, & Aaronson, 2002), and end-of-life preferences (Engelberg et al., 2005; Moorman & Carr, 2008; Shalowitz, Garrret-Myer, & Wendler, 2006; Steinhauser et al., 2000). Farber and colleagues (2003) describe these differences as reflecting the often highly divergent "cultural perspectives" of patients and their formal and informal caregivers around death and dying.

Although findings have been inconsistent, congruence in the end-of-life preferences and perceptions of elders and their family caregivers has been found to range from moderate to poor. There is some evidence of greater agreement around objective and measurable factors such as patient functioning and mobility, and less regarding subjective factors such as pain and depression (Desbiens & Mueller-Rizner, 2000; Engelberg et al., 2005; McPherson & Addington-Hall, 2003; Tang & McCorkle, 2003). Congruence may be more likely when surrogate decision-makers are younger and female (McPherson & Addington-Hall, 2003; Zettel-Watson, Ditto, Danks, & Smucker, 2008), family income is higher (Desbiens & Mueller-Rizner, 2000), the illness is of longer duration, or the patient is closer to death (Sneeuw et al., 2002). Notably, there is evidence that families who have

had explicit discussions about dying and the patient's wishes are more likely to agree with each other about end-of-life care preferences (Engelberg et al., 2005; Sulmasy, Terry, Weisman, Miller, Stallings, Vettese et al., 1998).

Despite gaps in our understanding of the correspondence between individual and family experiences of dying and preferences for end-of-life, very few studies have focused on congruence among paired patient-family caregiver dyads (Engelberg et al., 2005). And there remains a critical lack of knowledge about the shared and distinct challenges, concerns, and preferences of older adults and their family caregivers at the end of life (Vig et al., 2002). Empirical inquiry in this area may help to enhance familial understanding of older patients' concerns and the accuracy of surrogate decision-making, and to ultimately improve the quality of life at the end of life. The study described here uses qualitative methods to delve more deeply into the subjective experiences of terminally ill elders and their family caregivers, describe their end-of-life preferences and identify areas of congruence and incongruence.

Methods
Study Design
These data were collected as part of a larger longitudinal research study exploring the process and experience of end-of-life care provided to frail elders with advanced chronic disease enrolled in an innovative, fully "integrated" managed care program (Kramer & Auer, 2005). The design was an embedded case study (Scholz & Tietje, 2002), involving in-depth data collection with multiple sources of data. Case study research design makes it possible to examine processes, perceptions and outcomes regarding naturalistic phenomena of which the researcher seeks multiple perspectives (Yin, 2003). The results reported here address the congruent and incongruent end-of-life perceptions, challenges, concerns, and care preferences of elders and their primary family caregivers.

Research Site and Sample
Elder Care of Dane County, a not-for-profit organization, has provided community-based health and social services for older adults since 1976. The Elder Care Partnership (ECP) program, the largest program offered by this organization, provides comprehensive, fully integrated health, psychosocial, and long-term care to low-income frail elders. The program integrates practices that are consistent with clinical practice guidelines for quality palliative care (National Consensus Project, 2004). Detailed descriptions of the study and site can be found elsewhere (Kramer & Auer, 2005).

Study participants were purposively selected by interdisciplinary team members from the pool of elders (aged 65 years or older) enrolled in ECP. Enrollees had annual incomes below $10,000, seven to eight chronic medical conditions, and functional limitations in three or more Activities of Daily Living. Team members were asked to identify elders who were likely to die within 6 months, spoke English, were cognitively able to understand and respond to interview questions, and had a family member involved in their care. Once the elder completed consent procedures and agreed to participate, team members invited the identified primary family caregiver to participate in an interview with the Principal Investigator (PI; second author).

Data Collection

In-depth, semi-structured, face-to-face interviews, which ranged from 1 to 2 hours long, were conducted by the project PI, a university professor and Project on Death in America Social Work Leader. Elders and their identified family care-givers were interviewed separately at a time and place selected by the participant, most often in the participant's home. The interviews were not standardized in order to facilitate greater exploration of issues deemed most important to respondents (Padgett, 2008). Instead, each interview was structured around open-ended questions reflecting the study aims, including questions designed to explore the perceived challenges and concerns of the participants, their end-of-life preferences, and the extent to which they had discussed these issues with family members:

- What has been most difficult or challenging to you and your family members at this time?
- What are your [your family member's] concerns or worries?
- What is most important to you about the care you [your family member] receive[s] in your [their] last days?
- If you could plan it perfectly, what kind of death would you hope for [for the patient]? What would make a "good" death?

Additional questions and probes were used to explore participant preferences about the location of death, the desire for family members to be present, and the importance of family communication and saying "goodbye" during the elder's last days. In addition, the interviewer asked about the extent to which they had talked about the elders' end-of-life preferences, and their comfort or difficulty in doing so.

Data Analysis

All of the interviews were recorded on audiotape and transcribed verbatim, with participant consent. The researchers employed qualitative methods that entailed detailed readings and re-readings of each transcript, team coding, and thematic and conceptual analysis. Data analysis followed a form of *template analysis* (Crabtree & Miller, 1999) that begins with an a priori set of coding categories (i.e., a "template") based on the researchers' domains of interest (end-of-life challenges and worries or fears, care concerns, preferences, and family communication). Two researchers independently read the transcripts, identified segments that were relevant to the research domains, and used the preliminary coding template to search for and identify patterns and themes in the data. These themes were then tested within and across cases, and refined in order to generate broader and more integrated conceptual domains. Upon reaching theoretical saturation, a thematic conceptual matrix (Patton, 2002) was developed to examine the congruent (i.e., like) and incongruent (distinct) themes relevant to the domains of elder and family caregiver end-of-life challenges, concerns, and care preferences.

While no tests were conducted of inter-rater reliability, the research team employed several strategies to ensure analytic rigor. The protocol included: extended engagement, or the use of long interviews with extensive probing and clarification; independent team coding and peer debriefing; deviant case analysis in the development and testing of a final thematic schema; and careful auditing that involved documentation (including verbatim transcripts, field notes, and analytic memos) of the data collection and analytic process (Padgett, 2008).

Findings
Study Participants

Ten elders (five women and five men) and ten family caregivers (six women and four men) completed face-to-face interviews (see Table 1). The mean age of the elders was 85 years-old (range: 64-101), and family members were a mean 53 years-old

Table 1 Elder and Family Caregiver Dyads

Elder	Family Caregiver
97-year-old African-American female with heart disease	47-year-old African-American grandson; single, live-in caregiver
86-year-old white female with lung disease	50-year-old white daughter; lives separately
89-year-old white male with heart disease	56-year-old white son; married, lives separately
82-year-old white female with lung cancer	52-year-old white daughter; single, lives separately
101-year-old white female with heart disease	67-year-old white son; single, live-in caregiver
84-year-old white male with heart disease	47-year-old white daughter; divorced, lives separately (in same town)
80-year-old white male with heart disease and accident-related injuries	48-year-old white daughter-in-law (married to step-son); lives separately
86-year-old white male with prostate cancer	56-year-old daughter; single, live-in caregiver
82-year-old white female with lung disease and accident-related injuries	48-year-old white son; married, lives with elder
64-year-old white male with lung disease	55-year-old white wife; live-in

Table 2   Congruence & Incongruence among Elders & Family Caregivers

Domain	Themes	Incongruent		Congruent
		Elder	**Family**	**Both**
Challenges	Experiencing decline			X
	Accepting dependence	X		
	Providing adequate care		X	
	Living with uncertainty			X
Worries	Pain & suffering			X
	Meeting elders' care needs		X	
	Becoming a burden	X		
	Anticipating the impact on survivors			X
Concerns about EOL	Receiving competent, consistent & responsive care			X
Care	Managing pain			X
	Being treated with dignity and respect			X
	Living while dying			X
A "Good Death"	Dying at home			X
	Dying quickly, without suffering			X
	Avoiding life support			X
	Being prepared	X		
	Addressing spiritual needs addressed		X	

(range: 47-67). Family caregivers included four daughters, three sons, one daughter-in-law, one grandson, and one wife. Nine of the dyads were non-Hispanic white, and one was African American. Elders were enrolled in the program an average of 2.6 years (range: 1.5-4), and all had multiple chronic health conditions. The most debilitating diagnoses included serious heart disease ($n = 5$), lung disease ($n = 3$), and cancer ($n = 2$). Five of the elders lived alone and five lived with their family caregivers (four with an adult child and one with a spouse).

Domains of Care

Four domains of end-of-life care framed the results of our analysis: a) the *challenges* or day-to-day difficulties related to the patient's terminal illness; b) participants' *worries* or fears about the patient's death and dying; c) *care concerns* regarding the patient's end-of-life care by formal and informal caregivers; and d) participants' hopes and preferences for a *good death*. These domains reflect a range of end-of-life concerns and preferences that were expressed and elaborated on by study participants, some of which are shared or congruent, and others which are distinct to either elders or their family members (see Table 2).

Challenges

Elders and their family caregivers identified four primary illness-related challenges they struggled with on a daily basis.

Experiencing Physical and Functional Decline

Elders spoke articulately about their efforts to participate in normal daily activities in the face of decreased energy and declining physical and functional capacities, as is illustrated here:

> I like to walk. I can't get out and walk. I have to have a walker so sometimes the kids take me in a wheelchair and we can walk around the campgrounds, or we'll go down by the lake. I'd like to be able to walk, too. But I can't do it. I can't go up and down the stairs so I have to stay here and let somebody else go down and do my laundry. I haven't been down the stairs in the basement for two years. (83 year-old female elder)
>
> I can't do the things I want to do, like mow the lawn or walk down the block. It's hard to breathe . . . Yeah, feels like you're ready to die—takes your breath right away from you. (64-year-old male elder)

Family caregivers also struggled with the changes in their loved ones' functioning, often within the context of lifelong relationships:

> It's just that I can't be with him like I'd like to be . . . we've been married almost 37 years so it's a long time, and, just to see him going downhill like he is. (55-year-old wife)

Accepting Increasing Dependence

Closely associated with physical and functional decline, many elders struggled to contend with the diminished autonomy and increasing dependence on others:

> I miss driving . . . I have to depend on other people and I was always so independent. It bothers me when I have

to ask people to haul me around and pick me up, but they don't care, they don't say anything, but I—that's one thing that bugs me but I can't change it so I'll just go on the way it is. (80-year-old male elder)

Some family caregivers were aware that decreased autonomy could be challenging for the elders, but rather than viewing dependence as a challenge they emphasized the benefits of relying on others:

He was able to take his own baths and do everything and then wham-o, here he is. He's in bed all the time and somebody has to help him bathe or whatever . . . although I tell him it's *teamwork,* that we're doing this as a team. (56-year-old daughter)

Providing Adequate Care

Family caregivers spoke at length about caring for the elders, often emphasizing the challenges and responsibilities inherent in the role of family caregiver.

Basically, I'm her number one health advocate. I've had to deal with these situations where people didn't want [her] to go to the hospital and I knew she had to, or just on and on with different things that have happened. So, I just kind of focus on her. (48-year-old son)

The challenge of providing care was often experienced as stressful by family members, given the elder's changing medical needs and the complex nature of family history and relationships:

Part of my life is on hold right now because I'm staying here to take care of her. . . . I'm married and I have a wife and we want to enjoy our life together, so as painful as it is to see your parent leave your life, it's also going to be a big transition when I finally get on with my life . . . it's really a dichotomy because you feel selfish when you think about yourself and your own situation and what your preferences are and what you'd do if you were just living in your own house with your own family versus taking care of a parent. So, it's pretty hard. (48-year-old son)

Living with Uncertainty

Both elders and family caregivers talked about the difficulties they had in coping with their uncertain futures. Although all participants were aware that the elders had limited prognoses, many struggled with not knowing how and when their terminal decline would occur:

About death? I've had pains and stuff, you know, and I had to go to the hospital and all that. I don't know if I'm gonna come home again or not. You don't know that—if you're that bad—and these blood clots can move. They can hit you just like that and you're gone. (64-year-old male elder)

For me, it's never knowing when he's going into an attack, and if I'm at work . . . I told them at work—I said there'll be days when I can't come in because he isn't

good, or I'll have to leave because something's gone wrong. (55-year-old wife)

Worries or Fears about Dying

Elders and family caregivers were encouraged to talk about their concerns, worries, and fears related to dying. In response to direct questions, most of the elders initially denied any fears of death or dying. As the interviews progressed, however, elders and family caregivers raised a variety of concerns about the future. Four areas of concern or worry were expressed by a majority of the participants.

Pain and Suffering

The principal concern shared by elders and family caregivers was that the elder would experience unmanageable pain or physical discomfort as they were dying.

I'm concerned about pain and cancer, I never had anyone in my family that's had cancer, my ideas of it are strictly from novels or movies, so they give you enough pain medication to control the pain then you're going to be nauseated and sleepy and even [lose] your mind, hallucinating even, so that's not something I look forward to. (82-year-old female elder)

I guess I'm . . . afraid of the pain, if she might have a lot of pain. I don't know, it really is kind of terrifying. I don't know what it's going to be like when the, if the cancer really hits. The best thing would be if she would die from some secondary, related, symptomatic illness like pneumonia or something. (52-year-old daughter)

Meeting Elders' Increasing Needs

Family caregivers were particularly worried about their capacity to respond to the intensifying needs of the elders, and that they might lack the necessary supports and resources to continue providing care at home. Several participants feared having to place elders in long-term care institutions in the future:

I suppose my biggest concern . . . is that he will regress and have a physical deterioration that will make it virtually impossible for him to be able to continue in that apartment, making a full time placement in a nursing home type facility necessary. That's going to be hard in a lot of ways. There's the physical move and taking care of all the stuff that will need to be moved over there, and then there's just the emotional aspect for [Elder] in terms of being in a place where he just damn well doesn't want to be. (48-year-old daughter-in-law)

A related concern was that the elder might not be aware of—or might hide—signs of his or her decline.

I think probably one of my biggest concerns with my mother is whether or not she'll be totally honest and recognize when something is really wrong. And so that, that's got me some concern to the point when she did fall the last time and she was in the nursing home . . . she had fallen a couple of times earlier in the week and hadn't told anybody that she had been dizzy and that she had fallen and if she, if she had told anybody either her home nurse or us, that that was going on, then we would have intervened, so it raised questions about whether or not she could be on her own or not. (50-year-old daughter)

Family caregivers often feared a sudden decline in the elder's health, and, in particular, "something happening with no one around." Several family members expressed anxiety and guilt about going to work or returning to their own homes, and leaving the elder in the care of others.

Well, I worry every single day about her falling down and stuff like that, and what's going to be the next trigger that sends her back to the hospital for the next surgery that she can barely tolerate or not at all—that whole thing (48-year-old son)

Becoming a Burden

A major concern of most of the elders was the fear of experiencing a long trajectory of decline, and becoming a burden on their families:

Well, I'd like to go fast. I don't want to suffer a lot and make everybody else suffer a lot. That would be important. My husband had Alzheimer's and that was just pathetic, watching him for ten years go downhill . . . most families now-a-days are half crazy with trying to make a living . . . they have to spend so much time with the woman working and the man working, and then to add the care of an elderly patient is just too much for them, it overburdens them so that they, the parent or the aunt or grandmother, whoever it is, begins to feel well I don't want to bother my children with this, I'll just let it go which is what I do to some extent. (82-year-old female elder)

Family caregivers did not share the concern that their elders were becoming burdens; most did not question their responsibility to provide care and support for the elders.

Anticipating Survivors' Wellbeing

Many elders worried about the needs and wellbeing of their families after their impending death. They were primarily concerned about family members' grief and ability to cope with the loss:

Just to keep my daughter as calm as possible—that's the main thing. I don't want to upset her any more than I have to. What can you do? Your parents die, that's going to happen, so . . . there is nothing to be done about it but I want to, want her to be as calm as possible. (82-year old female elder)

One elder was also specifically anxious about the spiritual wellbeing of her children and grandchildren after she died:

Well, to know that they're taken care of—their health and they're able to—their religion—stay with that. And then I hear about some of them giving up religion and they're all becoming atheists—it makes me feel kind of blue. I don't like to hear that. (101-year-old female elder)

Some elder participants worried more about practical concerns (e.g., medical bills, taxes, or loss of income) that would affect their loved ones. Many expressed regrets that they would not be around to look out for family members after death.

Well, the thing I'd be concerned about is my wife and the kids, and the house and stuff, you know? All the bills should be paid, or whatever. Well, she'd be living here by herself, you know? And if she was taken care of, or whatever she has to do—I don't think she'd ever get remarried again, but I imagine it'd be tough for her to keep on rolling, keeping the house maybe. The taxes ain't cheap. (64-year-old male elder)

I just hope that the kids will get along fine, and the grandkids, that's it. And hope the world straightens out a little bit better. All this terrorism and stuff, I don't like that but that's way beyond my help. (80-year-old male elder)

Family caregivers echoed these concerns with their own worries about life after the elder's death. Some concerns were about their anticipation of grief and loss, but several caregivers worried about pragmatic matters such as arranging funeral plans and paying bills.

[My fears are] stupid. [Laughs], My worries are about her funeral, okay? That it will come at a really bad time, like when I'm in the middle of three hundred and forty report cards and my house is a mess, you know, and that kind of stuff that, that I won't know what to do. That there will be a division, and fighting like over the paintings and things like that [Laughs]. I want her to write people's names on the backs of the paintings so I won't have to deal with it. (50-year-old daughter)

Concerns about End-of-Life Care

In addition to their worries about dying, elders and family caregivers articulated their concerns and care preferences regarding the care the elders would receive from healthcare team members in their last days. Specifically, they reported four major preferences.

Receiving Competent, Consistent and Responsive Care

Elders and family caregivers felt that quality care required the involvement of skilled healthcare professionals who were competent, "consistent and responsive" to the elders' needs. For elders, it was of critical importance to feel they could depend on reliable caregivers that met their basic needs:

Well [hospice] volunteers means that no one person would come every week, instead you would probable get a stream of people coming in, none of whom you knew and I don't like that idea at all . . . . Just that whoever takes care of me shows me respect . . . taking good care of me. You know, keeping me clean and fed and whatever. If I can't eat—well that's another thing but . . . I just think to take good care of me, see that my needs were taken care of. (82-year-old female elder)

For family members, these concerns seemed to be associated with their anxieties about meeting the elders' escalating needs as death approached (see above). Their descriptions of adequate care often emphasized the medical and concrete aspects of care (e.g., keeping the elder safe and clean, and ensuring their adherence to medication regimens):

Her body is so fragile and her skin is so, you know, tender, so I mean for them making sure she's gets the proper hygiene. And medical, um, well granny won't take a lot of medical, but I mean, but they're there for any medical needs. But, I think, just trying to make her comfortable as possible. (48-year-old grandson)

Managing Pain

Elders and family caregivers were concerned that the elders receive good pain control and prompt alleviation of physical discomfort at the end of their lives. For several participants, this was a primary reason for choosing hospice or palliative care services:

Well that, the hospitals, they never used to give you enough painkiller to make enough difference because they said you were going to become addicted. Well what difference does it make at that point? And so I would want someone managing that and I . . . I think I would want to go to hospice and let them handle it. (86-year-old female elder)

I happen to be a big proponent of hospice-type transitions from life to death. And, I'm a big believer in you make the person comfortable. At that point, I don't care if he gets hooked on a particular drug. It's irrelevant. But if he could have his needs tended to, the pain alleviated, and the transition as smooth as possible, I'd rather see that—except to go quickly. (48-year-old daughter-in-law)

Being Treated with Dignity and Respect

Elders and family caregivers also agreed that respectful treatment was of paramount concern in end-of-life care. For elders, this meant appreciating their need for autonomy and control, and being cared for in a courteous, compassionate manner. Family members also articulated the importance of having providers who treated the elders with dignity and valued each patient as a unique, "whole person":

Just that, that whole, you know, just having respect and beauty and concern around. . . . But a nursing home staff in all fairness is totally overloaded, I mean so it's not like totally all their fault. It's our system's fault, it's like, we don't value that so much. (50-year-old daughter)

To try to meet the person on their own level. In my mother's case, in other words, to try and find out what is important to that person and take an interest in those things with them. Share with them those things. If someone thinks clipping coupons is important, than the social worker who's coming says look at all these coupons I found, we can go get such and such at so and so or if the person is a musician and the social worker would come and say well I have a new recording of so and so's orchestra doing such and such. (52-year-old daughter)

Living While Dying

Many of the elders thought it was important to continue living as they had their entire lives. "Focusing on living" instead of dying included eating the foods they loved, participating in activities they enjoyed (e.g., walking, sewing, card-playing, and socializing) with friends and family.

Just comradeship. . . . [Having] people that are around that I will talk with, or will talk with me, and you would miss them if you don't see them at least once a week, or more than that. (84-year-old male elder)

This concern was associated with the desire to be treated with dignity and respect, and to die at home in the context of intimate surroundings, people, and routines! Elders emphasized the critical importance of having a measure of control over their lives and choice in their care during the dying process.

Well, if I could eat—to get some decent food—and they wouldn't cut me off my martinis or beer. That's about all. (80-year-old male elder)

Although not often a primary concern, most family caregivers expressed an understanding of how important it was for the elder to continue "living while dying," and sought to provide them with opportunities to enjoy their cherished activities.

Well, I think she wants to maintain a sense of normalcy, that things are still the way they used to be as much as possible. So even if life is slipping away, she still can enjoy it. She can still feel at home. So little things, like being able to watch her favorite television shows. . . . Being able to get out—she likes to get out and drive around. You know, just anything that would make her feel normal. So eating the types of things that she's enjoyed in the past, being able to go to a movie with us, go for a drive with the relatives. All the types of things like that. (48-year-old son)

A "Good Death"

In response to a being asked to describe a good death, participants expressed their fundamental end-of-life preferences for the elders' final days.

Dying at Home

Almost all participants expressed a preference for the elder to die at home. Dying at home was viewed as a more "natural death," where elders could more easily be surrounded by friends and family, and their final wishes could be best met. Several family caregivers worried that the patient's needs might outstrip the supports and resources necessary to keep the elder at home until death, but preferred that the death take place at home if at all possible.

Dying Quickly, Without Suffering

For elders and family members, the ideal death was seen as one where the elder dies swiftly, "peacefully, and without pain." One patient summed this perspective up memorably:

> Just let me die. Quickly. Fast. And painlessly. . . . Stand out there and have lightening strike me, or anything that would do me in like that! (84-year-old male elder)

Many imagined a "natural" death, spending their last moments comfortably ensconced in a favorite chair or sitting in a garden surrounded by natural beauty. Some hoped they would simply be able to "go to sleep and not wake up":

> Good death would be able to roll out in a wheelchair onto a garden patio and be surrounded by beautiful flowers, you know, I mean that would be all right. Just that . . . having respect and beauty and concern around you. (50-year-old daughter)
>
> He would sit down in his chair and he wouldn't wake up. That would be ideal. (48-year-old daughter-in-law)

Avoiding High-tech Life Support

For most elders, the desire to die naturally meant not having to accept unwanted intervention, and not taking advantage of feeding or breathing "tubes," or other medical technologies meant to prolong their lives.

> Well, I don't want this—I don't want to be resuscitated. If I'm going I want to go, and that's supposed to prevent them from putting me on any machines. I don't want to wake up a lunatic or something, you know, be alive—breathing but not knowing what's going on. I don't want that. . . . I want to go—no life saving treatments for me. It might be a terrible thing to say. . . . It's my life. (80-year-old male elder)

For the most part, family caregivers reported that they respected these concerns and believed it important to follow their elders' preferences, even if they did not share them:

> Um yes, we, we talked, we talked about it and she just basically wants to be at home, not hooked up to any machines um, you know, just to die naturally, you know, just go. She don't want to go to a revival or resuscitory thing, you know, she dies, she just wants to die, you know. (47-year-old grandson)

Being Prepared

The elders expressed a preference to be made aware of their impending death so that they could "get things in order." Many worked to develop a sense of completion in their lives, had arranged their financial and other affairs, and felt to some extent prepared to die. Those who did not feel a sense of completion or closure reported that having time for preparation was quite important to them.

> Well, I wouldn't want to go in my sleep. I'd want to prepare better. I'd want some doctor to say "[Name], you only have two days, three days, six days," whatever and then I can prepare myself better—get things straightened out with the kids, get my will set, and just have a priest with me and that's all. I don't want to die in my sleep. (80-year-old male elder)

Family caregivers were not aware of and did not share the elders' desire to be prepared for death, although some shared regrets that they had not talked enough or spent enough time with elders when they were still "able to do things."

Addressing Spiritual Needs

Many family members hoped their loved ones would achieve "peace of mind" at the end of their lives, and felt this was an important component of a good death. This sense of peace was most often expressed in spiritual or religious terms; several family members hoped that elders would achieve "spiritual closure" through faith and prayer, and wanted them to have access to clergy to talk with about their spiritual concerns.

> I guess it's um, being taken care of spiritually . . . contacting the people at the church. And have somebody come talk to him, and um, give him a peace of mind. (56-year-old son)

Although we asked questions about faith, spirituality, and religion, there was a great deal of variability in the extent to which faith was important to the elders. Most denied that having their spiritual or faith needs addressed were essential to a "good death" in the way they were to family caregivers.

Communication about End-of-Life Care Preferences

As part of our analysis, the researchers examined the ways in which families talked about death and dying, and how family communication influenced the congruence between participants in expressed challenges, concerns, and preferences. When asked about the extent to which they had discussed dying or their care preferences with family members, the majority of elders and family members—six of the ten dyads—indicated they had not done so. Three elders believed the lack of communication was due to their own lack of desire to talk about dying or end-of-life care with family members. Two others reported that it was difficult to talk about these subjects with family, either due to their own or their family members' discomfort.

> It doesn't make me feel uncomfortable but I can't think of anything that I could, that I can add to it that I haven't already thought about. . . . No, I think I'd like to talk to them about that. They don't seem to want to talk about it—'cause it's an unpleasant thing and they don't always go for it—kind of push it back. But I want to talk a little more about this. (82-year-old male elder)

Four families indicated that they had talked about dying and discussed the elders' care preferences. Even though she had talked with her husband, one caregiver indicated that she found these conversations about dying and his care preferences extremely uncomfortable.

Table 3 Communication Patterns and Congruence in End-of-Life Care Preferences

Communication Pattern	Congruence	Incongruence
Communication Constraints	3	3
Open Communication	4	0

In order to examine the relationship, if any, between participants' communication patterns and congruence in end-of-life care preferences, we compared the responses of families who reported communication constraints with those who reported open communication. As illustrated in Table 3, the level of congruence was much higher among families reporting open communication regarding dying and end-of-life care. None of the four families with open communication and half of the six families with communication constraints shared end-of-life concerns or preferences that were not congruent. Examples of the latter include: the 84-year-old male elder who stated a preference to be alone at the time of death, and his 47-year-old daughter who reported he wished to be surrounded by family; the 101-year-old female elder who expressed a strong desire to be kept informed of her evolving health status whose 67-year-old son preferred her not to be informed of these changes; and the 64-year-old male elder who expressed a strong desire to die at home without the use of life-sustaining machines, contrasting his 55-year-old wife's preference for him to die at the hospital, with full access to medical and technological resources.

Discussion

The findings of this study were generally consistent with the empirical literature on congruence between patients and surrogate decision-makers, which suggests that agreement about dying and end-of-life care ranges from poor to moderate (Engelberg et al., 2005; Moorman & Carr, 2008; Mularski et al., 2004). Elder participants acknowledged their need for support and care as their illnesses progressed, but—in contrast to family caregivers—most strongly valued their independence, and wanted to maintain control over their lives and continue to participate in activities they enjoyed. This parallels the finding that family members often underestimate the patient's need for autonomy and control over their own care (Farber et al., 2003; McSkimming et al., 1999; Singer, et al., 1999; Vig & Pearlman, 2004). Elders were greatly concerned about becoming a burden on their families, echoing another well-documented finding, particularly with older patients (McPherson et al., 2007; Vig & Pearlman, 2004).

The lack of apparent spiritual or religious needs on the part of the elders may be due, in part, to the lack of minority elder participants; a wealth of prior research suggests spirituality is of primary importance to African Americans and Latinos at the end of life (Born, Greiner, Sylvia, & Ahluwalia, 2004; Waters, 2001). One African-American elder shared that she spent all of her waking hours in prayer, but she too denied a desire to talk with others about her faith. This may reflect a perception that spiritual needs are felt to be intrinsic, and not as something that requires intervention from others.

Family caregivers felt most challenged by the responsibilities of managing and providing adequate care, and were concerned about their capacity to meet their loved ones' physical and spiritual needs as the illness progressed. The preeminence of these concerns is consistent with the literature (Terry et al., 2006) and reflects the high level of cognitive, emotional, and physical investment made by family caregivers at the end of life (Waldrop et al., 2005). Although other researchers have found strong congruence around the importance of preparation and a sense of completion in determining a good death (Engelberg et al., 2005; Steinhauser et al., 2000), in this study only elder participants identified this as a significant preference. Unlike the elders, family caregivers were concerned about elders' spiritual wellbeing, and felt that achieving "peace of mind" was essential to experiencing a good death.

Despite these differences, elders and family caregivers reported many congruent concerns and preferences. Consistent with the literature on quality of life at the end of life, most elders and family caregivers preferred that the elder die at home (Tang & McCorkle, 2003; Steinhauser et al., 2000), and for death to come swiftly, without pain or suffering (Heyland et al., 2006; Vig & Pearlman, 2004). Experiencing loss related to the elders' physical, functional, and cognitive decline, and managing advanced illness in the face of an uncertain and unpredictable future were among the most difficult challenges reported by the elders and their care-givers. Accepting the inherent uncertainty and ambiguity of the dying process may indeed be one of the more significant challenges for terminally ill patients and their families (Bern-Klug, 2004; Gardner, 2008; McKechnie, Macleod & Keeling, 2007). Elders and family caregivers also shared concerns about the wellbeing of survivors following the patient's eventual death.

There was particularly consistent agreement regarding end-of-life care preferences, specifically around the importance of reliable, high-quality care, and the avoidance of life-sustaining treatment. Another shared concern was that elders be treated with dignity and respect by formal caregivers, and would be allowed to continue living until death, a finding echoed in the literature (Chochinov et al., 2002). A finding not compatible with prior literature was the shared preference of elders and family caregivers to avoid using life-sustaining treatment. Many studies suggest that family members are less likely than older patients to prefer life-support, and that surrogates often underestimate elders' preference for aggressive measures at the end of life (Hamel, Lynn, Teno, Covinsky, Wu, Galanos et al., 2000; Pruchno, Lemay, Field, & Levinsky, 2005). The present finding may be another artifact of a sample that includes few minority elders, who are more likely than white patients to prefer life-sustaining medical treatment (Phipps, True, Harris, Chong,

Tester, Chavin et al., 2003; Steinhauser et al., 2000). Nonetheless, the findings suggest the need for further exploration of patients and family preferences for life-sustaining treatment.

Replicating findings from prior research (Parker, Clayton, Hancock, Walder, Butow, Carrick et al., 2007; Teno, Lynn, Wenger, Phillips, Murphy, Connors et al., 1997), a minority of families had communicated with each other about end-of-life concerns and preferences. Despite the advantages of open family communication (Metzger & Gray, 2008), the literature on advance care planning and family communication suggests that less than 20% actually talk about dying and their preferences for care (Bradley & Rizzo, 1999; Rosnick & Reynolds, 2003; Teno et al., 1997). Lack of communication can contribute to family conflict between the elder and family surrogates, difficulties in decision-making and advance care planning, and ultimately to poorer quality end-of-life care (Kramer, Boelk, & Auer, 2006). This corroborates our finding that a lack of communication was associated with greater incongruence, and suggests the importance of future research on the impact of family conflict on end-of-life experiences and outcomes.

Conclusions & Implications

While many of these findings were consistent with the literature on congruence in patient and caregiver perceptions, the current study is unusual in that it compared the subjective experiences of older chronically and terminally ill patients with those of their matched family caregivers. This study confirms that end-of-life concerns and care preferences found with broader populations also apply to frail elders and their caregivers. The findings further suggest that there may be more family congruence around preferences for end-of-life care than around challenges, concerns, and wishes related to dying. Open family communication was associated with greater congruence in patient and family preferences, which supports prior findings that open communication is associated with better adjustment in family caregivers after the death of their loved ones (Kramer, 1997; Metzger & Gray, 2008). These results have important implications for intervention and research, as they highlight potential sources of unmet needs and conflict among dying elders and their family members.

Although there were more areas of congruence than incongruence among family members, the findings of this study suggest that healthcare professionals providing end-of-life care would be prudent to view family reports as imperfect proxies for elder's concerns, challenges, and preferences. Principle domains of incongruence included the elders' difficulties in accepting dependence, their fears of becoming a burden, and desire to be prepared for death. Unlike the elders, family caregivers were primarily concerned with providing adequate care to meet the elders' physical and spiritual care needs. The study highlights the need for more focused and comprehensive assessment of terminally ill elders and their family caregivers, and for sensitivity to potential differences in preferences and concerns.

It is perhaps not surprising that elders and family caregivers viewed the end-of-life experience somewhat differently, given their different ages, roles, and perspectives. Incongruence presents difficulties only when patients and caregivers with different views are unable to communicate openly and resolve differences with each other (de Haes & Teunissen, 2005). Family conflict and communication constraints can present significant barriers to the provision of quality care, the completion of advance directives, and the attainment of a "good death" (Covinsky, Fuller, Yaffe, Johnston, Hamel, Lynn et al., 2000; Kramer et al., 2006). Terminally ill elders and their families may therefore derive particular benefit from interventions that address congruent and incongruent experiences, and teach communication and family problem-solving skills around the end-of-life and end-of-life care. Working to enhance families' efforts to talk about and resolve differences, and to make informed decisions about care is fundamental to facilitating advance care planning, and reducing inappropriate procedures and hospitalizations.

There were some limitations to this study, which involved a small, non-representative sample of primarily white, low-income elders, recruited purposively from a unique comprehensive health and long-term care program in the Midwest. Casual generalizations should not, therefore, be made to other populations of terminally ill elders and family caregivers. The sample lacked heterogeneity in terms of race/ethnicity, and cultural factors have been shown to be important variables in end-of-life preferences (Phipps et al., 2003). There was also a good deal of variability in medical diagnosis, elders' living situations, and family caregivers' relationships to the elder, all of which may have influenced the findings.

Despite these limitations, this qualitative study identifies subjective concerns and care preferences of terminally ill elders and their family caregivers at the end of life. The findings highlight the need for more focused and comprehensive assessment of terminally ill elders and their family caregivers, and attention to potential differences in patient and family preferences and concerns. Further research into this population's unique needs and perceptions, including the dynamics of family communication and decision making at the end of life, is necessary to further healthcare efforts to better meet elders' psychosocial needs, enhance their wellbeing, and facilitate a "good death." Understanding elders' experiences and preferences, identifying areas of congruence and incongruence, and improving communication in families are essential to providing quality end-of-life care to all dying patients and their families.

References

Bern-Klug, M. (2004). The Ambiguous Dying Syndrome. *Health and Social Work, 29*(1), 55–65.

Born, W., Greiner, K., Sylvia, E., & Ahluwalia, J. (2004). Knowledge, attitudes, and beliefs about end-of-life care among inner-city African Americans and Latinos. *Journal of Palliative Medicine, 7*(2), 247–256.

Bradley, E., & Rizzo, J. (1999). Public information and private search: Evaluating the Patient Self-Determination Act. *Journal of Health Politics, Policy and Law, 24*(2), 239–273.

Chochinov, H., Hack, T., Hassard, L., Kristjianson, S., McClement, S., & Harlos, M. (2002). Dignity in the terminally ill: A cross-sectional, cohort study. *The Lancet, 360,*(9350), 2026–2030.

Cohen, S. R., & Leis, A. (2002). What determines the quality of life of terminally ill cancer patients form their own perspective? *Journal of Palliative Care, 18*(1), 48–58.

Covinsky, K., Fuller, J., Yaffe, K., Johnston, C., Hamel, M., Lynn, J., et al. (2000). Communication and decision-making in seriously ill patients: Findings of the SUPPORT project. *Journal of the American Geriatrics Society, 48*(5), S187–S193.

Crabtree, B., & Miller, W. (1999). Using codes and code manuals: A template organizing style of interpretation. In B. F. Crabtree & W.L. Miller (Eds.), *Doing qualitative research* (2nd ed., pp. 163–178). Thousand Oaks, CA: Sage.

de Haes, H., & Teunissen, S. (2005). Communication in palliative care: A review of recent literature. *Current Opinion in Oncology, 17*(4), 345–350.

Desbiens, N., & Mueller-Rizner, N. (2000). How well do surrogates assess the pain of seriously ill patients? *Critical Care Medicine, 28,* 1347–1352.

Emanuel, L., von Gunten, C., & Ferris, F. (2000). Gaps in end-of-life care. *Archives of Family Medicine, 9,* 1176–1180.

Engelberg, R., Patrick, D., & Curtis, J. (2005). Correspondence between patients' preferences and surrogates' understandings for dying and death. *Journal of Pain and Symptom Management, 30*(6), 498–509.

Farber, S., Egnew, T., Herman-Bertch, J., Taylor, T., & Guldin, G. (2003). Issues in end-of-life care: Patient, caregiver, and clinician perceptions. *Journal of Palliative Medicine, 6*(1), 19–31.

Field, M. J., & Cassel, C. K. (Eds.). (1997). *Approaching death: Improving care at the end of Life.* Institute of Medicine. Washington, DC: National Academy Press.

Gallo, W., Baker, M., & Bradley, E. (2001). Factors associated with home versus institutional death among cancer patients in Connecticut. *Journal of the American Geriatrics Society, 49,* 771–777.

Gardner, D. (2008). Cancer in a dyadic context: Older couples' negotiation of ambiguity and meaning in end-of-life. *Journal of Social Work in End-of-life and Palliative Care, 4*(2), 1–25.

Hamel, M., Lynn, J., Teno, J., Covinsky, K., Wu, A., Galanos, A., et al. (2000). Age-related differences in care preferences, treatment decisions, and clinical outcomes of seriously ill, hospitalized adults: Lessons from SUPPORT. *Journal of the American Geriatrics Society, 48*(5/Supplement), S176–S182.

Heyland, D., Dodek, P., Rocker, G., Groll, D., Garni, A., Pichora, D., et al. (2006). What matters most in end-of-life care: perceptions of seriously ill patients and their family members. *Canadian Medical Association Journal, 174*(5), 627–633.

Higginson, I., & Sen-Gupta, G. (2000). Place of care in advanced cancer: a qualitative systematic literature review of patient preferences. *Journal of Palliative Medicine, 3*(3), 287–300.

Kramer, B. J., & Auer, C. (2005). Challenges to providing end-of-life care to low-income elders with advanced chronic disease: Lessons learned from a model program. *The Gerontologist, 45,* 651–660.

Kramer, B. J., Boelk, A., & Auer, C. (2006). Family conflict at the end of life: Lessons learned in a model program for vulnerable older adults. *Journal of Palliative Care 9*(3), 791–801.

Kramer, B. J., Christ, G., Bern-Klug, M., & Francoeur, R. (2005). A national agenda for social work research in palliative and end-of-life care. *Journal of Palliative Medicine 8,* 418–431.

Kramer, D. (1997). How women relate to terminally ill husbands and their subsequent adjustment to bereavement. *Omega: Journal of Death and Dying, 34*(2), 93–106.

Laakkonen, M., Pitkala, K., & Strandberg, T. (2004). Terminally ill elderly patients' experiences, attitudes, and needs: A qualitative study. *Omega: Journal of Death and Dying, 49*(2), 117–129.

McCormick, T., & Conley, B. (1995). Patients' perspectives on dying and on the care of dying patients. *Western Journal of Medicine, 163*(3), 236–243.

McKechnie, R., Macleod, R., & Keeling, S. (2007). Facing uncertainty: The lived experience of palliative care. *Palliative and Supportive Care, 5,* 367–376.

McPherson, C., & Addington-Hall, (2003). Judging the quality of care at the end of life: Can proxies provide reliable information? *Social Science and Medicine, 56,* 95–109.

McPherson, C., Wilson, K., & Murray, M. (2007). Feeling like a burden: Exploring the perspectives of patients at the end of life. *Social Science & Medicine, 64*(2), 417–427.

McPherson, C., Wilson, K., Lobchuk, M., & Brajtman, S. (2008). Family caregivers' assessment of symptoms in patients with advanced cancer: Concordance with patients and factors affecting accuracy. *Journal of Pain Symptom Management, 35*(1), 70–82.

McSkimming, S., Hodges, M., Super, A., Driever, M., Schoessler, M., Franey, S. G., et al. (1999). The experience of life-threatening illness: Patients' and their loved ones' perspectives. *Journal of Palliative Medicine, 2*(2), 173–184.

Metzger, P., & Gray, M. (2008). End-of-life communication and adjustment: Pre-loss communication as a predictor of bereavement-related outcomes. *Death Studies, 32*(4), 301–325.

Moorman, S., & Carr, D. (2008). Spouses' effectiveness as end-of-life surrogates: Accuracy, uncertainty, and errors of overtreatment or undertreatment. *Gerontologist, 48*(6), 811–819.

Morrison, S. (2005). Health care system factors affecting end-of-life care. *Journal of Palliative Medicine, 8*(Supplement 1), S79–S87.

Mularski, R., Curtis, R., Osborne, M., Engelberg, R., & Ganzini, L. (2004). Agreement among family members and their assessment of the quality of dying and death. *Journal of Pain and Symptom Management, 28*(4), 306–315.

National Consensus Project (2004). *Clinical practice guidelines for quality palliative care.* Brooklyn, NY.

National Institutes of Health (NIH). (2004). *State-of-the-science conference on improving end-of-life care: Conference statement.* Bethesda, MD: National Institutes of Health.

Padgett, D. K. (2008). *Qualitative methods in social work research: Challenges and rewards* (2nd ed.). Thousands Oaks, CA: Sage Publications, Inc.

Parker, S., Clayton, J., Hancock, K., Walder, S., Butow, P., & Carrick, S. et al. (2007). A systematic review of prognostic/end-of-life communication with adults in the advanced stages of a life-limiting illness: Patient/care-giver preferences for the content, style, and timing of information. *Journal of Pain and Symptom Management, 34*(1), 81–93.

Patton, M. (2002). *Qualitative research and evaluation methods* (3rd ed.). Thousands Oaks, CA: Sage Publications, Inc.

Phipps, E., True, G., Harris, D., Chong, U., Tester, W., Chavin, S., et al. (2003). Approaching the end of life: Attitudes, preferences, and behaviors of African-American and white patients and their family caregivers. *Journal of Clinical Oncology, 21*(3), 549–554.

Pritchard, R., Fisher, E., Teno, J., Sharp, S., Reding, D., Knaus, W., et al. (1998). Influence of patient preferences and local health system characteristics on the place of death. (SUPPORT Investigators: Study to Understand Prognoses and Preferences for Risks and Outcomes of Treatment). *Journal of the American Geriatrics Society, 46*(10), 1242–1250.

Pruchno, R., Lemay, E., Field, L., & Levinsky, N. (2005). Spouse as health care proxy for dialysis patients: Whose preferences matter? *Gerontologist, 45*(6), 812–819.

Rosnick, C., & Reynolds, S. (2003). Thinking ahead: Factors associated with executing advance directives. *Journal of Aging & Health, 15*(2), 409–429.

Scholz, R. and Tietje, R. (2002). *Embedded case study methods: Integrating quantitative and qualitative knowledge.* Thousand Oaks, CA: Sage Publications.

Shalowitz, D., Garrett-Meyer, E., & Wendler, D. (2006). The accuracy of surrogate decision makers: A systematic review. *Archives of Internal Medicine, 166,* 493–497.

Singer P., Martin D., & Kellner M. (1999). Quality end-of-life care: patients' perspectives. *Journal of the American Medical Association, 281,* 163–168.

Sneeuw, K., Sprangers, M., & Aaronson, N. (2002). The role of health care providers and significant others in evaluating the quality of life of patients with chronic disease. *Journal of Clinical Epidemiology, 55*(11), 1130–1143.

Steinhauser A., Christakis N., Clipp E., McNeilly M., McIntyre L., & Tulsky J. (2000). Factors considered important at the end of life by patients, family, physicians, and other care providers. *Journal of the American Medical Association, 284*(19), 2476–2482.

Sulmasy, D., Terry, P., Weisman, C., Miller, D., Stallings, R., Vettese, M., et al. (1998). The accuracy of substituted judgments in patients with terminal disease. *Annals of Internal Medicine, 128*(8), 621–629.

SUPPORT Principal Investigators (1995). A controlled trial to improve care for seriously ill hospitalized patients: The study to understand prognosis and preferences for outcomes and risks for treatments (SUPPORT). *Journal of the American Medical Association, 274*(20), 1591–1598.

Tang, S., & McCorkle, R. (2003). Determinants of congruence between the preferred and actual place of death for terminally ill cancer patients. *Journal of Palliative Care 19*(4), 230–237.

Teno, J., Clarridge, B., Casey, V., Welch, L., Wetle, T., Shield, R., et al. (2004). Family perspectives on end-of-life care at the last place of care. *Journal of the American Medical Association, 291*(1), 88–93.

Teno, J., Lynn, J., Wenger, N., Phillips, R., Murphy, D., Connors, A., et al. (1997). Advance directives for seriously ill hospitalized patients: Effectiveness with the patient self-determination act and the SUPPORT intervention. SUPPORT Investigators. *Journal of the American Geriatric Society, 45*(4), 500–507.

Terry, W., Olson, L., Wilss, L., & Boulton-Lewis, G. (2006). Experience of dying: Concerns of dying patients and of carers. *Internal Medicine Journal, 36*(6), 338–346.

Thomas, C., Morris, S., & Clark, D. (2004). Place of death: Preferences among cancer patients and their carers. *Social Science & Medicine, 58,* 2431–2444.

Vig, E., Davenport, N., & Pearlman, R. (2002). Good deaths, bad deaths, and preferences for the end of life: A qualitative study of geriatric outpatients. *Journal of the American Geriatric Society, 50*(9), 1541–1548.

Waldrop, D., Kramer, B.J., Skretny, J., Milch, R., & Finn, W. (2005). Final transitions: Family caregiving at the end of life. *Journal of Palliative Medicine, 8*(3), 623–638.

Waters, C. (2001). Understanding and supporting African Americans' perspectives of end-of-life care planning and decision making. *Qualitative Health Research, 11,* 385–398.

Vig, E. & Pearlman, R. (2004). Good and bad dying from the perspective of terminally ill men. *Archives of Internal Medicine, 164*(9), 977–981.

Yin, R. (2003). *Case study research: Design and methods* (3rd ed.). Thousand Oaks, CA: Sage Publications.

Zettel-Watson, L., Ditto, P., Danks, J., & Smucker, W. (2008). Actual and perceived gender differences in the accuracy of surrogate decisions about life-sustaining medical treatment among older spouses. *Death Studies, 32*(3), 273–290.

Critical Thinking

1. What are the barriers to quality end-of-life care?

2. What were the major worries and fears about dying expressed by the elders and their family caregivers?

3. What were the end-of-life preferences for the elders in their final days?

Acknowledgements—The authors' extend their appreciation to Elder Care Partnerships staff and administration, and to End-of-Life committee members who provided ongoing support and consultation. Special thanks to the elders and their family members who offered their valuable insights.

UNIT 3

The Dying Process

Unit Selections

15. **Dying on the Streets: Homeless Persons' Concerns and Desires about End-of-Life Care,** John Song et al.
16. **Death and Dying Across Cultures,** Gihan ElGindy
17. **The Promise of Presence,** Paul Rosseau
18. **When Death Strikes without Warning,** Jennifer Couzin
19. **Are They Hallucinations or Are They Real?, The Spirituality of Deathbed and Near-Death Visions,** L. Stafford Betty
20. **Beyond Terror and Denial: The Positive Psychology of Death Acceptance,** Paul T.P. Wong and Adrian Tomer

Learning Outcomes

After reading this unit you should be able to:

- Talk somewhat knowingly about homeless persons' concerns/desires about end-of-life care.
- Relate to what nurses cross-culturally and via different religious backgrounds need to know in order to deal with persons at the end of life.
- Discuss the spirit hypothesis regarding deathbed and near-death visions.
- Point out weaknesses of the spirit hypothesis regarding deathbed and near-death visions.
- Discuss the various meanings of death acceptance and death denial.
- Talk with knowledge about sudden unexpected death in epilepsy.

Student Website
www.mhhe.com/cls

Internet References

American Academy of Hospice and Palliative Medicine
www.aahpm.org
Hospice Foundation of America
www.hospicefoundation.org
Hospice Care
http://hospice-cares.com
National Prison Hospice Association
www.npha.org
The Zen Hospice Project
www.zenhospice.org

While death comes at varied ages and in differing circumstances, for most of us there will be time to reflect on our lives, our relationships, our work, and what our expectations are for the ending of life. This is called the dying process. In recent decades, a broad range of concerns has arisen about that process and how aging, dying, and death can be confronted in ways that are enlightening, enriching, and supportive. Efforts have been made to delineate and define various stages in the process of dying so that comfort and acceptance of our inevitable death will be eased. The fear of dying may heighten significantly when actually given the prognosis of a terminal illness by one's physician. Awareness of approaching death allows us to come to grips with the profound emotional upheaval that will be experienced. Fears of the experience of dying are often more in the imagination than in reality. Yet, when the time comes and death is forecast for the very near future, it is reality, a situation that may be more fearful for some than others.

Perhaps you know someone who has communicated with and even "seen" a deceased family member or friend. What is really happening here? Is such an experience an hallucination or is it real? L. Stafford Betty looks into this "twilight zone" to determine if such is real or a mere hallucination.

Homeless individuals seem somewhat segregated from the rest of the population, yet what are their feelings about death away from home, as dying in one's home seemingly is the all-American way to die? John Song and colleagues address this issue in their article regarding homeless persons' concerns about end-of-life issues.

Death across cultures and religions, as to what nurses need to know, is presented by Gihan ElGindy. Nurses are at the "front line" on their eight-hour shifts in the hospital relating to patients,

© Fuse/Getty Images

thus they see patients as their health improves or deteriorates. Nurses, therefore, are pivotal in helping patients cope with the dying process.

Dr. Paul Rousseau's article reminds us to always follow up on something we promised, perhaps especially true when relating to an individual in the latter stages of a terminal illness. Not everyone dies a lingering death; some individuals die rather unexpectedly. Such is the case described by Jennifer Couzin as she addresses the devastating effect of epilepsy and sudden death.

Though we all will eventually die, American society tends to deny death—it won't happen to me. Paul T. P. Wong and Adrian Tomer's article highlights the importance to psychology of focusing on death acceptance, not death denial.

Dying on the Streets
Homeless Persons' Concerns and Desires about End-of-Life Care

Background: There is little understanding about the experiences and preferences at the end of life (EOL) for people from unique cultural and socioeconomic backgrounds. Homeless individuals are extreme examples of these overlooked populations; they have the greatest risk of death, encounter barriers to health care, and lack the resources and relationships assumed necessary for appropriate EOL care. Exploring their desires and concerns will provide insight for the care of this vulnerable and disenfranchised population, as well as others who are underserved.

Objective: Explore the concerns and desires for EOL care among homeless persons.

Design: Qualitative study utilizing focus groups.

Participants: Fifty-three homeless persons recruited from agencies providing homeless services.

Measurements: In-depth interviews, which were audiotaped and transcribed.

Results: We present 3 domains encompassing 11 themes arising from our investigation, some of which are previously unreported. Homeless persons worried about dying and EOL care; had frequent encounters with death; voiced many unique fears, such as dying anonymously and undiscovered; favored EOL documentation, such as advance directives; and demonstrated ambivalence towards contacting family. They also spoke of barriers to EOL care and shared interventions to improve dying among the very poor and estranged.

Conclusions: Homeless persons have significant personal experience and feelings about death, dying, and EOL care, much of which is different from those previously described in the EOL literature about other populations. These findings have implications not only for homeless persons, but for others who are poor and disenfranchised.

JOHN SONG, MD, MPH, MAT[1,2], DIANNE M. BARTELS, RN, MA, PHD[1,2], EDWARD R. RATNER, MD[1,2], LUCY ALDERTON, MPH[4], BRENDA HUDSON, MS[3], AND JASJIT S. AHLUWALIA, MD, MPH, MS[2,3]

[1]*Center for Bioethics, University of Minnesota, N504 Boynton, 410 Church Street S.E., Minneapolis, MN 55455, USA;*

[2]*Medical School, University of Minnesota, Minneapolis, MN, USA;*

[3]*Academic Health Center, University of Minnesota, Minneapolis, MN, USA;*

[4]*Worldwide Epidemiology, GlaxoSmithKline, Mail Stop UP4305, Collegeville, PA 19426-0989, USA.*

Background

There remain many deficiencies in how society addresses the needs of dying individuals.[1] One shortcoming is the fundamental assumptions behind end-of-life (EOL) care: it focuses on individuals with loved ones, health care, and a home. Society has not considered homeless persons, who often die without these resources. It is necessary to address EOL care in this population for several reasons. First, the high prevalence of homelessness in the United States, with estimates ranging up to several million,[2] and the disproportionate amount and severity of illness in this population[3,4] is a public health crisis. Homeless persons also suffer high mortality rates—several times the rate of domiciled populations[5-7]—and premature mortality (average ages of death in Atlanta, San Francisco, and Seattle are 44, 41, and 47).[8,9] In addition, homeless persons encounter many barriers to health care[10-12] and, it may be hypothesized, to EOL care. Homeless persons, for example, die with little medical care immediately prior to their deaths.[13] Finally, additional concerns are raised by the unique personal, cultural, and medical characteristics of homelessness. Given the immediacy of basic human needs while living without shelter, homeless persons' concerns beyond daily survival may be different from those of persons who do not worry about food or shelter.

Few studies have addressed EOL care for underserved or disenfranchised persons,[1] and existing work is limited as it reflects the concerns of people with health care and personal resources and relationships. Three studies have previously examined homeless persons and EOL care. One demonstrated that homeless persons are eager to address EOL issues,[14] and a second explored EOL scenarios among homeless persons.[15] A third study addressed ICU care preferences.[16] The first 2 studies, however, are limited by their small and homogeneous samples, and the third focused on one specific aspect of EOL care.

This work represents the first in-depth exploration of a homeless population and their attitudes towards EOL care. We hypothesized that they would have concerns different from those of other previously studied populations. We previously reported how life on the streets influences attitudes towards death and dying (Song et al. submitted for publication) The present paper's objective was to examine how homelessness influences concerns and desires about care at the time of death.

Design

We conducted a qualitative investigation utilizing focus groups of homeless individuals. The study was funded by the NIH/National Institute of Nursing Research and approved by the University of Minnesota Institutional Review Board.

Participants

Participants were recruited from 6 social service agencies that serve homeless persons in Minneapolis and St. Paul, MN. These agencies provide a variety of services, including food, shelter, and health care. Participants were required to be at least 18 years old, speak English, and able to give informed consent. Participants were required to have been homeless at least once in the last 6 months, ascertained by a demographic questionnaire consistent with the federal guidelines.[17]

Participants were recruited through a mixture of random and purposive sampling, utilizing key informants[18]; details of this procedure are detailed elsewhere (Song et al. submitted for publication). Six focus groups were held, with an average of 9 participants per group. Participants were compensated $20. Interim analyses were conducted, and interviews were held until theme saturation was achieved.

Table 1 Interview Guide for Focus Groups

Questions

General questions

Do you have any experience with a serious illness or injury or a close friend or relative who had a serious illness or injury or who has died?

Are you concerned about dying?

Do you think about dying, care while dying, or death? Is this an issue that concerns you?

Is this an issue that you would like to talk about more?

Specific questions

Do you have any one that you can talk to about these issues?

  Probes: Do you have family that you are in contact with? Do you have friends that you trust? Do you know any social workers, service providers, or health care providers whom you trust?

What concerns do you have regarding dying, care at the end of life, and death?

  Probes: Are you concerned about what happens to your body? Your health care? Pain, symptom management, discomfort? Are you concerned about being stuck on life support? Are you concerned about dying alone?

If you were sick or dying, are there people you trust or love that you can get support from? Who can make decisions for you?

  Probes: Do you have family that you are in contact with? Do you have friends that you trust? Do you know any social workers, service providers, or health care providers whom you trust? Have you ever heard of a living will or durable power of health attorney?

Describe a "good death."

  Probes: Where would you like to die? Who would you like to have by your side? Who do you need to make peace with? What would you like to have happen to your body? What are you afraid of when dying?

What stands in the way of you having a good death?

  Probes: What stands in the way of good health care? What would you need to die in comfort and dignity? What are some problems with services that you have encountered?

What kind of services would you say would be needed so that homeless people might die in comfort and with dignity?

Measurement

Interviews were conducted between July 2003 and January 2004. A semistructured interview guide consisting of open-ended questions was developed through a pilot study,[14] community consultants, and the EOL and homelessness literature (Table 1).

The sessions were audio-taped and investigators took field notes on the group process and nonverbal communication, which served to contextualize the interviews and verify congruence of verbal and nonverbal communication.[18] Audiotapes were transcribed, and Atlas ti software was used to facilitate analysis.

Analysis

Investigators utilized a modified consensual qualitative research (CQR) approach to analyze data, which has proven effective in evaluating complex psychosocial phenomena.[19] This method involves an inductive analytic process to identify themes, which the team derives by consensus and verifies by systematically checking against the raw data.[19] This CQR approach incorporates a 3-step process to identify salient themes; details of CQR utilized by this team are provided elsewhere (Song et al. submitted for publication).

Results

Fifty-three people participated in the 6 focus groups. The mean age of participants was 47, and 35% were female. Thirty-six percent were identified as Native American, 8% reported an advanced degree, and 40% responded that they experienced more than one living situation during the last 6 months (Table 2).

Main outcomes were participants' concerns about and wishes for EOL care. We found 11 themes grouped into 3 domains, by locus of concern: personal themes, relational concerns, and environmental influences (Table 3).

Personal Themes

This domain involves participants' experiences with and attitudes towards EOL care. These results represent internal dynamics and considerations—the experiences that have influenced participants' conceptions about EOL care, including their wishes and concerns about their own care. Within the "personal theme" domain, we found 6 themes: experience with EOL care, fears and uncertainties, advance care planning, preferences/wishes/hopes, spirituality/religion, and veteran status (Table 3).

Experience with End of Life Care

Participants consistently had experiences with serious illnesses and deaths of loved ones or acquaintances, or their own encounters with serious illness. These experiences influenced their beliefs and attitudes towards EOL care. Past experiences with death and EOL care were frequently poor and frightening:

> When she (my mom) got sick, they put her in a nursing home, and they denied me access . . . she deteriorated, she lost her hair, she was almost comatose . . . I never got to see her. What they did to her I'll never know. One thing I knew—when she saw me she said, 'Call a taxi; get me out of here.' . . . So everything right now is in a nightmare. I'm trying to find out how she

Table 2 Participant Demographics

Characteristics	%
Age, years	
<35	15
36–45	25
46–55	45
56–65	9
>65	6
Gender	
Female	35
Race	
Hispanic or Latino	2
Not Hispanic or Latino	2
American Indian or Alaskan Native	36
Asian	2
Black or African American	27
Native African	2
Hawaiian/other Pacific Islander	0
White	22
Not reported	7
Years of education	
5–8	8
9–11	39
12–15	32
16+	8
Not reported	13

died . . . nobody told me . . . In my mind I'm thinking she's still alive . . . I never thought I'd lose my mom, or not in this way, not this hideous mess that happened that I can't understand.

This perception of EOL care as being out of the control of patients and family was common: "My mother lacked two weeks being 94 years old when she passed away. She was forced into a nursing home . . . She lost her freedom . . ." So, too, was the feeling that EOL care was unresponsive to the suffering party: "It was a situation where he didn't want to come out of there, living off the machine. When the time came for him to start to die, they wanted us to resuscitate him . . . That kind of weighed heavy on me because I thought I was letting him down. The last of his hours, he was kind of in pain. I just kept asking the doctor to give him something for his pain. They never did."

Because experiences contributed to an attitude that care is imposed, most interventions are seen as an unwanted and invasive: "After I saw my mom die, I'm almost thinking alone would be better. I don't want to be hooked up to tubes and all that crap when it comes time for me to go." Loss of control was a common concern, "Once I got real sick and got [put] in a nursing home. I don't care how old I was, I can't deal with not

Table 3   Domains and Themes of EOL Care Expressed by Homeless People

Domain	Definitions	Representative quote(s)
Personal themes		
Experience with EOL care	Experience with deaths of loved ones, friends, and acquaintances on the streets or personal experiences with illness or injury, and the care received	I've had a lot of tragedy. My girlfriend died in my arms with my baby. She was four months pregnant at the time . . . and she comes back in my dreams. He had a stroke and was on dialysis. Me and him, being about the same age, it made me fear for my life.
Fears and uncertainties	Concerns and fears about dying and EOL care	Me? I'd just like to be remembered by somebody. The only thing I'm worried about is that I don't want to die on the streets. After I've passed, my biggest fear would be not making it back home to Canada and my reservation. . . . they'll throw you in a pauper's grave someplace and nobody's going to mourn you.
Preferences/ wishes/hopes	Possibilities related to what would be a "good death"	If that was to happen, I would want it to happen some place where it was noticeable. Yeah, you may be dead there for three, four years . . . I'll be somewhere where nobody could find me. But also, once you see the doctor, the doctor should spend a little more time and get to know you a little bit better and show a little more compassion.
Advance care planning/ documentation	Strategies to influence outcomes in the event of death or serious illness	You gotta have it wrote down, or else they'll do just what they want. I'm going to have one of those made out, a living will, because if I end up in the hospital, I don't think I'd want no life support keeping me alive. My will says that if I go into a diabetic coma or if I get hit by a car, they can start life-saving techniques, and then my brother Bob's name is on that. They are to call him and say John's in the hospital, doesn't look good; do you want to come down and sign the papers to pull the plug; we will try to keep him going for some time to see if he improves. If he doesn't improve, then come down. That is exactly how it's worded.
Spirituality/religion	Influence and role that an individual's spirituality or religious convictions has on dying and EOL care	Personally, death comes like peace, but like John said, we look forward to it if we're Christian because I can go and get my reincarnate body and dance without this one.
Veteran status	Thoughts about death and EOL care related to having served in the armed forces	Even though I'm a serviceman, if I was buried in a national cemetery, I feel that my soul would be lost. I went to get medical care, something that they guaranteed me for life. They looked at me and said, 'OK, you have an honorable discharge.' As a matter of fact, I have two. 'Do you have insurance on your job?' and I'm like, whoa. The insurance on my job, OK, when I signed these contracts you didn't say that my insurance would be primary. You said that you would take care of it. So the VA does nothing.
Relational themes		
Relationships with known people	How current relationships with family, friends, and peers affect desires and fears about dying and EOL care	Most of these guys, they don't want their family to know. They ask you what happened. Why are you homeless? What's the problem? But I notice that homeless people, or street punks, whatever you call them, whatever is right for them, prostitutes or whatever, sometimes these type of people, another street person they have known for years and seems more like a family member than their own family. For me that is considered a family member. They'd be there for me, but I wouldn't want them to make all them changes. It takes a lot of money to travel and I don't want them wasting money. Not because I ain't worth the money, but I don't want them.

Table 3 Domains and Themes of EOL Care Expressed by Homeless People (*continued*)

Domain	Definitions	Representative quote(s)
Relationships with strangers	How individuals' relationship with institutions and its representatives influence their views of dying and EOL care	Have a doctor, an intern, or even have a medical student for a doctor, come and work at a shelter for a week to two weeks, just to see how it is, to get woke up at 6:00 in the morning and booted out, and getting a cold bowl of cereal from the branch for breakfast, and just shadowing somebody that has been homeless or is homeless, just to feel what it's like to, if just to say 'I know this guy; he's homeless and this needs to be taken care of right away' and not making him wait. Then they will have an idea of what it's like being homeless. The doctor called me a goddamn drug addict and told me to get the hell out of his office.
Communication tools/ strategies	The communication between the subjects and their loved or valued ones, and strategies homeless persons have to communicate with loved ones during a health care crisis or if unable to communicate directly	My sister, I put her name on everything that I have. There can be contact with her and she will communicate with my daughter. My living will says my family will have no say or discussion of what is done. Basically, they don't know me, so why should they have a say in whether I live or not. I made sure to talk to him (nephew) on the telephone. It just came into my mind. I said, 'I'm going to leave this in your hands. I'm going down hill now.'
Environmental		
Environmental barriers/facilitators to good EOL care	Barriers or facilitators identified by subjects to good EOL care	They don't give you proper medical care because they know you are homeless. They think because we live in the streets, we're all junkies that don't feel no pain. Even if your family is not around at the hospital, there are these great hospice people. If you could spend your last time talking with them . . . that would be a good death. Living without life insurance, who's going to put me away—stuff like that? I had cancer just last year. My fear was being alone because my children ain't here. But I had support from the people at Listening House, friends.
Participant-suggested interventions	Interventions suggested by participants to improve dying and EOL care for homeless persons	What we do need is a shelter somewhere between Minneapolis and St. Paul that would be fully staffed 24/7 . . . and if you came out and just had surgery, you could go there . . .

EOL end of life.

having my freedom. There's no way. I need to be free . . . once you're in a nursing home or hospital you lose control."

Fears and Uncertainties

Participants expressed many fears and uncertainties similar to those of domiciled people: "Don't prolong my life. I don't want to carry on laying there as a vegetable . . ." However, the derivation of these fears may be different in this population—a combination of experience and the impotence and indignity of homelessness: "I was thinking of my friend Jeff wound up under the bridge. They look at it like another junkie guy, but he was trying really, really hard to work every day. And just to see him treated with little dignity was [not] right . . ."

Another common fear was dying anonymously, which may be unique to this population: "It makes a difference when you're homeless and you're dying by yourself. You're

here by yourself, no one to care"; and, "Me? I just want to be remembered by somebody." A dreaded consequence expressed by many was that their passing, and life, would go unnoticed and without memorialization. Similar fears include not being found and dying in a public place: "I wouldn't want to be under a bridge. If you die somewhere and not be found."

Participants also expressed many misconceptions and uncertainties about surrogate decision-making, persistent vegetative states and heroic treatments, and advance care planning: "A good buddy of mine that used to be a street person . . . fell out and ended up in a coma . . . There [were] doctors and nurses . . . calling, asking anybody to come down and say you were his family, just so you could sign a waiver to pull the plug." This was one of many urban EOL myths expressed by participants.

Another common concern was the final disposal of their body, a fear that appears unique to this population; they believed a homeless, disenfranchised person's body would be anonymously cremated, buried in a common grave, or used in medical experimentation: "I don't know if the city will just take me to the furnace down there and burn me." Participants were not aware of Minnesota state law that forbids cremation without consent of patient or family.

Preferences, Wishes, and Hopes

Participants expressed preferences and hopes, many echoing those articulated in the mainstream EOL literature, such as a wish for reconciliation with loved ones or avoiding heroic interventions. However, the wish for companionship had a unique twist in this disenfranchised population. While some desired reunion with their families, many more simply wanted anyone compassionate at the time of death, whether homeless friends or even anonymous care providers: "I would wish someone to be there, especially since I know my folks won't be."

Given the misconceptions and fears about body disposal, there were explicit and detailed desires that participants' bodies be laid to rest in a personally and culturally acceptable manner. Native Americans, for example, often stated a preference that their body be taken to native lands for proper burial.

Another common desire expressed was that EOL care focus on symptom management, particularly pain control. At the end of a long dialogue on pain control, one participant summed up the prevailing mood: "I'm kind of on the same page as him . . . if I'm dying, just give me my drugs. Make sure I'm loaded; then I'm cool. I'm not going to sell it to anybody; I just want to . . . Let me go in peace."

Finally, participants desired simply to be treated with respect: "deal with us not as some sleaze bag out for trouble, but we are just homeless." A lack of respect fostered fear of dying among subjects: "Right now I'm afraid of dying mostly because I don't have nothing. It's like a disgrace or shame to me to die that way . . . Even though I can't hear it and I won't know it, talking about, 'He was a tramp. He was a no-good tramp.'"

Advance Care Planning

A major finding is the importance of advance care planning and documentation for this isolated population: "My fear is being found on the street, but no one knowing how to help me or who I am." It appears that this desire for advance care planning arises from several concerns. One is, as reflected above, anonymity and estrangement. Given the belief that EOL care is paternalistic and unresponsive, advance care planning was also seen as a way to maintain control: "In '73, I was actually declared brain dead . . . I regained consciousness . . . my only real fear about death is that the doctor tried too aggressively to keep me alive, and because of this, I created a living will."

For some participants advance care planning meant discussion with significant others and/or appointment of a proxy; however, the most cited forms of advance care planning included written documentation of wishes or contact information, personal identification, or written directive or other advance care planning document. One participant voiced a typical strategy to dictate circumstances of his death: "In my wallet, I have a card with my sister's name and a phone number. Do I want to be buried in Minnesota? Hell no!"

When speaking of surrogate decision-makers, nearly all who had thought of this issue or who had appointed one chose surrogates who were not related; they were most often service providers; friends; and, occasionally, romantic partners.

Sprituality/Religion

Spirituality and religion were means of finding comfort and solace when confronting death while homeless: "Can you die alone? I remember when Bill Cosby's son died on the street . . . nobody came to touch him and hold him, but if he's a child of God, then God was holding him and taking him home." Despite the physical reality of dying alone, religion made it possible to believe that, spiritually, one was not alone.

Veteran Status

Many opinions about EOL care related to prior military experience. Participants identified veteran status as either a positive or negative factor. Some, for example, felt reassured they would have care or even a grave provided by the U.S. government: "If I drop dead or die or get my head blown off, if my parents don't do it or my family, put me in the national cemetery, too, with other veterans, my brothers." Others feared poor VA care or did not want burial in a veteran's cemetery.

Relational Themes

A second major domain was "relational themes," which we organized into 3 categories: relationships with known people, relationships with strangers, and communication tools/strategies. This domain captures how current personal and institutional relationships affect attitudes towards EOL care.

Relationships with Known People/Burden to Others

Relationships were described as complex, fractured, or nonexistent. Many were estranged from their family of origin. Some homeless persons viewed dying as an opportunity for reconciliation, though they were uncertain whether this would happen: "Truthfully, I couldn't honestly say who would and who wouldn't [be there]. I'll just have to see when I get there . . . Sometimes when they say they'll be there, they're never there."

A majority of participants did not want contact with their families while dying or after their deaths. There were several reasons for this preference, including the assertion that their families, "abandoning" them in life, had no right to claim a relationship or authority in death: "I got 6 sisters and five brothers . . . but, dead is dead. So don't cry; help me while I breathe, not when I'm stiff and frozen." This rejection extended into surrogate decision-making: "My living will says my family will have no say or discussion of what is done. Basically, they don't know me, so why should they have a say in whether I live or not." Others feared that their families would not be compassionate: "They'd be saying, 'bury him like he lived,' or 'we don't want nothing to do with him.'" Some did not want to be a burden on their families, either emotionally or financially, or feared revealing their circumstances and homelessness: "When I die, don't tell them. I don't want them to know that I'm homeless." Finally, many others did not want their families contacted because they had found, while living on the streets, trusted friends and service providers to serve as surrogates.

Relationships with Strangers

Most respondents commented that society, including police, medical professionals, and social service agency staff, does not treat them with respect or compassion. When discussing physicians, one respondent insisted: "We are homeless. They say, 'well this guy's homeless . . . You ain't got to worry about it.'" They cited slow and poor service at health care facilities, and felt betrayed by the social services system. Based on these experiences, they expected poor care at the EOL: "He'd a died more dignified if they [the counselors] actually sat down and listened to him, instead of saying, 'we're too busy; get out of here . . .'"

However, not all comments were negative. Compassionate providers were described gratefully. Several respondents claimed a particular social service provider as their most trusted confidant and indicated that this individual should be contacted as a surrogate decision-maker. "John," said one respondent, referring to a street case manager, "knows what I want. I trust him."

Communication Tools/Strategies
Those who did wish communication or reconciliation at the EOL had different strategies to insure that this occurred. These strategies were often inventive and adapted to the disenfranchised lives many led. Many, for example, carried phone numbers of loved ones or left them with various social service providers. Although in jest, this comment demonstrates how difficult communication may be: "If I was going to die in three months, I'd probably rob a bank . . . I figure if I robbed a bank, I would get caught. [My family] heard about it in the newspaper and call me up . . . "

Environmental Factors

Our final domain's common thread is the environment in which dying occurs and the structural boundaries of EOL care. We organized it into 2 categories: barriers/facilitators to good EOL care and participant-suggested interventions.

Barriers/Facilitators to Good EOL Care

Health care professionals' attitudes were most often cited as a barrier to good EOL care, while others found care inaccessible or inadequate because of financial or insurance insufficiencies. Because of poverty, even the simplest aspects of EOL care cause worry in this population: "My goal is to get me some type of burial plan. $300 won't bury nobody at this table. Then I wouldn't mind it so much, but right now I'm afraid of dying mostly because I don't have nothing." Inappropriate care also resulted because of preconceptions about homeless persons, such as the denial of pain medication for fear of abuse. Respondents also complained about the lack of respite or hospice facilities and programs; once discharged from the hospital, they only have shelters to go to.

Participant-Suggested Interventions

Finally, participants suggested many interventions to improve care for dying homeless people. Some were educational, directed towards both health care providers and homeless people. Another frequently suggested intervention was some form of advance care planning or document to preserve autonomy: "It's a legal document. Let's say that's your wish, but it's not written anywhere, and someone says, 'keep him on the respirator.' They [would] . . . unless you written it down." Indeed, any kind of identification was considered essential and encouraged for a disconnected population. Finally, homeless participants demanded special accommodations to facilitate dying among this population.

Discussion

In our study, homeless participants demonstrated more differences than similarities in their attitudes and beliefs towards EOL care compared to other populations studied.[20-25] First, many participants have had personal experiences with death, dying, and EOL care. These experiences led them to view EOL care as paternalistic, unresponsive, and poor. Other unique concerns expressed include fear of dying anonymously, without memorialization or remembrance; fear of not being found or identifiable in death; and worry about the final resting place of their bodies. These concerns are all new to the EOL literature.

Another unexpected finding is participants' advocating advance care planning, especially the appointment of surrogate decision-makers and the preparation of advance care documents, such as living wills. These findings are interesting, given the current disfavor toward advance care documents[1] and the intuition that homeless individuals would not value or utilize documentation. According to participants, documents serve different functions among a population that is anonymous, voiceless, or lacks obvious surrogate decision-makers.

Important relational findings were also expressed. Though some participants wished reconcilement and contact, a greater number did not want their families contacted when seriously ill, when dying, or after death. These desires derived from several different reasons, including avoiding emotional and financial burdens on their families, shame, and anger over abandonment. Many had made surrogate decision-making plans that did not include family.

Relationships with institutions also figured prominently in the EOL experiences and desires of homeless persons—which is expected given the role institutions play in the daily lives of homeless persons, providing food, shelter, and other necessities. These relationships were occasionally positive. Participants spoke of trusted service providers, such as shelter personnel, some of whom were even designated as surrogate decision-makers. Most often, though, relationships with systems of care were described as poor, and contributed to give views of dying.

Participants spoke of "environmental" contexts or contributors to EOL care, noting multiple barriers to EOL care, including poor relationships, lack of insurance or finances, poor health care, lack of respect, and lack of knowledge of available resources or rights. Some participants, though, cited factors that led to satisfactory health care experiences or positive expectations of EOL care, such as advance care planning, facilitation of health care by social service workers, and physician advocacy.

Finally, subjects suggested interventions for improving EOL care for homeless or underserved persons. These included patient and provider education, advance care planning, living wills and other documentation, and special programs and facilities for dying or seriously ill homeless persons. A Medline and web search yields no reports of specific efforts focused on dying homeless individuals. Clearly, interventions are needed to serve this population.

The recent NIH state-of-science statement on improving EOL care reported that insufficient research has focused on individuals from different cultural and socioeconomic backgrounds.[1] While there is a growing body of evidence that these individuals may experience disparities in EOL care,[23–29] relatively little attention has been paid to the desires of these populations or interventions to improve their care.[1] Our study provides new and important information on EOL issues among homeless persons, among the most unfortunate of overlooked populations.

Our study's limitations include the selection of subjects from one urban area, a high number of Native Americans represented, and potential selection bias, as our participants are those who accessed service providers. The findings of our study are not necessarily generalizable. Rather, our data are exploratory, examining a previously unknown health-related phenomena: we are among the first to characterize in-depth the EOL concerns and desires of a vulnerable and disenfranchised population from their perspective.

Conclusions

Our study demonstrates that homeless persons have extensive, and often unique, concerns about dying and EOL care. The experiences and circumstances of homelessness inform and influence a view of death and EOL care unlike previously reported findings in the study of EOL care. Our work has implications for further study of this population, as well as study of other underrepresented and underserved populations. This work also suggests examining interventions to improve care for this and other vulnerable populations.

Notes

1. National Institutes of Health State-of-the-Science Conference Statement on Improving End-of-Life Care December 6–8, 2004. Available at www.consensus.nih.gov/2004/2004EndOf LifeCareSOS024html.htm. Accessed March 16, 2006.

2. Burt MR. Homelessness: definitions and counts. In: Baumohl J, ed. Homelessness in America. Phoenix, AZ: Oryx Press, 1996:15–23.

3. Breakey WR, Fischer PJ, Kramer M. Health and mental problems of homeless men and women in Baltimore. *JAMA* 1989; 262:1352–7.

4. Gelberg L, Linn LS. Assessing the physical health of homeless adults. *JAMA* 1989; 262:1973–9.

5. Barrow SM, Herman DB, Cordova PBA. Mortality among shelter residents in New York City. *Am J Public Health* 1999; 89:529–34.

6. Hibbs JR, Benner L. Mortality in a cohort of homeless adults in Philadelphia. *N Engl J Med* 1994; 331:304–9

7. Cheung AM, Hwang SW. Risk of death among homeless women: a cohort study and review of the literature. *CMAJ* 2004; 170(8):1243–7.

8. Hwang SW, Orav EJ, O'Connell JJ, Lebow JM, Brennan TA. Causes of death in homeless adults in Boston. *Ann Intern Med* 1996; 126:625–8.

9. King County Public Health 2004. Available at www.metrokc. gov/HEALTH/hchn/2004-annual-report-HD.pdf. Accessed January 20, 2006.

10. Gallagher TC, Andersen RM, Koegel P, Gelberg L. Determinants of regular source of care among homeless adults in Los Angeles. *Med Care* 1997; 35(8):814–30.

11. Gelberg L, Andersen RM, Leake BD. Healthcare access and utilization. *Health Serv Res.* 2000; 34(6):1273–1314.

12. Gelberg L, Thompson L. Competing priorities as a barrier to medical care among homeless adults in Los Angeles. *Am J Public Health* 1997; 87:217–20.

13. Hwang SW, O'Connell JJ, Lebow JM, Bierer MF, Orav EJ, Brennan TA. Health care utilization among homeless adults prior to death. *J Health Care Poor Underserved* 2001 Feb; 12(1):50–8.

14. Song J, Ratner E, Bartels D. Dying while homeless: Is it a concern when life itself is such a struggle? *J Clin Ethics.* Fall 2005; 16(3):251–61.

15. Tarzian A, Neal M, O'Neil J. Attitudes, experiences, and beliefs affecting end-of-life decision-making among homeless individuals. *J Palliat Med.* Feb 2005, Vol. 8, No. 1: 36–48.

16. Norris W, Nielson E, Engelberg R, Curtis JR. Treatment preferences for resuscitation and critical care among homeless persons. *Chest* 2005; 127(6):2180–7.

17. Stewart B. McKinney Homeless Assistance Act (42 U.S.C. 11431 et seq.)

18. Bernard HR. Reseach Methods in Cultural Anthropology. Beverly Hills, CA: Sage Publications 1988.

19. Hill CE, Thompson BJ, Williams EN. A guide to conducting consensual qualitative research. *Couns Psychol* 1997; 25:517–72.

20. Singer PA, Martin DK, Kelner M. Quality end of life care: patients' perspectives. *JAMA* 1999; 281:163–8.
21. Steinhauser KE, Clipp CC. In search of a good death: observations of patients, families, and providers. *Ann Intern Med.* 2000; 132:825–31.
22. Vig EK, Pearlman RA. Quality of life while dying: a qualitative study of terminally ill older men. *J Am Geriatr Soc* 2003 Nov; 51(11):1595–601
23. Born W, Greiner KA, Sylvia E, Butler J. Ahluwalia JS. Knowledge, attitudes, and beliefs about end-of-life care among inner-city African Americans and Latinos. *J Palliat Med.* 2004 7(2): 247–56.
24. Blackhall LJ, Murphy ST, Frank G. Ethnicity and attitudes toward patient autonomy. *JAMA* 1995;274:820–5.
25. Caralis PV, Davis B, Wright K, Marcial E. The influence of ethnicity and race on attitudes toward advance directives, life-prolonging treatments, and euthanasia. *J Clin Ethics* 1993;4(2):155–65.
26. Carrese JA, Rhodes LA. Western bioethics on the Navajo reservation. *JAMA* 1995;274:826–9.
27. Daneault S, Labadie J. Terminal HIV disease and extreme poverty: a review of 307 home care files. *J Palliat Care* 1999; 15:6–12.
28. Degenholtz HB, Thomas SB, Miller MJ. Race and the intensive care unit: disparities and preferences for end-of-life care. *Crit Care Med.* 31(5 Suppl):S373–8, 2003 May.
29. Cleeland CS, Gonin R, Baez L et al. Pain and treatment of pain in minority patients with cancer. *Ann Intern Med* 1997;127:813–6.

Critical Thinking

1. Because homeless individuals do not have a "home," what would you expect their attitudes to be toward end-of-life issues: similar to or rather different from a population with a "home?"

2. What were the six personal themes that related to homeless individuals' attitudes toward end-of-life care?

3. What were the two relational themes that impacted on homeless persons' attitudes toward end-of-life care?

Corresponding Author: **John Song,** MD, MPH, MAT; Center for Bioethics, University of Minnesota, N504 Boynton, 410 Church Street S.E., Minneapolis, MN 55455, USA (e-mail: songx006@umn.edu).

Acknowledgments—The authors would like to thank the clients and staff of St. Stephen's shelter; Holy Rosary Church; Listening House; Hennepin County Outreach Services; Health Care for the Homeless, Minneapolis; and Our Saviors Church who were so generous with their time, thoughts, and dedication to serving others. We would also like to thank LeeAnne Hoekstra for administrative support, Tybee Types for transcription, and Karen Howard for manuscript preparation. This study was funded by the National Institute of Nursing Research, National Institutes of Health, grant RO3 NR008586-02.

Death and Dying across Cultures

GIHAN ELGINDY, RN, MSN

Death and dying is a universal human experience throughout the globe. Yet human beings' beliefs, feelings and practices in regard to this experience vary widely between different religions and cultures. As nurses, it is amazing how much we need to learn in order to incorporate sensitivity to unique religious and/or cultural needs into our daily practice. For patients from diverse cultures, quality of care means culturally appropriate care. We need to remember that dying is difficult enough; no one needs to undergo additional stress or suffering as a result of cultural misunderstanding.

As we all learn in nursing school, the patient is the focus of our care. Therefore, patients—and their families—from cultures we may not be familiar with should be viewed as a source of knowledge about their special religious/cultural needs and norms. In many cases, accommodating these needs in a hospital setting is not that difficult, but it definitely requires creativity and just a few extra minutes of our time.

Often, just being aware of our own perceptions and religious/cultural practices, and possessing a degree of openness toward other individuals' unique needs, is more than enough to lead our basic common sense in caring competently for dying patients from diverse cultural backgrounds during this difficult time.

However, we must resist the temptation to make generalizations or assumptions that all individuals from the same cultural, ethnic or religious background are exactly alike. Within many ethnic populations, such as Hispanics/Latinos, there is a great deal of diversity in terms of cultural practices, geographic origin, etc. Above all, it's important to realize whether you are dealing with recent immigrants to the U.S. or with first- or second-generation individuals.

Q: As an ICU nurse, I care for dying patients every shift. Often when there is a Hispanic or Latino patient dying or deteriorating, I have to face a crowd of family and friends all day, regardless of the visible visiting hours sign, posted in Spanish. The frustration is mutual. In addition, sometimes the families request to place a special food item in a special location next to the patient's bed. I know how much this item must mean to them but many of our inflexible unit policies do not promote such practices. What is the best approach to resolve this issue?—Mary John, RN

A: Yes, it is true that America's health care facilities have many inflexible polices that do not allow much room for promoting diverse cultural/religious rituals or practices. This is a conflict that we nurses face every day and need to work on through ongoing dialog. It can often be difficult to accommodate a patient's wishes without changing these old, dry polices that ignore many individuals' needs, even during their last minutes of life.

In the situation you have described, to fully understand these families' requests we need to understand their culture, too. Hispanics/Latinos are predominantly Christians, yet they encompass varied cultural backgrounds and traditions. Sometimes when a Hispanic/Latino person is sick or dying, close family members such as the spouse, children, parents, etc. may all sit in a circle around a carefully selected food item, such as a fruit dish, placed in the middle of the room. They may spend most of the night praying and conducting special religious practices around this fruit dish. As a result, it becomes a holy dish that holds a great religious significance; the family believes that the holy object can assist their sick or dying loved one. At the end of the night, the family carries the holy fruit dish to the nurse or other care providers, expecting their full compliance in placing it next to the patient to facilitate healing, recovery or a peaceful death.

A simple discussion with the family explaining hospital and unit policies will usually lead nowhere. To please everyone and maintain a positive environment—including compliance with unit policies—the best approach is to place the holy fruit dish or food item in a sealed plastic bag, placing it exactly as the family specifies and explaining to them the perishable item's time limitation depending on fermentation status and weather conditions. Allowing the item to remain in place for several hours—such as only eight, 10 or 24 hours—will be very much appreciated and calming to everyone. It is very important to remember to ask the family what they want you to do with this item when the time is over.

Q: I recently encountered my first Jehovah's Witness patient, a child who was dying from a simple bleeding condition. It was very painful to watch his parents repeatedly refusing a blood transfusion that could easily save the boy's life. Then I heard the physician trying to obtain a court order that would enable him to act as the child's guardian so he could administer the needed blood transfusion. What a relief, he was able to save the child's life. But I still do not fully understand why the parents were so angry. Will you kindly explain this, and why they were refusing a simple treatment that has saved millions of lives? —B.B., Kansas.

A: It is very hard and often very painful for care providers to have to watch the process of slow death, or to do nothing for a dying patient whom they think they can save. Many times, we tend to forget that there is a limit to our role and that we need to realize and accept this.

To help you understand why this young patient's parents were so resistant to the child being given a blood transfusion, let me first explain the significance of blood in the Jehovah's Witness faith. Jehovah's Witnesses believe blood is sacred, representing life. Because of the Bible's command to "keep abstaining from . . . blood," their religion prohibits the ingestion of blood and the transfusion of blood and/or blood products. Some artificial blood products may be permissible but never natural human blood or its byproducts.

Often, Jehovah's Witnesses who require medical or surgical treatment will request the use of nonblood alternatives. To be a culturally competent care provider means recognizing that adult patients have a right to make this choice. Therefore, obtaining the patient's clear written permission before performing any auto-transfusion procedure is the safest practice for both the provider and the receiver. Failure to do so constitutes violating the patient's bill of rights and can lead to litigation or legal actions.

However, under U.S. law, providing care to a Jehovah's Witness patient who is a minor (as in the case you describe) differs from caring for a Jehovah's Witness adult. For minors, the physician can obtain a court order allowing administration of blood or blood products against the parents' will if he or she knows the procedure can and will save the child's life. The reason behind the physician's action is to protect the minor's life until he/she becomes an adult and can make his/her own faith decision. Of course, when physicians take this action it is not surprising that care providers, especially nurses, will face angry parents.

In future, to resolve this issue easily and safely for everyone, it would be helpful for you to learn about the bloodless treatment alternatives that are available for Jehovah's Witness patients. If the facility where you work is unable to provide these alternatives, be aware of the health care centers in your area that are specialized and authorized to manage Jehovah's Witness patients. Contacting the Witnesses' Hospital Liaison Committee in your area to obtain more information on bloodless treatment options, patient transfers and/or consultation can also be very helpful. This service is available 24 hours a day, seven days a week.

Q: I had a dying Muslim patient. I tried to provide her with spiritual support but instead I made her upset. I told her, innocently, that I would call the priest for her. Her tears and facial expressions were alarming enough to send a message of pain. Will you please explain what went wrong? In the future, how can I provide appropriate assistance to Muslims patients who are dying?—Linda

A: Before answering your questions, I need to explain an Islamic concept/principal first. In Islam there is no religious figure, such as a priest or rabbi, through which one communicates with Allah (God) on one's deathbed. Muslims communicate directly with Allah anytime and anywhere as they wish. In other words, they don't need a human religious figure to act as a spiritual "middleman." Nor do they need to give confession to absolve their sins before they die.

Secondly, while it was culturally inappropriate in itself to offer to send a Catholic priest to comfort a Muslim patient, what really made this patient upset was probably that she perceived your action as a message that she was about to die. After death, Islam, like many other religions, requires conducting a prayer for the dead, asking for Allah's mercy and forgiveness before burial takes place. This prayer may be performed by an Imam—a respected member of the community who, through his memorizing of the Quran (Muslim holy book), leads prayers—or by a Shiekh, or Islamic Scholar, who is a knowledgeable person who spent most of his life studying Islam and usually earns a PhD degree in Islamic Shariah (or "Islamic Laws Jurisprudence"). Therefore, even if you had offered to call an Imam or Shiekh instead of a priest, the patient would probably still have been upset, because she would have interpreted this as meaning that her death was imminent.

In the future, the most culturally appropriate way to assist a dying Muslim patient is to offer them the Quran and to facilitate their prayers.

Critical Thinking

1. In relating to dying patients, why is it important that nurses be well versed in how different cultures and religions view dying and death?

2. What beliefs do Jehovah's Witnesses have regarding medical attention which differ significantly from other religions?

3. What is different regarding the Muslin religion and other religions' views on dying and death?

Editor's Note—Meet Minority Nurse's cultural competence expert: GIHAN ELGINDY, RN, MSN, an internationally recognized authority on cross-cultural issues in nursing. Her advice column is designed to answer your questions about incorporating cultural competence into your nursing practice and resolving cultural conflicts in today's diverse health care workplace. Do you need expert advice on how to provide culturally sensitive care to patients from a particular ethnic or religious background? Are you looking for ways to increase understanding and acceptance of cultural differences in your work environment? Our expert can help!

Send your Cultural Competence Q&A questions to pam.chwedyk@alloyeducation.com.

The Promise of Presence

Regrets, I've had a few . . . Frank Sinatra, *I Did It My Way*

PAUL ROUSSEAU, MD

He was a 65-year-old man with widely metastatic colon cancer and unrelenting pain and vomiting, likely due to progressive bowel obstruction. His wife of 40 years was constantly at his bedside, leaving only to get food or to shower in the communal family bathroom.

"Mr. Roberts. I'll be back later and check on you before I go home. We have the pain medication at the right dose now, and your nausea is much better—it's the first time you've smiled since we met. That's a good thing!" With dying. success is measured by small miracles, and controlling pain and reducing vomiting are small miracles.

"Thanks, doc. I'll see you later. And doc . . . thank you."

As I left his room, his wife followed me into the hallway "Dr. Rousseau, his pain seems so much better, and the vomiting has stopped. I know he's dying, but I just want him comfortable." Then there was a pause, and I knew the question was coming: "How long do you think he has? Our three children are on their way, and we just need to know."

I had been asked that question hundreds of times, and an answer always tangled my heart: underestimate, and confidence may be lost if the person lives longer, overestimate, and families may procrastinate and be upset that they did not have more time. But Mr. Roberts was dying and it could be hours to maybe a day or two. I told Mrs. Roberts I thought he would die soon, likely within a day. But that I would be back later to check on both of them. She thanked me, and went back into the room and gently closed the door, her title slowly changing from wife to widow. And with that I was gone, 2 more consults pending, and a need to follow up on 3 consults completed the day before.

As I hurried down the hall, the clock on the wall told me it was late in the afternoon. Both consults would require discussions that would tear at grieving hearts and claim their innocence of mortality. And the follow-ups? They would likely require extended conversations as well—one regarding a do-not-resuscitate order, the other withdrawal of life support.

By the time I finished the consults and the follow-ups, 5 hours had passed and my mind was foggy from emotion and sadness. With consults and notes finished, I headed down the hall to the cafeteria, purchased a cup of coffee, and began the walk to the parking garage. As I drove home, my mind rehashed the grief and sorrow of the day, but I was soon in my house, far from the turmoil of the hospital, checking my mail and the news of the day, then heading to bed and the safety of slumber.

The next morning, I awoke to a page for a new consult, and after arriving at the hospital, suddenly remembered I had not gone back to check on Mr. Roberts before I left the night before. Exhaustion had overwhelmed my memory. I rushed to his floor and searched for his chart, but it was gone. Then I ran and peered into his room and saw housekeeping cleaning his bed in anticipation of the next patient. Mr. Roberts had died. I sat at the nurses' station physically and emotionally sick—I was nauseous and ashamed. I told both he and his wife I would "be back," and I had failed them—I did not return. Oh sure, I had plenty of excuses, the new consults and follow-ups that required hours of conversation, the lateness of the day, and my physical and emotional exhaustion, but they were all supported by flimsy scaffolds that reeked of intolerable excuses. I was not there in their time of need, when I told them I *would* be there. I had failed the Roberts, plain and simple, and I had failed the principle of nonabandonment. If I did not think I could return, I should have said so. And with death, there is no second chance; no time to make things right—death is final, a judge without compassion or remorse.

My heart cried and my anguish overwhelmed—I knew what I had to do. I nervously telephoned Mrs. Roberts, and after an awkward hello and heartfelt condolences, apologized for my absence. Tears passed through our distance, but even in the presence of loss, she was gracious, repeatedly telling me she understood, that I had given her husband a comfortable death, and that that was worth everything to her and her children. As I listened to Mrs. Roberts, I was humbled by the gentle benevolence of her understanding—a wife, mired in the grief of loss, comforting a physician who failed his promise to be present. What irony.

But now, as I look back, I understand that such troubling and life-altering "sentinel events" frame our careers—it is what we do with these events that define our character. The importance and value of the promise of presence cannot be stressed enough—if we promise presence, we must be present, because all we have are our words, and our words are our honor and our gift to patients and their families. And presence—being in the moment with the patient and their family—can be a soothing balm when disease continues an unrelenting march.[1] Its value is mystical and comforting, even as death sits at the bedside waiting for its next remains. My only concern is that the uncertain and unfolding landscape of medicine may relegate the promise of presence to the trash heap of clinical detachment, desktop medicine, and handheld gadgets such as iPhones and iPads, further distancing the physician from the bedside and leaving patients and families alone and struggling with difficult journeys. But I hope I am wrong. After all, as physicians, if we promise to be there, to be present, we must fulfill that promise, we must "be back"—for we may not have another chance.

Acknowledgment—I would like to thank Mr. and Mrs. Roberts for reminding me of the value of the promise of presence so early in my career.

Declaration of Conflicting Interests—The author(s) declared no conflicts of interest with respect to the authorship and/or publication of this article.

Funding—The author(s) received no financial support for the research and/or authorship of this article.

Reference

I. Rousseau P. Presence. *J Clin Oneal.* 2010; 28(22):3668–3669.

Critical Thinking

1. Physicians are often asked. "Doc, how long do I have to live?" when diagnosed with a terminal illness. Would you wish to have a timetable if given such a prognosis?

2. How honest do you feel medical doctors should be in "telling" the patient if she/he has a terminal prognosis? Should the doctor assess the situation with the patient and her/his family before deciding whether or not to tell. According to the American Medical Association's policy in the 1980s, it is the patient's right to know if the illness is terminal.

When Death Strikes without Warning

After years of neglect, a devastating effect of epilepsy, sudden death, is drawing new scrutiny.

JENNIFER COUZIN

The call came on a Thursday, 21 February 2002, while Jeanne Donalty sat at her desk at work. Her son Chris, a 21-year-old senior at a Florida college, had stopped breathing. His girlfriend found him on his bed, surrounded by the books he'd been studying and a summer job application. Paramedics were unable to revive him, and just like that, Chris Donalty was gone.

Chris Donalty had had epilepsy—he suffered his first seizure in school when he was 9 years old—but his mother at first saw no clear line connecting his death and the disease for which he was being treated. An autopsy found no visible cause of death, and it was shortly after that that Jeanne Donalty discovered a term she had never heard before: SUDEP.

Sudden unexpected death in epilepsy, SUDEP was first written up in *The Lancet* in 1868 by a British physician; he described the phenomenon as "sudden death in a fit." Neurologists today are familiar with SUDEP, which is thought to follow a seizure, and most specialists have lost patients in this way. "Four or five times a year, someone will not come to my clinic because they have a SUDEP death," says Mark Richardson, a neurologist at King's College London. Most victims, like Chris Donalty, are in their 20s or 30s.

SUDEP has been little studied and is rarely discussed in the medical and scientific communities. Families often learn of it only after a relative's death. In the United Kingdom, which is well ahead of the United States in tracking SUDEP, it's estimated that SUDEP strikes at least 500 people a year. It's thought to explain between 8% and 17% of deaths in people with epilepsy. Among those with frequent seizures, the number may be as high as 40%. This increased risk, recognized only recently, underscores that SUDEP is more likely to occur if seizures are more frequent or treatment is inadequate.

Chris Donalty was in that high-risk group: Despite taking his medications as prescribed, he suffered seizures regularly for 2 years before his death. But he never told his parents—because, they now believe, he did not want to lose his driver's license. "I don't know of any other disease that can be fatal where patients aren't aware of" that risk, says his mother.

Driven largely by grieving families, more doctors are discussing risk of SUDEP with patients, and research is picking up. A few studies are focusing on what happens to breathing and heart rhythm during seizures. In the U.K., researchers and advocates hope to set up a nationwide registry of SUDEP cases. The U.S. National Institutes of Health (NIH) will host several dozen specialists at its Bethesda, Maryland, campus this fall in a first-ever meeting on SUDEP. Still, the epilepsy community is divided on what to tell patients about the risk of sudden death—and exactly what should be done about it.

In from the Shadows

Epilepsy, characterized by recurrent seizures caused by abnormal electrical activity in the brain, has long carried a stigma. Some say this may explain why physicians swept SUDEP under the rug: They didn't want to magnify existing fears, especially because no way to prevent it is known. "There was a real concern that the main message should be, 'You can live a completely normal life with epilepsy,'" says Jane Hanna, who helped found the nonprofit Epilepsy Bereaved in Wantage, U.K., after her 27-year-old partner died of SUDEP shortly after he was diagnosed. Even textbooks on epilepsy omitted mention of SUDEP.

But this discretion carried drawbacks, burying historical knowledge of SUDEP cases and slowing clinical investigation, says Lina Nashef, a neurologist at King's College Hospital in London. Until the early 20th century, many people with epilepsy lived in asylums or other institutions, where staff recognized that patients sometimes died during or after seizures. But the collective memory of these deaths faded as antiepilepsy drugs became widely available and patients began living independently. Most who die of SUDEP now do so at home, unobserved.

Nashef began investigating SUDEP as a research project for a postgraduate degree in 1993, interviewing 26 families who had lost someone to sudden death. Although nearly all the deaths occurred without witnesses, Nashef was often told of signs, such as a bitten tongue, that occur after a seizure. The evidence in other cases was more circumstantial: One young man in his late teens, whose seizures were triggered by flickering light from television and computer screens, was found dead at a computer terminal in the library.

Nashef identified a handful of characteristics that the SUDEP victims shared. All but three were battling regular seizures, though sometimes not more than two or three a year. And all had suffered from a particular type, called generalized tonic-clonic or, colloquially, grand mal seizure. Such seizures, the kind most people associate with epilepsy, are accompanied by a loss of consciousness and violent jerking motions and affect large swaths of the brain.

What Goes Wrong?

Digging deeper into SUDEP, Nashef and others have focused on two life-sustaining functions: respiration and heartbeat. Most physicians now believe that SUDEP stems from arrested breathing, called apnea, or heartbeat, called asystole.

One broader question is whether apnea or asystole strike even during seizures that aren't fatal. Neurologists Maromi Nei and her mentor, Michael Sperling, both at Thomas Jefferson University in Philadelphia, provided an early clue in 2000 when they described electrocardiogram patterns from 43 people with epilepsy. Although none died of SUDEP, 17 of these patients had cardiac abnormalities during or right after seizures, including significant arrhythmias and, in one case, no heartbeat at all for 6 seconds.

More recently, Nei and her colleagues investigated hospital records from 21 people who later died, apparently of SUDEP, and compared their heart rhythms with those from the original study, to see whether the SUDEP cohort had some signs of susceptibility. The biggest difference, they reported in 2004, was not the prevalence of arrhythmias but "a greater degree of heart rate change," says Nei, with heart rate soaring by about 80 beats per minute during seizures that struck while they slept. Seizures tend to boost heart rate because they can provoke the autonomic nervous system, especially when the brain regions stimulated are those that trigger such "fight-or-flight" reactions. These data hinted that the phenomenon is exaggerated in those who later die of SUDEP.

"Four or five times a year, someone will not come to my clinic because they have a SUDEP death."

—Mark Richardson, King's College London

Now Nei is implanting devices under the left collarbone of 19 people with intractable epilepsy to gather data on their heart rhythm over a span of 14 months. Neurologist Paul Cooper of Hope Hospital near Manchester, U.K., is beginning a similar study with 200 people.

Both studies follow a related and troubling report in 2004 from *The Lancet*. There, a group of British researchers described cardiac data from 377 seizures in 20 patients gathered over 2 years. Four of the 20 had perilous stretches of asystole and later had pacemakers permanently implanted to jump-start their hearts if needed.

What might be behind this effect? Asystole isn't always dangerous, although it sounds alarming; it can happen even during some fainting spells. A normal heart starts beating again on its own—which leads clinicians to wonder whether the hearts of patients struck by SUDEP may harbor invisible defects. One possibility is that over time, repeated seizures can scar and damage the organ. Another is that a genetic defect may be causing both heart rhythm problems and epilepsy.

Earlier this year, Nashef, King's College geneticist Neeti Hindocha, and their colleagues intrigued epilepsy specialists with a report on a family with a rare form of inherited epilepsy, including two members who died from SUDEP. The researchers, after gathering DNA from the living, found that all 10 family members who had epilepsy also carried a previously undescribed mutation in a gene called *SCN1A,* which was responsible for their disease. A so-called ion channel gene, *SCN1A* helps control electrical signaling between cells. Similar genes have been linked to epilepsy and sudden cardiac death. The authors postulated that the SUDEP deaths in this family were also caused by *SCN1A,* which could have disrupted heart rhythm or brain-stem function in addition to triggering epilepsy. A group at Baylor College of Medicine in Houston, Texas, is now studying whether ion channel genes that can freeze the heart are also present in brain tissue.

If cardiac defects like these are behind SUDEP, "it might be something preventable," says Stephan Schuele, director of the Comprehensive Epilepsy Center at Northwestern Memorial Hospital in Chicago, Illinois. People with gene defects that cause sudden cardiac death, for example, receive pacemakers that can shock their hearts into beating again. Perhaps, doctors say, the same could be done for epilepsy—if they can determine who's at risk of SUDEP to begin with.

Missing Clues

But Schuele, who's looking for other causes of SUDEP, notes that despite a few reports pointing to genetics, "there is no direct evidence" that asystole is killing people with epilepsy. Schuele wonders if the body's way of stopping seizures in the brain could also be disturbing vital brainstem function in some patients. These mechanisms, which are just starting to be explored and involve surges of certain neurotransmitters, may go overboard and cause chaos in the autonomic nervous system, which governs heart rate and respiration.

The detective work is slow and arduous, in part because so few cases of SUDEP have come to light from epilepsy monitoring units in hospitals, where vital signs are recorded—perhaps, Schuele suggests, because health workers are loath to admit that a SUDEP death occurred on their watch. Last

August, neurologists Philippe Ryvlin of the Hospices Civils de Lyon in France and Torbjörn Tomson of the Karolinska Hospital in Stockholm, Sweden, began surveying 180 hospitals in Europe for information on SUDEP deaths or "near-misses" that required resuscitation. Two months ago, they extended their search worldwide, collecting cases from as far away as India and the United States. They expect to conclude their collection and analysis in about a year.

Just four cases have been published. The most detailed, in 1997 on a patient in Bristol, U.K., reported that that person's brain waves went flat before the pulse faded, perhaps causing a failure of the brain region that controls breathing. This suggests that heart failure could be a consequence, not a cause, of SUDEP. Still, "the mechanism of that brain-activated shutdown is very mysterious," says Ryvlin. "Nobody knows what it could be."

There are clues that respiration is key. By monitoring it in hospitalized epilepsy patients, Nashef found that episodes of apnea were common during seizures. And a mouse strain used for decades to test epilepsy drugs has the disconcerting habit of dying from respiratory failure after a severe seizure. That was "generally considered a nuisance," says Carl Faingold, a neuropharmacologist at Southern Illinois University in Springfield, until he and a handful of others realized the mice could be used to study SUDEP. At Boston College, biologist Thomas Seyfried found that putting the mice in an oxygen chamber during seizures prevented death in all of them.

Faingold considered whether the neurotransmitter serotonin, which functions in the brain's respiratory network, might play a role. He gave the mice the antidepressant Prozac, a serotonin booster, and found that though their seizures remained the same, they were at least 90% less likely to die afterward.

Faingold is disappointed that the mouse work has received little attention and no financial support from NIH—his SUDEP research is funded by an epilepsy advocacy group—and its relevance to humans has been questioned. Because no one can predict who will die of SUDEP or when, "if you don't have a way of investigating [SUDEP] in animals, you're very limited," he says.

Acknowledging the Unmentionable

Meanwhile, doctors face a more pressing question: what to tell their patients about SUDEP. "I admit, I am still trying to figure out the best way to do this," says Elizabeth Donner, a pediatric neurologist at the Hospital for Sick Children in Toronto, Canada. She has grown more willing to share the information, but still, "sometimes we worry in telling people about this phenomenon . . . we could actually make their lives worse." Already, one of the toughest aspects of epilepsy is its unpredictability. "When you add in a statement that some people die, and we don't know why and we can't predict it and we can't prevent it, that can be very scary."

U.K. national guidelines in 2004 recommended that physicians discuss SUDEP with everyone who has epilepsy. In reality, a survey of British neurologists published 2 years ago showed, "nobody told anybody anything," says Cooper. Cooper and some other physicians believe that the 30% or so of patients whose epilepsy does not respond to medication—or those reluctant to take it—ought to be told of SUDEP, because they are at a higher risk than people whose epilepsy is controlled. The latter group, he believes, does not need to know about SUDEP.

That perspective doesn't sit well with epilepsy advocates. "Anecdotally, we're aware of deaths every year in people with second or third seizures," says Hanna of Epilepsy Bereaved. "It does worry me a bit if there's going to be some basic clinical practice that just cuts the line with people who seem to have the most serious epilepsy."

Jeanne Donalty still struggles with her family's ignorance of SUDEP while Chris was alive. "I'm not insensitive to how hard this is for a physician," she says. If she had known of SUDEP then, "I would have been upset; . . . who wouldn't be? But I think you have the right to have all the knowledge about the disease that is out there, so that you can make your decisions based on that knowledge." When it comes to sharing information on SUDEP, says Donalty, "to me, it's easy. You tell everybody."

Critical Thinking

1. What is SUDEP? Do you know someone who has experienced SUDEP?

2. What does recent research suggest is the cause of SUDEP?

3. What are some of the problems involved in research on SUDEP?

Are They Hallucinations or Are They Real? The Spirituality of Deathbed and Near-Death Visions

L. STAFFORD BETTY, PHD

When I try to unpack the many meanings of the word "spirituality," I try not to forget that the word comes from "spirit," and that one of the main meanings of "spirit" is, as my dictionary puts it, "a supernatural being or essence." Thanatologists have long been aware that people very near death, especially if they have *not* been heavily sedated, frequently "see spirits." French historian Philippe Ariès reports that a thousand years ago throughout Western Europe, most slowly dying people saw such spirits—presumably because sedation was unknown (M. Morse, 1990, p. 60). Even today, with heavy sedation the rule rather than the exception, some hospice nurses report that seeing and communicating with spirits is a "prevalent theme" of the dying patients they provide care for (Callanan & Kelley, 1992, p. 83). Usually these spirits bring comfort and a sense of wonder, not only for the dying, but also for the family of the dying. To put it another way, they "spiritualize" death. They suggest to all concerned that this world is not the only one, but that a "spiritual" world awaits the deceased. What is the nature of these spirits and the world they apparently live in? Is the "romance of death" generated by them a false comfort, a useful fiction, or is there something real and sturdy about them? In this article we will look at the evidence on both sides of the question, then come to a tentative conclusion.

Typical Deathbed or Near-Death Visions

According to Callanan and Kelley, visions of the dying come in two types. The first, and more common, are sightings of spirits who come, for the most part, to greet and encourage those who are dying. Most spirits are recognized by the one dying as a dead relative or friend. These spirits may visit for minutes or even hours; they are not seen by those at the bedside of the dying person, but it is often obvious that the dying person is communicating with an unseen presence or presences. Dozens of such communications are recorded by Callanan and Kelley, of which the following is typical: "Martha described several visitors unseen by others. She knew most of them—her parents and sister, all of whom were dead—but couldn't identify a child who appeared with them" (Callanan & Kelley, pp. 87–88). Martha goes on to explain to her nurse, "They left a little while ago. They don't stay all the time; they just come and go. . . . sometimes we talk, but usually I just know that they're here. . . . I know that they love me, and that they'll be here with me when it's time" (p. 88).

The other type of vision is a transcendental glimpse of the place where the dying think they're going. "Their descriptions are brief—rarely exceeding a sentence or two—and not very specific, but usually glowing" (p. 99). At the end of Tolstoy's famous novella "The Death of Ivan Ilych," Ivan exclaims on his deathbed, "So that's what it is! What joy!" (1993, p. 63)—the last words he ever spoke. His words are typical of visions of this second kind. But since there is no way to ascertain whether this type of vision is veridical or hallucinatory, I won't give much attention to it. Suffice it to say that those who have such visions invariably report them as glimpses of a real world, not as chimeras.

So we will be concentrating on the visions that people close to death have of beings, not of places. Are these visions more than likely veridical? Are they sightings of real beings that any of us, properly equipped, could see, and who exist in their own right whether we see them or not? Or are they hallucinations? Are they as the word is commonly used, sensory perceptions that are unrelated to outside events—in other words, seeing or hearing things that aren't there?

I should add here that two types of people close to death have visions of deceased spirits: (1) those dying slowly, often of cancer, who see spirits at their bedside, and (2) those not necessarily dying who have a potentially fatal experience that culminates in a near-death experience (NDE). Those dying slowly are usually aware of their surroundings and can communicate simultaneously with both the living and the dead—as if they have one foot in this world and one in the next. Those who meet dead relatives or friends during NDEs are completely cut off from our world as they communicate with the deceased. Yet the descriptions of these spirits given by NDErs after their return from the "Other World" are the same as the descriptions given by the slowly dying. The spirits are usually recognizable, loving, and supportive. Sometimes they are described as "takeaway spirits" or "greeters."

The Argument for the Spirit Hypothesis

Social scientists usually have little patience with any theory that takes seriously the reality of beings on the "Other Side." Words used to describe them like "transcendental" or "spiritual" are often looked at with suspicion if not dismissed as nonsense. But there are excellent reasons for taking them seriously. I will list them under four headings.

1. First, persons near death usually insist that the phantasms they see are not hallucinations, but living spirits existing in their own right. This insistence is especially impressive when the dying person is an atheist or materialist who does not believe in life after death. "I'm an atheist. I don't believe in God or Heaven," a 25-year-old woman named Angela, and dying of melanoma, declared to her nurse (Callanan & Kelley, p. 89). Blind and partially paralyzed, she nevertheless had a vision, and it changed her outlook on death. "I don't believe in angels or God," she told her nurse, "but someone was here with me. Whoever it was loves me and is waiting for me. So it means I won't die alone" (p. 90).

Angela's claim is of course easy to dismiss. One can claim, not without reason, that Angela hallucinated a takeaway spirit to ease her despair in the face of eternal extinction. NDErs are typically just as adamant about the reality of the spirits they encounter while out of their body, and social scientists usually react to these claims in the same skeptical fashion. But the sheer volume of such claims by persons near death is impressive. And it is all the more impressive when put alongside similar claims made by other visionaries *not* near death. Conant's study of bereaved but otherwise healthy widows (1996), to take but one example, reveals the same insistence by some of the widows that the spirits who visited them were real. Conant reports that the "vividness of the experience amazed them. The comparison to hallucinations was voiced simultaneously five times and was always rejected. These were *not* hallucinations" (p. 186). Some of the widows "seemed to be amazed by the emotional power of the experience more than by its vividness because of the conviction they had been in contact with the spirit of the deceased [husband]" (p. 187). Not all the widows in the study were confident that the spirits of their

husband actually paid them a visit; most felt that their culture discouraged a "spiritual interpretation" of their visions, and several worried about "the connotation of craziness" (p. 188) that such an interpretation carried. But all agreed that the vision "feels real" (p. 194). And all, even the most skeptical, derived "reassurance that life after death was possible for the deceased . . . as well as for themselves when they would eventually die" (p. 192). I myself am impressed enough by all these visions, especially their feeling of "realness," to keep an open mind about their ontological status. Not so Conant herself. While acknowledging that such visions "served as a safe haven to help mend the trauma of loss, as an inner voice to lessen current social isolation, as an internal reworking of self to meet new realities, and as reassurance of the possibility of immortality" (p. 195), she describes them as "vivid hallucinations." The ontological status of the visions is never discussed. She appreciates that the visions are useful fictions and therefore salutary, but the possibility that they might be real apparently never occurred to her.

Conant's study is especially relevant to our study for two reasons. First, even though she is not studying visions of the dying or potentially dying, the visions of her collection of widows seem to be of the same quality. Though invisible to everyone else, they are convincingly real to the one having the vision, they are recognizable, and they usually convey a message of reassurance. Second, Conant is a cautious, thoroughgoing social scientist with, if anything, a bias against drawing transcendental conclusions based on her research. What she wanted to show was that visions of the deceased should be regarded as successful coping mechanisms, not as delusions that should be discouraged. Her interests run in a completely different direction from mine, yet I find her useful. When two minds so differently attuned find a common ground, there is often something important going on.

2. The second prong of the argument for the reality of spirits comes from a careful analysis of them. The spirits of persons who are identified by NDErs or by the slowly dying have one thing in common: They are almost always spirits of the deceased. You might ask yourself why all these hallucinations are so tidy. Everywhere else hallucinations are higgledy-piggledy. Aunt Adelaide alive on earth is just as likely to be hallucinated as Aunt Jill who died five years before. But these hallucinations, if that's what they are, have sorted themselves out. With uncanny regularity only the dead show up. Why should that be?

The materialist might answer that it would be *illogical* to hallucinate someone you thought was still alive. After all, a person can't be living on earth and living on the Other Side at the same time. If you had a vision of someone alive on this side of the veil, that would be *proof* you were hallucinating and would undercut the benefit you might derive from the hallucination. So the subconscious mind sorts out who's died and who hasn't. It keeps track. And when your time is up, it decks out a nice dead relative for you to hallucinate, a nice dead relative to take care of you when you finally die. Your fear of death vanishes. So the argument goes. But this argument is not as convincing as it might first appear. After all, how logical *are* hallucinations? Hallucinations are made of memory fragments, and those fragments are no more orderly as they come and go in the theater of the mind than the stuff of our daydreams. Zen masters compare the behavior of this mental detritus to a pack of drunken monkeys. And Aldous Huxley refers to them as "the bobbing scum of miscellaneous memories" and as "imbecilities—mere casual waste products of psycho-physiological activity" (1945, pp. 126–127). The materialist's line of reasoning is plausible up to a point, but it overlooks the almost random nature of hallucinations.

But let us grant for the sake of argument that it does have force. I think I can show that whatever force we grant it for the moment is not good enough in the face of the facts. Here is why.

Let us say I am very sick in my hospital bed and have a near-death experience. I see in my vision my grandpa, long dead, and my cousin Manny, whom I think to be very much alive. They present themselves as spirits, and I recognize them as such, but I am confused. For how can Manny be a spirit since he's alive in the flesh? I come out of my NDE, and I express this confusion to the loved ones gathered around me. But they know something I don't know. They know that Manny was killed in an automobile accident two days before. They didn't tell me because they thought it would upset me. There are quite a few cases like this in the literature, and one whole book, a classic, devoted to them (Barrett, 1926). More recently, Callanan and Kelley presented three cases like this in their book on the slowly dying (Chapter Seven), and the Guggenheims (1995) devote a whole chapter to them in their study of after-death communications (ADCs). Here is why I think these cases are so important. If I believe my dear Aunt Mary and Uncle Charlie and my five siblings and my wife and dozens of other relatives and friends, *including my cousin Manny,* are all alive, why should I hallucinate only my cousin Manny from among all these possibilities? Why should my hallucination be so well informed and so selective? It could be a coincidence, but there are too many cases like this for them all to be coincidences. There is always the possibility that I could have known telepathically that Manny, and only Manny from among those I just named, was dead. But if I had never had any powerful telepathic experiences before, isn't this explanation *ad hoc?* I think the best explanation for Manny's appearance alongside my grandpa in my vision is that the newly dead Manny *actually came* (in spirit), along with grandpa, to greet me during my NDE. He was not a hallucination after all. He was not a delusion. He should be taken at face value.

3. The third prong of the argument derives from the physiology of near-death experiences. Recent research by a team of Dutch doctors, led by van Lommel (van Lommel, van Wees, Meyers, & Elfferich, 2001), makes it clear that the typical features of the NDE, including

meetings with deceased relatives, occur while the electro-encephalogram (EEG) is flat-lined—in other words, when the brain is inactive and the whole body is "clinically dead." Van Lommel summarizes the findings:

From these studies [involving 344 cardiac patients studied over an 8-year period] we know that . . . no electric activity of the cortex of the brain (flat EEG) must have been possible, but also the abolition of brain stem activity like the loss of the cornea reflex, fixed dilated pupils and the loss of the gag reflex is a clinical finding in those patients. However, patients with an NDE [18% of the total] can report a clear consciousness, in which cognitive functioning, emotion, sense of identity, and memory from early childhood was possible, as well as perception from a position out of and above their "dead" body. (van Lommel, no date)

Van Lommel elaborates further: Even though the EEG is flat, people

experience their consciousness outside their body, with the possibility of perception out of and above their body, with identity, and with heightened awareness, attention, well-structured thought processes, memories and emotions. And they also can experience their consciousness in a dimension where past, present and future exist at the same moment, without time and space, and can be experienced as soon as attention has been directed to it (life review and preview), and even sometimes they come in contact with the "fields of consciousness" of deceased relatives. And later they can experience their conscious return into their body. (van Lommel, no date)

Van Lommel then asks the obvious question: "How could a clear consciousness outside one's body be experienced at the moment that the brain no longer functions during a period of clinical death with flat EEG?" (van Lommel et al., 2001).

What does all this mean for our thesis? It means that the typical elements of the NDE, including meetings with deceased relatives, are not hallucinations. Hallucinations are produced by an *active* brain, one whose wave pattern would be anything but flat. What, then, could account for the visions of deceased loved ones? It appears that the dying person or nearly dead person, free from her physical body for a few moments, enters a world, an ethereal world, close by but undetectable by the physical senses. She looks like a corpse to an outside observer, but she is having the experience of a lifetime—in another dimension. An experience of what? She says an experience of real beings, embodied beings, dead people she recognizes. Is there any good reason to keep our minds closed to this possibility, given the unintelligibility of the alternative?

4. The fourth and last prong of the argument is, like the one we've just looked at, exclusively concerned with the near-death experience, and not the visionary experiences of the slowly dying who do not have an

NDE. Glimpsing spirits of deceased relatives is a standard feature of the NDE, so anything that argues for the veridicality of the NDE *as a whole* gives support for our thesis.

There is quite a bit that does. I will organize it under three headings.

First, many reports of things seen by NDErs having an out-of-body experience (OBE) turn out to be veridical. There are hundreds of examples in the serious literature on NDEs. One woman saw a shoe sitting on an upper-story ledge of her hospital—a shoe invisible from the street or from her room—as she drifted out of the building during her NDE; the shoe, upon inspection, turned out to be exactly where she said it was. Another woman took a trip to see her sister and later reported what her sister was doing and wearing at the time—a report later verified by the surprised sister who wondered how she knew. A five-year-old child described in detail, and with impressive accuracy, what happened when her body was being resuscitated while she, out of her body, watched from near the ceiling of her hospital room. In fact it is common for NDErs to describe their resuscitations while they are clinically dead. Michael Sabom, an Atlanta cardiologist, conducted an experiment involving resuscitation accounts to see how accurate they were:

> Sabom asked twenty-five medically savvy patients to make educated guesses about what happens when a doctor tries to get the heart started again. He wanted to compare the knowledge of "medically smart" patients with the out-of-body experiences of medically unsophisticated patients.

> He found that twenty-three of the twenty-five in the control group made major mistakes in describing the resuscitation procedure. On the other hand, none of the near-death patients made mistakes in describing what went on in their own resuscitations. (M. Morse, 1990, p. 120)

It is difficult to account for the accuracy of NDE accounts if NDErs are hallucinating. Why should hallucinations be so accurate? Why should they yield far more accuracy than the accounts of imagined resuscitations provided by "medically savvy" patients relying on their memory?

Second, NDEs are often profoundly life-changing. Melvin Morse did an extensive "Transformations study" to quantify what every NDE researcher already knew: that people who have a deep, well-developed—or "core"—NDE are dramatically transformed by their experience. He reported "amazing results": "After we finished analyzing the data from the more than four hundred people who participated in the research project, we discovered that the near-death experience causes many long-term changes" (M. Morse, 1992, p. 60). He grouped them under four headings: decreased death anxiety, increase in psychic abilities, higher zest for living, and higher intelligence. In the exhaustive study referred to above, van Lommel and his cohorts reported that the "transformational processes after

an NDE were very similar" and encompassed "life-changing insight, heightened intuition, and disappearance of fear of death" (van Lommel et al., 2001, p. 3).

The question that is natural to ask at this point is, Can hallucinations transform the people who have them? D. Morse, a clinical psychologist and hard-nosed materialist until he had his own NDE, has this to say about hallucinations:

> Descriptions given of hallucinations are often hazy and contain distortions of reality, while NDE descriptions are usually normally ordered and lifelike. Hallucinations are often accompanied by anxiety feelings, while NDEs are generally calm and peaceful. Hallucinations afterwards rarely cause life-changing occurrences as do NDEs. (D. Morse, 2000, pp. 48–49)

NDErs, like the widows we surveyed above, typically insist on the "realness" of their experience and that it is this realness that gives them hope of seeing their loved ones again. This quality of "realness," and the transformative quality that derives from it, is verified by van Lommel. He found in follow-up studies that most of his patients who did not have an NDE (the control group) did not believe in an afterlife, whereas those who had one "strongly believed in an afterlife" (no date, p. 8) and showed "positive changes." Furthermore, these changes were more apparent at the eight-year follow-up than the two-year (p. 8). Something deeply and lastingly transformed this second group of people. Which is more likely: That a hallucination did this, or that an overwhelming slap in the face by something very real did it?

Third, near-death researchers, beginning with Moody (1975), have consistently identified the "core features" of the NDE, and claim that these features recur in individuals having very little in common other than their NDE. It appears that NDEs from cultures as different as Japan, India, sub-Saharan Africa, and the West all exhibit these core features. Now, it is known that hallucinations vary radically from person to person—so much so that it would be surprising if one person's hallucination was at all similar to his next-door neighbor's, not to mention someone's from a different culture. How can the similarity in this core experience be explained? If by hallucination, then obviously not by any ordinary hallucination.

Rather than go out on a limb and posit a universal hallucination that all humans carry seed-fashion deep in their brains, most NDE researchers suspect the commonality is explainable by a common environment, or world, that opens up to the NDEr. In other words, they all see much the same thing because the world that opens up to them is not infinitely variable, like hallucinations, but is simply the way it is. It is real, in other words; and reality, while it admits of considerable variation and can be interpreted in a variety of ways, is malleable only up to a point. Beyond that point, all NDErs experience very much the same thing—just as an Inuit and a Zulu, in spite of radically different cultures and geographies, would experience the one world that belongs to us all and be able to talk about it meaningfully to each other. The Zulu and the Inuit might have different feelings about the spirits they met in their respective NDEs, but they would at least be able to say they encountered beings, many whom they recognized, that did not belong to the world of the living.

So again we must choose: Is it more reasonable to explain away the core experience as hallucinatory, or as a reflection of something that is real and is encountered? The only skeptical theory that makes sense is the "seed theory" I mentioned above. It is not a preposterous explanation, but is it the more likely? We must each decide for ourselves. Given the other prongs of the argument presented here, however, it seems much more likely, at least up to this point, that the spirits we see during our NDEs or as we near death after a long illness are what they seem to be: real beings from the world we might be about to enter.

The Weakness in the Spirit Hypothesis

It would be dishonest of me to fail to point out the weak link in the spirit hypothesis I've been defending up to this point. Melvin Morse appreciates it fully and asks the question:

> But we shouldn't forget about the woman who saw Elvis in the light, should we? As one skeptic pointed out, "If these experiences are real and not just dreams, how can you explain Elvis?" Or Buddha? How can NDEs of children be explained where they see pet dogs, or elementary school teachers who are still alive? They show up in some NDEs too. How can they be explained? (M. Morse, 1992, p. 128)

The skeptic asks a good question, and the skeptic in me worries more than a little about the idiosyncratic features of some NDEs, especially as found in children. Morse presents a cornucopia of cases involving children, and quite a few play into the skeptic's hands as he dredges the literature for signs of hallucination. For example, take the NDE of a five-year-old who nearly drowned in a swimming pool. Now a scientist in his forties of distinguished reputation, "Tom" recalls passing down a long tunnel toward the Light. All seems quite normal for an NDE until he sees "God on a throne. People—maybe angels—were below looking up at the throne." He goes on: "I sat on the lap of God, and he told me that I had to go back. 'It's not your time,' he said. I wanted to stay but I came back" (M. Morse, 1990, p. 167). Suffice it to say that very few NDErs report seeing God sitting on a throne. In another case, eight-year-old Michelle had an NDE during a diabetic coma. In typical NDE fashion she felt herself float out of her body and watched the resuscitation effort, later describing it in accurate detail. Eventually she was allowed to make a decision to return or not to return to her body, a typical feature of the NDE. But Michelle expressed her will to return in a novel manner: "In front of me were two buttons, a red one and a green one. The people in white kept telling me to push the red button. But I knew I should push the green one because the red one would mean I wouldn't come back. I pushed the green one instead and woke up from the coma" (M. Morse, 1990, p. 39).

Is there really a red and a green button in a world beyond ours? Does God really sit on a throne and talk to little children in that world? Not a chance, I would say. "Then the NDErs must have been hallucinating these bizarre features of the NDE," says the skeptic, "and if these are hallucinations, then doesn't it stand to reason that the entire experience is a hallucination?"

I raised this question to Greyson, editor of the *Journal of Near-Death Studies,* and this was his reply:

> As for Melvin Morse's 8-year-old patient who pushed the green button to return from her coma, I also find it hard to believe that the button was "real." But then I also have difficulty taking as concretely "real" a lot of things described by NDErs, including, in SOME cases, encounters with deceased loved ones and religious figures. I do not think that these are hallucinations, however, or that the experiencers are lying or fabricating memories. What I think is happening is that they are interpreting ambiguous or hard-to-understand phenomena in terms that are familiar to them.
>
> Many NDErs tell us that what they experienced was ineffable—and THAT I believe wholeheartedly. I think that what happens after death is so far beyond our feeble understanding that there is no way for us to describe it accurately in words. Although experiencers may understand fully while they are "on the other side," once they return to the limitations of their physical brains, they have to unconsciously force-fit their memories of incomprehensible events into images they CAN understand. That's why we hear Christians talk about seeing Jesus or Mary, and we hear Hindus talking about yamatoots (messengers of Yama, the god of the dead), and we hear NDErs from "advanced" Western societies—but not NDErs from "primitive" societies—talk about tunnels. (One NDEr who was a truck driver told me about traveling through a chrome tailpipe, an image he could relate to.)
>
> Many NDErs talk about not wanting to return, and yet here they are, so they have to construct some reason to explain their return. Westerners often say that a deceased relative or religious figure told them it was not yet their time, or their work was not finished. That's an acceptable and believable reason for a time-conscious and achievement-oriented Westerner to return. On the other hand, it is common for Indians to say that they were told a mistake had been made, and that the yamatoots were supposed to have taken Ravi Singh the incense-maker, not Ravi Singh the baker. That kind of "bureaucratic bungling," I am told, is more believable in India, as it is typical of the way things often happen in their society. I suspect that an 8-year-old girl with limited understanding had to come up with a concrete image like pushing a green button to return. She did not hallucinate the button, but after the fact her mind came up with that interpretation of what really happened to her to effect her return. It was a misinterpretation rather than a hallucination.

Am I splitting hairs? I don't think so. A hallucination is a perception that occurs in the ABSENCE of any sensory stimulation. I think NDErs DO "see" SOMETHING that is "really" there—but it is so far beyond our understanding that they have to interpret it subsequently in terms of familiar images. It is more like an illusion than a hallucination. If at night you imagine out of thin air that there is a person in your room, that is a hallucination. But if, in the darkness, you misinterpret a hat-rack for a person in your room, that is an illusion, an imprecise interpretation of something that is really there rather than something that sprang up solely from your imagination. That's what I think a lot of NDE imagery is: imprecise interpretations of things that are comprehensible in the bright light of the NDE, but incomprehensible in the dim light of our physical brains. (Personal communication, January 10, 2005)

Greyson has given us a rich, plausible account of the idiosyncratic features of NDEs. But the skeptic might remain dubious. After all, if there really is a world beyond ours, it is hard to imagine what in it would be confused with a green and a red button. To deal with this challenge, I veer slightly away from Greyson's analysis. It seems more plausible to me that the subconscious imagination of the NDEr is *actively supplying material* for the experience; or, alternatively, that someone else over there is actively supplying it for the benefit of the NDEr. In other words, the mysterious world entered into by the NDEr is made more approachable and intelligible—more *friendly* is perhaps a better word—by his own imagination or someone else's (a spirit guide's?) interpretive or artistic power. Whatever be the case, on balance there are, in my judgment, far too many indicators that the NDE is an experience of another world that exists *in the main* independently of the experiencer, even though certain reported features of it might be explainable by a coloring of the experience or by faulty memory of exactly what happened. The claim that the *entire experience* is a hallucinated fictive world strikes me as incredible. Nevertheless, there is room, based on all the evidence at our disposal, for such a claim. It is not a claim with no basis.

A final clarification of my position is in order. I believe that visions of the dying or nearly-dying are a combination of real transcendental material and imaginative projection. For example, Julian of Norwich, very near death when she had her famous visions of the dying Christ, could not have seen Krishna or Vairocana Buddha: They would have had no meaning for her, and the Mind who assisted her in coloring the vision, or alternatively her own imagination, would not have allowed such a thing. Nor could a South American Indian shaman have glimpsed Christ while entranced. But their visions are not purely the stuff of imagination either: were there no transcendental "canvas" to project them onto, there would not have been any vision. As for glimpses of the dying, especially deceased relatives, these visions are much closer to the realities they seem to be. I don't believe they are so much projections outward from dying persons, as projections "toward" them from deceased relatives

who come to greet them. If the skeptic insists on reducing all transcendental phenomena to hallucination, we will not be able to agree on much. We *would* agree, however, that all these visions are, to some extent, cultural, personal, and historical. And we also would agree that most hallucinations in normal subjects (as when a moose charges a sleep-deprived sledder in the Arctic) are not grounded in a transcendental world. In contrast to the visions we have been studying, they exist only in the mind of the subject. They are truly hallucinations.

The Relevance of This Study to the Spirituality of Death

I agree with Lucy Bregman, in her article in this issue, that the word "spirituality" is a wonderful word in search of a meaning. As I tried to show in my opening paragraph, I think the word must be anchored in a transcendent world if it is to retain its distinctive meaning. Otherwise it can become a synonym for *mystique* or *romance*—as when we speak of the spirituality of motherhood or of a sunset or of golf. Each of these can provide wonderful experiences, but they are not what we have in mind when we speak of the *spirituality of death.* As Sherwin Nuland (1995) showed us in his award-winning book *How We Die,* death is not usually a time of wonderful experiences. It is frequently, however, a time of healing experiences, as when long estranged relatives or friends are coerced by death's finality into an act of mutual forgiveness. Perhaps it is not stretching too far the meaning of the word *spirituality* to apply it to such meaningful moments. But there is a time when the word is ideally applicable. That is when a person close to death glimpses a world he or she is about to enter—what we will call the spiritual world, a world where spirits reside, and where the dying will reside when he or she becomes a spirit.

My grandmother transmitted to her family something of the excitement of that world shortly before she died. A devout Christian, she became comatose, or apparently comatose, hours before her death at 94. None of us could reach her, even when whispering our love into her ear. But then my mother happened to whisper that she would soon be with Jesus. So suddenly that we were startled, her eyes opened and her face lit up in great excitement. Like Ivan Ilych, she died joyously. She had a foretaste of the eternal world, the world where spirits reside, and her spirit practically jumped out of her body. Hers was a spiritual experience in the truest sense of the word. The *spirituality of death* may mean many things, but Granny epitomized its meaning for all of us.

But I am not concerned with linguistics or etymology. What I have tried to show here is that books are available to get us ready for death. So are the dying. Callanan and Kelley tell the following story:

> Bobby [who was dying] had spoken clearly for the first time in three days.
>
> "He told us, 'I can see the light down the road and it's beautiful,'" Bill said.

This glimpse of the other place gives immeasurable comfort to many, and often is perceived as a final gift from the one who died.

"I've never been a religious person, but being there when Bobby died was a real spiritual experience," his sister said later. "I'll never be the same again."

Bill echoed her sentiments at the funeral. "Because Bobby's death was so peaceful, I'll never be as scared of death," he said. "He gave me a little preview of what lay beyond it for him, and, I hope, for me." (p. 102)

Whether dying persons are telling us of their glimpse of the next world or conversing with people we can't see, we should consider ourselves immensely blessed when it happens. If we don't make the mistake of assuming they are "confused," we are likely to feel some of the excitement they convey. For we are witnessing the momentary merging of two worlds that at all other times remain tightly compartmentalized and mutually inaccessible. That merging is what I mean by the spirituality of death

References

Barrett, W. (1926). *Death-bed visions*. London: Methuen.

Callanan, M., & Kelley, P. (1992). *Final gifts*. New York: Bantam.

Conant, R. (1996). Memories of the death and life of a spouse: The role of images and *sense of presence* in grief. In D. Klass, P. Silverman, & S. Nickman (Eds.), *Continuing bonds: New understandings of grief*. Washington, DC: Taylor & Francis.

Guggenheim, B., & Guggenheim, J. (1995). *Hello from heaven!* New York: Bantam.

Huxley, A. (1945). Distractions—I. In C. Isherwood (Ed.), *Vedanta for the western world*. Hollywood: Vedanta Press.

Moody, R. (1975). *Life after life*. New York: Bantam.

Morse, D. (2000). *Searching for eternity*. Memphis: Eagle Wing.

Morse, M. (1990). *Closer to the light*. New York: Ivy.

Morse, M. (1992). *Transformed by the light*. New York: Ivy.

Nuland, S. (1995). *How we die*. New York: Vintage.

Tolstoy, L. (1993). *The Kreutzer Sonata and other short stories*. New York: Dover.

van Lommel, P., van Wees, R., Meyers V., & Elfferich, I. (2001). Near-death experience in survivors of cardiac arrest: A prospective study in the Netherlands. *Lancet, 358*(9298). Retrieved from World Wide Web: . . ./get_xml.asp?booleanTerm=SO=The+Lancet+AND+SU+Near+Death+Experiences&fuzzy Term

van Lommel, P. (no date). A reply to Shermer: Medical evidence for NDEs. Retrieved June 26, 2005 from the World Wide Web: www.skepticalinvestigations.org/whoswho/vanLommel.htm.

Critical Thinking

1. After reading this article, what are your personal beliefs regarding deathbed and near-death visions?

2. What are the strengths/weaknesses of the spirit hypothesis?

3. What "evidence" can you present to support the idea that some individuals do indeed have deathbed and/or near-death visions?

Beyond Terror and Denial: The Positive Psychology of Death Acceptance

Paul T. P. Wong and Adrian Tomer

Death remains the biggest threat as well as the greatest challenge to humanity. It is the single universal event that affects all of us in ways more than we care to know (Greenberg, Koole, & Pyszczynski, 2004; Wass & Neimeyer, 1995; Yalom, 2008). Because of the unique human capacity of meaning-making and social construction, death has evolved into a very complex and dynamic system, involving biological, psychological, spiritual, societal, and cultural components (Kastenbaum, 2000). Whatever meanings we attach to death may have important implications for our well-being. Thus, at a personal level, death attitudes matter: Death defines personal meaning and determines how we live (Neimeyer 2005; Tomer, 2000; Tomer, Eliason, & Wong, 2008).

At the cultural level death also makes its ubiquitous presence felt in a broad spectrum of social functions, from family, religion, and the entertainment industry to medical care (Kearl, 1989). How we relate to our own mortality is in turn mediated by family, society, and culture (Kastenbaum, 2000). In sum, all human activities are framed by death anxiety and colored by our collective and individual efforts to resolve this inescapable and intractable existential given.

In the post-9/11 era, the ever-present threat of terrorist attacks has injected into our collective awareness the unpredictable nature of mortal danger and mass destruction. Death attitudes even play a vital role in national security: Death-defying suicide bombers have changed the landscape of geopolitical warfare, and victory in the war on terror depends in part on our ability to live with death threat.

In a wired global village, our death attitudes are further affected by the 24-hour news coverage of natural and man-made disasters around the world, from catastrophic earthquakes to genocides. Death has invaded our living rooms in grisly detail. Our passive acceptance of the endless coverage of carnage and atrocity betrays a love–hate relationship with death: We are simultaneously repelled by its terror and seduced by its mysteries. The popular appeal of violent video games, TV dramas, and Hollywood movies provide further evidence of our morbid fascination with death. In short, our relationship with death cannot be reduced to terror; a complete psychology of death needs to move beyond terror and denial and start investigating positive attitudes toward death.

The ubiquity of images of death may be seen as an opportunity. Lifting of the taboo may have paved the way for death to emerge as a popular subject for both psychological research and public education.

From Death Denial to Death Acceptance

All through history, human beings have pondered the meaning of mortality and developed elaborate defense mechanisms against the terror of death both at the individual and cultural levels. We now have a huge literature on death denial and terror management (Pyszczynski, Greenberg, & Solomon, 2002).

The problem with death denial is that no matter how hard we try to suppress and repress death awareness, anxiety about our demise can still manifest itself in a variety of symptoms, such as worries, depression, stresses, and conflicts (Yalom, 2008). Another problem with death denial is that it is doomed to fail. Sooner or later, various events in life, such as terminal illness or the death of a loved one, will thrust us right in front of the stark reality of mortality. Yalom (2008) maintained that both covert and conscious death anxiety, if not adequately addressed, may undermine our well-being and prevent us from fully engaging in life. To be obsessed with fear of death can prevent us from living fully and vitally because so much energy will be spent in the denial and avoidance of death. We keep on worrying about death to the extent that we are not free to live. We may avoid loving in order to avoid the pain of separation. Yalom pointed out that "some refuse the loan of life to avoid the debt of death" (p. 108). From an existential perspective, to live fully and happily, we need to engage what we most fear.

Considering the above, it is high time for psychologists to focus on the process of death acceptance. There are numerous reasons for embarking on this positive exploration of a traditionally dark subject matter. These include a fuller understanding of the meaning of life and a better preparation for living well and dying well. Indeed, research on the good death constitutes a new frontier of the current positive psychology movement. We need to learn how to talk about death in a way that is liberating, humanizing, and life-enhancing. Through an increased understanding of death acceptance we may learn to treat each other with respect and compassion.

The Different Meanings of Death Acceptance

Elisabeth Kubler-Ross (1969, 2009) was largely responsible for making death a legitimate topic for research and medicine. Her stage-model of coping with death (denial, anger, bargaining, depression, and acceptance) has left a lasting impact on our understanding of the psychological reactions to death. She has identified some defense mechanisms (denial and bargaining) and negative emotional reactions (anger and depression) involved in coming to terms with the reality of death. In the final stage, denial, fear, and hostility give way to embracing the inevitable end. However, her sequential stage concept has been widely criticized. For example, Bonanno (2009) has recently found that in coping with bereavement, most people can come to death acceptance without struggling through the previous stages. Only research explicitly designed to study death acceptance will reveal the pathways and mechanisms of coming to terms with death in a constructive way.

Nearly 25 years ago, Wong and his associates undertook a comprehensive study of death acceptance (Gesser, Wong, & Reker, 1987–1988). In addition to death fear and death avoidance, they identified three distinct types of death acceptance: (a) neutral death acceptance, facing death rationally as an inevitable end of every life; (b) approach acceptance, accepting death as a gateway to a better afterlife; and (c) escape acceptance, choosing death as a better alternative to a painful existence. The Death Attitude Profile (DAP) was later revised as DAP-R (Wong, Reker, & Gesser, 1994). Both instruments have been widely used. Neimeyer, Moser, and Wittkowski (2003) confirm that DAP-R remains the preferred instrument to assess death acceptance.

The Dual-System Model of Coping with Death

Imagine yourself as a marine serving in Afghanistan, knowing that every time you are on patrol duty, you may be blown to pieces by an improvised explosive device. How would you carry out your mission in spite of the imminent mortal danger? Any professional soldier knows that it does not pay to live in terror, because excessive fear will paralyze you and reduce your combat effectiveness and increase the likelihood of getting killed. Similarly, denial may also be fatal. Wong's

(in press) dual-system model of achieving the good life can be readily applied to the challenge of how to cope with death anxiety while striving for life-enhancing goals.

According to this model, one has to depend on the cooperation and interaction between approach and avoidance systems. These two complementary tendencies represent two different motivations and life orientations. The defensive tendency to avoid pain, suffering, dangers, anxieties, and death serves a protective function. It is the tendency to seek security and self-preservation in a chaotic and often dangerous world. It involves various defense mechanisms, both unconscious and conscious, to safeguard our psychological and physical integrity. It also involves coping behaviors to reduce threats and negative outcomes. Those who take a defensive stance toward life and death tend to be very cautious and timid, afraid of making changes or taking risks. Paradoxically, their defensive orientation may actually increase their level of fear and anxiety.

The approach system is primarily concerned with pursuing worthwhile life goals, such as career success, raising a happy and healthy family, or defending national security. Engagement in such life-expanding projects cannot be maintained without dealing with setbacks, negative thoughts, and fear of untimely death. Optimal functioning depends on transforming the negative to strengthen the positive, thus, involving worth approach and avoidance systems.

Positively oriented individuals are willing to confront the crisis and create opportunities for growth. Their preferred tendency is to take on the difficult tasks and risk even death in order to achieve some significant life goals. They are primarily motivated by their desire to accomplish their life mission, whatever the risks, because they have found something worth dying for. Death exposes the fragility of life and the futility of everyday busyness and strivings. Death focuses and clarifies. The terror of death teaches us what really matters and how to live authentically. The human quest for meaning and spirituality occupies the center stage, while death anxiety belongs to the background. Thus, the sting of death is swallowed up by our engagement in a meaningful life. In sum, the positive orientation is more concerned with what makes life worth living in spite of suffering and death anxiety. Kahlil Gibran (1994) expressed this idea well: "It is life in quest of life in bodies that fear the grave" (p. 104).

Terror Management Theory (TMT) Vs. Meaning Management Theory (MMT)

According to terror management theory (TMT; Pyszczynski, Greenberg, Solomon, Arndt, & Shimel, 2004; Pyszczynski, Greenberg, Solomon, & Maxfield, 2006), avoidance of death anxiety is the primary motive while the quest for positive meaning is secondary, because the latter is used as a way to shield us from the terror of death. Meaning creation and maintenance are primarily considered to fulfill a defensive purpose. Symbolic immortality is a particular type of meaning. One attains symbolic immortality by living up to, or even better, exceeding prevalent standards of value (Goldenberg, Pyszczynski, Greenberg,

& Solomon, 2001). Because the concept of symbolic immortality is so close to the concept of self-esteem, derogation of the self or derogation of one's culture or system of value are likely to produce a defensive reaction. Moreover, an increase in mortality salience is likely to increase one's propensity to defend self and/or the belief/meaning system (Psyzczynski, 2006). To sum up, while TMT does not negate the existence of a growth motivation (e.g., Pyszczynski, Greenberg, & Goldenberg, 2003), the search for meaning and meaning making are considered from a defensive perspective. In contrast, according to meaning management theory (MMT), the quest for meaning is a primary motive, because we are meaning-seeking and meaning-making creatures living in a world of meanings. Thus, the pressing question for most people is, How should I live? How can I live a good, fulfilling life?

The negative defensive life orientation focuses on anxiety, terror, and unconscious defensive reactions. The positive life orientation focuses on growth, authenticity, and meaning. It advocates proactive and transformative confrontation with the human condition in its totality. When people are exposed to mortality salience, both TMT and MMT would predict an increase in pro-culture and pro-esteem activities, but for very different reasons. The former is for minimizing terror, but for the latter, it is for maximizing meaning, fulfillment, and joy.

From the perspective of MMT, the heart and soul of overcoming death anxiety and living an authentic happy life lies in the human capacity for meaning making and meaning reconstruction (Neimeyer, 2001; Tomeretal., 2008; Wong, 2008). More specifically, it is the life-enhancing and life-expanding quest for meaning that enables us to live fully in the light of death. Ryan and Deci (2004), based on their self-determination theory (SDT), also emphasized the idea that healthy people seek authentic meaning, as opposed to the defensive or contingent self-esteem emphasized in TMT.

What we need to achieve a complete psychology of death is a good articulation between defense-oriented theories such as TMT and growth-oriented models such as SDT and MMT that emphasize the meaning seeking/making as basic human motivation.

We have just begun the dialog on death acceptance. We still know very little about the pathways and stages of death acceptance. We also remain uninformed about the individual differences and contextual variables in shaping the process of death acceptance. We can only speculate about the optimal ways of combining death denial and death acceptance to achieve well-being in various situations. Finally, so much can be done to apply the concepts and empirical knowledge of death acceptance to clinical populations (Banfman, 2002; Frankl, 1986; Yalom, 2008; Wong, in press). This special issue represents some of the preliminary efforts to explore the new frontier of the positive psychology of death acceptance.

References

Banfman, F. (2002). A matter of life and death. Clinical Nursing Research, 11, 103–115.

Bonanno, G. A. (2009). The other side of sadness: What the new science of bereavement tells us about life after loss. New York, NY: Basic Books.

Frankl, V. (1986). The doctor and the soul: From psychotherapy to logotherapy. New York, NY: Vintage Books.

Gesser, G., Wong, P. T. P., & Reker, G. T. (1987–1988). Death attitudes across the life-span: The development and validation of the Death Attitude Profile (DAP). Omega: The Journal of Death and Dying, 18, 113–128.

Gibran, K. (1994). The prophet. London, UK: Senate Press.

Greenberg, J., Koole, S. L., & Pyszczynski, T. (Eds.) (2004). Handbook of experimental existential psychology. New York, NY: Guilford Press.

Goldenberg, C., Pyszczynski, T., Greenberg, J., & Solomon, S. (2001). Understanding human ambivalence about sex: The effects of stripping sex of meaning. The journal of Sex Research, 39, 310–320.

Kastenbaum, R. (2000). The psychology of death (3rd ed.). New York, NY: Springer. Kearl, M. C. (1989). Endings: A sociology of death and dying. New York, NY: Oxford University Press.

Kubler-Ross, E. (1969). On death and dying. New York, NY: Macmillan.

Kubler-Ross, E. (2009). On death and dying (40th anniv. ed.). Abingdon, UK: Routledge.

Neimeyer, R. A. (2001). Meaning reconstruction and the experience of loss. Washington, DC: American Psychological Associatioin.

Neimeyer, R. A. (2005). From death anxiety to meaning making at the end of life: Recommendations for psychological assessment. Clinical Psychology: Science and Practice, 12, 354–357.

Neimeyer, R A., Moser, R., & Wittkowski, J. (2003). Assessing attitudes toward death: Psychometric considerations. Omega: The Journal of Death and Dying, 47, 45–76.

Pyszczynski, T., Greenberg, J., & Goldenberg, J. (2003). Freedom versus fear: On the defense, growth, and expansion of the self. In M. R. Leary & J. P. Tangney (Eds.), Handbook of self and identity (pp. 314–343). New York, NY: Guilford Press.

Pyszczynski, T., Greenberg, J., & Solomon, S. (2002). In the wake of 9/11: The psychology of terror. Washington, DC: American Psychological Association.

Pyszczynski, T., Greenberg, J., Solomon, S., Arndt, J., & Shimel, J. (2004). Why do people need self-esteem? A theoretical and empirical review. Psychological Bulletin, 130, 535–468.

Pyszczynski, T., Greenberg, J., Solomon, S., & Maxfield, M. (2006). On the unique psychological import of the human awareness of mortality: Themes and variations. Psychological Inquiry, 17, 328–356.

Ryan, R. M., & Deci, E. L. (2004). Avoiding death or engaging life as accounts of meaning and culture: Comment on Pyszczynski et al. (2004). Psychological Bulletin, 130, 173–177.

Tomer, A. (Ed.). (2000). Death attitudes and the older adult: Theories, concepts, and applications. Philadelphia, PA: Brunner-Routledge.

Tomer, A., Eliason, G. T., & Wong, P. T. P. (2008). Existential and spiritual issues in death attitudes. New York, NY: Lawrence Erlbaum Associates.

Wass, H., & Neimeyer, R. A. (Eds.). (1995). Dying: Facing the facts. Washington, DC: Taylor & Francis.

Wong, P. T. P. (in press). A dual-system model of making life worth living. In P. T. P. Wong (Ed.), The human quest for meaning (2nd ed.). New York, NY: Routlege.

Wong, P. T. P. (2008). Meaning management theory and death acceptance. In A. Tomer, G. T. Eliason, & P. T. P. Wong (Eds.), Existential and spiritual issues in death attitudes (pp. 65–88). Mahwah, NJ: Lawrence Erlbaum Associates.

Wong, P. T. P., Reker, G. T., & Gesser, G. (1994). Death Attitude Profile—Revised: A multidimensional measure of attitudes toward death. In R. A. Neimeyer (Ed.), Death anxiety handbook: Research instrumentation and application (pp. 121–148). Washington, DC: Taylor & Francis.

Yalom, I. D. (2008). Staring at the sun: Overcoming the terror of death. San Francisco, CA:Jossey-Bass.

Critical Thinking

1. What are the different meanings of death acceptance?

2. Do we both accept and deny death in the Western world today?

3. What is the difference in terror management theory and meaning management theory?

UNIT 4

Ethical Issues of Dying and Death

Unit Selections

21. **Ethics and Life's Ending,** Robert D. Orr and Gilbert Meilaender
22. **Obituary for Jack Kevorkian,** Associated Press
23. **At the Bottom of the Slippery Slope,** Wesley J. Smith
24. **Hospitals Embrace Palliative Care,** Bridget M. Kuehn
25. **Cannabis Use in Long-Term Care: An Emerging Issue for Nurses,** Roxanne Nelson
26. **I Was a Doctor Accustomed to Death, But Not His,** Marc Agronin

Learning Outcomes

After reading this unit you should be able to:

- Understand the difference between a durable power of attorney and a living will.

- Understand the importance of having a living will and the limitations of such legal documents.

- Understand the complexities of administering and the use of cannabis in a medical setting for the betterment of patients who are in end care.

- Gain an appreciation for the difficulty in determining issues relationship between extra-ordinary and ordinary measures of treating patients and withholding and withdrawing life support.

- Make distinctions between providing medical treatment for illness and providing end of life care.

- Realize that palliative care is a subspecialty of medicine.

- Understand that sometimes the best medical care is not providing a cure but providing care, support, and comfort.

Student Website

www.mhhe.com/cls

Internet References

Articles on Euthanasia: Ethics
http://ethics.acusd.edu/Applied/Euthanasia
Euthanasia and Physician-Assisted Suicide
www.religioustolerance.org/euthanas.htm
The Sociology of Death: Moral Debates of Our Times
www.Trinity.Edu/~mkearl/death-5.html#eu
The Kevorkian Verdict
www.pbs.org/wgbh/pages/frontline/kevorkian
Living Wills (Advance Directive)
www.mindspring.com/~scottr/will.html
Not Dead Yet
www.notdeadyet.org
UNOS: United Network for Organ Sharing
www.unos.org

One of the concerns about dying and death that is pressing hard upon our consciences is the question of helping the dying to die sooner with the assistance of the physician. Public awareness of the horrors that can visit upon us by artificial means of ventilation and other support measures in a high-tech hospital setting has produced a literature that debates the issue of euthanasia—a "good death." As individuals think through their plans for care when dying, there is a steady increase in the demand for control of that care. The case of Terri Schiavo had brought national attention to the need for more clarity in end-of-life directives and the legitimacy of passive euthanasia. Another controversial issue is physician-assisted suicide. Is it the function of the doctor to assist patients in their dying—to actually kill them at their request? The highly publicized suicides in Michigan, along with the jury decisions that found Dr. Jack Kevorkian innocent of murder, as well as the popularity of the book *Final Exit,* make these issues prominent national and international concerns. Legislative action has been taken in some states to permit this, and the issue is pending in a number of others. We are in a time of intense consideration by the courts, by the legislatures, and by the medical and nursing professions of the legality and the morality of providing the means by which a person can be given the means to die. Is this the role of healthcare providers? The pro and contra positions are presented in several of the unit's

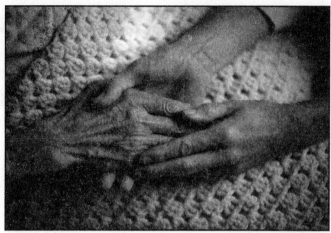

articles. Although the issue is difficult and personally challenging, as a nation we are in the position of being required to make difficult choices. There are no "right" answers; the questions pose dilemmas that require choice based on moral, spiritual, and legal foundations.

Ethics and Life's Ending

An Exchange

ROBERT D. ORR AND GILBERT MEILAENDER

Feeding tubes make the news periodically, and controversies over their use or non-use seem unusually contentious. But feeding tubes are not high technology treatment; they are simple, small-bore catheters made of soft synthetic material. Nor are they new technology; feeding tubes were first used in 1793 by John Hunter to introduce jellies, eggs, sugar, milk, and wine into the stomachs of patients unable to swallow. Why does this old, low-tech treatment generate such controversy today? The important question is not whether a feeding tube *can* be used, but whether it *should* be used in a particular situation.

Too often in medicine we use a diagnostic or therapeutic intervention just because it is available. This thoughtless approach is sometimes called the technological imperative, i.e., the impulse to do everything we are trained to do, regardless of the burden or benefit. Kidney failure? Let's do dialysis. Respiratory failure? Let's use a ventilator. Unable to eat? Let's put in a feeding tube. By responding in this way, the physician ignores the maxim "the ability to act does not justify the action." Just because we know how to artificially breathe for a patient in respiratory failure doesn't mean that everyone who cannot breathe adequately must be put on a ventilator. Such a response also represents a failure to do the moral work of assessing whether the treatment is appropriate in a particular situation.

The moral debate about the use or non-use of feeding tubes hinges on three important considerations: the distinction between what in the past was called "ordinary" and "extraordinary" treatments; the important social symbolism of feeding; and a distinction between withholding and withdrawing treatments.

It was recognized many years ago that respirators, dialysis machines, and other high-tech modes of treatment are optional. They could be used or not used depending on the circumstances. However, it was commonly accepted in the past that feeding tubes are generally not optional. Part of the reasoning was that feeding tubes are readily available, simple to use, not very burdensome to the patient, and not very expensive. They were "ordinary treatment" and thus morally obligatory.

Ordinary [versus] Extraordinary

For over four hundred years, traditional moral theology distinguished between ordinary and extraordinary means of saving life. Ordinary means were those that were not too painful or burdensome for the patient, were not too expensive, and had a reasonable chance of working. These ordinary treatments were deemed morally obligatory. Those treatments that did involve undue burden were extraordinary and thus optional. This distinction was common knowledge in religious and secular circles, and this language and reasoning was commonly applied in Western society.

As medical treatments became more complicated, it was recognized that this distinction was sometimes not helpful. The problem was that the designation appeared to belong to the treatment itself, rather than to the situation. The respirator and dialysis machine were categorized as extraordinary while antibiotics and feeding tubes were classed as ordinary. But real-life situations were not that simple. Thus began a change in moral terminology first officially noted in the *Declaration on Euthanasia* published in 1980 by the Catholic Church's Sacred Congregation for the Doctrine of the Faith in 1980: "In the past, moralists replied that one is never obligated to use 'extraordinary' means. This reply, which as a principle still holds good, is perhaps less clear today, by reason of the imprecision of the term and the rapid progress made in the treatment of sickness. Thus some people prefer to speak of 'proportionate' and 'disproportionate' means."

This newer and clearer moral terminology of proportionality was used in secular ethical analysis as early as the 1983 President's Commission report, *Deciding to Forgo Life-Sustaining Technologies.* The "ordinary/extraordinary" language, however, continues to be seen in the medical literature and heard in the intensive care unit. Reasoning on the basis of proportionality requires us to weigh the burdens and the benefits of a particular treatment for a particular patient. Thus a respirator may be proportionate (and obligatory) for a young person with a severe but survivable chest injury, but it may be disproportionate (and thus optional) for another person who is dying of lung cancer. The same is true for (almost) all medical treatments, including feeding tubes. There are two treatments that always remain obligatory, as I shall explain below.

A second aspect of the discussion about the obligation to provide nutritional support, especially in secular discussions but also in religious debate, was the symbolism of food and water—feeding is caring; nutrition is nurture; food and water are not treatment, and therefore they are never optional. The reasoning commonly went as follows: we provide nutritional support for vulnerable infants because this is an important part of "tender loving care." Shouldn't we provide the same for vulnerable adults as well?

Certainly when a patient is temporarily unable to swallow and has the potential to recover, artificially administered fluids and nutrition are obligatory. Does that obligation change if the prognosis is poor?

This aspect of the debate continued through the 1970s and '80s. It appeared to be resolved by the U.S. Supreme Court in its 1990 decision in *Cruzan v. Director, Missouri Department of Health* when five of the nine Justices agreed that artificially administered fluids and nutrition are medical treatments and are thus optional. Since *Cruzan* medical and legal professions have developed a consensus that feeding tubes are not always obligatory. This debate is ongoing, however, and in some minds the symbolism of feeding remains a dominant feature.

Starvation

A parallel concern to the symbolism entailed in the use of fluids and nutrition is the commonly heard accusation, "But you will be starving him to death!" when discontinuation of a feeding tube is discussed. This is incorrect. Starvation is a slow process that results from lack of calories and takes several weeks or months. When artificially administered fluids and nutrition are not used in a person who is unable to swallow, that person dies from dehydration, not starvation, and death occurs in five to twelve days. Dehydration is very commonly the last physiologic stage of dying, no matter what the cause.

"But that is no comfort! Being dehydrated and thirsty is miserable." Yes and no. Being thirsty is miserable, but becoming dehydrated need not be. The only place in the body where thirst is perceived is the mouth. There is good empirical evidence that as long as a person's mouth is kept moist, that person is not uncomfortable, even if it is clear that his or her body is becoming progressively dehydrated.

I said earlier that there are two treatments that are never optional: these are good symptom control and human presence. Therefore, when a person is becoming dehydrated as he or she approaches death, it is obligatory to provide good mouth care, along with other means of demonstrating human caring and presence, such as touching, caressing, gentle massage, hair-brushing, talking, reading, and holding.

Withholding [versus] Withdrawing

A third feature of the debate over feeding tubes is the issue of withholding versus withdrawing therapy. Thirty years ago, it was common teaching in medicine that "it is better to withhold a treatment than to withdraw it." The thinking was that if you stop a ventilator or dialysis or a feeding tube, and the patient then dies from this lack of life support, you were the agent of death. Therefore, it would be ethically better not to start the treatment in the first place. Then, if the patient dies, death is attributable to the underlying disease and not to your withdrawal of life support.

Slowly, with help from philosophers, theologians, attorneys, and jurists, the medical profession came to accept that there is no moral or legal difference between withholding and withdrawing a treatment. In fact, it may be ethically better to withdraw life-sustaining treatment than it is to withhold it. If there is a treatment with a very small chance of helping the patient, it is better to give it a try. If it becomes clear after a few days or weeks that it is not helping, then you can withdraw the treatment without the original uncertainty that you might be quitting too soon, and now with the comfort that comes from knowing you are not the agent of death.

However, even if there is no professional, moral, or legal difference, it still may be psychologically more difficult to withdraw a treatment that you know is postponing a patient's death than it would have been not to start it in the first place. Turning down the dials on a ventilator with the expectation that the patient will not survive is more personally unsettling than is merely being present with a patient who is actively dying. Withdrawal of a feeding tube can be even more unsettling, especially if the professional involved has any moral reservations about the distinction between ordinary and extraordinary means, or about the symbolism of artificially administered fluids and nutrition.

Some develop this part of the debate with moral concern about intentionality. They contend that your intention in withdrawing the feeding tube is that the patient will die, and it is morally impermissible to cause death intentionally. In actuality, the intention in withdrawing any therapy that has been proven not to work is to stop postponing death artificially.

With these aspects of the debate more or less settled, where does that leave us in making decisions about the use or non-use of feeding tubes? The short-term use of a feeding tube for a patient who is unable to swallow adequate fluids and nutrition for a few days, because of severe illness or after surgery or trauma, may be lifesaving and is almost always uncontroversial. Such usage may even be morally obligatory when the goal of treatment is patient survival and a feeding tube is the best way to provide needed fluids and nutrition.

A feeding tube is sometimes requested by a loved one as a last-gasp effort to postpone death in a patient who is imminently dying and unable to swallow. This is almost always inappropriate. Good mouth care to maintain patient comfort and hygiene is obligatory, but in such cases maintenance of nutrition is no longer a reasonable goal of treatment. In fact, introduction of fluids may even lead to fluid overload that can cause patient discomfort as the body's systems are shutting down.

Long-Term Use

The situation that can generate ethical quandaries, front-page news, and conflicts in court is the long-term use of feeding tubes. And these situations are not as neatly segregated into proportionate or disproportionate usage.

Long-term use of a feeding tube remains ethically obligatory for a patient who is cognitively intact, can and wants to survive, but is permanently unable to swallow, an example being a patient who has been treated for malignancy of the throat or esophagus. Protracted use of a feeding tube is also morally required in most instances when it is uncertain whether a patient will regain awareness or recover the ability to swallow—for instance, immediately after a serious head injury or a disabling stroke.

Long-term use of a feeding tube becomes controversial in patients suffering from progressive deterioration of brain function (e.g., Alzheimer's dementia), or in patients with little or no likelihood of regaining awareness after illness or injury (e.g., the permanent vegetative state). Thus, the most perplexing feeding-tube questions involve patients who are unable to take in adequate fluids and nutrition by themselves but who have a condition that by itself will not soon lead to death. The reasoning is, the patient has no fatal condition; he or she can be kept alive with the simple use of tube feedings; therefore we are obligated to use a feeding tube to keep this person alive.

Alzheimer's dementia is the most common type of brain deterioration, afflicting five percent of individuals over sixty-five and perhaps as many as 50 percent of those over eighty-five. It is manifested by progressive cognitive impairment, followed by physical deterioration. This process generally takes several years, often a decade, and is ultimately fatal. In its final stages it almost always interferes with the patient's ability to swallow. Eventually the individual chokes on even pureed foods or liquids. Continued attempts at feeding by mouth very commonly result in aspiration of food or fluid into the airway, frequently leading to pneumonia. Aspiration pneumonia will sometimes respond to antibiotics, but other times it leads to death. Such respiratory infections are the most common final event in this progressive disease.

Feeding tubes have been commonly used in the later stages of Alzheimer's. The reasoning has been that this patient is not able to take in adequate fluids and nutrition and he is not imminently dying. Several assumptions then follow: a feeding tube will improve his comfort, will prevent aspiration pneumonia, and will ensure adequate nutrition which will in turn prevent skin breakdown and thus postpone his death. However, empirical evidence, published in the *Journal of the American Medical Association* in 1999, has shown each of these assumptions to be incorrect: using a feeding tube in a patient with dementia does not prevent these complications, nor does it prolong life.

In addition, there are several negative aspects to using a feeding tube in a person with advanced cognitive impairment. There are rare complications during insertion, some merely uncomfortable, some quite serious. Having a tube in one's nose is generally uncomfortable; even having one coiled up under a dressing on the abdominal wall can be annoying. Because the demented patient doesn't understand the intended purpose of the feeding tube, he or she may react by trying to remove it, requiring either repeated re-insertions or the use of hand restraints. In addition, using a feeding tube may deprive the patient of human presence and interaction: hanging a bag of nutritional fluid takes only a few seconds, as opposed to the extended time of human contact involved in feeding a cognitively impaired person.

End Stage Alzheimer's

There is a slowly developing consensus in medicine that feeding tubes are generally not appropriate for use in most patients nearing the end stage of Alzheimer's disease. This belief can be supported from a moral standpoint in terms of proportionality. And yet feeding tubes are still rather commonly used. A recently published review of all U.S. nursing home patients with cognitive impairment found that an average of 34 percent were being fed with feeding tubes (though there were large state-to-state varia-

tions, from nine percent in Maine, New Hampshire, and Vermont to 64 percent in Washington, D.C.).

The cases we read about in the newspaper—in which families are divided and court battles fought—most often involve patients in a permanent vegetative state (PVS). This is a condition of permanent unawareness most often caused by severe head injury or by the brain being deprived of oxygen for several minutes. Such deprivation may be the result of successful cardiopulmonary resuscitation of a patient whose breathing or circulation had stopped from a cardiac arrest, near-drowning, strangulation, etc. In a PVS patient, the heart, lungs, kidneys, and other organs continue to function; given good nursing care and artificially administered fluids and nutrition, a person can live in this permanent vegetative state for many years.

A person in a PVS may still have reflexes from the spinal cord (grasping, withdrawal from pain) or the brain stem (breathing, regulation of blood pressure), including the demonstration of sleep-wake cycles. He may "sleep" for several hours, then "awaken" for a while; the eyes are open and wander about, but do not fix on or follow objects. The person in a PVS is "awake, but unaware" because the areas of the upper brain that allow a person to perceive his or her environment and to act voluntarily are no longer functioning.

Uncertainty

Some of the clinical controversy about nutritional support for persons in a PVS is due to uncertainty. After a head injury or resuscitation from a cardiac arrest, it may be several weeks or months before a patient can rightly be declared to be in a PVS—months during which the provision of nutritional support via feeding tubes is often very appropriate. Loved ones usually remain optimistic, hoping for improvement, praying for full recovery. The length of time from brain damage to declaration of a PVS can extend, depending on the cause of the brain injury, from one month to twelve months. And just to muddy the waters even further, there are rare instances of delayed improvement after many months or even a few years, so that the previously unaware patient regains some ability to perceive his or her environment, and may even be able to say a few words. These individuals are now in a "minimally conscious state." More than minimal delayed improvement is exceedingly rare. (Treatment decisions for persons in a minimally conscious state are perhaps even more controversial than are those for PVS patients, but that discussion must wait for another time.)

The greatest ethical dilemma surrounding the use or non-use of nutritional support for persons in a PVS arises from the fact that they are not clearly dying. With good nursing care and nutrition, individuals in this condition have survived for up to thirty-five years. Those who advocate continued nutritional support argue thus: this person is alive and not actively or imminently dying; it is possible to keep him alive with minimal effort; this human life is sacred; therefore we are obligated to continue to give artificially administered fluids and nutrition.

It is hard to disagree with the various steps in this line of reasoning. (Some utilitarians do disagree, however, claiming that a patient in a PVS is "already dead" or is a "non-person." Those who believe in the sanctity of life must continue to denounce this line of thought.) Let us stipulate the following: the person in a PVS is alive; he can be kept alive for a long time; his life is sacred. But does the obligation to maintain that severely compromised human life necessarily follow from these premises?

Let's first address the issue of whether he is dying. One could maintain that his physical condition is such that he will die soon but for the artificial provision of fluids and nutrition. Thus the permanent vegetative state could be construed to be lethal in and of itself. However, that fatal outcome is not inevitable since the saving treatment is simple. How does this differ from the imperative to provide nourishment for a newborn who would die without the provision of fluids and nutrition? There are two differences. Most newborns are able to take in nutrition if it is placed in or near their mouths. PVS patients can't swallow, so the nutrition must be delivered further down the gastrointestinal tract. As for sick or premature infants, they have a great potential for improvement, growth, and development. The PVS patient has no such potential.

Kidney Failure

Rather than a newborn, a better analogy for this aspect of the discussion would be a person with kidney failure. The kidney failure itself is life-threatening, but it is fairly easily corrected by dialysis three times a week. If the person has another condition that renders him unaware of his surroundings, or a condition that makes life a continuous difficult struggle, most would agree that the person is ethically permitted to stop the dialysis even if that means he will not survive. The ultimate cause of death was treatable, so that death could have been postponed, possibly for years. However, other mitigating circumstances may make the dialysis disproportionate, and so one should be allowed to discontinue this death-postponing treatment in a person who is not imminently dying.

Someone coming from a mechanistic perspective can easily and comfortably decide that a person in a PVS with no potential for recovery has no inherent value and is even an emotional drain on loved ones and a financial drain on society. But what about a person of faith? Does the sanctity of life, a basic tenet of Christianity, Judaism, and Islam, dictate that life must always be preserved if it is humanly possible to do so? Our moral intuitions tell us the answer is no.

It might be possible to postpone the death of a patient from end-stage heart failure by doing one more resuscitation. It might be possible to postpone the death of someone with end-stage liver disease by doing a liver transplant. It might be possible to postpone the death of someone with painful cancer with a few more blood transfusions or another round of chemotherapy. But these therapies are often not used—because the burden is disproportionate to the benefit. Thus the timing of death is often a matter of choice. In fact, it is commonly accepted that the timing of 80 percent of deaths that occur in a hospital is chosen.

Believers do not like to use the words "choice" and "death" in the same sentence. Doing so recalls acrimonious contests about the "right to life" versus the "right to choose" that are the pivotal point in debates about abortion, assisted suicide, and euthana-

sia. And certainly belief in the sanctity of human life obligates believers to forgo some choices. But does this belief preclude all choices? No: life is full of difficult choices. This is true for believers and nonbelievers alike. Believers may have more guidance about what choices to make and perhaps some limits on options, but we still are faced with many choices—such as choices about the use or non-use of feeding tubes.

When engaging in moral debate on matters of faith, it is important not to focus exclusively on one tenet of faith to the exclusion of others. In debating the use of feeding tubes—or of any mode of treatment for that matter—one must not ignore the concepts of finitude and stewardship by focusing only on the sanctity of life.

If belief in the sanctity of human life translated automatically into an obligation to preserve each human life at all costs, we would not have to debate proportionate and disproportionate treatments. We would simply be obligated to use all treatments available until they failed to work. However, because of the Fall, human life is finite. All of us will die. Since that is inevitable, God expects us to care wisely for our own bodies and for those of our loved ones, and also for our resources. Healthcare professionals similarly must be wise stewards of their skills and services.

Taking into consideration the scriptural principle of stewardship and the tradition of proportionate treatment, I conclude that there must be some degree of discretion in the use or non-use of feeding tubes. There are clearly situations where a feeding tube must be used. There are other situations where a feeding tube would be morally wrong. But there are many situations where the use of a feeding tube should be optional. And this means that one individual of faith might choose to use a tube when another might choose not to use it.

Personal Values

Because of the patient's personal values, someone might choose to continue artificially administered fluids and nutrition for a loved one in a permanent vegetative state for many years. Another might choose to continue for one year and then to withdraw it if there was no sign of awareness. Still another might choose to stop after three months or one month.

What might those discretionary personal values include? Such things, among others, as an assessment of how to deal with uncertainty, concern about emotional burden on loved ones, and cost of care. Though beliefs in the sanctity of human life and in the obligation to care for vulnerable individuals are not optional for persons of faith, an assessment of whether or not to use a given technology requires human wisdom and thus entails some discretion.

Gilbert Meilaender

There is much to agree with in Robert D. Orr's measured discussion of the moral issues surrounding the use of feeding tubes, there are a few things that seem to me doubtful or in need of clarification, and then there is one major issue that requires greater precision.

Accepted Claims

It may be useful to note first some claims of Dr. Orr that few would dispute.

- Feeding tubes are a rather low-tech form of care.
- Our ability to do something does not mean that we should do it.
- Any distinction between "ordinary" and "extraordinary" care (if we wish to use that language) cannot simply be a feature of treatments but must be understood as patient-relative. What is ordinary treatment for one patient may be extraordinary for another, and what is ordinary treatment for a patient at one point in his life may become extraordinary at another point when his illness has progressed to a new stage.
- There is no crucial moral difference between withholding or withdrawing a treatment. (Dr. Orr actually writes that there is "no moral or legal difference" between these. The issue of legality is, I suspect, sometimes more complicated, but I take him to be correct insofar as a strictly moral judgment is involved.)
- There are circumstances, some noted by Dr. Orr, in which the use of feeding tubes seems clearly required and is relatively uncontroversial.
- Patients in a persistent vegetative state are not dying patients. (I don't quite know how to combine this with Dr. Orr's statement a few paragraphs later that the permanent vegetative state "could be construed to be lethal in and of itself." In general, I don't think his article ever really achieves clarity and precision on this question, and it will turn out to be a crucial question below.)
- A commitment to the sanctity of human life does not require that we always do everything possible to keep a person alive.

There are also places where Dr. Orr's discussion seems to me to be doubtful or, at least, underdeveloped. Among these are the following:

- The idea that the terms "proportionate" and "disproportionate" are more precise than the (admittedly unsatisfactory) language of "ordinary" and "extraordinary" is, at best, doubtful. On what scale one "weighs" benefits and burdens is a question almost impossible to answer. Even more doubtful is whether we can "weigh" them for someone else. My own view is that when we make these decisions for ourselves, we are not in fact "weighing" anything. We are deciding what sort of person we will be and what sort of life will be ours. We are making not a *discovery* but a *decision*. And if that is true, then it is obvious that we have not discovered anything that could necessarily be transferred and applied to the life of a different patient. In general, the language of "weighing" sounds good, but it is almost impossible to give it any precise meaning.
- No *moral* question was resolved by the Supreme Court's *Cruzan* decision. It established certain legal boundaries, but it did no more than that.

- I suspect that—despite the growing consensus, which Dr. Orr correctly describes—he is too quick to assume that the "symbolism" issue can be dispensed with, and too quick to assume that feeding tubes are "treatment" rather than standard nursing care. A consensus may be mistaken, after all. It is hard to see why such services as turning a patient regularly and giving alcohol rubs are standard nursing care while feeding is not. To take an example from a different realm of life, soldiers are combatants, but the people who grow the food which soldiers eat are not combatants (even though the soldiers could not continue to fight without nourishment). The reason is simple: they make not what soldiers need to fight but what they need, as we all do, in order merely to live. Likewise, we might want to think twice before endorsing the view that relatively low-tech means of providing nourishment are treatment rather than standard nursing care.

Intention

- Dr. Orr's discussion of the role of "intention" in moral analysis is, putting it charitably, imprecise. Obviously, if a treatment has been shown not to work, in withdrawing it we do not intend or aim at the patient's death. We aim at caring for that person as best we can, which hardly includes providing treatment that is useless. But the crucial questions will turn on instances in which the treatment is not pointless. If we stop treatment in such cases, it is harder to deny that our aim is that the patient should die.
- Dr. Orr's seeming willingness to allow the state of a patient's cognitive capacities to carry weight—or even be determinative—in treatment decisions is troubling. Obviously, certain kinds of higher brain capacities are characteristics that distinguish human beings from other species; however, one need not have or be exercising those capacities in order to be a living human being. Allowing the cognitive ability of a patient to determine whether he or she is treated will inevitably lead to judgments about the comparative worth of human lives.

If Dr. Orr is correct in arguing that the use of feeding tubes in end-stage Alzheimer's patients is of no help to those patients and may sometimes be burdensome to them, we would have no moral reason to provide them with tube feeding. This judgment, however, has nothing at all to do with "proportionality." It has to do, simply, with the two criteria we ought to use in making treatment decisions—usefulness and burdensomeness. If a treatment is useless or excessively burdensome, it may rightly be refused.

This brings us to the most difficult issue, which clearly troubles Dr. Orr himself, and which is surely puzzling for all of us: the patient in a persistent vegetative state. We cannot usefully discuss this difficult case, however, without first getting clear more generally on the morality of withholding or withdrawing treatment. As I noted above, on this issue the language of proportionality is unlikely to be of much use for serious moral reflection.

Morality of Treatment

At least for Christians—though, in truth, also much more generally for our civilization's received medical tradition—we begin with what is forbidden. We should never aim at the death of a sick or dying person. (Hence, euthanasia, however good the motive, is forbidden.) Still, there are times when treatment may rightly be withheld or withdrawn, *even though* the patient may then die more quickly than would otherwise have been the case. How can that be? How can it be that, as a result of our decision, the patient dies more quickly, yet we do not aim at his death? This is quite possible—and permissible—so long as we aim to dispense with the treatment, not the life. No one need live in a way that seeks to ensure the longest possible life. (Were that a moral requirement, think of all the careers that would have to be prohibited.) There may be many circumstances in which we foresee that decisions we make may shorten our life, but we do not suppose that in so deciding we are aiming at death or formulating a plan of action that deliberately embraces death as a good. So in medical treatment decisions the question we need to answer is this: Under what circumstances may we rightly refuse a life-prolonging treatment without supposing that, in making this decision, we are doing the forbidden deed of choosing or aiming at death?

The answer of our medical-moral tradition has been the following: we may refuse treatments that are either *useless* or *excessively burdensome.* In doing so, we choose not death, but one among several possible lives open to us. We do not choose to die, but, rather, how to live, even if while dying, even if a shorter life than some other lives that are still available for our choosing. What we take aim at then, what we refuse, is not life but treatment—treatment that is either useless for a particular patient or excessively burdensome for that patient. Especially for patients who are irretrievably into the dying process, almost all treatments will have become useless. In refusing them, one is not choosing death but choosing life without a now useless form of treatment. But even for patients who are not near death, who might live for a considerably longer time, excessively burdensome treatments may also be refused. Here again, one takes aim at the burdensome treatment, not at life. One person may choose a life that is longer but carries with it considerable burden of treatment. Another may choose a life that is shorter but carries with it less burden of treatment. Each, however, chooses life. Neither aims at death.

Rejecting Treatments

It is essential to emphasize that these criteria refer to treatments, not to lives. We may rightly reject a treatment that is useless. But if I decide not to treat because I think a person's life is useless, then I am taking aim not at the treatment but at the life. Rather than asking, "What if anything can I do that will benefit the life this patient has?" I am asking, "Is it a benefit to have such a life?" If the latter is my question, and if I decide not to treat, it should be clear that it is the life at which I take aim. Likewise, we may reject a treatment on grounds of excessive burden. But if I decide not to treat because it seems a burden just to have the life this person has, then I am taking aim not at the burdensome treatment but at the life. Hence, in deciding whether it is appropriate and permissible to withhold or withdraw treatment—whether, even if life is thereby shortened, we are aiming only at the treatment and not at the life—we have to ask ourselves whether the treatment under consideration is, for this patient, either useless or excessively burdensome.

Against that background, we can consider the use of feeding tubes for patients in a persistent vegetative state. (I set aside here the point I noted above—that we might want to regard feeding simply as standard nursing care rather than as medical treatment. Now we are asking whether, even on the grounds that govern treatment decisions, we have good moral reason not to feed patients in a persistent vegetative state.)

Is the treatment useless? Not, let us be clear, is the life a useless one to have, but is the treatment useless? As Dr. Orr notes—quite rightly, I think—patients "can live in this permanent vegetative state for many years." So feeding may preserve for years the life of this living human being. Are we certain we want to call that useless? We are, of course, tempted to say that, in deciding not to feed, we are simply withdrawing treatment and letting these patients die. Yes, as Dr. Orr also notes, these patients "are not clearly dying." And, despite the sloppy way we sometimes talk about these matters, you cannot "let die" a person who is not dying. It is hard, therefore, to make the case for treatment withdrawal in these cases on the ground of uselessness. We may use those words, but it is more likely that our target is a (supposed) useless life and not a useless treatment. And if that is our aim, we had better rethink it promptly.

Is the treatment excessively burdensome? Alas, if these patients could experience the feeding as a burden, they would not be diagnosed as being in a persistent vegetative state. We may wonder, of course, whether having such a life is itself a burden, but, again, if that is our reasoning, it will be clear that we take aim not at a burdensome treatment but at a (presumed) burdensome life. And, once more, if that is our aim, we had better rethink it promptly.

Choosing Life

Hence, although these are troubling cases, Dr. Orr has not given us good or sufficient arguments to make the case for withdrawing feeding tubes from patients in a persistent vegetative state. I have not suggested that we have an obligation always and at any cost to preserve life. I have simply avoided all comparative judgments of the worth of human lives and have turned aside from any decisions which, when analyzed carefully, look as if they take aim not at a dispensable treatment but at a life. "Choosing life" does not mean doing whatever is needed to stay alive as long as possible. But choosing life clearly means never aiming at another's death—even if only by withholding treatment. I am not persuaded that Dr. Orr has fully grasped or delineated what it means to choose life in the difficult circumstances he discusses.

Critical Thinking

1. Why are each of these a problem: the distinction between extraordinary and ordinary treatments? the social symbolism of feeding? and the distinction between withholding and withdrawing of treatments?

2. Why do real-life situations complicate the distinction between extraordinary and ordinary treatments?

3. What does the author argue are never optional treatments for the dying?

MR. ORR is the Director of Ethics and a professor of family medicine at the University of Vermont College of Medicine. **MR. MEILAENDER** is a member of the President's Council on Bioethics. From "Ethics & Life's Ending: An Exchange," by Robert D. Orr and Gilbert Meilaender, *First Things*, August/September 2004, pages 31–38.

Jack Kevorkian

Jack Kevorkian, the retired pathologist who captured the world's attention as he helped dozens of ailing people commit suicide, igniting intense debate and ending up in prison for murder, has died in a Detroit-area hospital after a short illness. He was 83.

Kevorkian, who said he helped some 130 people end their lives from 1990 to 1999, died about 2:30 A.M. at William Beaumont Hospital in Royal Oak, close friend and prominent attorney Mayer Morganroth said. He had been hospitalized since last month with pneumonia and kidney problems.

An official cause of death had not been determined, but Morganroth said it likely will be pulmonary thrombosis.

"I had seen him earlier and he was conscious," said Morganroth, who added that the two spoke about Kevorkian's pending release from the hospital and planned start of rehabilitation. "Then I left and he took a turn for the worst and I went back."

Nurses at the hospital played recordings of classical music by composer Johann Sebastian Bach for Kevorkian before he died, Morganroth said.

Kevorkian was freed in June 2007 after serving eight years of a 10- to 25-year sentence for second-degree murder. His lawyers had said he suffered from hepatitis C, diabetes and other problems, and he had promised in affidavits that he would not assist in a suicide if he was released.

In 2008, he ran for Congress as an independent, receiving just 2.7 percent of the vote in the suburban Detroit district. He said his experience showed the party system was "corrupt" and "has to be completely overhauled from the bottom up."

His life story became the subject of the 2010 HBO movie, "You Don't Know Jack," which earned actor Al Pacino Emmy and Golden Globe Awards for his portrayal of Kevorkian. Pacino paid tribute to Kevorkian during his Emmy acceptance speech and recognized the world-famous former doctor, who sat smiling in the audience.

Pacino said during the speech that it was a pleasure to "try to portray someone as brilliant and interesting and unique" as Kevorkian and a "pleasure to know him."

Kevorkian himself said he liked the movie and enjoyed the attention it generated, but told The Associated Press that he doubted it would inspire much action by a new generation of assisted-suicide advocates.

"You'll hear people say, 'Well, it's in the news again, it's time for discussing this further.' No it isn't. It's been discussed to death," he said. "There's nothing new to say about it. It's a legitimate ethical medical practice as it was in ancient Rome and Greece."

Eleven years earlier, he was sentenced in the 1998 death of a Lou Gehrig's disease patient—a videotaped death shown to a national television audience as Kevorkian challenged prosecutors to charge him.

"The issue's got to be raised to the level where it is finally decided," he said on the broadcast by CBS' "60 Minutes."

Nicknamed "Dr. Death" because of his fascination with death, Kevorkian catapulted into public consciousness in 1990 when he used his homemade "suicide machine" in his rusted Volkswagen van to inject lethal drugs into an Alzheimer's patient who sought his help in dying.

For nearly a decade, he escaped authorities' efforts to stop him. His first four trials, all on assisted-suicide charges, resulted in three acquittals and one mistrial.

Murder charges in earlier cases were thrown out because Michigan at the time had no law against assisted suicide; the Legislature wrote one in response to Kevorkian. He also was stripped of his medical license.

People who died with his help suffered from cancer, Lou Gehrig's disease, multiple sclerosis, paralysis. They died in their homes, an office, a Detroit island park, a remote cabin, the back of Kevorkian's van.

Kevorkian likened himself to Martin Luther King and Gandhi and called prosecutors Nazis, his critics religious fanatics. He burned state orders against him, showed up at court in costume, called doctors who didn't support him "hypocritic oafs" and challenged authorities to stop him or make his actions legal.

"Somebody has to do something for suffering humanity," Kevorkian once said. "I put myself in my patients' place. This is something I would want."

Devotees filled courtrooms wearing "I Back Jack" buttons. But critics questioned his publicity-grabbing methods, aided by his flamboyant attorney Geoffrey Fieger until the two parted ways before his 1999 trial.

"I think Kevorkian played an enormous role in bringing the physician-assisted suicide debate to the forefront," Susan Wolf, a professor of law and medicine at University of Minnesota Law School, said in 2000.

"It sometimes takes a very outrageous individual to put an issue on the public agenda," she said, and the debate he engendered "in a way cleared public space for more reasonable voices to come in."

Even so, few states have approved physician-assisted suicide. Laws went into effect in Oregon in 1997 and

Washington state in 2009, and a 2009 Montana Supreme Court ruling effectively legalized the practice in that state.

In a rare televised interview from prison in 2005, Kevorkian told MSNBC he regretted "a little" the actions that put him there.

"It was disappointing because what I did turned out to be in vain. . . . And my only regret was not having done it through the legal system, through legislation, possibly," he said.

Kevorkian's ultimate goal was to establish "obitoriums" where people would go to die. Doctors there could harvest organs and perform medical experiments during the suicide process. Such experiments would be "entirely ethical spinoffs" of suicide, he wrote in his 1991 book "Prescription: Medicide—The Goodness of Planned Death."

His road to prison began in September 1998, when he videotaped himself injecting Thomas Youk, a 52-year-old Lou Gehrig's disease patient, with lethal drugs. He gave the tape to "60 Minutes."

Two months later, a national television audience watched Youk die and heard Kevorkian say of authorities: "I've got to force them to act." Prosecutors quickly responded with a first-degree murder charge.

Kevorkian acted as his own attorney for most of the trial. He told the court his actions were "a medical service for an agonized human being."

In his closing argument, Kevorkian told jurors that some acts "by sheer common sense are not crimes."

"Just look at me," he said. "Honestly now, do you see a criminal? Do you see a murderer?"

The U.S. Supreme Court twice turned back appeals from Kevorkian, in 2002, when he argued that his prosecution was unconstitutional, and in 2004, when he claimed he had ineffective representation.

In an interview at the time Kevorkian was released from prison, Youk's brother Terrence said his brother received "a medical service that was requested and, from my point of view, compassionately provided by Jack. It should not be a crime."

But Tina Allerellie became a fierce critic after her 34-year-old sister, Karen Shoffstall, turned to Kevorkian in 1997. She said in 2007 that Shoffstall, who suffered from multiple sclerosis, was struggling with depression and fear but could have lived for years longer.

"(Kevorkian's) intent, I believe, has always been to gain notoriety," Allerellie said.

Born in 1928, in the Detroit suburb of Pontiac, Kevorkian graduated from the University of Michigan's medical school in 1952 and became a pathologist.

Kevorkian said he first became interested in euthanasia during his internship year when he watched a middle-aged woman die of cancer. She was so emaciated, her sagging, discolored skin "covered her bones like a cheap, wrinkled frock," Kevorkian wrote.

After building a suicide device in 1989 from parts he found in flea markets, he sought his first assisted-suicide candidate by placing advertisements in local newspapers. Newspaper and TV interviews brought more attention.

On June 4, 1990, he drove his van to a secluded park north of Detroit. After Janet Adkins, 54, of Portland, Ore., met him there, he inserted a needle into her arm and, when she was ready, she flipped the switch that released a lethal flow of drugs.

He later switched from his device to canisters of carbon monoxide, again insisting patients took the final step by removing a clamp that released the flow of deadly gas to the face mask.

Kevorkian's fame—or notoriety—made him fodder for late-night comedians' monologues and sitcoms. His name became cultural shorthand for jokes about hastening the end of life.

Even admirers couldn't resist. Adam Mazer, the Emmy-winning writer for "You Don't Know Jack," got off one of the best lines of the 2010 Emmy telecast.

"I'm grateful you're my friend," Mazer said, looking out at Kevorkian. "I'm even more grateful you're not my physician."

When asked in 2010 how his own epitaph should read, Kevorkian said it should reflect what he believes to be his "real virtue."

"I am quite honest. I have trouble lying. I don't like people who lie."

Critical Thinking

1. Why is Jack Kevorkian so popular and controversial?
2. What will be the lasting legacy of Jack Kevorkian?
3. After he was released from prison, what role did Jack Kevorkian have in the "right to die" debate in the United States?

At the Bottom of the Slippery Slope

Where euthanasia meets organ harvesting.

WESLEY J. SMITH

In 1992, my friend Frances committed suicide on her 76th birthday. Frances was not terminally ill. She had been diagnosed with treatable leukemia and needed a hip replacement. Mostly, though, she was depressed by family issues and profoundly disappointed at where her life had taken her.

Something seemed very off to me about Frances's suicide. So I asked the executor of her estate to send me the "suicide file" kept by the quintessentially organized Frances and was horrified to learn from it that she had been an avid reader of the (now defunct) *Hemlock Quarterly,* published by the aptly named Hemlock Society (which was since merged into the assisted-suicide advocacy group, Compassion and Choices). The HQ taught readers about the best drugs with which to overdose and gave precise instructions on how to ensure death with a plastic bag—the exact method used by Frances to end her life.

I was furious. Frances's friends had known she was periodically suicidal and had intervened to help her through the darkness. The Hemlock Society had pushed Frances in the other direction, giving her moral permission to kill herself and then teaching her how to do it. This prompted the first of the many articles I have written over the years against assisted-suicide advocacy. It appeared in the June 28, 1993, *Newsweek* and warned about the cliff toward which assisted-suicide advocacy was steering our society:

We don't get to the Brave New World in one giant leap. Rather, the descent to depravity is reached by small steps. First, suicide is promoted as a virtue. Vulnerable people like Frances become early casualties. Then follows mercy killing of the terminally ill. From there, it's a hop, skip, and a jump to killing people who don't have a good "quality" of life, perhaps with the prospect of organ harvesting thrown in as a plum to society.

The other shoe—"organ harvesting"—has now dropped. Euthanasia was legalized in Belgium in 2002. It took six years for the first known coupling of euthanasia and organ harvesting, the case of a woman in a "locked in" state—fully paralyzed but also fully cognizant. After doctors agreed to her request to be lethally injected, she asked that her organs be harvested after she died. Doctors agreed. They described their procedure in a 2008 issue of the journal *Transplant International:*

This case of two separate requests, first euthanasia and second, organ donation after death, demonstrates that organ harvesting after euthanasia may be considered and accepted from ethical, legal, and practical viewpoints in countries where euthanasia is legally accepted. This possibility may increase the number of transplantable organs and may also provide some comfort to the donor and her family, considering that the termination of the patient's life may be seen as helping other human beings in need for organ transplantation.

The idea of coupling euthanasia with organ harvesting and medical experimentation was promoted years ago by the late Jack Kevorkian, but it is now becoming mainstream. Last year, the Oxford bioethicist Julian Savulescu coauthored a paper in *Bioethics* arguing that some could be euthanized, "at least partly to ensure that their organs could be donated." Belgian doctors, in particular, are openly discussing the nexus between euthanasia and organ harvesting. A June 10 press release from Pabst Science Publishers cited four lung transplants in Leuven from donors who died by euthanasia.

What's more, Belgian doctors and bioethicists now travel around Europe promoting the conjoining of the two procedures at medical seminars. Their PowerPoint presentation touts the "high quality" of organs obtained from patients after euthanasia of people with degenerative neuro/muscular disabilities.

Coupling organ donation with euthanasia turns a new and dangerous corner by giving the larger society an explicit stake in the deaths of people with seriously disabling or terminal conditions. Moreover, since such patients are often the most expensive for whom to care, and given the acute medical resource shortages we face, one need not be a prophet to see the potential such advocacy has for creating a perfect utilitarian storm.

Some might ask, if these patients want euthanasia, why not get some good out of their deaths? After all, they are going to die anyway.

But coupling organ harvesting with mercy killing creates a strong emotional inducement to suicide, particularly for people who are culturally devalued and depressed and, indeed, who might worry that they are a burden on loved ones and society. People in such an anguished mental state could easily come to believe (or be persuaded) that asking for euthanasia and organ donation would give a meaning to their deaths that their lives could never have.

And it won't stop there. Once society accepts euthanasia/ organ harvesting, we will soon see agitation to pay seriously disabled or dying people for their organs, a policy that Kevorkian once advocated. Utilitarian boosters of such a course will argue that paying people will save society money on long-term care and allow disabled persons the satisfaction of benefiting society, while leaving a nice bundle for family, friends, or a charitable cause.

People with serious disabilities should be alarmed. The message that is being broadcast with increasing brazenness out of Belgium is that their deaths are worth more than their lives.

Critical Thinking

1. How did this article link organ harvesting with Kevorkian's campaign to give patients the "right to die"?

2. How does physician aid in dying give society a stake in the deaths of people with seriously disabling terminal conditions?

3. How does organ donation give those who would seek physician aid in dying a meaning for their suicides?

WESLEY J. SMITH is a senior fellow at the Discovery Institute's Center on Human Exceptionalism, a lawyer for the Patients Rights Council, and a special consultant for the Center for Bioethics and Culture.

Hospitals Embrace Palliative Care

BRIDGET M. KUEHN

Despite advances in medicine and medical technology, there is a growing population of aging patients with complex health problems who are poorly served by even the best intensive care units. To help these patients, who often have multiple chronic conditions or various complications of acute conditions, hospitals are turning to palliative care, which focuses on symptom management, communication, and other means to improve quality of life for patients and their families.

Palliative care may be delivered in concert with curative or life-prolonging medical care and is not prognosis dependent. These features distinguish it from hospice care, which offers symptom management for patients who are facing a terminal illness and no longer wish to undergo life-prolonging treatments, as well as other kinds of support for these patients and their families.

Between 2000 and 2005, the number of hospitals with palliative care programs grew by 96% from 632 to 1240, according to the Center to Advance Palliative Care, which analyzed data from the 2007 American Hospital Association Annual Survey of Hospitals.

The field of palliative and hospice care became formally recognized as a subspecialty by the American Board of Medical Specialties in 2006. A record 10 specialty groups—anesthesiology, emergency medicine, family medicine, obstetrics and gynecology, internal medicine, pediatrics, physical medicine and rehabilitation, psychiatry and neurology, radiology, and surgery—endorse hospice and palliative medicine as a subspecialty of their fields.

Also in 2006, the Accreditation Council for Graduate Medical Education (ACGME) decided to begin accrediting hospice and palliative medicine fellowship programs. Starting in 2008, physicians will for the first time be able to become board certified in hospice and palliative care and the first fellowship programs will be able to seek ACGME accreditation.

Unmet Needs

Recognition of vast unmet needs among aging and dying patients and concerns about the cost of caring for a growing aging population have helped drive the growth of palliative care in hospitals.

"Not every patient can be cured—in fact, the vast majority of patients live for a long time with significant chronic diseases that pose enormous burdens, not only on the patient but also on the family caregivers," said Diane E. Meier, MD, director of the Center to Advance Palliative Care, in New York City. Modern medicine and high technology simply do not have a fix for those problems, she said.

In fact, technology has blurred the line between illness and end of life, said Patricia A. Grady, PhD, RN, director of the National Institute of Nursing Research (NINR) in Bethesda, Md, leaving individuals and health care workers with several questions: How and when should life-prolonging technology be used? When should its use end and who should make that decision? How are these difficult decisions made?

A 1997 report from the Institute of Medicine, *Approaching Death: Improving Care at the End of Life* (http://www.nap.edu/catalog.php?record_id=5801#toc), outlined many deficiencies in the way that seriously ill and dying patients are treated in the United States and acted as a catalyst for change. Four of the chief concerns cited in the report were

- Needless suffering by many patients at the end of life when they do not receive appropriate supportive care or when they receive unnecessary or ineffective invasive treatments;
- Legal, organizational, and economic factors that impede the delivery of the best care for these individuals;
- Inadequate education for health care professionals about end-of-life care;
- Lack of research to support evidence-based end-of-life care.

Cost pressures and limited capacity also have forced hospitals to reconsider how they care for the most critically ill, said Meier. Hospitals have adopted a model in which patients are treated and quickly discharged, but not all patients fit this model. For example, a person who undergoes surgery for a total hip replacement may develop a complication such as pneumonia or a stroke and then spend weeks or months in the intensive care unit due to one complication after another. While relatively few patients fall into this category, she said, those who do stay in the hospital for extended periods of time and have high costs per day.

Palliative care offers an alternative model for caring for these patients, Meier said. "It not only improves the quality of care for that category of patients, but it's also a very efficient model of delivering care because it involves bringing appropriate care, as opposed to unnecessary, expensive, and futile care, to patients," she said.

J. Cameron Muir, MD, president of the American Association of Hospice and Palliative Medicine, said there is an emerging body of evidence suggesting that appropriate discussion of the goals of care among clinicians, patients, and their families, as well as aggressive symptom management, improves the quality of care and reduces hospital costs and length of stay (Meier DE. *J Hosp Med.* 2006;1[1]:21-28).

A New Model

In traditional intensive care settings, a patient may be seen by multiple specialists who communicate primarily through the patient's medical chart, said Meier. Often there is no primary care physician coordinating the patient's care, so some symptoms or problems facing the patient or the patient's family may fall through the cracks. Communication between the health care team, the patient, and the patient's family also may be compromised.

Palliative care, on the other hand, brings together an interdisciplinary team of physicians, nurses, and social workers who work closely to assess the needs and wishes of a patient and family members and to establish and carry out a treatment plan accordingly, Meier explained. The team places a special emphasis on assessing and managing such symptoms as pain, anxiety, depression, insomnia, constipation, and shortness of breath. To ensure good communication, the team also gathers information from all the treating physicians and translates it into language that the patient, family members, and the primary care physician can understand.

For patients who wish to be treated at home, the team brings its clinical expertise to planning and carrying out an effective, safe, and sustainable discharge plan, which can reduce readmission rates. Meier explained that traditionally, in hospitals without a palliative care team, a social worker with little knowledge of the patient's health care needs is charged with coordinating patient discharges. This can lead to a patient going home without necessary medicines or equipment, and many quickly return to the hospital via the emergency department, she said.

Meier emphasized that unlike hospice, which provides only supportive care to terminally ill patients, palliative care is appropriate for any patient with complex medical needs, and it can be provided in conjunction with curative or life-prolonging treatments. "It is as appropriate for a 24-year-old coming into the hospital with a new diagnosis of leukemia for whom the goal is cure, but who has enormous symptom burden and enormous family distress, as it is for a person with advanced dementia and repeated aspiration pneumonia," she explained.

Building Capacity

Recent growth in hospital-based palliative care and related growth in home hospice care has allowed more individuals to choose to die at home. Between 1990 and 2000, US census data show a 17% decrease in the number of individuals who died in the hospital, Muir said. Yet much remains to be accomplished in this arena, given that 85% of US residents report that they would prefer to die at home but only 50% do so (based on the 2000 census figures).

Many efforts are already under way to support, expand, and improve palliative care. To strengthen the evidence base for palliative care, the NINR is conducting and supporting multidisciplinary research on such issues as symptom assessment, advanced directives, improving communication between the patient, family, and the health care team, and cultural competency.

Although previous studies have consistently found that palliative care reduces symptoms, improves patient satisfaction, and reduces costs, many of the studies have been small, have looked at different types of palliative care programs, or had other methodological problems that make it difficult to make comparisons and draw conclusions across studies. To help provide a clearer picture, Meier and colleagues at Mount Sinai School of Medicine are launching a 5-year multimember, prospective study of palliative care for patients with cancer. Thousands of patients will be included in the study.

In 2006, the Aetna Foundation, the Brookdale Foundation, the JEHT Foundation, and the John A. Hartford Foundation joined the Robert Wood Johnson Foundation in supporting the latter's Center to Advance Palliative Care. The center, which was launched in 1999 to provide technical support to hospitals for the development and maintenance of palliative care programs, offers extensive Web-based resources for leaders of palliative care programs and has recently added distance learning by offering audio conferences. Interactive Webinars and online courses also are being developed.

The American Academy of Hospice and Palliative Medicine, which began in 1988 with 250 founding members, has grown to include more than 2600 members. Muir said the academy is shifting its focus from the start-up phase of the field to maintaining and advancing the field, including building the workforce of physicians trained in palliative care. In the past 12 to 15 years, the number of fellowships in palliative and hospice medicine have grown from 5 to more than 50, Muir said. To continue that growth and provide funding for existing programs, the academy is working to gain Medicare and other funding sources for fellowships in the field at both traditional academic programs and community based academic hospice programs. Securing funding for faculty development also is a priority.

Another key priority is convincing the Centers for Medicare & Medicaid Services to recognize palliative care as a subspecialty. Such recognition will ensure that palliative care physicians can bill the agency for services rendered to Medicare and Medicaid recipients and will likely lead to more commercial payers covering such care, Muir said. Some commercial payers, convinced by data showing quality improvements and cost savings associated with palliative care, have already begun to do so.

Meanwhile, continued growth of hospital-based palliative care programs is expected. The most vulnerable patients receive high-quality care and hospital resources are used efficiently, Meier said. "It's a win-win."

Critical Thinking

1. Define palliative care.
2. Explain why palliative care is described as a "new model." How does it differ from the old way, and is it really a solution?

Cannabis Use in Long-Term Care: An Emerging Issue for Nurses

Conflicting laws at the state and federal levels put nurses in the middle.

Roxanne Nelson

The use of cannabis as a medicinal agent is a hotly debated and contentious issue in the United States. Cannabis has been touted as a treatment for many conditions, including nausea and anorexia caused by chemotherapy, AIDS-related wasting, neuropathic pain, spasticity associated with multiple sclerosis, and glaucoma. Its use for medical purposes has enjoyed strong support among professional health care organizations and the public at large; 14 states and the District of Columbia now allow its use, although regulations and qualifications vary widely. (The advocacy group Americans for Safe Access dedicates a site to explaining those laws state by state: http://bit.ly/gs7hIw.)

Although the U.S. Department of Justice announced in 2009 that users and distributors of medical cannabis wouldn't be pursued as long as they followed state laws, the federal government has resisted any change to the drug's illegal status at the national level.

This isn't only an issue of state laws conflicting with federal law; even within states that permit medical cannabis, the rules about its use in the institutional setting may be hazy. These ill-defined regulations can put health care professionals in a precarious position. And because many nursing homes rely on federal or state funding, there are unanswered questions as to whether health care providers can legally provide or administer any form of medical cannabis to residents.

"There are issues of loss of licenses and certifications," said Allen St. Pierre, executive director of the National Organization for the Reform of Marijuana Laws, or NORML. "The idea of a Schedule I drug being used or tolerated at a facility that's licensed by a state or federal government is anathema."

But this isn't a new issue, and for NORML it began even before the advent of "medical cannabis proper," according to St. Pierre. In 1990, he said, NORML would take calls from organizations that provided homes away from home for families and patients dealing with painful diseases. In these cases, said St. Pierre, "we would have older teenagers, who, with their physician's recommendation, wanted to use cannabis on site."

The legal counsels or managers of such organizations were caught between wanting to provide the best possible health care for people at a very difficult time in their lives and trying not to jeopardize the operation for future clients, given that this was a clear violation of the law. St. Pierre contends that the conflict—between providing good health care and breaking the law—has wrapped itself around nearly every tier of the health care industry.

Federal vs. State Rules

Cannabis sativa is available in leaf form (known as marijuana, pot, weed, or reefer) or in various extracted forms (as hashish or oil) and can be taken in a variety of ways (smoked, ingested, or vaporized). It's best known as a recreational drug, although its medicinal properties have been documented for thousands of years. It was legally available in the United States until the beginning of the 20th century. In 1937 the first federal laws against cannabis use were passed. (For more on the history of cannabis in the United States, see "A Brief History of Medical Marijuana" in *Time:* http://bit.ly/3NFI7d.)

Cannabis is currently listed as a Schedule I drug, which means that the government doesn't recognize any medical value. Despite the federal laws, a growing number of states are liberalizing their laws and allowing patients varying degrees of access to cannabis. Although firm numbers remain somewhat elusive, it's believed that the percentage of older users is growing. If that's true, it would indicate that long-term care facilities will increasingly have to address the situation. (This year NORML plans to roll out the NORML Senior Alliance, which will offer information to older adults about the medical uses of cannabis.)

One of the main problems is that many state laws don't specifically address the use of cannabis in nursing homes and other institutions. For example, Alaska law doesn't require any facility monitored by its Department of Administration to accommodate cannabis users. In Montana, smoking is prohibited in all health care facilities, but cannabis may be used in other forms; individual facilities may set their own rules, including under what conditions and circumstances cannabis use would be permitted. Maine, on the other hand, permits nursing homes and inpatient hospice workers to act as registered caregivers for patients using medical cannabis.

Another pressing concern is that these facilities often receive federal funding, either directly through Medicare or indirectly through Medicaid. This places administrators in an awkward position, having to choose between complying with federal law (and maintaining funding) and permitting access to cannabis to residents who rely on it.

"We may only find out what will happen if a brave nursing home takes the risk and does the right thing for its patients," said Mary Lynn Mathre, MSN, RN, an addiction specialist and president of the nonprofit group Patients Out of Time. "Given the Obama administration's statement about not interfering with medical marijuana patients who are getting legal recommendations from their care provider, it seems very wrong to *not* allow nursing home patients to use it because the facility receives federal funding." She added that "it would be great to see nursing home administration organizations pass a formal resolution recognizing this potential problem and asking the federal government to allow patients the option to use this medicine as they would any other medicine."

Nursing's Stance on the Issue

Overall, nursing organizations, including the American Nurses Association and more than a dozen state nursing associations, support supervised access to medical cannabis. But if experts are correct, and the number of older adult cannabis users escalates in nursing homes and assisted living facilities, nurses may find themselves in a rather unusual situation. Aside from possibly violating federal drug laws, there are other issues to consider. Who dispenses the cannabis? What is the dosage? How will the facility obtain it?

California has been a pioneer in exploring the issue of medicinal cannabis use, having been the first state in the nation to pass an initiative that loosened its laws and allowed for medical usage.

"In California, we have laws that protect patients' rights," said Deborah Burger, RN, copresident of the California Nurses Association (National Nurses United), which supports the use of medical cannabis. "If patients have been prescribed the medication, they should get it. Nurses in those areas are bound by California law to advocate on behalf of the patient." And if California nurses have had problems with it, Burger hasn't heard about it. "I haven't heard that there were any issues with nursing homes refusing to allow patients to use it," she said.

Sometimes the "don't ask, don't tell" approach is the best option, according to Mathre. "I can tell you that many hospice nurses turn a blind eye to cannabis use in the home because they know it helps." She explained that during a legislative committee hearing on a medical cannabis bill in Wisconsin, a nurse who represented her hospice organization spoke in favor of the legislation and acknowledged the problem that nurses in this situation face. "They may be witnessing illegal activity, but they pretend not to see or know what's going on because, in their hearts, they know the patient benefits from the use of cannabis."

Critical Thinking

1. Why is cannabis great medicine?
2. How do state and local laws interfere with medical treatments involving cannabis?
3. Why are nursing home administrators in an awkward position when using medical cannabis in treating the elderly?

From *American Journal of Nursing*, April 2011, pp. 19–20. Copyright © 2011 by Lippincott, Williams & Wilkins/Wolters Kluwer Health. Reprinted by permission via Rightslink.

I Was a Doctor Accustomed to Death, But Not His

Working in nursing homes taught me about old age—but I was unprepared for my grandfather's last days.

MARC AGRONIN

I currently live and work in Miami as a doctor for old people—the very profession so derided in my early years of training. To be more specific, I am the psychiatrist at the Miami Jewish Health Systems, the site of one of the largest nursing homes in the United States. Although people sometimes call my place of work "God's waiting room," they miss a much bigger picture.

True, the average age of my patients is about 90 years old, meaning that I see a lot of people close to 100. The 80-year-olds who come to see me are like teenagers on my scale of things, and the 70-year-olds—babies! And true, my job is to tend to all of the maladies and infirmities of aging that I learned about in my medical and psychiatric training. But as I have learned from countless older individuals, the true scales of aging are not one-sided; the problems of aging must be weighed against the promises. In my work as a geriatric psychiatrist I have learned that aging equals vitality, wisdom, creativity, spirit, and, ultimately, hope. And for an increasing number of aged individuals, these vital forces are growing by the day.

In the spring of 1997 my beloved grandfather passed away. A week before his death, I stood vigil at his bedside while he flickered between confusion and insensibility. The once-brilliant mind of this retired doctor was soaked in a pool of morphine, and most rational thinking had already drowned. He insisted on wearing a large pair of sunglasses in the darkened room. He cursed and growled when I held his arms as he staggered into the bathroom.

I am not certain that he even recognized me on that final visit, as by then his lifelong persona had largely separated from the person. Nevertheless, his voice came to me as I watched him lying in bed, breathing slowly: "Notice the abnormal rate and pitch of the breath sounds," I imagined him saying; "they are quiet at first but become increasingly labored until they stop for a moment—called

apnea—and then the pattern repeats. This is known as Cheyne-Stokes respiration, and it is often seen just prior to death." I pictured the seriousness of my grandfather's face as he taught me to observe the ebb and flow of the respirations and then quizzed me to make certain that I had absorbed the lesson. The distinctive cadence of his voice alternated between curt instructions and impatient pauses, waiting for my answer. He had a way of repetitively flipping his outstretched hand at the wrist as he spoke, one finger extending out like Michelangelo's God, as if to say, "It can be this way, or that, but you must choose one!"

The practice of medicine was his life, and he had taught me with both an earnestness and a severity about caring for patients. My grandfather had experienced the urgency of his work while serving as a field surgeon in the U.S. Army Air Corps stationed on Okinawa during World War II. This sensibility was reinforced after the war in his fifty years as a general practitioner in the small industrial town of Kaukauna, Wisconsin. In both circumstances the survival of a patient depended on his own wit and hands; there were few colleagues or other resources to help out.

My grandfather had an instinctive sense of independence, no doubt fashioned in his childhood. He was born in 1914 and grew up in a small town in Ukraine near Kiev, alone with his mother and grandmother after his father left for America. He survived the poverty and deprivation of rural Russia during World War I and recalled hiding in haystacks or in the forest to escape from the murderous pogroms of the Cossacks. At the age of twelve he came to America in the steerage of a transatlantic steamer, landing at Ellis Island with other similarly huddled masses. My grandfather remembered seeing the gleaming torch of the Statue of Liberty as the ship glided into New York harbor. He remembered the sweet, precious taste of an orange that he ate, for the first time, while on board. His subsequent journey in America slowly took him west along the rail-lines; he lived with relatives in New York, Chicago, Madison, and, finally, Appleton, Wisconsin.

Before becoming a doctor, my grandfather was, in succession, a milkman, a boxer, and a scientist. His appearance lent itself to each job, as he had the quick, thin legs of a deliveryman; the box-shaped, muscular trunk of a pugilist; and the round, balding, and bespectacled face of an intellectual. Photographs of him from youth to old age always show a dapper man, whether dressed in uniform, scrubs, or coat and tie. In 1938 he married my grandmother, and they stayed together for life. She was the consummate doctor's wife, who raised their three children, managed the books, and kept the home quiet, kosher, and revolving smoothly around his frenetic schedule. As a doctor my grandfather worried incessantly about his patients, but he hid it behind his obsessive work habits and sometimes-gruff demeanor. By the early 1970s probably half of Kaukauna's residents were either current or former patients, a good many of them having been birthed into his hands. Neighbors, strangers, and family alike all made visits to his modest-sized, spartan clinic, where he was renowned as a diagnostician. There weren't many secrets in our large extended family living throughout Wisconsin, but whatever they were, he knew and kept them hidden as a good doctor should.

Until the year before his death, aging had been a relatively benign process for my grandfather. He practiced medicine and surgery until the age of eighty and then retired not because he felt any desire to but because it just seemed logical. When he became ill, however, aging caught up to him quite quickly. In the summer of 1996 he was diagnosed with an aggressive form of prostate cancer. Suddenly, he needed me for support and advice, and we spoke nearly every day about how to manage some of his physical discomfort. Of course, as a newly minted psychiatrist I was of little value to his medical management, and I left that up to my uncle, who had taken over his practice. But our conversations were not really about my grandfather's pain; they were, it seemed to me, cover for dealing with aging and death.

As the de facto family historian I also knew that I had to record his life stories, and so at Thanksgiving we sat down on the porch of my grandparents' house for a taped interview. The life review was almost too painful for him, however, and he broke down crying at several points. I had never seen him cry before, let alone show sadness, but I persisted with the camera, knowing that time was short. In my work with older individuals it is always painful to witness the crumbling of their composure in the face of

loss and grief, but I can steel my own emotions because I rarely know what the person was once like. But such was not the case with my grandfather, and I vacillated between denial and despair. As I was saying my good-byes and leaving my grandparents' home at the end of the weekend, he pulled me aside and stated rather perfunctorily that this was probably the last time I would see him. His words were sterile and clinical—a doctor's way of parting with a patient. But I knew that this was his best effort at saying good-bye. A doctor myself, I brushed off his words in the same manner I might use leaving the clinic at day's end— "No, Grandpa; I'll see you soon. Call me tomorrow."

I reflected on these moments as I sat at his bedside that spring and tried to contain my emotions. He was not only my grandfather, but also my mentor, my inspiration, and, from my earliest childhood days, my own doctor. But now his life of eighty-three years was drawing to a close, and I was standing witness at the point where aging meets death. Shortly after my grandparents passed away, I compressed much of my grief into an odd fantasy that in the afterlife they had moved down to Miami Beach and were experiencing eternal bliss together, with endless sunny beaches and Early Bird specials. Florida, I imagined, was actually some form of Shangri-La where all of our deceased elderly could be found happily wandering around if we just looked hard enough.

No other period of life has such a feared and mysterious ending. Childhood ends with the budding of puberty and the new challenges of adolescence. Adolescence passes away in the excitement of pulsating hormones, shedding its awkward, uncertain skin in the journey into young adulthood. The subsequent stages of adulthood bring undiscovered treasures of love, children, work, and spirit. Even in the face of failure or lost opportunities, there is always hope for something new. But aging seems to bring this process to a halt. The horizon is unknown except for the single fact that a true ending will come . . .

Critical Thinking

1. What is "God's waiting room"?
2. If the doctor's conversations were not really about his grandfather's pain and treatment; what were they really about?
3. Comment on the following quote: "Even in the face of failure or lost opportunities, there is always hope for something new."

MARC AGRONIN, M.D., a graduate of Harvard University and Yale Medical School, is a board-certified geriatric psychiatrist. He is the author of "How We Age: A Doctor's Journey into the Heart of Growing Old."

UNIT 5
Funerals

Unit Selections

27. **The Contemporary American Funeral,** Michael R. Leming and George E. Dickinson
28. **Building My Father's Coffin,** John Manchester
29. **Dealing with the Dead,** Jennifer Egan
30. **Mourning in a Digital Age,** Bruce Feiler
31. **10 Burdens Funeral Directors Carry,** Caleb Wilde
32. **Memorial videos give lasting farewell,** Jeff Strickler
33. **Speaking from beyond the grave,** Jeff Strickler

Learning Outcomes

After reading this unit you should be able to:

- Know the needs of the bereaved.

- Understand the social function of the funeral.

- Assist and support children when they attend funerals.

- Know how planning and producing a funeral is an important part of grief work.

- Understand how physical objects connected with the dead can facilitate therapeutic grieving.

- Understand how digital resources affect funeral planning and ways to support the bereaved.

Student Website
www.mhhe.com/cls

Internet References

The Alcor Life Extension Foundation
www.alcor.org
Funeral Consumers Alliance
www.funerals.org
Funerals and Ripoffs
www.funerals-ripoffs.org
The Internet Cremation Society
www.cremation.org

Decisions relating to the disposition of the body after death often involve feelings of ambivalence—on one hand, attachments to the deceased might cause one to be reluctant to dispose of the body and on the other hand, practical considerations make the disposal of the body necessary. Funerals or memorial services provide methods for disposing of a dead body, remembering the deceased, and helping survivors accept the reality of death. There are also public rites of passage that assist the bereaved in returning to routine patterns of social interaction. In contemporary America, 79 percent of deaths involve earth burial and 21 percent involve cremation. These public behaviors, along with the private process of grieving, comprise the two components of the bereavement process.

This unit on the contemporary American funeral begins with a general article on the nature and functions of public bereavement behavior by Michael R. Leming and George E. Dickinson. Leming and Dickinson provide an overview of the present practice of funeralization in American society, including traditional and alternative funeral arrangements. They also discuss the functions of funerals relative to the sociological, psychological, and theological needs of adults and children.

The remaining articles in this section reflect upon the many alternative ways in which funerals, rituals, and final dispositions for the deceased may be constructed.

© Design Pics/Darren Greenwood

Article 27

The Contemporary American Funeral

MICHAEL R. LEMING AND GEORGE E. DICKINSON

Paul Irion (1956) described the following needs of the bereaved: reality, expression of grief, social support, and meaningful context for the death. For Irion, the funeral is an experience of significant personal value insofar as it meets the religious, social, and psychological needs of the mourners. Each of these must be met for bereaved individuals to return to everyday living and, in the process, resolve their grief.

The psychological focus of the funeral is based on the fact that grief is an emotion. Edgar Jackson (1963) indicated that grief is the other side of the coin of love. He contends that if a person has never loved the deceased—never had an emotional investment of some type and degree—he or she will not grieve upon death. As discussed in the opening pages of Chapter 2, evidence of this can easily be demonstrated by the number of deaths that we see, hear, or read about daily that do not have an impact on us unless we have some kind of emotional involvement with those deceased persons. We can read of 78 deaths in a plane crash and not grieve over any of them unless we personally knew the individuals killed. Exceptions to the preceding might include the death of a celebrity or other public figure, when people experience a sense of grief even though there has never been any personal contact.

In his original work on the symptomatology of grief, Erich Lindemann (1944) stressed this concept of grief and its importance as a step in the resolution of grief. He defined how the emotion of grief must support the reality and finality of death. As long as the finality of death is avoided, Lindemann believes, grief resolution is impeded. For this reason, he strongly recommended that the bereaved persons view the dead. When the living confront the dead, all of the intellectualization and avoidance techniques break down. When we can say, "He or she is dead, I am alone, and from this day forward my life will be forever different," we have broken through the devices of denial and avoidance and have accepted the reality of death. It is only at this point that we can begin to withdraw the emotional capital that we have invested in the deceased and seek to create new relationships with the living.

On the other hand, viewing the corpse can be very traumatic for some. Most people are not accustomed to seeing a cold body and a significant other stretched out with eyes closed. Indeed, for some this scene may remain in their memories for a lifetime. Thus, they remember the cold corpse, not the warm, responsive person. Whether or not to view the body is not a cut-and-dried decision. Many factors should be taken into account when this decision is made.

Grief resolution is especially important for family members, but others are affected also—the neighbors, the business community in some instances, the religious community in most instances, the health-care community, and the circle of friends and associates (many of whom may be unknown to the family). All of these groups will grieve to some extent over the death of their relationship with the deceased. Thus, many people are affected by the death. These affected persons will seek not only a means of expressing their grief over the death, but also a network of support to help cope with their grief.

Sociologically, the funeral is a social event that brings the chief mourners and the members of society into a confrontation with death. The funeral becomes a vehicle to bring persons of all walks of life and degrees of relationship to the deceased together for expression and support. For this reason in our contemporary culture the funeral becomes an occasion to which no one is invited but all may come. This was not always the case, and some cultures make the funeral ceremony an "invitation only" experience. It is perhaps for this reason that private funerals (restricted to the family or a special list of persons) have all but disappeared in our culture. (The possible exception to this statement is a funeral for a celebrity—in which participation by the public may be limited to media coverage.)

At a time when emotions are strong, it is important that human interaction and social support become high priorities. A funeral can provide this atmosphere. To grieve alone can be devastating because it becomes necessary for that lone person to absorb all of the feelings into himself or herself. It has often been said that "joy shared is joy increased;" surely grief shared is grief diminished. People need each other at times when they have intense emotional experiences.

A funeral is in essence a one-time kind of "support group" to undergird and support those grieving persons. A funeral provides a conducive social environment for mourning. We may go to the funeral home either to visit with the bereaved family or to work through our own grief. Most of us have had the experience of finding it difficult to discuss a death with a member of the family. We seek the proper atmosphere, time, and place. It is during the funeral, the wake, the shivah, or the visitation with the bereaved family that we have the opportunity to express our condolences and sympathy comfortably.

Anger and guilt are often deeply felt at the time of death and will surface in words and actions. They are permitted within the funeral atmosphere as honest and candid expressions of grief, whereas at other times they might bring criticism and reprimand. The funeral atmosphere says in essence, "You are okay, I am okay; we have some strong feelings, and now is the time to express and share them for the benefit of all." Silence, talking, feeling, touching, and all means of sharing can be expressed without the fear of their being inappropriate.

Another function of the funeral is to provide a theological or philosophical perspective to facilitate grieving and to provide a context of meaning in which to place one of life's most significant experiences. For the majority of Americans, the funeral is a religious rite or ceremony (Pine, 1971). Those grievers who do not possess a religious creed or orientation will define or express death in the context of the values that the deceased and the grievers find important. Theologically or philosophically, the funeral functions as an attempt to bring meaning to the death and life of the deceased individual. For the religiously oriented person, the belief system will perhaps bring an understanding of the afterlife. Others may see only the end of biological life and the beginning of symbolic immortality created by the effects of one's life on the lives of others. The funeral should be planned to give meaning to whichever value context is significant for the bereaved.

"Why?" is one of the most often asked questions upon the moment of death or upon being told that someone we know has died. Though the funeral cannot provide the final answer to this question, it can place death within a context of meaning that is significant to those who mourn. If it is religious in context, the theology, creed, and articles of faith confessed by the mourners will give them comfort and assurance as to the meaning of death. Others who have developed a personally meaningful philosophy of life and death will seek to place the death in that philosophical context.

Cultural expectations typically require that we dispose of the dead with ceremony and dignity. The funeral can also ascribe importance to the remains of the dead. In keeping with the specialization found in most aspects of American life (e.g., the rise of professions), the funeral industry is doing for Americans that necessary task they no longer choose to do for themselves.

The Needs of Children and Their Attendance at Funerals

For children, as well as for their elders, the funeral ceremony can be an experience of value and significance. At a very early age, children are interested in any type of family reunion, party, or celebration. To be excluded from the funeral may create questions and doubts in the minds of children as to why they are not permitted to be a part of an important family activity.

Another question to be considered when denying the child an opportunity to participate in postdeath activities is what goes through the child's mind when such participation is denied. Children deal with other difficult situations in life, and when denied this opportunity, many will fantasize. Research suggests that these fantasies may be negative, destructive, and at times more traumatic than the situation from which the children are excluded.

Children also should not be excluded from activities prior to the funeral service. They should be permitted to attend the visitation, wake, or shivah. (In some situations it would be wise to permit children to confront the deceased prior to the public visitation.) It is obvious that children should not be forced into this type of confrontation, but, by the same token, children who are curious and desire to be involved should not be denied the opportunity.

Children will react at their own emotional levels, and the questions that they ask will usually be asked at their level of comprehension. Two important rules to follow: Never lie to the child, and do not over answer the child's question.

At the time of the funeral, parents have two concerns about their child's behavior at funerals. The first concern is that the child will have difficulty observing the grief of others—particularly if the child has never seen an adult loved one cry. The second concern is that parents themselves become confused when the child's emotional reactions may be different than their own. If the child is told of a death and responds by saying, "Oh, can I go out and play?" the parents may interpret this as denial or as a suppressed negative reaction to the death. Such a reaction can increase emotional concern by the parents. However, if the child's response is viewed as only a first reaction, and if the child is provided with loving, caring, and supportive attention, the child will ordinarily progress into an emotional resolution of the death.

The final reasons for involving children in postdeath activities are related to the strength and support that children give other grievers. They often provide positive evidence of the fact that life goes on. In other instances, because they have been an important part of the life of the deceased, their presence is symbolic testimony to the immortality of the deceased. Furthermore, it is not at all unusual for children to change the atmosphere surrounding bereavement from one of depression and sadness to one of laughter, verbalization, and celebration. Many times children do this by their normal behavior, without any understanding of the kind of contribution being made.

Critical Thinking

1. What are the three basic needs of the bereaved according to Paul Iron?

2. Explain the following quote by Edgar Jackson: "Grief is the other side of the coin of love."

3. How can one help children when they attend funerals?

Building My Father's Coffin

My dad spent his life writing books. His final, impractical request gave us a story like no other.

This is an excerpt from John Manchester's upcoming memoir. It appeared on his Open Salon blog.

JOHN MANCHESTER

In his last years my father, the writer William Manchester, told me, "When I die. I want you children to build my coffin." He'd gotten the idea sometime in the '70s, when a Wesleyan chemistry professor died, and his sons, following a Catalan custom, spent the night before the funeral building his coffin in their basement. My dad explained, "It will give you and your sisters a focus for your grief."

I nodded and held my tongue. It was pointless to explain what he already knew: My sisters had never done any carpentry, and my own modest skills had diminished since I'd become afflicted by carpal tunnel syndrome.

It was a focus, all right, not for grief but for worry. How were we going to build it? In the last spring of his life, as he declined, I prayed he would just forget about it.

But the morning after he died I found a list of instructions on his desk. No. 5: "My body is to be placed in a plain pine box. I would like my children to make the box."

Fuck. We really had to build it.

Down at the funeral home, I explained to the director how we planned to build the coffin. I felt awkward asking, but there were questions only he could answer. What were the interior measurements needed to accommodate the body? He told me, and I wrote them down. What about securing the lid? He would screw it onto the box. Good. As we spoke, I remembered my father telling me how funeral homes make their money selling fancy coffins, and wondered why this guy wasn't trying to sell me one. But then he told me about one homemade coffin he'd encountered. "The family made it years ahead of time, and by the time the person died, it had warped." He gave me a look: *You don't want to know the details.* There was his sales pitch, and I was tempted to go with it.

I had also heard a story about a funeral where the homemade coffin disintegrated as the pallbearers carried it, and the body fell out. My worst fear. That's what made me determined that ours would be the sturdiest, most reliable casket since Napoleon's seven-layered sarcophagus beneath the Invalides in Paris.

How were we going to build it? I called my older son, Shawn, who was an engineering major. He was already far more competent with his hands than my father, sisters and me combined. Home for the weekend from college, he devised a plan for the box. I vetted it with a friend of mine, a master cabinetmaker. It seemed up to snuff, but we still didn't have tools.

I called my sister, who was living in Florida. She was busy working and would have to scramble just to get to the funeral. So she'd join us in the coffin-building only in spirit.

I called my other sister, who was in Connecticut for the summer, and discussed the coffin. She explained that her mother-in-law's partner, David, would be happy to help us. "He's a professional. He teaches carpentry. He has a fully equipped workshop in his garage."

David invited us down to his place in Connecticut the following Saturday. It was only a two-hour drive from our house in Massachusetts. By the time we got off the phone, I felt relieved: We had Shawn's plan, good tools, and David to help us.

My wife, Judy, and I pulled into the driveway. David and Shawn stood in front of the garage around a couple of sawhorses with some boards on top.

Judy said, "Thank God they've already started."

I agreed.

It was one of those perfect days, the kind that comes only once or twice a year in New England. I smiled, remembering my father telling me, "One of the crucial things in my writing is my use of irony." He would have enjoyed the irony of this task on this day. It was in striking contrast to what I'd pictured all those years—us building the coffin in my father's gloomy basement storeroom.

For years I had a vision of me and my sisters making the coffin on top of our sad, warped Ping-Pong table, up to our waists in the tens of thousands of pages of his papers that filled the room.

I heard the bang of a hammer, looked over at Shawn and David around the sawhorse, and remembered why I was here. David looked at my worried face, rubbed his hands together, and gave me a smile that said, "This is going to be fun." His only question was how to do it.

He looked at Shawn's plan, nodded his head, then handed it back and said diplomatically, "Let's make it up as we go along." He looked down at the boards on the sawhorse, frowning, then turned and looked at the side of the garage, pointing: "It's a door." He added, "I know how to make a door."

He thought another moment, then nodded. "The sides and top are also doors." Following the measurements given by the funeral director, he cut the assembly to size. We had the first door. The rest was easy: four more doors for the sides and one for the top, and we'd be done.

I lost myself in the rhythm of making it. When we were done screwing the sides to the bottom, I asked, "Are you sure it's strong enough?" David picked up a length of strapping and said, "I think it's fine, but just for you we'll box all the edges with this." When that was done even I was pretty confident that it would hold my father, and the strapping lent it a kind of elegance.

After lunch David looked at the box and shook his head. "It's going to be hard to carry, hard to keep hold of, with us crowded in three to a side." I saw us pallbearers at the funeral dropping it and gave David a look. He said, "We'll make rails." We went to the hardware store and got two 1-inch dowels and lag bolts.

By this point we were both starting to feel pride in our work. David said, "Let's stain it."

I said, "No, it's supposed to be a plain pine box. Besides, if we leave it bare, people at the funeral will realize we built it." He nodded.

My sister, who had watched from the porch, put in a symbolic screw.

We stood around it, admiring its simple elegance. Still, I had to ask David, "Are you sure it's strong enough?"

He said, "Only one way to find out—take it for a test drive."

Judy bravely volunteered. We lifted it to the ground and she climbed in. Someone said, "Maybe we should put the lid on."

She said, "No, this is fine." We hauled her around the yard. The neighbors, out working in their yards, put down their clippers and rakes and gawked. Why not? How often did they, or anyone else for that matter, get an opportunity to watch their neighbors building a coffin on a sunny Saturday?

As we carried her, Judy laughed along with the rest of us. What else to do? Later I asked her, "How did it feel?"

"It scared the hell out of me."

We finished our tour of the lawn and let her out. The coffin was rock solid. We congratulated ourselves: "Look at that thing!" "It only took five hours!" I thanked Shawn and David.

As Judy and I pulled out of the driveway, I gave the coffin a last look and felt the excitement of the day dissolve. Sometime later that evening the funeral director would discreetly steal it away, then place my father's body in it. The next time we would see it would be at the funeral.

He would not be buried in it. His instructions stated that following the funeral, he would be cremated. It felt weird to have gone to all that trouble, just to have the coffin burned up a few days later. But its purpose was never practical. My father was a storyteller at heart, and this made a good one. It even had poetic potential: something about all those trees sacrificed to make all his books offering up a few boards for his last story.

Critical Thinking

1. Why would a father ask his children to build his coffin?
2. What is the function of becoming involved in funeral planning and implantation?
3. Explain the following quote: "It will give you and your sisters a focus for your grief."

JOHN MANCHESTER'S music has been heard worldwide for the last 25 years on TV, radio and the Internet. You can also hear it on his MySpace page and at Manchester Music Library.

Dealing with the Dead

JENNIFER EGAN

In 1980, when my mother co-owned an art gallery in San Francisco, she and her assistant were robbed at gunpoint by two jittery escaped convicts, who mistook the gallery for a cash business and openly discussed shooting them when the cash failed to materialize. The ordeal ended without serious harm (thanks to the miraculous arrival of a delivery man, who frightened the convicts away), but my mother never again wanted to wear the skirt she'd had on that day: a long black wraparound with a geometric pattern of magenta flowers and thick green stems. I appropriated the skirt, cut it short, took it with me to college, and wore it through my twenties. I never forgot its awful history; on the contrary, that history sharpened my pleasure in wearing it. The very act of tying the skirt around my waist felt restorative—as if, by paving over my mother's horrific experience with ordinary life, I were repairing an imbalance.

I was near the end of my twenties before I lost someone I was close to: my mother's mother, whose three-tiered necklace of small fake pearls I inherited. I wore that necklace constantly, even after it became clear that I would destroy it unless I put it aside. I had the same impulse when my father died, six years later, and, five years after that, my stepfather. From my father's closet, I borrowed a navy-blue wool V-neck, from my stepfather's a gray-and-burgundy argyle sweater. For years, on any given winter day I wore one of those two sweaters, partly for the obvious reason—wearing the garment of a person I loved was like being wrapped in a protective force field. But what drove me was also a kind of defiance. When the clock stops on a life, all things emanating from it become precious, finite, and cordoned off for preservation. Each aspect of the dead person is removed from the flux of the everyday, which, of course, is where we miss him most. The quarantine around death makes it feel unlucky and wrong—a freakish incursion—and the dead, thus quarantined, come to seem more dead than they already are. Those sweaters did more than remind me of their original owners; the sheer ordinariness of working in them, spilling on them, taking them off at the end of the day, and tossing them on the floor helped to diffuse that dour hush. Borrowing from the dead is a way of keeping them engaged in life's daily transactions—in other words, alive.

When my father-in-law, whom I adored, died a year and a half ago, I began with almost unseemly speed to lobby my mother-in-law for one of his sweaters. She gave me a few to choose from, two of which I kept: a scratchy green sweater that's too warm for everyday wear, and a vest, ginger-colored and wonderfully roomy, just as my stepfather's argyle sweater was for years, until I accidentally put it in the dryer and it shrank to fit me exactly. I'd forgotten, in the years since my father and stepfather died, what it was like to first wear their clothing. Starting fresh with my father-in-law's vest brought it back: the garment smelled so much like him—coffee, pepper, burning wood—that when I held it under my children's noses and asked, "Who does this smell like?" they both cried, startled, "Grandpa!"

After a few weeks, the vest went from smelling like Grandpa to smelling like me, until the latter fact was so pronounced that I had it dry-cleaned, at which point it became, in some sense, mine. But always on loan, to such an extent that I think Joe's vest each time I pull it from my closet, and I find the notion so heartening that I recently marvelled to my husband at his reluctance to avail himself of this obvious way to feel connected with—surrounded by—his father, whom I know he misses. "There are more sweaters!" I exhorted him. "I only took two." My husband paused a moment before replying, disconcerted, "What can I say? I don't have the impulse to wear them. I think about him constantly, but it's not bound up in physical things."

Of course, a loan from someone dead is—like any loan—temporary. It can't be renewed, and, eventually, the physical object begins to wear down. My grandmother's necklace broke on an East Village corner; the cheap plastic pearls went flying into the street. I gathered up as many as I could and sealed them in an envelope, which I've since lost track of. My father's and stepfather's sweaters are beginning to look threadbare, despite multiple repairs. This reminds me of how long it's been since I saw their owners. I find it ever harder to remember how it felt to be in a room with either of those men, but I know how their sweaters feel against my skin. I plan to wear them until they unravel into shreds.

Critical Thinking

1. How can wearing something associated with the dead facilitate grieving?
2. Explain the following quotation: "Of course, a loan from someone dead is—like any loan—temporary."
3. Explain the following quotation: "My father's and stepfather's sweaters are beginning to look threadbare, despite multiple repairs. This reminds me of how long it's been since I saw their owners. I find it ever harder to remember how it felt to be in a room with either of those men, but I know how their sweaters feel against my skin. I plan to wear them until they unravel into shreds."

Source: New Yorker; 10/11/2010, Vol. 86 Issue 31, p68.

Mourning in a Digital Age

BRUCE FEILER

I have found myself in a season of loss. Every few weeks for the last six months, friends in the prime of life have suffered the death of a close family member. These deaths included a mother, a father, a sister, a brother, a spouse and, in one particularly painful case, a teenage child who died on Christmas morning.

The convergence of these passings brought home an awkward truth: I had little idea how to respond. Particularly when the surviving friend was young, the funeral was far away and the grieving party did not belong to a religious institution, those of us around that friend had no clear blueprint for how to handle the days following the burial.

In several of these cases, a group of us organized a small gathering. E-mails were sent around, a few pizzas and a fruit salad were rounded up, someone baked a cake. And suddenly we found ourselves in what felt like the birth pangs of a new tradition.

"It's a secular shiva," the hostess announced.

So what exactly were we creating? Grieving has been largely guided by religious communities, from celebratory Catholic wakes, to the 49 days of mourning for Buddhists, to the wearing of black (or white) in many Protestant traditions, to the weeklong in-house condolence gatherings that make up the Jewish tradition of shiva. Today, with religiosity in decline, families dispersed and the pace of life feeling quickened, these elaborate, carefully staged mourning rituals are less and less common. Old customs no longer apply, yet new ones have yet to materialize.

"We're just too busy in this world to deal with losing people," said Maggie Callanan, a hospice nurse for the last 30 years and the author of "Final Gifts," an influential book about death and dying. "And yet we have to."

Ms. Callanan and others in the field point to the halting emergence of guidelines to accommodate our high-speed world, in which many people are disconnected from their friends physically, yet connected to them electronically around the clock.

One puzzle I encountered is the proper way to respond to a mass e-mailing announcing a death.

"We still feel it's nice to pick up the phone or send a card," said Danna Black, an owner of Shiva Sisters, an event-planning company in Los Angeles that specializes in Jewish funeral receptions. "But if the griever feels comfortable sending out an e-mail, you can feel comfortable sending one back. Just don't hit Reply All."

Facebook presents its own challenges. The site's public platform is an ideal way to notify a large number of people, and many grievers I know have taken comfort in supportive messages from friends. Like CaringBridge, CarePages and similar sites, social networks can become like virtual shiva locations for faraway loved ones.

But Megory Anderson, the founder of the Sacred Dying Institute in San Francisco (it seeks to bring spirituality to the act of dying), said problems arise when grievers begin encroaching on the personal space of others.

"The safest thing is to share your own story," she said. Since everyone grieves differently, she cautions against sharing private details of other family members, loved ones or the deceased themselves. She also recommends sending a private message to grievers instead of writing on their wall.

Especially in a world in which so much communication happens online, the balming effect of a face-to-face gathering can feel even more magnified. The Jewish tradition of sitting shiva offers an appealing template. Named after the Hebrew word for "seven," shiva is a weeklong mourning period, dating back to biblical times, in which immediate family members welcome visitors to their home to help fortify the soul of the deceased and comfort the survivors. Though many contemporary Jews shorten the prescribed length, the custom is still widely practiced.

The "secular shivas" we organized had a number of notable differences that proved crucial to their success. First, we organized them for Jews and non-Jews alike. Second, no prayers or other religious rituals were offered. Third, we held them away from the home of the griever, to reduce the burden. And finally, we offered the grieving party the option of speaking about the deceased, something not customary under Jewish tradition.

I recently reached out to the guests of honor, and, along with a few professionals, tried to identify a few useful starting points.

Don't wait for the griever to plan. As Ms. Callanan observed: "One thing you can assume with a grieving person is that they're overwhelmed with life. Suddenly keeping up with the bills, remembering to disconnect the hoses or shoveling the sidewalk no longer seem necessary." With a traditional shiva, the burden falls on the family to open their home to sometimes hundreds of people. If you are considering a "secular shiva," insist on doing the planning yourself, from finding a location, to notifying guests, to ordering food.

By invitation only. Traditional shivas are open houses; they're communitywide events in which friends, neighbors and colleagues can stop by uninvited. Our events were more restricted, with the guest of honor suggesting fewer than a dozen invitees. "An old-fashioned shiva would have felt foreign to me," said my friend Karen, who lost her mother last summer. "I'm more private. If it was twice the size, I wouldn't have felt comfortable."

"Would you like to share a few stories?" At the event we held for Karen, she opted to speak about her mom. For 45 emotional minutes, she talked about her mother's sunny disposition, her courtship, her parenting style. It was like watching a vintage movie.

"I liked speaking about my mom," she told me. "One, I hadn't had time to fully grieve because I was so focused on my dad. And two, there was something each of you could come away with about who my mom was in the world."

At a later event, a Catholic friend who had lost her brother chose not to speak about him. She felt too fragile, she later explained. Instead she handed out CDs with a photo montage of her brother's life. "I think if I hadn't had the pictures, I would have felt the need to talk about him."

The comfort of crowds. While I came away from these events convinced we had hit on a new tool for our circle of friends, I was quickly warned not to assume our model was universal.

"Introverts need to grieve, too," Ms. Andrews said. "For some, a gathering of this kind might be a particular kind of torture."

My friend who lost her brother had that reaction initially. "On the way over, I had some misgivings," she said. "I was still crying every time I mentioned his name." But the event surprised her, she said. "Seeing all my friends gathered, I couldn't help but be happy. There was a reaffirming glimmer."

Six months after my string of losses began, it hardly feels over. What I've taken away from the experience is a reminder of what I've seen often in looking at contemporary religion. Rather than chuck aside time-tested customs in favor of whiz-bang digital solutions, a freshening of those rituals is often more effective. Our "secular shivas" took some advantages of the Internet (e-mail organizing, ordering food online); coupled them with some oft-forgotten benefits of slowing down and reuniting; and created a nondenominational, one-size-doesn't-fit-all tradition that can be tinkered to fit countless situations.

Like all such traditions, they may not soften the blow of a loss, but they had the unmistakable boon of reaffirming the community itself.

Critical Thinking

1. What is a "secular shiva"? How does the digital age contribute to it?

2. How can Internet communication contribute the emotional support provided to loved ones at the time of death?

3. How is it that the "secular shiva" can soften the blow of loss but does little to create an affirming community of social support?

10 Burdens Funeral Directors Carry

I wrote this article over the weekend and I wasn't going to publish it until Wednesday, but since I just spent my entire night [11 PM to 5:45 AM] picking up three deceased persons, I thought it's probably appropriate to post it now. After I hit "publish," I'll be off to bed and back to work by noon. Ah, the joys of a small family business.

CALEB WILDE

The following burdens are not necessarily funeral service specific, but many, if not all, come with this profession. Those of us who stay in this profession do so because we find serving others in their darkest hour extremely rewarding, yet there are burdens to be borne. Here's ten.

One. A Lack of Personal Boundaries.

The phone rings at 3 AM in the morning with a hospice nurse on the other end of the line telling you that so-and-so has died, that so-and-so's family is requesting your services and that the family of so-and-so is ready for you to come and pick up so-and-so.

The phone rings at 6 PM the next day. Someone needs to see so-and-so . . . he simply can't believe so-and-so is dead and must come to the funeral home at once to see so-and-so.

Two. Depression.

While those of us who stay in this business do so because we love serving people, the lack of personal boundaries can lead to depression.

Depression, because my son's baseball game was at 6 PM, but somebody in so-and-so's family needed to see so-and-so this very minute. Depression because the emotional needs of others somehow always trump my personal life needs. And all of a sudden "I'm not a good father" and "I'm not happy with my life."

Three. Psychosis.

Psychologist Carl Rogers described how he "literally lost my 'self,' lost the boundaries of myself . . . and I became convinced (and I think with some reason) that I was going insane." When we in human service, and death service, become pulled into the whole narrative of death and dying, we can lose ourselves.

Four. Smells.

An iron stomach I have not. Putrid smells, this business has many. This is a burden that comes home with me . . . a burden that my wife often notices shortly after I walk through the door.

Five. Life Secrets, Death Secrets and Practice Secrets.

When a person commits suicide or dies from an overdose, there are times when the family simply wants to keep the manner of death a secret from the public.

I don't mind carrying the burden of a secret, but when you live in a small town where suspicion can run rampant, secrets can become heavy.

Some things we see will remain with us forever. They are so disturbing, so terrible that we do the world a favor by not sharing them.

Six. Isolation by Profession.

Death makes us different . . . not necessarily unique, just different. This difference creates a chasm between us and those not immersed in death. Sure, police, doctors, psychologist, etc. have chasms created by their professions, but ours—because of the fear, sadness and undefined hours of our practice—creates us into something other.

Seven. Death itself.

Death can be a beautiful experience in the life of a family. But when that death is tragic and unexpected, death is a heavy burden for both the family and for those who serve the family. Specifically, when the death is a young person, our entire staff becomes agitated and moody.

Eight. Workaholism.

Many funeral homes are small businesses that don't have enough staff for shift work. In order to serve our families (so that they'll return), we have learned that the way to overcome the depression and potential psychosis that can come with a lack of personal boundaries is to marry the business. We make the work our life. Such work addiction pleases the families we work for, but can leave our personal families destitute.

And while many of us don't carry the burden of workaholism, we do carry the burden of fighting off the addiction.

Nine. Death Logistics Stress.

Every business has stress. Some more and some less. And while funeral service can't claim a quantitative difference in stress, it can claim to have its very own type of stress. To grasp the type of stress surrounding a funeral, imagine planning a wedding in five days, except where there's joy, sadness exists, and where there's usually a bride, a dead body lies in state.

Ten. Dress clothes . . .

. . . in the summer heat. Dress clothes in the dead of winter. We are one of the few—armed service members are the only others I can think of—professions that wears suits outdoors as a matter of practice. There's nothing like having sweat drip down your back and into your crack. Well, nothing except maybe freezing your dress shoe covered toes in a foot of snow.

Critical Thinking

1. What are the special burdens that funeral directors carry?

2. What are negative coping mechanisms employed by funeral directors in dealing with the special burdens of funeral service?

3. What are positive coping mechanisms employed by funeral directors in dealing with the special burdens of funeral service?

Memorial Videos Give Lasting Farewell

JEFF STRICKLER

Shortly before Connie Dunlap died in October, she sat in front of a camera focused in a tight close-up and talked about her faith and how it shaped her battle against cancer. "Our legacy is usually money or property that we pass down to our children and grandchildren," she says softly but earnestly. "But I think a legacy of faith and our life is much more valuable."

The Forest Lake resident, who was 68, had called the Rev. Alan Naumann and asked him to record a farewell message to be shared with her family after her death. "It was important for her to know that her grandchildren, who were too young to remember her, would one day get to know her," said Naumann, who also is a videographer.

Memorial videos are the latest twist on the video slide shows of snapshots chronicling a life that are often shown at funerals. Aging baby boomers, completely comfortable in the medium of video, are using it not only to look back but also to leave a final message for the future. They share insights from their life and impart advice. Some are somber, others lighthearted.

This new kind of video—sometimes called legacy or end-of-life videos—is becoming so popular that some funeral homes are being outfitted with video projection systems and churches that used to frown on them are embracing them.

Once you've seen one of the videos, advocates say, you'll understand why.

"The emotional impact of these is so powerful," said Ken Kurita, owner of Videon Productions in Excelsior, who made a memorial video for his father's recent funeral. "Which memory would you rather take with you [from a funeral]: the lifeless body lying in a casket, or the living, breathing person you loved, complete with all their mannerisms, their smile, their sense of humor?"

Kurita's father, who died in January at age 83, used his video to recall boyhood anecdotes and even worked in a little humor. "That was my dad," Kurita said, tearing up slightly as he watched the video in his editing booth. "This is all about life's treasured moments."

Sometimes, even the videographers are moved by the end result. Mike Madden from Moviescreen Films in St. Paul was recording a wedding when he coaxed the camera-shy father of the bride to sit down and give a 3-minute interview. The man died unexpectedly three weeks later.

The daughter told him the interview "is one of the most precious things she has," he said.

While the number of videos being shown at funerals is on the rise, just wait a decade, Naumann said. A lot of the work he does now involves people who want to get their stories on record while they're still sharp in their minds.

"We're shooting stuff that we'll have on file for years" before it's needed for memorials, he said.

A Pioneer

Naumann, who is credited with making one of the earliest memorial videos in 1988, said it came out of his dual background. In addition to being a minister, he's the owner of Minneapolis-based Memory Vision. In the late '80s, he was serving as the chaplain at Hillside Cemetery in northeast Minneapolis. He bought a video camera and started experimenting with it. One of those experiments was a video biography, and when he showed part of it at the subject's funeral, he knew immediately that he was onto something special.

"It was overwhelming," he said.

Still, memorial videos didn't catch on right away. For one thing, editing video was a laborious task because the tapes couldn't be cut and spliced like film. It wasn't until the digital revolution enabled editors to use a computer to mimic film editing that the memorials started to gain popularity.

It also took persuading to get some churches to allow them. Naumann made a video about a Roman Catholic nun, only to have her parish priest reject the idea as conflicting with the solemnity of the funeral mass.

"I called him up, clergy to clergy, and explained how the video was going to show all the wonderful things this woman did to help people," he said. "He finally agreed to let us show it. He was so impressed by the video that after the funeral, he started showing it to other groups. He became its biggest supporter."

Wide Price Range

The cost of a memorial video varies tremendously. Prices start as low as $200 for an electronic photo album to as much as $20,000 for one with exclusive music and interviews with relatives and friends. But a typical video consisting of an interview with the subject costs $1,000 to $2,000.

Memorial videographers take great pride in their interviews. Their goal is to have the subject reveal something that will surprise everyone. Kurita even managed to do that when he did the video with his father, Dr. Kenji Kurita.

Being of Japanese-American descent, he was sent to a so-called relocation camp at the start of World War II. He eventually enlisted in the Army and was assigned to one of the Japanese-American battalions. The younger Kurita always assumed that his patriotic father was bitter about having been sent to a pseudo-prison. When he did his interview, his father set him straight, and, in the process, drove home the video's potential to influence future generations.

"Many subjects see this as their last chance to tell people what's important to them," Kurita said. "He wanted to tell us not to waste time being angry and bitter over what happened in the past. He said to use that energy to follow your dreams."

Just Do It

While professional videographers would like you to hire them, many of them believe so strongly in the medium that they encourage people to do their own memorial video.

"If you can't afford to hire me, at least get a video camera, put it in front of Grandma and Grandpa and record them," Kurita insisted. "Everyone has a story, and we need to get those stories now."

Naumann is gathering material for a class on do-it-yourself memorial videos. But don't wait for that, he said.

"I got a call the other day from a woman who said, 'My mother just turned 90. When do you think I should start recording her story?'" he recalled. "And I said, 'How about yesterday?'"

Critical Thinking

1. How can memorial videos lead to a improved funeral service?

2. Do you think it is appropriate to include a memorial in a funeral service?

3. What is the role of memorial videos in the future of funeral service? Will it have increased popularity or will it be a dying augmentation?

Speaking from Beyond the Grave; High-tech Headstones Use QR Codes to Link to Photos and Videos of the Dearly Departed

JEFF STRICKLER

Karen Shragg didn't go with traditional granite for her grandmother's headstone.

She went high-tech.

The marker features a QR code that allows visitors to a Richfield cemetery to read her grandmother's biography and view photographs of her, as well.

"This is just fantastic," Shragg said. "It's revolutionary."

The idea of sticking a QR code onto a headstone is the brainchild of a Twin Cities–based outfit determined to drag the industry into the 21st century.

More than just a marketing gambit aimed at a techno-obsessed society, it's an opportunity to document family stories before they fade away, said Norm Taple, president of Katzman Monument Co., which launched the QR codes in 2011. His company is believed to be one of four in the nation offering the QR code service.

"It's a chance for future generations to make a connection with a loved one," Taple said. "There's no emotional connection when all you can look at is a headstone, probably a dirty headstone, at that. We've got people telling their own stories, speaking directly to future generations."

The QR code allows people with smartphones to access a website paying tribute to the dearly departed. Cemetery visitors can read the deceased's biography, study their family tree, look at pictures or even watch videos of them talking about their lives.

The practice grew out of the surging popularity of memorial videos—sometimes called legacy or end-of-life-videos—in which people tape messages to be played at their funerals. Taple wondered why videos should be limited to funerals.

Thus was born the "interactive memorial." It's accessed via the QR code, which is on a 1-1/2-inch-square sticker similar to the renewal tabs used on license plates that can be attached anywhere on the tombstone. It's free with the purchase of a headstone from Katzman Monument, or you can add it to an existing tombstone for $150.

"As long as a cemetery is in an area with cellphone coverage—which these days is just about everywhere—it will work," he said.

Taple's company has been around for a little more than a year. Or a little over 77 years, depending on how you count.

It was started by Taple's grandfather, Jack Katzman, who opened shop at the corner of 19th Street and Nicollet Avenue in 1935. In 1981, with no one in the family interested in taking over the business, he closed it. Taple, his brother, Loren, and a longtime family friend, Michael Gregerson, decided to "reconstitute" the company, but in a technology-centric mode.

Instead of a brick-and-mortar showroom—which none of them could staff because they all have full-time jobs—they set up shop as an online business. Customers who log on to their website, katzmanmonument.com, can do everything electronically, including uploading photographs or other artwork to be etched into the granite.

"There are still companies where, when you walk in, there's a guy with a pencil and pad of sketch paper," he said. "This is an industry that has been missing the boat as far as the rest of the world goes."

Depending on how computer-savvy you are or how complex you want to make the memorial, you can do it yourself or arrange for the monument company to do it for you, either piecemeal or in its entirety. There are forms in which you can type biographies and fill in family trees. If you need help, prices range from $1 a piece to scan nondigital photos, to $45 to convert a VHS tape to digital format, to $215 to produce a 30-photo montage or $550 to shoot a simple video.

You can change the memorial at any time. "Anybody with a smartphone can access it and see it," Taple said, "but only one person has the log-in code that enables them to edit it."

Shragg, who is director of Wood Lake Nature Center and author of the book "Grieving Outside the Box" in which she interviewed people who dealt with grief in unusual ways, said it was insightful to work on her grandmother's QR memorial.

"I wish I had known about them [QR memorials] before I wrote the book," she said. "Any memorial—like the benches we dedicate [at Wood Lake]—is a way of calling attention to a person who was important in your life but is no longer here. But the QR code took it to a new level. It was a way to show people who my grandmother was."

The Rev. Alan Naumann, who also is a videographer, often helps people in hospice record a farewell message. He was doing that with a man in Rochester recently when he mentioned the QR code memorial.

"As we were getting done, I asked him one last question: If you could say something to the people who come to look at your headstone, what would you tell them?" Naumann said. The man said he'd advise his heirs to focus on the things that are important in life. "So then I told him that we can make that happen, and he got so excited about the fact that his life could still have an impact after he was gone.

"Legacy isn't just about money," Naumann continued. "The most important legacy we can leave behind are the lessons we learned and the values that steered our life. And to be able to do that in your own voice is very powerful."

Most cemeteries have embraced the idea. The only resistance Taple has encountered has come from Fort Snelling National Cemetery, which is subject to policies set on a national level. The Department of Veterans Affairs maintains a list of emblems that have been approved for inclusion on grave markers; QR codes aren't on it.

"It's all about uniformity," Taple said. "They don't want a marker to be unique. Well, these were your loved ones, and they were unique in many ways."

He's hoping that the VA will change its policies once it realizes the codes' potential, which he's convinced is almost limitless. His company is working with the creators of a veterans' memorial where visitors will be able to access the personal stories of 600 war dead.

"We're going to reach out to all 600 families," he said. "It's a wonderful opportunity. It's so much better than just a name etched into a monument."

Critical Thinking

1. What is the social benefit of the high-tech headstones that allow the dead to speak beyond the grave?

2. Do you think it is appropriate to have high-tech headstones that allow the dead to speak beyond the grave?

3. What is the role of high-tech headstones that allow the dead to speak beyond the grave? Will it have increased popularity or will it be a dying augmentation to cemeteries?

UNIT 6

Bereavement

Unit Selections

34. **The Grieving Process,** Michael R. Leming and George E.Dickinson
35. **The Normal Process of Grieving,** Harvard Medical School
36. **A guide to getting through grief,** Harvard Medical School
37. **Disenfranchised Grief?,** Kenneth J. Doka
38. **Challenging the Paradigm: New Understandings of Grief,** Kenneth J. Doka
39. **We've Been Misled about How to Grieve,** Nicholas Kohler
40. **Shades of Grief: When Does Mourning Become a Mental Illness,** Virginia Hughes
41. **11 Ways to Comfort Someone Who's Grieving,** Harvard Medical School

Learning Outcomes

After reading this unit you should be able to:

- Understand normal feelings and behaviors related to the grieving process.

- Understand the concept of disenfranchised grief and how grieving can become disenfranchised.

- Become a critical reader of research related to the grieving process.

- Understand how changes in the social environment will have effects on the bereavement process.

- Understand the limitation of stages in describing "normal" grieving.

- Understand high-risk factors that can predispose an individual to complicated grieving.

- Understand ways in which one can assist others who are experiencing trauma in grieving.

Student Website

www.mhhe.com/cos

Internet References

Bereaved Families of Ontario
www.bereavedfamilies.net
The Compassionate Friends
www.compassionatefriends.org
Grief in a Family Context
www.indiana.edu/~famlygrf/sitemap.html
Widow Net
www.widownet.org

In American society many act as if the process of bereavement is completed with the culmination of public mourning related to the funeral or memorial service and the final disposition of the dead. For those in the process of grieving, the end of public mourning only serves to make the bereavement process a more individualized, subjective, and private experience. Private mourning of loss for most people, while more intense at its beginning, continues throughout their lifetime. The nature and intensity of this experience is influenced by the relationship of the mourner to the deceased, the age of the mourner, and the social context in which bereavement takes place.

This unit on bereavement begins with three general articles on the bereavement process and describes and discusses the active coping strategies related to the bereavement process and the four tasks of bereavement. The fourth and fifth articles by Kenneth J. Doka provide an alternative perspective on the understanding of the bereavement process. The next two articles discuss much of the misinformation most people assume about grieving. The final articles are focused on bereavement and helping strategies employed by professional and lay supporters of the bereaved.

© Design Pics/Kristy-Anne Glubish

The Grieving Process

MICHAEL R. LEMING AND GEORGE E. DICKINSON

Grief is a very powerful emotion that is often triggered or stimulated by death. Thomas Attig makes an important distinction between grief and the grieving process. Although grief is an emotion that engenders feelings of helplessness and passivity, the process of grieving is a more complex coping process that presents challenges and opportunities for the griever and requires energy to be invested, tasks to be undertaken, and choices to be made (Attig, 1991).

Most people believe that grieving is a diseaselike and debilitating process that renders the individual passive and helpless. According to Attig (1991, p. 389):

It is misleading and dangerous to mistake grief for the whole of the experience of the bereaved. It is misleading because the experience is far more complex, entailing diverse emotional, physical, intellectual, spiritual, and social impacts. It is dangerous because it is precisely this aspect of the experience of the bereaved that is potentially the most frustrating and debilitating.

Death ascribes to the griever a passive social position in the bereavement role. Grief is an emotion over which the individual has no control. However, understanding that grieving is an active coping process can restore to the griever a sense of autonomy in which the process is permeated with choice and there are many areas over which the griever does have some control.

Coping with Grief

The grieving process, like the dying process, is essentially a series of behaviors and attitudes related to coping with the stressful situation of a change in the status of a relationship. Many individuals have attempted to understand coping with dying as a series of universal, mutually exclusive, and linear stages. Not all people, however, will progress through the stages in the same manner.

Seven behaviors and feelings that are part of the coping process are identified by Robert Kavanaugh (1972): shock and denial, disorganization, volatile emotions, guilt, loss and loneliness, relief, and reestablishment. It is not difficult to see similarities between these behaviors and Kübler-Ross's five stages (denial, anger, bargaining, depression, and acceptance) of the dying process. According to Kavanaugh (1972, p. 23), "these seven stages do not subscribe to the logic of the head as much

as to the irrational tugs of the heart—the logic of need and permission."

Shock and Denial

Even when a significant other is expected to die, at the time of death there is often a sense in which the death is not real. For most of us our first response is, "No, this can't be true." With time, our experience of shock diminishes, but we find new ways to deny the reality of death.

Some believe that denial is dysfunctional behavior for those in bereavement. However, denial not only is a common experience among the newly bereaved but also serves positive functions in the process of adaptation. The main function of denial is to provide the bereaved with a "temporary safe place" from the ugly realities of a social world that offers only loneliness and pain.

With time, the meaning of loss tends to expand, and it may be impossible for one to deal with all of the social meanings of death at once. For example, if a man's wife dies, not only does he lose his spouse, but also his best friend, his sexual partner, the mother of his children, a source of income, and so on. Denial can protect an individual from some of the magnitude of this social loss, which may be unbearable at times. With denial, one can work through different aspects of loss over time.

Disorganization

Disorganization is the stage in the bereavement process in which one may feel totally out of touch with the reality of everyday life. Some go through the 2- to 3-day time period just before the funeral as if on "automatic pilot" or "in a daze." Nothing normal "makes sense," and they may feel that life has no inherent meaning. For some, death is perceived as preferable to life, which appears to be devoid of meaning.

This emotional response is also a normal experience for the newly bereaved. Confusion is normal for those whose social world has been disorganized through death. When Michael Leming's father died, his mother lost not only all of those things that one loses with a death of a spouse, but also her caregiving role—a social role and master status that had defined her identity in the 5 years that her husband lived with cancer. It is only natural to experience confusion and social disorganization when one's social identity has been destroyed.

Volatile Reactions

Whenever one's identity and social order face the possibility of destruction, there is a natural tendency to feel angry, frustrated, helpless, and/or hurt. The volatile reactions of terror, hatred, resentment, and jealousy are often experienced as emotional manifestations of these feelings. Grieving humans are sometimes more successful at masking their feelings in socially acceptable behaviors than other animals, whose instincts cause them to go into a fit of rage when their order is threatened by external forces. However apparently dissimilar, the internal emotional experience is similar.

In working with bereaved persons over the past 20 years, Michael Lemming has observed that the following become objects of volatile grief reactions: God, medical personnel, funeral directors, other family members, in-laws, friends who have not experienced death in their families, and/or even the person who has died. Mild-mannered individuals may become raging and resentful persons when grieving. Some of these people have experienced physical symptoms such as migraine headaches, ulcers, neuropathy, and colitis as a result of living with these intense emotions.

The expression of anger seems more natural for men than expressing other feelings (Golden, 2000). Expressing anger requires taking a stand. This is quite different from the mechanics of sadness, where an open and vulnerable stance is more common. Men may find their grief through anger. Rage may suddenly become tears, as deep feelings trigger other deep feelings. This process is reversed with women, notes Golden. Many times a woman will be in tears, crying and crying, and state that she is angry.

As noted earlier, a person's anger during grief can range from being angry with the person who died to being angry with God, and all points in between. Golden's mentor, Father William Wendt, shared the story of his visits with a widow and his working with her on her grief. He noticed that many times when he arrived she was driving her car up and down the driveway. One day he asked her what she was doing. She proceeded to tell him that she had a ritual she used in dealing with her grief. She would come home, go to the living room, and get her recently deceased husband's ashes out of the urn on the mantle. She would take a very small amount and place them on the driveway. She then said, "It helps me to run over the son of a bitch every day." He concluded the story by saying, "Now that is good grief." It was "good" grief because it was this woman's way of connecting to and expressing the anger component of her grief.

Guilt

Guilt is similar to the emotional reactions discussed earlier. Guilt is anger and resentment turned in on oneself and often results in self-deprecation and depression. It typically manifests itself in statements like "If only I had . . . ," "I should have . . . ," "I could have done it differently . . . ," and "Maybe I did the wrong thing." Guilt is a normal part of the bereavement process.

From a sociological perspective, guilt can become a social mechanism to resolve the **dissonance** that people feel when unable to explain why someone else's loved one has died.

Rather than view death as something that can happen at any time to anyone, people can **blame the victim** of bereavement and believe that the victim of bereavement was in some way responsible for the death—"If the individual had been a better parent, the child might not have been hit by the car," or "If I had been married to that person, I might also have committed suicide," or "No wonder that individual died of a heart attack, the spouse's cooking would give anyone high cholesterol." Therefore, bereaved persons are sometimes encouraged to feel guilt because they are subtly sanctioned by others' reactions.

Loss and Loneliness

Feelings of loss and loneliness creep in as denial subsides. The full experience of the loss does not hit all at once. It becomes more evident as bereaved individuals resume a social life without their loved one. They realize how much they needed and depended upon their significant other. Social situations in which we expected them always to be present seem different now that they are gone. Holiday celebrations are also diminished by their absence. In fact, for some, most of life takes on a "something's missing" feeling. This feeling was captured in the 1960s love song "End of the World."

> Why does the world go on turning?
>
> Why must the sea rush to shore?
>
> Don't they know it's the end of the world
>
> Cause you don't love me anymore?

Loss and loneliness are often transformed into depression and sadness, fed by feelings of self-pity. According to Kavanaugh (1972, p. 118), this effect is magnified by the fact that the dead loved one grows out of focus in memory—"an elf becomes a giant, a sinner becomes a saint because the grieving heart needs giants and saints to fill an expanding void." Even a formerly undesirable spouse, such as an alcoholic, is missed in a way that few can understand unless their own hearts are involved. This is a time in the grieving process when anybody is better than nobody, and being alone only adds to the curse of loss and loneliness (Kavanaugh, 1972).

Those who try to escape this experience will either turn to denial in an attempt to reject their feelings of loss or try to find surrogates—new friends at a bar, a quick remarriage, or a new pet. This escape can never be permanent, however, because loss and loneliness are a necessary part of the bereavement experience. According to Kavanaugh (1972, p. 119), the "ultimate goal in conquering loneliness" is to build a new independence or to find a new and equally viable relationship.

Relief

The experience of relief in the midst of the bereavement process may seem odd for some and add to their feelings of guilt. Michael Leming observed a friend's relief 6 months after her husband died. This older friend was the wife of a minister, and her whole life before he died was his ministry. With time, as she built a new world of social involvements and relationships of which he was not a part, she discovered a new independent person in herself whom she perceived was a better person than she had ever before been.

Relief can give rise to feelings of guilt. However, according to Kavanaugh (1972, p. 121): "The feeling of relief does not imply any criticism for the love we lost. Instead, it is a reflection of our need for ever deeper love, our quest for someone or something always better, our search for the infinite, that best and perfect love religious people name as God."

Reestablishment

As one moves toward reestablishment of a life without the deceased, it is obvious that the process involves extensive adjustment and time, especially if the relationship was meaningful. It is likely that one may have feelings of loneliness, guilt, and disorganization at the same time and that just when one may experience a sense of relief, something will happen to trigger a denial of the death.

What facilitates bereavement and adjustment is fully experiencing each of these feelings as normal and realizing that it is hope (holding the grieving person together in fantasy at first) that will provide the promise of a new life filled with order, purpose, and meaning.

Reestablishment occurs gradually, and often we realize it has been achieved long after it has occurred. In some ways it is similar to Dorothy's realization at the end of *The Wizard of Oz*—she had always possessed the magic that could return her to Kansas. And, like Dorothy, we have to experience our loss before we really appreciate the joy of investing our lives again in new relationships.

Four Tasks of Mourning

In 1982 J. William Worden published *Grief Counseling and Grief Therapy*, which summarized the research conclusions of a National Institutes of Health study called the Omega Project (occasionally referred to as the Harvard Bereavement Study). Two of the more significant findings of this research, displaying the active nature of the grieving process, are that mourning is necessary for all persons who have experienced a loss through death and that four tasks of mourning must be accomplished before mourning can be completed and reestablishment can take place.

According to Worden (1982), unfinished grief tasks can impair further growth and development of the individual. Furthermore, the necessity of these tasks suggests that those in bereavement must attend to "grief work" because successful grief resolution is not automatic, as Kavanaugh's (1972) stages might imply. Each bereaved person must accomplish four necessary tasks: (1) accept the reality of the loss, (2) experience the pain of grief, (3) adjust to an environment in which the deceased person is missing, and (4) withdraw emotional energy and reinvest it in another relationship (Worden, 1982).

Accept the Reality of the Loss

Especially in situations when death is unexpected and/or the deceased lived far away, it is difficult to conceptualize the reality of the loss. The first task of mourning is to overcome the natural denial response and realize that the person is dead and will not return.

Bereaved persons can facilitate the actualization of death in many ways. The traditional ways are to view the body, attend the funeral and committal services, and visit the place of final disposition. The following is a partial list of additional activities that can assist in making death real for grieving persons.

1. View the body at the place of death before preparation by the funeral director.
2. Talk about the deceased person and the circumstances surrounding the death.
3. View photographs and personal effects of the deceased person.
4. Distribute the possessions of the deceased person among relatives and friends.

Experience the Pain of Grief

Part of coming to grips with the reality of death is experiencing the emotional and physical pain caused by the loss. Many people in the denial stage of grieving attempt to avoid pain by choosing to reject the emotions and feelings that they are experiencing. As discussed by Erich Lindemann (1944), some do this by avoiding places and circumstances that remind them of the deceased. Michael Leming knows one widow who quit playing golf and quit eating at a particular restaurant because these were activities that she had enjoyed with her husband. Another widow found it extremely painful to be with her dead husband's twin, even though he and her sister-in-law were her most supportive friends.

Worden (1982, pp. 13–14) cites the following case study to illustrate the performance of this task of mourning:

> One young woman minimized her loss by believing her brother was out of his dark place and into a better place after his suicide. This might not have been true, but it kept her from feeling her intense anger at him for leaving her. In treatment, when she first allowed herself to feel anger, she said, "I'm angry with his behavior and not him!" Finally she was able to acknowledge this anger directly.

The problem with the avoidance strategy is that people cannot escape the pain associated with mourning. According to Bowlby (cited by Worden, 1982, p. 14), "Sooner or later, some of those who avoid all conscious grieving, break down—usually with some form of depression." Tears can afford cleansing for wounds created by loss, and fully experiencing the pain ultimately provides wonderful relief to those who suffer while eliminating long-term chronic grief.

Assume New Social Roles

The third task, practical in nature, requires the griever to take on some of the social roles performed by the deceased person or to find others who will. According to Worden (1982), to abort this task is to become helpless by refusing to develop the skills necessary in daily living and by ultimately withdrawing from life.

An acquaintance of Michael Leming's refused to adjust to the social environment in which she found herself after the death of her husband. He was her business partner, as well as her best and only friend. After 30 years of marriage, they had no children, and she had no close relatives. She had never learned to drive a car. Her entire social world had been controlled by her former husband. Three weeks after his funeral she went into the basement and committed suicide.

The alternative to withdrawing is assuming new social roles by taking on additional responsibilities. Extended families who always gathered at Grandma's house for Thanksgiving will be tempted to have a number of small Thanksgiving dinners at different places after her death. The members of this family may believe that "no one can take Grandma's place." Although this may be true, members of the extended family will grieve better if someone else is willing to do Grandma's work, enabling the entire family to come together for Thanksgiving. Not to do so will cause double pain—the family will not gather, and Grandma will still be missed.

Reinvest in New Relationships

The final task of mourning is a difficult one for many because they feel disloyal or unfaithful in withdrawing emotional energy from their dead loved one. One of Michael Leming's family members once said that she could never love another man after her husband died. His twice-widowed aunt responded, "I once felt like that, but I now consider myself to be fortunate to have been married to two of the best men in the world."

Other people find themselves unable to reinvest in new relationships because they are unwilling to experience again the pain caused by loss. The quotation from John Brantner at the beginning of this chapter provides perspective on this problem:

"Only people who avoid love can avoid grief. The point is to learn from it and remain vulnerable to love."

However, those who are able to withdraw emotional energy and reinvest it in other relationships find the possibility of a newly established social life. Kavanaugh (1972, pp. 122–123) depicts this situation well with the following description:

At this point fantasies fade into constructive efforts to reach out and build anew. The phone is answered more quickly, the door as well, and meetings seem important, invitations are treasured and any social gathering becomes an opportunity rather than a curse. Mementos of the past are put away for occasional family gatherings. New clothes and new places promise dreams instead of only fears. Old friends are important for encouragement and permission to rebuild one's life. New friends can offer realistic opportunities for coming out from under the grieving mantle. With newly acquired friends, one is not a widow, widower, or survivor—just a person. Life begins again at the point of new friendships. All the rest is of yesterday, buried, unimportant to the now and tomorrow.

Critical Thinking

1. Describe the seven behaviors and feelings that are part of coping with grief and loss.

2. What are the four tasks of mourning and how can the loss of closure relative to these tasks lead to impaired grieving?

3. How can relief and reinvestment in new relationships be important in normal grieving?

The Normal Process of Grieving

People often experience fluctuating emotions for months.

When people talk about grieving, they often describe an experience akin to being at sea. Wave after wave of emotion envelops them, and just when they think they're recovering, a new wave hits them. Yet with time, most people manage to reach equilibrium. While significant losses are never forgotten, the feelings of grief become less intense and more manageable.

The following experiences are all part of the normal spectrum of grieving and can last from six to 12 months.

Yearning. Survivors repeatedly want to reunite with the person who died in some way, and may even want to die themselves in order to be with their loved one.

Deep sadness. People often experience waves of deep sadness and regret about the loved one. Crying and even sobbing jags are also normal.

Other negative emotions. Anger, remorse, and guilt are all common negative emotions as well.

Vivid memories. It's common to think of the deceased often and recall vivid memories of times together. Images of the deceased—or even the sound of a loved one's voice—may emerge without warning.

Somatic disturbances. Grief affects people physically as well as mentally. It's normal for people to have sleep problems, changes in appetite, digestive difficulties, dry mouth, or fatigue after a loss. Occasional bouts of restlessness and agitation are also common.

Disbelief. It takes people a long time to truly accept that a loved one has died. People often forget at times that a loved one is gone—until some reminder brings the reality searing back.

Apathy. It's typical for people to withdraw or disengage at times while grieving. They may become irritable toward others.

Emotional surges. Although some of the worst emotions and disturbances ebb with time, the grieving process also involves surges of emotions. Holidays, anniversaries, birthdays, and other significant events can trigger bouts of raw grief.

Factors that Make Grieving Harder

As if the normal process of grief were not challenging enough, the following events or factors may make it even harder. In some people, these factors can cause grief to become complicated and prolonged.

Conflict in relationships. People who had an ambivalent, angry, conflicted, or a highly dependent relationship with the deceased may find it hard to grieve.

Multiple deaths. If the loss occurs in conjunction with deaths of other loved ones, the grieving process can become magnified.

Mental illness. People who already have depression, anxiety, or another mental illness may have an amplified response to a loss and experience a more intense bereavement.

Traumatic death. A death that was unexpected, untimely, traumatic, or violent sets the stage for a more difficult grieving process.

Caregiving. People who provided care to their loved ones before they died are likely to feel the loss more acutely than others, in part because they structured so much of their time to be with their loved ones. They may be haunted by images from the final days. In other cases, they may be at a loss to know how to spend their time.

Social isolation. People who have few friends, family members, or other sources of social support may feel abandoned as they navigate the grieving process. Elderly people who outlive their spouses and friends, for example, may suffer more because they are suffering relatively alone.

Critical Thinking

1. What are the eight experiences that are part of "normal" grieving?

2. What are the six factors that make grieving harder for the bereaved?

3. How does time influence experiences of "normal grieving"?

HIRSCH M, ED. *Coping with Grief and Loss: A Guide to Healing* (Harvard Health Publications, 2010). For more references, please see www.health. harvard.edu/mentalextra.

A Guide to Getting Through Grief

Focus on the essentials and try to let people know what support you need.

Losing a close friend or family member can be devastating. All the small details of daily life—getting out of bed, making meals, going to appointments, taking care of children, handling responsibilities at work—may seem monumentally hard or inconsequential. It is important for people to let the nonessentials slide and focus on ways to get through this difficult time.

Dr. Michael Hirsch, a psychiatrist at Massachusetts General Hospital and medical editor of Harvard Medical School's Special Health Report *Coping with Grief and Loss: A Guide to Healing,* offers the following advice. Although some tips may seem basic, they are vital for enabling people who are grieving to work through the process.

Tend to the Essentials

People who are grieving a loved one's loss may neglect their own health and well-being. In spite of the emotional pain, it's important that you attend to the basics—making the literal, eat-your-vegetables choices—to maintain your physical health.

Eat well. A well-balanced diet is essential as you withstand the stress of grieving. That means eating plenty of vegetables, fruits, and lean proteins, and drinking plenty of water and other healthy liquids. If your appetite is diminished, try eating small portions more frequently. A daily multivitamin can cover any missing nutrients.

Take necessary medications. Grief makes people more vulnerable to illness, so it's important that you keep taking your regular medications.

Get enough sleep. Grief is exhausting. If you feel tired, nap to make up for a sleep deficit. Paradoxically, doing more exercise is likely to improve your energy. Watch your caffeine and alcohol intake, as these substances can interfere with sleep.

Exercise every day. A simple walk, a bike ride, yoga, or a harder workout can ease agitation, anger, and depression. Depending on your needs, xercise can provide you with a distraction when you need a break from grieving, or offer you some quiet time to focus on your loss.

Avoid risky behavior. In the wake of a profound loss, people often justify using dangerous coping strategies—such as drinking too much alcohol (more than one drink a day for women or two for men), using drugs, or engaging in impulsive or self-destructive behavior. The short-term relief of pain is likely not to be worth it if the pattern of dangerous behavior persists or intensifies, leading to further losses.

Delay big decisions. Grief can cloud thought processes, and people who make abrupt decisions may regret them later. Many experts suggest that you wait a year, if possible, before moving, changing jobs, clearing out keepsakes, and making other momentous decisions.

Practice self-care. People who are grieving should regularly ask, "What would help me most today?" The answer may vary from day to day and even from hour to hour. Sometimes you need to cry, or talk to a friend, or just take a break from grieving.

Turn to Family and Friends

Dr. Alan D. Wolfelt, a grief counselor and author of *Healing Your Grieving Heart,* suggests that people who are grieving identify three friends or family members who can provide support on a regular basis in the first weeks and months after a loss. Perhaps they have practical help to offer (such as cooking meals), or are not judgmental and willing to listen. The following tips may also be helpful.

Tell people what helps. People who are grieving may need to say, "I just need to cry right now," or "There's nothing you can do to fix this. It would help if you just stay with me for an hour." If you want to talk about the person you've lost, you may need to let others know. For example, it might help if you say, "I miss her so much. I just want to talk about her, but I feel like everyone is afraid to say her name."

Embrace mixed feelings. It is entirely normal to have mixed emotions about the loss and about your loved one. It helps to express these so that other people understand what you are going through. Some of the things you can say:

- "I feel so angry about his death. It seems so useless."
- "I'm relieved that Mom isn't suffering anymore, but I miss her terribly."
- "My relationship with my dad was really difficult. I'm feeling a lot of things right now—not just sadness."
- "I know you think I should be over this, but I'm not."

Take away uncertainty. Often, people aren't sure how to act around you when you are grieving. Although it may be difficult for you to express what you need while you are grieving a loss, the following directions might help others understand how they can support you:

- "If you really want to help, clearing up the kitchen or vacuuming would be great."

- "Hugs just make me feel worse right now. What I need is a little time alone."
- "I can't bear to be alone tonight, but I don't want to talk. Could you stay and just watch TV with me?"
- "I feel so mad about everything. I'm irritated with people all the time."

Find others who understand. People who have also lost a loved one may be more understanding. Ask them outright: "What helped you? How did you get through this awful time?" When friends and family can't help in these ways, support groups often can.

Leave the door open. People who are grieving sometimes may wish that everyone else would just go away and leave them alone to sort through their feelings. If you express this need too forcefully, though, you may drive people so far away that they are not going to be there when you do need them. Here are some ways of expressing the need for solitude while leaving the door open to future support:

- "I just want to go home and go to bed right now. Would you call me tomorrow, though?"
- "I feel so upset these days, I can't settle on anything. Please don't take it personally."
- "I'm just not up to that right now. Maybe in a few weeks. Will you try me again?"

Realize that everyone grieves differently. People who experience the same loss often grieve in different ways. For example, other parent who loses a child may need to cry and talk frequently, while the othe might work incessantly and act increasingly distant. Both are trying desperately to deal with their pain and loss. Professional insight from a grief counselor can be valuable when grieving drives a wedge between you and your spouse, family members, or other loved ones.

Commemorating a Loved One

Remembering and honoring the person who died helps people keep memories alive. Sometimes it helps shape meaning from loss. You can commemorate a loved one in various ways.

Artwork. Creating art can help you explore your feelings, chronicle the life of the person who died, or express your ideas of an after-life. For example, you can create a memory quilt incorporating meaningful scenes and fabrics. Children struggling with grief may find creating art—whether it's with clay, colored pens, paints, or collage supplies—particularly helpful.

Journal. Some people create a journal to memorialize a loved one's life. You can also develop a timeline of important dates and events. The journal can include pictures, stories, sayings, and well-loved recipes. Friends and family may want to contribute as well.

Memory box. You can use pictures, objects, and art supplies to make a memory box for display or keepsakes. When you are ready to go through your loved one's belongings, you can set aside items for the memory box.

Slide show. You can use favorite pictures, songs, and sayings to create a poignant multimedia remembrance of your loved one's life. Or splice old videos together and copy them onto DVDs for others to enjoy.

Photo wall. You can create a collage or remembrance wall from photos taken at different times and events.

Good cause. Sometimes people leave instructions about how they want to be remembered through memorial gifts to various causes, such as medical research, peace efforts, and scholarship funds. If not, you can think about how best to honor your loved one.

Peaceful spot. A peaceful nook with a comfortable chair, lighting, photos, inspirational books, or other important objects can serve as a spot to honor your loved one. Some people create serene outdoor spots, such as a fountain in a garden. Or you could walk regularly through a nature preserve, or visit a spot your loved one enjoyed.

Garden. Planting a garden or a tree can be a wonderful way to remember someone.

Gravesite. In many cultures, the gravesite is a focal point for commemorating the loved one, particularly on special days such as birthdays, anniversaries, or holy days. You can plant flowers there, say a prayer, or simply visit for a few moments of contemplation.

Prayer. Spirituality is of great comfort to many people. Depending on your own views, spiritual practices can include saying prayers, lighting incense or a candle, creating a shrine, or meditating.

Echo. You can create an "echo" of your loved one, by doing something silly, pleasurable, or solemn that they once did. This might involve giving a holiday toast, traveling, playing well-loved music, cracking a bad joke, or performing acts of kindness.

References

Hirsch M, ed. *Coping with Grief and Loss: A Guide to Healing* (Harvard Health Publications, 2010).

Moules NJ, et al. "The Soul of Sorrow Work: Grief and Therapeutic Interventions with Families," *Journal of Family Nursing* (Feb. 2007): Vol. 13, No. 1, pp. 117–41.

Running A, et al. "When There Is Nothing Left to Do, There Is Everything Left to Do," *American Journal of Hospice & Palliative Care* (Dec. 2007–Jan. 2008): Vol. 24, No. 6, pp. 451–54.

Wolfelt A. *Healing Your Grieving Heart: 100 Practical Ideas* (Companion Press, 2001).

Critical Thinking

1. What are the essential basics in "getting through" the grieving process?
2. How can family and friends be important in "getting through" the grieving process?
3. Describe some of the many ways in which one can commemorate a loved one and how this can help people "get through" the grieving process?

Disenfranchised Grief

Kenneth J. Doka

Introduction

Ever since the publication of Lindemann's classic article, "Symptomatology and Management of Acute Grief," the literature on the nature of grief and bereavement has been growing. In the few decades following this seminal study, there have been comprehensive studies of grief reactions, detailed descriptions of atypical manifestations of grief, theoretical and clinical treatments of grief reactions, and considerable research considering the myriad variables that affect grief. But most of this literature has concentrated on grief reactions in socially recognized and sanctioned roles: those of the parent, spouse, or child.

There are circumstances, however, in which a person experiences a sense of loss but does not have a socially recognized right, role, or capacity to grieve. In these cases, the grief is disenfranchised. The person suffers a loss but has little or no opportunity to mourn publicly.

Up until now, there has been little research touching directly on the phenomenon of disenfranchised grief. In her comprehensive review of grief reactions, Raphael notes the phenomenon:

> There may be other dyadic partnership relationships in adult life that show patterns similar to the conjugal ones, among them, the young couple intensely, even secretly, in love; the defacto relationships; the extramarital relationship; and the homosexual couple. . . . Less intimate partnerships of close friends, working mates, and business associates, may have similar patterns of grief and mourning.

Focusing on the issues, reactions, and problems in particular populations, a number of studies have noted special difficulties that these populations have in grieving. For example, Kelly and Kimmel, in studies of aging homosexuals, have discussed the unique problems of grief in such relationships. Similarly, studies of the reactions of significant others of AIDS victims have considered bereavement. Other studies have considered the special problems of unacknowledged grief in prenatal death, [the death of] ex-spouses, therapists' reactions to a client's suicide, and pet loss. Finally, studies of families of Alzheimer's victims and mentally retarded adults also have noted distinct difficulties of these populations in encountering varied losses which are often unrecognized by others.

Others have tried to draw parallels between related unacknowledged losses. For example, in a personal account, Horn compared her loss of a heterosexual lover with a friend's loss of a homosexual partner. Doka discussed the particular problems of loss in nontraditional relationships, such as extramarital affairs, homosexual relationships, and cohabiting couples.

This article attempts to integrate the literature on such losses in order to explore the phenomenon of disenfranchised grief. It will consider both the nature of disenfranchised grief and its central paradoxical problem: the very nature of this type of grief exacerbates the problems of grief, but the usual sources of support may not be available or helpful.

The Nature of Disenfranchised Grief

Disenfranchised grief can be defined as the grief that persons experience when they incur a loss that is not or cannot be openly acknowledged, publicly mourned, or socially supported. The concept of disenfranchised grief recognizes that societies have sets of norms—in effect, "grieving rules"—that attempt to specify who, when, where, how, how long, and for whom people should grieve. These grieving rules may be codified in personnel policies. For example, a worker may be allowed a week off for the death of a spouse or child, three days for the loss of a parent or sibling. Such policies reflect the fact that each society defines who has a legitimate right to grieve, and these definitions of right correspond to relationships, primarily familial, that are socially recognized and sanctioned. In any given society these grieving rules may not correspond to the nature of attachments, the sense of loss, or the feelings of survivors. Hence the grief of these survivors is disenfranchised. In our society, this may occur for three reasons.

1. The Relationship Is Not Recognized

In our society, most attention is placed on kin-based relationships and roles. Grief may be disenfranchised in those situations in which the relationship between the bereaved and deceased is not based on recognizable kin ties. Here the closeness of other non-kin relationships may simply not be understood or appreciated. For example, Folta and Deck noted, "While all of these studies tell us that grief is a normal phenomenon, the intensity of which corresponds to the closeness of the relationship, they fail to take this (i.e., friendship) into account. The underlying assumption is that closeness of relationship exists only among spouses and/or immediate kin." The roles of lovers, friends, neighbors, foster parents, colleagues, in-laws, stepparents and stepchildren, caregivers, counselors, co-workers, and roommates (for example, in nursing homes) may be long-lasting and intensely interactive, but even though these relationships are recognized, mourners may not have full opportunity to publicly grieve a loss. At most, they might be expected to support and assist family members.

Then there are relationships that may not be publicly recognized or socially sanctioned. For example, nontraditional relationships, such as extramarital affairs, cohabitation, and homosexual relationships have tenuous public acceptance and limited legal standing, and they face negative sanctions within the larger community. Those involved in such relationships are touched by grief when the relationship is terminated by the death of the partner, but others in their world, such as children, may also experience grief that cannot be acknowledged or socially supported.

Even those whose relationships existed primarily in the past may experience grief. Ex-spouses, past lovers, or former friends may have limited contact, or they may not even engage in interaction in the present. Yet the death of that significant other can still cause a grief reaction because it brings finality to that earlier loss, ending any remaining contact or fantasy of reconciliation or reinvolvement. And again these grief feelings may be shared by others in their world such as parents and children. They too may mourn the loss of "what once was" and "what might have been." For example, in one case a twelve-year-old child of an unwed mother, never even acknowledged or seen by the father, still mourned the death of his father since it ended any possibility of a future liaison. But though loss is experienced, society as a whole may not perceive that the loss of a past relationship could or should cause any reaction.

2. The Loss Is Not Recognized

In other cases, the loss itself is not socially defined as significant. Perinatal deaths lead to strong grief reactions, yet research indicates that many significant others still perceive the loss to be relatively minor. Abortions too can constitute a serious loss, but the abortion can take place without the knowledge or sanctions of others, or even the recognition that a loss has occurred. It may very well be that the very ideologies of the abortion controversy can put the bereaved in a difficult position. Many who affirm a loss may not sanction the

act of abortion, while some who sanction the act may minimize any sense of loss. Similarly, we are just becoming aware of the sense of loss that people experience in giving children up for adoption or foster care, and we have yet to be aware of the grief-related implications of surrogate motherhood.

Another loss that may not be perceived as significant is the loss of a pet. Nevertheless, the research shows strong ties between pets and humans, and profound reactions to loss.

Then there are cases in which the reality of the loss itself is not socially validated. Thanatologists have long recognized that significant losses can occur even when the object of the loss remains physically alive. Sudnow for example, discusses "social death," in which the person is alive but is treated as if dead. Examples may include those who are institutionalized or comatose. Similarly, "psychological death" has been defined as conditions in which the person lacks a consciousness of existence, such as someone who is "brain dead." One can also speak of "psychosocial death" in which the persona of someone has changed so significantly, through mental illness, organic brain syndromes, or even significant personal transformation (such as through addiction, conversion, and so forth), that significant others perceive the person as he or she previously existed as dead. In all of these cases, spouses and others may experience a profound sense of loss, but that loss cannot be publicly acknowledged for the person is still biologically alive.

3. The Griever Is Not Recognized

Finally, there are situations in which the characteristics of the bereaved in effect disenfranchise their grief. Here the person is not socially defined as capable of grief; therefore, there is little or no social recognition of his or her sense of loss or need to mourn. Despite evidence to the contrary, both the very old and the very young are typically perceived by others as having little comprehension of or reaction to the death of a significant other. Often, then, both young children and aged adults are excluded from both discussions and rituals.

Similarly, mentally disabled persons may also be disenfranchised in grief. Although studies affirm that the mentally retarded are able to understand the concept of death and, in fact, experience grief, these reactions may not be perceived by others. Because the person is retarded or otherwise mentally disabled, others in the family may ignore his or her need to grieve. Here a teacher of the mentally disabled describes two illustrative incidences:

> In the first situation, Susie was 17 years old and away at summer camp when her father died. The family felt she wouldn't understand and that it would be better for her not to come home for the funeral. In the other situation, Francine was with her mother when she got sick. The mother was taken away by ambulance. Nobody answered her questions or told her what happened. "After all," they responded, "she's retarded."

The Special Problems of Disenfranchised Grief

Though each of the types of grief mentioned earlier may create particular difficulties and different reactions, one can legitimately speak of the special problem shared in disenfranchised grief.

The problem of disenfranchised grief can be expressed in a paradox. The very nature of disenfranchised grief creates additional problems for grief, while removing or minimizing sources of support.

Disenfranchising grief may exacerbate the problem of bereavement in a number of ways. First, the situations mentioned tend to intensify emotional reactions. Many emotions are associated with normal grief. Bereaved persons frequently experience feelings of anger, guilt, sadness and depression, loneliness, hopelessness, and numbness. These emotional reactions can be complicated when grief is disenfranchised. Although each of the situations described is in its own way unique, the literature uniformly reports how each of these disenfranchising circumstances can intensify feelings of anger, guilt, or powerlessness.

Second, both ambivalent relationships and concurrent crises have been identified in the literature as conditions that complicate grief. These conditions can often exist in many types of disenfranchised grief. For example, studies have indicated the ambivalence that can exist in cases of abortion, among ex-spouses, significant others in nontraditional roles, and among families of Alzheimer's disease victims. Similarly, the literature documents the many kinds of concurrent crises that can trouble the disenfranchised griever. For example, in cases of cohabiting couples, either heterosexual or homosexual, studies have often found that survivors experience legal and financial problems regarding inheritance, ownership, credit, or leases. Likewise, the death of a parent may leave a mentally disabled person not only bereaved but also bereft of a viable support system.

Although grief is complicated, many of the factors that facilitate mourning are not present. The bereaved may be excluded from an active role in caring for the dying. Funeral rituals, normally helpful in resolving grief, may not help here. In some cases the bereaved may be excluded from attendance. In other cases they may have no role in planning those rituals or in deciding whether even to have them. Or in cases of divorce, separation, or psychosocial death, rituals may be lacking altogether.

In addition, the very nature of the disenfranchised grief precludes social support. Often there is no recognized role in which mourners can assert the right to mourn and thus receive such support. Grief may have to remain private. Though they may have experienced an intense loss, they may not be given time off from work, have the opportunity to verbalize the loss, or receive the expressions of sympathy and support characteristic in a death. Even traditional sources of solace, such as religion, are unavailable to those whose relationships (for example, extramarital, cohabiting, homosexual, divorced) or acts (such as abortion) are condemned within that tradition.

Naturally, there are many variables that will affect both the intensity of the reaction and the availability of support. All the variables—interpersonal, psychological, social, physiological—that normally influence grief will have an impact here as well. And while there are problems common to cases of disenfranchised grief, each relationship has to be individually considered in light of the unique combinations of factors that may facilitate or impair grief resolution.

Implications

Despite the shortage of research on and attention given to the issue of disenfranchised grief, it remains a significant issue. Millions of Americans are involved in losses in which grief is effectively disenfranchised. For example, there are more than 1 million couples presently cohabiting. There are estimates that 3 percent of males and 2–3 percent of females are exclusively homosexual, with similar percentages having mixed homosexual and heterosexual encounters. There are about a million abortions a year; even though many of the women involved may not experience grief reactions, some are clearly "at risk."

Disenfranchised grief is also a growing issue. There are higher percentages of divorced people in the cohorts now aging. The AIDS crisis means that more homosexuals will experience losses in significant relationships. Even as the disease spreads within the population of intravenous drug users, it is likely to create a new class of both potential victims and disenfranchised grievers among the victims' informal liaisons and nontraditional relationships. And as Americans continue to live longer, more will suffer from severe forms of chronic brain dysfunctions. As the developmentally disabled live longer, they too will experience the grief of parental and sibling loss. In short, the proportion of disenfranchised grievers in the general population will rise rapidly in the future.

It is likely that bereavement counselors will have increased exposure to cases of disenfranchised grief. In fact, the very nature of disenfranchised grief and the unavailability of informal support make it likely that those who experience such losses will seek formal supports. Thus there is a pressing need for research that will describe the particular and unique reactions of each of the different types of losses; compare reactions and problems associated with these losses; describe the important variables affecting disenfranchised grief reactions; assess possible interventions; and discover the atypical grief reactions, such as masked or delayed grief, that might be manifested in such cases. Also needed is education sensitizing students to the many kinds of relationships and subsequent losses that people can experience and affirming that where there is loss there is grief.

Critical Thinking

1. What is the meaning of disenfranchised grief?

2. How can grief be enfranchised?

3. Why does Dr. Doka believe that the proportion of disenfranchised grievers in the general population will rapidly increase in the future?

KEN DOKA, PhD, is a professor of gerontology at the College of New Rochelle in New York. He became interested in the study of death and dying quite inadvertently. Scheduled to do a practicum in a facility that housed juvenile delinquents, he discovered that his supervisor had changed the assignment. Instead, Doka found himself counseling dying children and their families at Sloan-Kettering, a major cancer hospital in New York.

This experience became the basis of two graduate theses, one in sociology entitled "The Social Organization of Terminal Care in Two Pediatric Hospitals," and the other in religious studies entitled "Pastoral Counseling to Dying Children and Their Families." (Both were later published.) His doctoral program pursued another longstanding interest: the sociology of aging. In 1983, Dr. Doka accepted his present position at the College of New Rochelle where he specializes in thanatology and gerontology.

Active in the Association for Death Education and Counseling since its beginnings, Dr. Doka was elected its president in 1993. In addition to articles in scholarly journals, he is the author of *Death and Spirituality* (with John Morgan, 1993), *Living with Life-Threatening Illness* (1993) and *Disenfranchised Grief: Recognizing Hidden Sorrow* (1989), from which the following selection is excerpted. His work on disenfranchised grief began in the classroom when a graduate student commented, "If you think widows have it rough, you ought to see what happens when your ex-spouse dies."

Challenging the Paradigm: New Understandings of Grief

KENNETH J. DOKA, PhD

Introduction

In 1989, Wortman and Silver published a controversial yet influential article entitled "The Myths of Coping With Loss," in which they identified five "myths" that were widely accepted by professionals treating bereavement:

- Depression and distress are inevitable in grief.
- Distress is necessary, and its absence is problematic.
- Survivors must "work through" a loss.
- Survivors can expect to recover from a loss.
- Survivors can reach a state of resolution.

The research, in Wortman and Silver's evaluation, did not support the widespread acceptance of these propositions.

Wortman and Silver's article crystallized a challenge to what might be called the *grief work hypothesis*. This hypothesis was really a conceptual belief that one must work through powerful feelings in order to detach from the deceased, reinvest in life, and recover from and resolve the loss. Originally derived from Freud's seminal 1917 article "Mourning and Melancholia," (Freud, 1957) the concept is pervasive in self-help books. Staudacher (1991), for example, expresses this notion:

> Simply put, *there is only one way to grieve* [emphasis in original]. That way is to go through the core of grief. Only by experiencing the necessary emotional effects of your loved one's death is it possible for you to eventually resolve the loss. (p. 3)

Although the grief work hypothesis was evident in much work in the field, especially in trade and self-help literature, it was not universally accepted. In the professional literature, the hypothesis was continually challenged in one way or another and coexisted with other ideas and approaches. In many ways, Wortman and Silver had over-simplified some very subtle and nuanced approaches to the understanding of grief and loss, but their article had great heuristic value, bringing forth many modifications and challenges to these early and popular understandings of grief.

The past 15 years have seen an increasing number of challenges to the early paradigms. In this chapter, I will describe five significant ways in which earlier understandings or paradigms of grief have been challenged. I will also discuss three current challenges to the field and two others that are likely to occur in the not-too-distant future.

Five New Understandings of Grief

1. Extending the Definition of Grief

One of the basic questions in the field relates to the definition of grief. Is grief a reaction to the death of a significant person, or can it be more broadly understood as a reaction to loss? Freud's illustration of grief in "Mourning and Melancholia" is a bride left standing at the altar. Most contemporary work emphasizes grief as a reaction to death. Yet confusion over the issue still remains. The major death-related professional organization founded in the United States (though international in membership) was called the Association for Death Education and Counseling (ADEC). The Australian counterpart is called NALAG, the National Association for Loss and Grief. Yet, it remains unclear if the differences between these organizations, in terms of focus or mission, are, in fact, significant.

However, recent work has begun to emphasize grief as a more widespread reaction to loss. Some of this loss is certainly related to dying or death. For example, there has been long-standing recognition that people grieve *secondary losses;* that is, losses that follow a primary loss and engender additional grief. For example, a parent who has experienced the death of a child may mourn not only the loss of the child but also the absence of the child's friends, who were often present in the home. Rando's (1986, 2000) work on anticipatory mourning further develops the idea that losses other than death can generate grief. The original concept of anticipatory grief was that at the onset of a life-limiting disease, a person anticipated a future death and mourned that expected loss. Rando considerably expanded the concept to include anticipatory mourning, which she defined as a response to all the losses encountered—past, present, and future—in the course of an illness. For example, both patient and family may mourn the progressive disabilities and role losses that accompany the disease, as well as the loss of dreams, such as for an idyllic retirement, that now seem unlikely to be fulfilled. Rando's sensitivity to the myriad forms of loss is illustrated in *The Treatment of Complicated Mourning* (1993), in which she discusses tangible losses, such as an object that is stolen or a fire that destroys one's home, and intangible or symbolic losses, such as a divorce.

My work on disenfranchised grief (Doka, 1989, 2002) also addresses the wide range of losses that engender grief, stressing that the very lack of recognition of the grief experienced in such losses complicates grief. Some of these losses involved deaths that were unacknowledged by others—such as the deaths of former spouses, lovers, friends, and even animal companions. The work also emphasized the effects of other types of losses—such as incarceration, divorce, or infertility—that can generate significant grief. The concept of disenfranchised grief emphasizes that every society has "grieving rules" that determine a socially conferred "right to grieve." Generally, for example, these rules give family members the right to grieve the deaths of other family members. But in many situations—including non-death-related losses—a person might experience a significant loss but be deprived of the opportunity to publicly acknowledge the loss, openly mourn, and receive social support. This is disenfranchised grieving.

Harvey (1998) also notes the pervasiveness of loss and suggests the need for a larger psychology of loss that would complement and move beyond the study of dying and death. This shift is a critical one, as it allows the application of the study of grief to areas such as divorce and job loss, and allows the study to draw from the considerable literature around stress, coping, and adaptation (i.e., seeing grief as a type of stress reaction and mourning as a form of coping or adaptation).

However, the danger exists that grief will be trivialized. If every loss evokes "grief," the word becomes less important and signifies little. The antidote is to support research that clarifies the grief reactions and outcomes in a wide array of losses, allowing comparisons between grief reactions and outcomes from a death with those from other losses.

2. The Application of New Models

Most of the early models of grief were drawn from the work of Kubler-Ross (1969) and emphasized that people were likely to experience grief by going through a series of predictable reactions, or stages. Kubler-Ross originally studied the ways adults with life-threatening illness coped with impending death, but her work quickly was applied to the process of grief, in which a person was expected to experience a relatively linear movement through denial, bargaining, anger, and depression to reach a state of acceptance. This understanding of grief has become widespread.

Despite the popular embrace of these stages, most of the newer models have avoided the language and assumptions of stage theories. Worden (1982) broke new ground in his book *Grief Counseling and Grief Therapy* by conceptualizing mourning as a series of four tasks:

1. To accept the reality of the loss
2. To work through the pain of grief
3. To adjust to an environment where the deceased is missing.
4. To withdraw emotional energy and invest it in another relationship (In the second and third editions (1991, 2002), this task was revised to read "To emotionally relocate the deceased and move on with life," a modification that is discussed later in this chapter.)

While Worden's tasks clearly identified grief and mourning with death, they represented a significant paradigm shift from the predominant stage theories. Worden's task model was not linear; people worked on whatever issues arose in the process of mourning. The model stressed individuality (different survivors completed the tasks differently) and autonomy (survivors could choose when they were ready to tackle any task).

I recognized the value of Worden's approach and suggested a fifth task: to rebuild spiritual systems challenged by the loss (Doka, 1993). This task recognizes that some losses challenge personal spiritual belief systems, causing individuals to question and possibly redefine their faith.

After Worden, other models appeared. Rando (1993), for example, proposed the "R" processes of mourning: recognizing the loss; reacting to the separation; recollecting and reexperiencing the deceased and the relationship; relinquishing the old attachments to the deceased and the old assumptive world; readjusting to move adaptively into the new world without forgetting the old; and reinvesting. Stroebe and Schut (1999) offered a dual-process model, suggesting that successful coping in bereavement means oscillating between loss-oriented and restoration-oriented processes.

Both these models, along with Worden's task model, reaffirmed that mourning was more than simply a series of affective responses to loss. In addition, the new models asserted that mourning involved not only a response to the loss of another but also an effort to manage life in a world altered by significant loss.

All these new models offer value to counselors in assisting bereaved persons. Stage models suggested a limited role for counselors: interpreting the reactions of bereaved persons and helping them move through the stages. The newer models allow a more significant role, in which the counselor helps the bereaved person understand what factors are complicating the completion of certain tasks or processes and develops interventions that can help the person adapt to loss.

The models also have implications for group programs. One way to evaluate a program is to determine the underlying model. Programs based on newer models should do more than simply allow participants to express affect. They should reflect the variety of tasks and processes that are part of the experience of grief and mourning.

3. Beyond Affect

While research from Lindemann (1944) has emphasized that grief is manifested in many ways—including cognitive, physical, emotional, behavioral, and spiritual reactions—much attention has been placed on affect, to the exclusion of other responses. This focus reflects a general Western preoccupation with affect in counseling and therapy (see Sue & Sue, 1999). A number of writers have stressed reactions to loss other than affect; two will serve as examples.

Neimeyer (2001) emphasizes that the reconstruction of meaning is a critical issue—if not *the* critical issue—in grief, adding strong cognitive and spiritual components to the study of grief. Neimeyer's "narrative" approach to therapy helps people "reweave" the narrative of their lives, which has been torn apart by significant loss.

Martin and Doka (2000) suggest a continuum of grieving styles ranging from the intuitive to the instrumental. Intuitive grievers experience, express, and adapt to grief in strongly affective ways. Instrumental grievers, on the other hand, are likely to experience muted affective reactions. Their experience is more likely to be cognitive and behavioral, and they will favor such strategies for expression and adaptation to loss. Martin and Doka's work

strongly challenges the notion that expressing feelings is the most effective way to adapt to loss. The work began as an attempt to understand the grieving patterns of males; the authors now see these patterns as related to, but not determined by, gender.

Other researchers have strongly challenged the idea that expression of feelings and emotions in grief should be encouraged and that a lack of open affect suggests difficulty. In his social-functioning approach, Bonanno (2004) suggests that adaptation to loss is facilitated when grief-related distress is minimized and positive affect is accentuated. Similarly, Nolen-Hoeksema, McBride, and Larson (1997) suggest that excessive rumination might not be helpful and, in fact, is associated with poor outcomes. The excessive processing of loss can exacerbate distress. Resilient individuals minimize rumination by distraction—shifting their attention in a positive direction. However, Nolen-Hoeksema and her associates also found that deliberate avoidance and suppression of grief were maladaptive.

These insights have important implications for grief counselors, grief groups, and grief curricula. The ideas reflected in the newer models reaffirm that grief is more than emotion. They suggest that leaders should try to move their groups beyond shared anguish to discussions of effective ways to cope with grief and should encourage the recognition of positive memories and experiences, even within a state of grief. These concepts reaffirm the individuality of the grief experience and discourage dogmatic, one-size-fits-all strategies.

4. Beyond Coping

Early work in the field tended to emphasize the difficulty of coping with loss and focused on restoring a sense of equilibrium while slowly and painfully withdrawing emotional energy from the deceased. The perception of the survivor was primarily passive, besieged to cope with changes out of his or her control.

This concept was strongly challenged in the work of Catherine Sanders (1989). In her phase model of grief, Sanders suggested that the process of grieving involves a series of phases, and most people follow a common sequence. The first phase is *shock,* as the person begins to feel the impact of the death. In each phase, Sanders related the psychological, cognitive, and physical sequelae of grief. For example, in the shock phase, physical symptoms may include weeping, tremors, and loss of appetite. Bereaved persons may experience psychological distancing, egocentric phenomena, or preoccupation with thoughts of the deceased. Cognitive manifestations at this phase may include disbelief, restlessness, and a heightened state of alarm or a sense of unreality or helplessness. In each of the phases, Sanders recognized both he individuality and the multiplicity of grief reactions—a significant advance over the stage theory (Kubler-Ross, 1969).

The second phase, Sanders said, is *awareness of loss.* Here the funeral rituals are over and support has ebbed. Until now, shock and support have acted as a buffer. Now, as the shock recedes and family and friends withdraw, the primary grievers experience the full force of their loss. This is a period of high emotional and cognitive arousal; separation anxiety is intense and stress is prolonged. Grief is both raw and deeply painful. The bereaved person becomes exhausted and needs to withdraw from others to conserve limited energy.

Sanders proposed *conservation-withdrawal* as the third phase of bereavement. This is a long (possibly endless) phase of grief. The grieving person seems to be functioning, and pain is more chronic than acute. But the person feels physically weak and helpless—going through the motions rather than actively living life. Bereaved persons in this phase often express a belief that they are in state of hibernation, a sort of holding pattern as they struggle to adapt to the loss.

Sanders said that in the first and second phases, people are motivated largely by unconscious or biological factors. In this phase, she suggested that people have three choices. In the face of extreme physical and psychological stress, some may consciously or unconsciously seek their own death rather than live without the person who died. Others may assume that the necessary major life adjustments require more strength and power than they possess. They may choose the status quo, living the rest of their lives in a diminished state of chronic grief. Still others may decide to move forward and adjust to their loss.

According to Sanders, bereaved persons who choose to move forward often experience a fourth phase: *healing/the turning point.* In her research, many persons could point to a moment when they consciously decided that their lives needed to change. In one vignette, a widow recalled hearing her young granddaughter ask her mother, "Why does Grandma always cry?" The widow resolved then and there that she would not be remembered as "the grandma who always cried." In this phase, people reconstruct their identities and lives, and enjoy restored physical health, increased energy, and psychological vigor.

Finally, those who experience the turning point move to a fifth phase that Sanders called *renewal.* While they still experience occasional bad days and episodic moments of grief, they experience a new level of functioning characterized by enhanced self-awareness, increased levels of energy, personal revitalization, and the renewal of social ties. At this phase, the bereaved person has learned to live without the physical presence of the loved one, while retaining an internal sense of the deceased person's presence. Sanders noted that in this phase, people could often process and even enjoy memories of the deceased without the high emotional arousal experienced earlier in the grieving process.

Later, Sanders began to develop the notion of a sixth phase: *fulfillment.* In this phase, the grieving person can look back on his or her own life in a way that integrates the loss into the fabric of that life. While the loss was neither expected nor welcomed, the person can no longer imagine what life would be like without the loss (Doka, 2006).

Sanders was one of the first theorists to affirm that people had choices in the mourning process. Her writing emphasized that bereaved persons were active participants in the mourning process rather than passive copers with little control. Her renewal phase presaged such trends in contemporary bereavement theory as grief as a transformative experience (Neimeyer, 2001; Prend, 1997; Schneider, 1994), in which loss can lead to significant personal growth as the bereaved person struggles to adapt to life without the deceased. These concepts are supported in the research of Calhoun and Tedeschi (2004), which emphasizes the human capacity for reliance and notes that loss may trigger growth and change.

This work emphasizes that the point of therapy is not to "recover" from the loss. Rather, it suggests therapists can pose a larger question: "How will this loss change you?" The question implies an active response. Grieving persons are not passive: While they might have no choice about grief, they do have choices about what they will do with their loss.

5. Continuing Bonds

The Freudian notion that the work of grief is to detach from the deceased and reinvest in other relationships has been strongly challenged. In 1987, Attig compared "letting go" in grief to letting go of an adult child. By that Attig meant that even though there may be less physical presence, the connective bonds and sense of presence remain strong. Synthesizing other work, I suggested in the *Encyclopedia of Death* (Doka, 1984) that rather than emotionally withdraw, survivors might find ways to creatively retain their attachments to the loss object. Using his own research, Worden (1991) revised the wording of his fourth task from the Freudian concept of withdrawing emotional energy from the deceased to relocating the deceased, emphasizing that the bond between the deceased and the survivor continues, albeit in a different form.

In other work, LaGrand (1999) described a connection he labeled "extraordinary experiences," in which bereaved persons recounted dreams, sense experiences, and other phenomena after the death of someone they loved. Often these experiences were therapeutic—reaffirming a bond and offering comfort. Such experiences are so common that I suggest counselors routinely ask bereaved persons about them—they may be comforted by the experiences but reluctant to bring them up.

The challenge to the idea of withdrawal received its fullest treatment in the groundbreaking book *Continuing Bonds: New Understandings of Grief*, edited by Klass, Silverman, and Nickman (1996). The editors emphasize that throughout history and across cultures, bereaved persons have maintained bonds with their deceased. The research in this book deeply challenges the idea that emotional withdrawal is essential or even desirable.

Counselors should assure clients that the goal of grief therapy is not to abolish memories of the deceased. The amelioration of grief means that over time the intensity of the grief experience lessens and the bereaved person functions as well as (or perhaps even better than) before the loss, although surges of grief may occur even years later, brought on by significant transitions or other experiences. The point is that relationships continue even beyond death, and the grief process has no final end point.

However, not all bonds with the deceased are helpful. Some persons may retain connections to a loved one who has died that impair relationships with others or adaptation to the loss. Recent research described by Stroebe (2006) suggests that bonds may be supportive for some persons but maladaptive for others. The therapeutic challenge is to recognize that not all attachments are positive.

Current Challenges

These new understandings have received considerable attention and widespread acceptance. Three current challenges may further modify the way we understand grief.

1. Increasing Diversity: The Challenge of Culture

The United States and many other nations are becoming increasingly racially and ethnically diverse. Much of the research has been based on white, middle-class samples, so it may not be possible to generalize our understanding of grief. A more diverse society will cause us to rethink basic questions. For example, what does loss actually mean? Different societies, with different patterns of attachment and different expectations about life and death, may respond to a loss quite differently. What, for example, is the impact of a child's death in a society with high levels of infant and child mortality?

A more diverse society may challenge what we believe we know about grief. Different cultures may have distinct ways of describing the experience of grief, as well as their own modes of expressing grief and adapting to loss. It may be that the only thing all cultures share is that each one responds and adapts to loss. We may be able to learn from other cultures—their rituals and methods of expression and adaptation may teach us effective strategies and offer insights on different approaches to dealing with loss.

The issue of diversity also has programmatic implications for hospices and bereavement programs. How sensitive are programs to ethnic and cultural differences? Are there significant differences in participation or withdrawal from grief programs or bereavement groups? Do other programs reflect sensitivity to diversity? Do "interfaith services" truly reflect religious and cultural diversity? As Islam and other nonwestern faiths grow in the United States and many other western nations, is this growth reflected in the religious affiliations of chaplains and the nature of spiritual care? Are resources on grief—such as books or brochures—available in all the languages spoken in our communities?

Social class is another aspect of diversity, and strategies and programs need to acknowledge the differences. Are fees for services based on a sliding scale? Social class also encompasses differences in life style. For example, for many lower income families, photographs are a luxury. A common activity in children's groups involves creating photographic montages and picture boxes. Such exercises may isolate lower income children or expend a precious and not easily replaced resource.

Sexual orientation is yet another source of diversity. How inclusive are groups and materials? Are bereavement groups solely for widows and widowers or also for partners? Would bereaved unmarried partners—either gay or straight—be comfortable in the grief groups offered, or is it clear that the groups are meant to serve heterosexual widowed spouses?

Sue and Sue (2003) remind us that counseling is a culture itself, with its own distinct values. How well do these values match the values and approaches of the cultures being served?

2. The Challenge of Research and Evidence-Based Practice

As Neimeyer (2000) notes, little research has been done on the actual methods of grief counseling and grief therapy. In the past, we simply assumed that these methods worked. Grief counseling requires the integration of theory, practice, and research. Interventions need to be theoretically grounded and empirically assessed. Evidence-based practice is becoming the standard.

This standard has implications for practitioners, including the need for constant evaluation of grief programs. How can we be sure that the programs we offer are effective? On what evidence do we base programs?

More integration is needed between clinical practice and research. This integration is facilitated when researchers and theoreticians explore the practice applications of their work and when clinicians take an empirical approach to therapy—constantly assessing how well their therapy is helping the client adapt to loss. Research on the link between theory and practice will likely cause us to reassess and reevaluate the concepts and models that underlie the study of grief.

3. The Challenge of Technology

The challenge to research and evaluate is especially clear with regard to the many resources offered through the Internet. Online resources include grief information, grief groups, chat rooms, counseling, and opportunities for memorialization. Yet there has been little evaluation of these resources and little study of their efficacy.

The Internet may offer support for bereaved persons, but it may itself be a source of grief. The exponential increase in cyberspace relationships raises questions for the study of attachment and loss. If close relationships can form online, will these people constitute a future class of disenfranchised grievers? Will these relationships raise new questions regarding the processes of death notification?

On the Horizon

Two additional issues are likely to affect future understanding of grief. The first one is the move to add a "grief" category to the forthcoming *DSM-V.* One of the proposals before the American Psychiatric Association is on *complicated grief* (formerly called *traumatic grief*). Jacobs and Prigerson and others (see Jacobs & Prigerson, 2000; Prigerson & Maciejewski, 2006) suggest that certain symptoms evident early in the process of grieving predict problematic outcomes, and they recommend early intervention. For years, the field has eschewed a medical model of grief and avoided using terms like "symptoms." Grief, it is argued, is a normal part of the life cycle, not an illness. These proposals challenge that notion, asserting that at least some experiences of grief show evidence of psychiatric illness. The proposals are a sign of increasing recognition that there is a need for correction, that the emphasis on the normalcy of loss and grief has led to the neglect of problematic variants. Receptiveness to these proposals is probably also fueled by the growth of managed care in the United States and the need to have a clear grief-related diagnostic code. Regardless of the motivation, adding a diagnostic category for grief will constitute a paradigm shift.

The second issue is the demographic change as the baby boomers age. Many of them are experiencing the loss of their parents; in a few decades, they will face their own deaths. Also, each generation develops unique forms of attachment; many boomers have developed extremely close attachments to their children, so their deaths may create different problems for their offspring than in previous generations. This is a generation that has challenged and changed every institution it has experienced in its collective journey through the life cycle. Boomers demand choices in programs and avoid programs that ignore individual differences. They tend to trust individuals rather than institutions. They want to be active participants in programs rather than passive recipients. The baby boomers will surely change the ways we encounter loss, death, and grief.

Over the past 15 years, our understanding of grief has experienced major modifications. Changes and challenges are likely to continue to affect how we think about and respond to loss. As a popular Baby Boom song, Dylan's *"The World it Is a Changin"* put it "the wheel is still in spin."

References

Attig, T. (1987). Grief, love and separation. In C. Corr and R. Pacholski (Eds.), *Death: Completion and discovery.* Lakewood, OH: Association for Death Education and Counseling.

Bonnano, G. (2004). Loss, trauma and human resilience: Have we underestimated the human capacity to thrive after extremely aversive events? *American Psychologist, 59,* 20–28.

Calhoun, L. G., & Tedeschi, R. G. (2004). The foundations of posttraumatic growth: New considerations. *Psychological Inquiry, 15,* 93–102.

Doka, K. J. (1984). Grief. In R. Kastenbaum and B. Kastenbaum (Eds.), *Encyclopedia of death.* Phoenix, AZ: Oryx Press.

Doka, K. J. (1989). *Disenfranchised grief: Recognizing hidden sorrow.* Lexington, MA: Lexington Press.

Doka, K. J. (1993). The spiritual crises of bereavement. In K. J. Doka (with J. Morgan) (Ed.), *Death and spirituality* (pp. 185–195). Amityville, NY: Baywood Publishing Co.

Doka, K. J. (2002). *Disenfranchised grief: New directions, challenges, and strategies for practice.* Champaign, IL: Research Press.

Doka, K. (2006). Fulfillment as Sanders' sixth phase of bereavement: The unfinished work of Catherine Sanders. *Omega: The Journal of Death and Dying, 52,* 141–149.

Freud, S. (1957). Mourning and melancholia. London: Hogarth.

Harvey, J. (1998). *Perspectives on loss: A sourcebook.* Philadelphia: Brunner/Mazel.

Jacobs, S., & Prigerson, H. (2000). Psychotherapy of traumatic grief: A review of evidence for psychotherapeutic treatments. *Death Studies, 21,* 471–498.

Klass, D., Silverman, P., & Nickman, S. (Eds.). (1996). *Continuing bonds: New understandings of grief.* Washington, DC: Taylor & Frances.

Kubler-Ross, E. (1969). *On Death and Dying.* New York: Macmillan.

LaGrand, L. (1999). *Messages and miracles: Extraordinary experiences of the bereaved.* St. Paul, MN: Llewellyn Publications.

Lindemann, E. (1944). Symptomatology and management of acute grief. *American Journal of Psychiatry, 101,* 141–148.

Martin, T., & Doka, K. J. (2000). *Men don't cry, women do: Transcending gender stereotypes of grief.* Philadelphia: Brunner/Mazel.

Neimeyer, R. A. (2000). Grief therapy and research as essential tensions: Prescriptions for a progressive partnership. *Death Studies, 24,* 603–610.

Neimeyer, R. A. (2001). *Meaning reconstruction and the meaning of loss.* Washington, DC: American Psychological Association.

Nolen-Hoeksema, S., McBride, A., & Larson, J. (1997) Rumination and psychological distress among bereaved partners. *Journal of Personality and Social Psychology, 72,* 855–862.

Prend, A. (1997). *Transcending loss.* New York: Berkley Books.

Prigerson, H., & Maciejewski, P. (2006). A call for sound empirical testing and evaluation for complicated grief proposed for *DSM-V. Omega, The Journal of Death and Dying, 52,* 9–20.

Rando, T. A. (1986). *Loss and anticipatory grief.* Lexington, MA: Lexington Books.

Rando, T. A. (1993). *The treatment of complicated mourning.* Champaign, IL: Research Press.

Rando, T. A. (2000). *Clinical dimensions of anticipatory mourning: Theory and practice in working with the dying, their loved ones, and their caregivers.* Champaign, IL: Research Press.

Sanders, C. (1989). *Grief: The mourning after – Dealing with adult bereavement.* New York: Wiley.

Staudacher, C. (1991). *Men and grief.* Oakland, CA: New Harbinger Publications.

Stroebe, M., & Schut, H. (1999). The dual process model of coping with bereavement: Rationale and description. *Death Studies, 23,* 197–224.

Stroebe, M. (2006, April). *Continuing bonds in bereavement: Toward theoretical understanding.* Keynote presentation to the Association of Death Education and Counseling, Albuquerque, NM.

Sue, D.W., & Sue, D. (2003). *Counseling the culturally diverse: Theory and practice.* New York: John Wiley and Sons.

Worden, J. W. (1982, 1991, 2002). *Grief counseling and grief therapy: A handbook for the mental health practitioner* (eds.1–3). New York: Springer.

Wortman, C., & Silver, R. C. (1989). The myths of coping with loss. *Journal of Clinical Counseling, 57,* 349–357.

Critical Thinking

1. According to Dr. Doka, what are the five significant ways in which earlier understandings or paradigms of grief have been challenged?

2. Describe the three current challenges that may further modify the way we understand grief.

3. How will demographic changes change the way in which Americans grieve?

We've Been Misled about How to Grieve

Why it may be wise to skip the months of journalling and group talk we've been taught we need.

NICHOLAS KÖHLER

Many years ago, Nancy Moules, a pediatric oncology nurse who specializes in grief, got a call from a family member of one of her clients, a woman in her late 20s whose six-year-old daughter had died of leukemia a month or so earlier. The relative told Moules the woman was carrying an urn full of her daughter's ashes everywhere she went; that if you met her for lunch she'd get a table for three; that, in a nutshell, the family was concerned about how she was coping. Sure enough, when Moules later met the client for lunch, they ate with the ashes at the table. "So, are you wondering why I invited you out?" Moules asked. "Oh no, I know," the woman said. "Somebody phoned you, they're worried about me. They think I'm crazy." Moules probed further: "Do *you* think it's crazy?" she asked. "No," said the woman. "F—k them. This is the last human, physical connection that I have to her and I'll put her down when I'm ready to put her down."

For Moules, who now lectures on grief as a nursing prof at the University of Calgary, the young mother's story helps illustrate the sometimes paradoxical relationship many of us have with the emotions accompanying a loved one's death. "There's all these cultural expectations of grief that are contradictory," she says. "One is, 'Get over it, you should be over it by now!' And the other is, 'What's wrong with you that you aren't continuing to feel it? Didn't you love the person?' And we turn all those judgments inward."

Many of these expectations have, over the past four decades, been set by Elisabeth Kübler-Ross, a Swiss-born psychiatrist who used her interviews with a handful of dying patients in Chicago in the mid-'60s as the basis for a theory of grief that quickly gripped the world's imagination and never let go. *On Death and Dying,* her milestone 1969 book, proposed that a person confronting his or her own death passes through five stages—denial,

anger, bargaining, depression and, finally, acceptance. The analysis was backed by no solid research—indeed, as Ruth Davis Konigsberg's new book *The Truth About Grief: The Myth of Its Five Stages and the New Science of Loss* notes, scientific studies around grief remain surprisingly scant even now, and Kübler-Ross hit upon her stages only after getting a book deal and at the end of a bout of writer's block. In an era in which the old customs of black armbands and crepe no longer applied, Kübler-Ross became widely embraced as a grief guru— no matter that her research had always been limited to the dying. Soon an industry had grown up around the funeral business that found it convenient to guide the bereaved through her stages.

"Grief culture" has stigmatized the common response of resilience, branding it "cold"

Published the year after her death in 2004 and co-written with David Kessler, Kübler-Ross's *On Grief and Grieving* stamped her imprimatur onto a field that she'd largely come to define anyway (better that she remain associated with that than, say, her later interest in contacting the dead via seance). She still does, though academics now pooh-pooh her work: Konigsberg refers to a 2008 Hospice Association of Ontario report that identifies Kübler-Ross as the most recommended resource for bereavement support in that province. Her stages now colour the way we discuss everything from divorce to coming out of the closet to beating addiction.

Yet in *The Truth About Grief*—the title is tongue-in-cheek, as one-size-fits-all models like Kübler-Ross's actually prove incomplete—Konigsberg, a journalist who has worked as an editor at *New York* and *Glamour* magazines, argues stage theory has promoted a view of grief as long and debilitating, when recent research actually suggests people usually accept a loved one's death quickly, experience a few months of pining for the deceased, and are over it all in as little as six to 12 months—a natural evaporation of sadness. Kübler-Ross's stages interrupt that process by casting grief as a "journey" we must "work" through, a notion that heralded a whole industry of "death services" and created standards of grief all of us feel we must now labour to meet. All this served to shift the emphasis away from the deceased and toward those left behind, whose important work it now was to overcome loss. The old mourning rites may be gone, Konigsberg writes, "but they have been replaced by conventions for grief, which are more restrictive in that they dictate not what a person wears or does in public but his or her inner emotional state."

For all that grief work, studies show people who undergo bereavement counselling emerge from grief no more quickly than people who don't—except in the lengthiest cases, where the death of an intimate has likely exposed underlying depression (a condition now often called "complicated grief"). Konigsberg marshals more research suggesting Kübler-Ross's stages don't accurately describe what we typically experience after a death, and argues that adherence to the model does more harm than good in that the doctrine "has actually lengthened the expected duration of grief and made us more judgmental of those who stray from the designated path."

Beamsville, Ont., resident Sandy McBay, whose husband of 35 years, Rick, died suddenly in December of an aortic dissection—"Just in case, I love you," he told her as they awaited the ambulance—found herself as blindsided as anyone despite two decades of work in palliative care and bereavement support. In leading therapy sessions, McBay often encounters a tacit faith in Kübler-Ross. "A lot of people expect they're going to grieve that way," she says. "They are pleasantly surprised, some of them at least, to realize—'Okay, just because I'm not doing it the way I've heard it's supposed to be done doesn't mean I'm doing it wrong.'" Rather than anger or depression, many instead report feelings of yearning. McBay, whose husband was a teacher and choir director, is no different. "I was there when he died, so I know he's not coming back," she says. "But when I am home and looking around and seeing the life that we created together—I look at my 1.3-acre property and go, 'What am I going to do?' Just—him simply not being there."

What to do with such feelings? In fact, the long, agonizing ordeal Kübler-Ross and her disciples have long steeled us for isn't the norm. Here Konigsberg outlines research led by George Bonanno, a psychology prof at Columbia University's Teachers College, that "tracked elderly people whose spouses died of natural causes, and the single largest group—about 45 per cent—showed no signs of shock, despair, anxiety, or intrusive thoughts six months after their loss," Konigsberg writes. "A much smaller group—only about 15 per cent—were still having problems at 18 months." Such numbers belie popular notions that widows and widowers find the second year worse than the first. While Konigsberg takes care not to pathologize those who suffer prolonged turmoil, she argues that what she calls the "grief culture" has stigmatized the more common response of resilience and strength by branding it "cold," even "pathological." Actually, she says, "You probably already have what you need to get through this on your own. If after six months or a year you find you're still having trouble, you should probably seek professional help."

Before that threshold, though, it may be wise to skip the months of disclosure, journaling and group talk that the bereavement services sector, channelling Kübler-Ross, says we need lest our grief fester. ("Telling your story often and in detail is primal to the grieving process," Kübler-Ross tell us. "Grief must be witnessed to be healed.") All that vocalizing may be just the trouble. Reminiscent of the critiques around critical-incident stress debriefing, an intense talk therapy aimed at preventing post-traumatic stress disorder, some studies now say grief can be aggravated by chit-chat. Konigsberg cites another Bonanno study that found bereaved people who did not communicate their "negative emotions" had fewer health complaints than those who did, opening up the tantalizing possibility that tamping down bad feelings "might actually have a protective function."

Not everyone agrees with all this. Mel Borins, a Toronto family physician who lectures doctors on grief, calls complicated grief "underestimated and I think quite common—more than 15 percent of people get left with unfinished business." And assuming one does tie up those emotional loose ends, what exactly does it feel like to dispense with grief and yet go on remembering the dead? It's a question Konigsberg's book isn't designed to answer, though Kübler-Ross's insistence on "acceptance" cries out for quibbling. Indeed, it's that punishing commitment to recovery that Moules, the Calgary nursing prof, most often sees in those she counsels. "Many people come and say, 'I must be doing this grieving thing wrong, because I still feel something,'" she says, adding: "You will feel that loss for the rest of your life. It won't be as consuming, it won't be as absolutely devastating, as unfathomable as it was. But you never get over it." She recalls the young mother who carted around her daughter's ashes. Several weeks after that lunch, Moules got a call from the woman inviting her to her daughter's inurnment. Finally she was ready to lay the ashes down. But never her daughter.

"Many people say, 'I must be doing this grieving thing wrong, because I still feel something'"

—Nancy Moules

Critical Thinking

1. Why do people who avail themselves of grief counseling emerge no more quickly than those who don't?

2. Explain the following quotation: "You probably already have what you need to get through this on your own. If after six months or a year you find you're still having trouble, you should probably seek professional help."

3. Why did a Bonanno study conclude that bereaved people who did not communicate their "negative emotions" had fewer health complaints than those who did?

Shades of Grief: When Does Mourning Become a Mental Illness?

The new edition of a psychiatric manual called *DSM-5* tackles what to do when mourning becomes complicated or leads to depression.

Virginia Hughes

Sooner or later most of us suffer deep grief over the death of someone we love. The experience often causes people to question their sanity—as when they momentarily think they have caught sight of their loved one on a crowded street. Many mourners ponder, even if only abstractedly, their reason for living. But when are these disturbing thoughts and emotions normal—that is to say, they become less consuming and intense with the passage of time—and when do they cross the line to pathology, requiring ongoing treatment with powerful antidepressants or psychotherapy, or both?

Two proposed changes in the "bible" of psychiatric disorders—the *Diagnostic and Statistical Manual of Mental Disorders* (*DSM*)—aim to answer that question when the book's fifth edition comes out in 2013. One change expected to appear in the *DSM-5* reflects a growing consensus in the mental health field; the other has provoked great controversy.

In the less controversial change, the manual would add a new category: Complicated Grief Disorder, also known as traumatic or prolonged grief. The new diagnosis refers to a situation in which many of grief's common symptoms—such as powerful pining for the deceased, great difficulty moving on, a sense that life is meaningless, and bitterness or anger about the loss—last longer than six months. The controversial change focuses on the other end of the time spectrum: it allows medical treatment for depression in the first few weeks after a death. Currently the *DSM* specifically bars a bereaved person from being diagnosed with full-blown depression until at least two months have elapsed from the start of mourning.

Those changes matter to patients and mental health professionals because the manual's definitions of mental illness determine how people are treated and, in many cases, whether the therapy is paid for by insurance. The logic behind the proposed revisions, therefore, merits a further look.

Abnormal Grief

The concept of pathological mourning has been around since Sigmund Freud, but it began receiving formal attention more recently. In several studies of widows with severe, long-lasting grief in the 1980s and 1990s, researchers noticed that antidepressant medications relieved such depressive feelings as sadness and worthlessness but did nothing for other aspects of grief, such as pining and intrusive thoughts about the deceased. The finding suggested that complicated grief and depression arise from different circuits in the brain, but the work was not far enough along to make it into the current, fourth edition of the *DSM*, published in 1994. In the 886-page book, bereavement is relegated to just one paragraph and is described as a symptom that "may be a focus of clinical attention." Complicated grief is not mentioned.

Over the next few years other studies revealed that persistent, consuming grief may, in and of itself, increase the risk of other illnesses, such as heart problems, high blood pressure and cancer. Holly G. Prigerson, one of the pioneers of grief research, organized a meeting of loss experts in Pittsburgh in 1997 to hash out preliminary criteria for what she and her colleagues saw as an emerging condition, which they termed traumatic grief. Their view of its defining features: an intense daily yearning and preoccupation with the deceased. In essence, it is the inability to adjust to life without that person, notes Mardi J. Horowitz, professor of psychiatry at the University of California, San Francisco, and another early researcher of the condition. Prigerson, then an assistant professor at the Western Psychiatric Institute and Clinic in Pittsburgh, hoped the meeting would begin the process of finding enough evidence to support changing the *DSM*. "We knew that grief predicted a lot of bad outcomes—over and above depression and anxiety—and thought it was worthy of clinical attention in its own right," says Prigerson, now a professor of psychiatry at Harvard Medical School.

A spate of studies since then—not only of widows but of parents who had lost a child, tsunami survivors and others—has further confirmed and refined that initial description. In 2008 researchers got their first hint of what complicated grief disorder looks like at the neurological level. Mary-Frances O'Connor of U.C.L.A. scanned the brains of women who had lost their mother or a sister to cancer within the past five years. She compared the results of women who had displayed typical grief with those suffering from prolonged, unabated mourning. When, while inside the scanner, the study participants looked at images of the deceased or words associated with the death, both groups showed a burst of activity in neurological circuits known to be involved in pain. The women with prolonged grief, however, also showed a unique neural signature: increased activity in a nub of tissue called the nucleus accumbens. This area, part of the brain's reward center, also lights up on imaging scans when addicts look at photographs of drug paraphernalia and when mothers see pictures of their newborn infant. That does not mean that the women were addicted to their feelings of grief but rather that they still felt actively attached to the deceased. Meanwhile clinical studies have shown that a combination of cognitive therapy approaches used to treat major depression and post-traumatic stress may help some people with complicated grief work through it.

As these and other studies began to pile up, a few researchers turned to complex statistical analysis to validate more precisely the exact combination of features that define the condition. In 2009, more than 10 years after the Pittsburgh panel, Prigerson published data collected from nearly 300 grievers she had followed for more than two years. By analyzing which of some two dozen psychological symptoms tend to cluster together in these participants, she devised the criteria for complicated grief: the mandatory presence of daily yearning plus five out of nine other symptoms for longer than six months after a death. This is exactly the type of rigorous, quantitative study that is needed before a condition makes it into the *DSM*. "People who meet the criteria for complicated grief do not necessarily meet criteria for either depression or post-traumatic stress disorder," says Katherine Shear, a professor of psychiatry at Columbia University. "If you didn't have this disorder [in the *DSM*], then those people would not get treatment at all."

Controversial Treatment

The case for diagnosing people as depressed and treating them accordingly when they are still newly bereaved is more contentious. Although some symptoms of grief and depression overlap (sadness, insomnia), the two conditions are thought to be distinct. Grief is tied to a particular event, for example, whereas the origins of a bout of clinical depression are often more obscure. Antidepressants do not ease the longing for the deceased that grievers feel. So in most cases, treating grieving people for depression is ineffective.

A few studies, however, have suggested that mourning may trigger depression in the same way that other major stresses—such as being raped or losing one's job—can bring about the condition. If so, some people who grieve may also be clinically depressed. It seems unfair, advocates of changing the *DSM* argue, to make mourners wait so long for medical help when anyone else can be treated for depression after just two weeks of consistent depression. "On the basis of scientific evidence, they're just like anybody else with depression," says Kenneth S. Kendler, a member of the *DSM-5* Mood Disorder Work Group, which reviews all proposed changes to the manual related to anxiety, depression and bipolar disorder (a condition characterized by extreme mood swings). It is for this reason that the group recently suggested deleting the clause that specifies a two-month wait before mourners can receive a diagnosis of, and therefore treatment for, depression.

Critics of the move counter that it will lead to unwarranted diagnoses and overtreatment. "It's a disastrous and foolish idea," says Allen Frances, who chaired the task force that produced the fourth edition of the *DSM*. He worries about how the *DSM-5* may be used by sales representatives from pharmaceutical companies to urge doctors to write more prescriptions. Indeed, Frances believes that changes in the edition that he oversaw inadvertently sparked an unwarranted explosion of diagnoses for bipolar disorder in children. Prigerson, for her part, predicts a general backlash against the idea that mourners might ever need psychiatric treatment. "There will be vitriolic debates when the public fully appreciates the fact that the *DSM* is pathologizing the death of a loved one within two weeks," she says.

In many ways, parsing the differences between normal grief, complicated grief and depression reflects the fundamental dilemma of psychiatry: mental disorders are diagnosed using subjective criteria and are usually an extension of a normal state. So any definition of where normal ends and abnormal begins will be the object of strongly held opinions. As Frances says, "There is no bright line—it is always going to be a matter of judgment."

Critical Thinking

1. What is the DSM-5 and why is it important for grievers who are experiencing problematic grief?

2. When is grieving pathological and when does it need professional intervention?

3. Why is the categorization of bereavement as being pathological problematic to the critics of the move to change the DSM?

11 Ways to Comfort Someone Who's Grieving

If you have a friend or relative who is grieving, it can be hard to know how to console him or her. If it seems that nothing you can do or say helps, don't give up. You can't take the pain away, but your presence is more important than it seems. Accept that you can't fix the situation or make your friend or relative feel better. Instead just be present and offer hope and a positive outlook toward the future. Accept that the person's grieving will be a gradual process.

It is sometimes difficult to know what to say to a bereaved person. If you find yourself tongue-tied or uncertain of what to do in the face of someone's loss, here are some steps you might try.

1. **Name names.** Don't be afraid to mention the deceased. It won't make your friend any sadder, although it may prompt tears. It's terrible to feel that someone you love must forever be expunged from memory and conversation. (This suggestion does not apply in cultures in which mentioning the dead is taboo or bad luck, however.)

2. **Offer hope.** People who have gone through grieving often remember that it is the person who offered reassuring hope, the certainty that things will get better, who helped them make the gradual passage from pain to a renewed sense of life.

3. **Make phone calls.** Call to express your sympathy. Try to steer clear of such phrases as "It's God's will" or "It's for the best" unless the bereaved person says this first. Your friend or relative may need you even more after the first few weeks and months, when other people may stop calling.

4. **Write a note.** If you had a relationship with the deceased, try to include a warm, caring, or funny anecdote that shows how important to you he or she was. If you didn't know the deceased, offer your sympathy and assure the bereaved that he or she is in your thoughts or prayers.

5. **Help out.** Be specific when offering help. Volunteer to shop or do laundry, bring dinner, pass on information about funeral arrangements, or answer the phone. Pitch in to clean up the kitchen. A lawyer might volunteer to help with the estate. A handy person might button up the house as winter approaches.

6. **Be sensitive to differences.** People mourn and grieve in different ways. Religion plays a big role in how death is treated; so do ethnic, cultural, and family backgrounds. Avoid criticizing the funeral arrangements or memorial service. Also, try not to impose your beliefs about death on your friend.

7. **Make a date.** Ask your friend to join you for a walk or meal once a week. Be aware that weekends are often very difficult, and suggest an activity. Low-stress activities may be best: watch a video at home together versus going out to a movie. Sometimes just being there without saying much is enough—it may even be exactly what your friend wants.

8. **Listen well instead of advising.** A sympathetic ear is a wonderful thing. A friend who listens even when the same story is told with little variation is even better. Often, people work through grief and trauma by telling their story over and over. Unless you are asked for your advice, don't be quick to offer it.

9. **Express your feelings.** If you share your friend's sorrow, say so. It's even all right to blurt out that you don't know what to say. Most likely, nothing you say will turn the tide, but your sympathetic presence may make your friend feel slightly less alone. (One caveat: try not to express your feelings so emphatically that your friend has to take care of you.)

10. **Handle anger gently.** People who are grieving sometimes direct angry feelings toward the closest target. If that happens to be you, try to be understanding. That is, wait until well after

the person has cooled down before raising your concern in a nonthreatening way.

11. **Keep your promises.** If you offer to do anything, follow through. This is especially important where promises to children are involved. Losing a loved one is abandonment enough.

Critical Thinking

1. Why should one not be afraid to mention the deceased?

2. Why should one be specific when offering help?

3. Why is helping people express anger often problematic? What can you do if this becomes a problem?

Test-Your-Knowledge Form

We encourage you to photocopy and use this page as a tool to assess how the articles in *Annual Editions* expand on the information in your textbook. By reflecting on the articles you will gain enhanced text information. You can also access this useful form on a product's book support website at www.mhhe.com/cls

NAME:

DATE:

_____

TITLE AND NUMBER OF ARTICLE:

_____

BRIEFLY STATE THE MAIN IDEA OF THIS ARTICLE:

_____

LIST THREE IMPORTANT FACTS THAT THE AUTHOR USES TO SUPPORT THE MAIN IDEA:

_____

WHAT INFORMATION OR IDEAS DISCUSSED IN THIS ARTICLE ARE ALSO DISCUSSED IN YOUR TEXTBOOK OR OTHER READINGS THAT YOU HAVE DONE? LIST THE TEXTBOOK CHAPTERS AND PAGE NUMBERS:

_____

LIST ANY EXAMPLES OF BIAS OR FAULTY REASONING THAT YOU FOUND IN THE ARTICLE:

_____

LIST ANY NEW TERMS/CONCEPTS THAT WERE DISCUSSED IN THE ARTICLE, AND WRITE A SHORT DEFINITION:

NOTES

NOTES

NOTES

NOTES

NOTES

NOTES

NOTES

NOTES

NOTES